The present work is the first variorum edition of Milton's work to be published since that of H. J. Todd, which first appeared in 1801. It is published jointly by Routledge & Kegan Paul and the Columbia University Press, and all texts used are those of the Columbia edition of Milton's work.

In addition to providing interpretative criticism, the variorum commentary provides information of all kinds, from the history and meaning of words to the history and meaning of ideas. The work furnishes a body of variorum notes and discussions uniting all available scholarly illumination of the texts on all levels from the semantic and syntactical to those of deliberate or unconscious echoes of other works in all the languages known to Milton.

The present book, Volume Four of the *Variorum Commentary*, consists of a long introduction to *Paradise Regained*, and a line by line commentary on the poem which is more elaborate than any that is to be found in earlier editions of the poem. *Paradise Regained*, though never popular, is nevertheless a great work, and in composing the commentary, Professor MacKellar's purpose has been to make more clear its essential meaning and to enlarge the 'fit audience' of those who can see it as a poem of timeless truth. The commentary is followed by a perceptive essay on style and verse form of the poem by Edward R. Weismiller.

A Variorum Commentary on

the Poems of John Milton

MERRITT Y. HUGHES

General Editor

THE COMPLETE SERIES

A Variorum Commentary on

The Poems of
John Milton

Volume Four

PARADISE REGAINED

WALTER MacKELLAR

With a review of Studies of Style and Verse Form by
EDWARD R. WEISMILLER

New York
COLUMBIA UNIVERSITY PRESS
1975

Published in the United States 1975 by
Columbia University Press, New York
Copyright © 1975 Columbia University Press
International Standard Book Number: 0 231 08883 3
Library of Congress catalog card number: 70 129962
Printed in Great Britain

Publication of this VARIORUM COMMENTARY ON THE POEMS OF JOHN MILTON was made possible by funds granted by the Carnegie Corporation of New York. That Corporation is not, however, the author, owner, or proprietor of this publication, and is not to be understood as approving by virtue of its grant any of the statements made or views expressed therein.

Contents

Preface

Paradise Regained has never been a popular poem, nor is it likely ever to evoke the same interest as *Paradise Lost*, its counterpart, with which it has too often been mistakenly compared. Nevertheless it is a great poem, but until recent years critical appreciation of it, as indeed of much of Milton's other work, has been preoccupied with aspects of the poem which he would have regarded as of relatively minor significance: that is with his literary art, as if that were an end in itself, and with values which in his estimation are secondary. But it has always found a 'fit audience' of those who have understood that it is to be read as an expression of what Milton saw to be man's fundamental needs, which lie not in the world of material things, however he may conquer that world, but in the understanding of his own nature as a spiritual being, and of his moral obligations; not in knowledge as it is presented by science, which tells man only what he *can* do, but in religious and moral knowledge, or wisdom, which alone can tell man what he *ought* to do.

In Christ's successive temptations in the wilderness we should see the deceptive allurements which constantly endanger the moral health of the individual man and of society as a whole; and we should see that against these allurements the only defence is such sophistication as Christ possessed: that is the possession of such a set of values that one cannot be deceived by anything. Milton, however, was no facile optimist who believed that imperfect man by his own unaided powers can overcome evil; only by rigorous adherence to his moral obligations and by reliance upon the same divine spiritual assistance, upon which Christ, 'the great exemplar', relied, can righteousness be made to prevail in the world.

In composing the following commentary my purpose has been to make more clear, I hope, than has hitherto been done, what I am persuaded is the essential meaning of *Paradise Regained*, as it has just been summarily stated above; and thus, I also hope, to enlarge the 'fit audience' of those who can see it as a poem of timeless truth.

In the notes, Greek and Latin classical authors are generally referred to and quoted from editions in the Loeb Classical Library. For the sake of brevity the poems of Claudian are cited by their numbers, followed in parentheses by the numbers of the volumes and pages in L.C.L. Giles Fletcher's *Christs Victorie and Triumph in Heaven and Earth* is treated as a single poem in four parts and cited by the number of its parts.

In the course of my work I have incurred many debts for which I take this opportunity to express my gratitude. Those to earlier commentators on Milton's works are duly acknowledged where I refer to them. Dr Karl J. Sax I have to thank for the friendly generosity with which he read my manuscript and saved me from errors which had escaped my vigilance. I have also to thank my friend Mr James W. Downs for the benefit of his exquisite taste and judgment in various matters. For much advice and assistance I offer what must be very inadequate thanks to Professor Mary Tibbetts Freeman of Ithaca, New York, to Professors Harry Caplan and James Hutton of Cornell University, and to my fellow editors, Professors Douglas Bush, Merritt Y. Hughes, and A. S. P. Woodhouse.

It remains to acknowledge my debt to the late Professor Charles Grosvenor Osgood of Princeton who, over the years of a long and devoted friendship, contributed more than any other to my sympathetic appreciation of Milton, 'one transcendent poet', as he called him. My gratitude for what he gave me can best be expressed by dedicating to his memory the following work, for he was 'him selfe a true poem, a composition and patterne of the best and honourablest things'.

WALTER MaCKELLAR

Acknowledgments

For generous permission to quote from copyright books and articles I am indebted to the following publishers and authors: to the Clarendon Press for quotations from Douglas Bush's *English Literature in the Earlier Seventeenth Century*, from Frank Kermode's 'Milton's Hero', *Review of English Studies*, n.s. 4 (1953), 329, and from John M. Steadman's *Milton and the Renaissance Hero*; to Eric Partridge for quotations from *Paradise Regained*, ed. E. H. Blakeney; to the Johns Hopkins Press for quotations from Elizabeth Marie Pope's *Paradise Regained: the Tradition and the Poem*; to the Odyssey Press for quotations from *John Milton: Complete Poetry and Major Prose*, ed. Merritt Y. Hughes; to the University of Minnesota Press for quotations from Douglas Bush's *Mythology and the Renaissance Tradition*, and Arnold Stein's *Heroic Knowledge: an Interpretation of Paradise Regained and Samson Agonistes*; to Dick Taylor, Jr., for quotations from 'Grace as a Means of Poetry: Milton's Pattern for Salvation', *Tulane Studies in English* 4 (1954), 57–90; to Princeton University Press for quotations from Maurice Kelley's *This Great Argument: a Study of Milton's De Doctrina Christiana as a Gloss upon Paradise Lost*; to Zera S. Fink for a quotation from *The Classical Republicans*; to the University of Michigan Press for a quotation from Herbert H. Petit's 'The Second Eve of *Paradise Regained*', *Papers of the Michigan Academy of Science, Arts, and Letters* 44 (1959), 369; to the University of Toronto Press and Dick Taylor, Jr., for quotations from 'The Storm Scene in *Paradise Regained*', *University of Toronto Quarterly* 24 (1954–5), 359–76; to the University of Toronto Press and A. S. P. Woodhouse for quotations from 'Theme and Pattern in *Paradise Regained*', *University of Toronto Quarterly* 25 (1955–6), 167–82; to Cornell University Press for quotations from Douglas Bush's *Paradise Lost in Our Time*, from Allan H. Gilbert's *A Geographical Dictionary of Milton*, and from Irene Samuel's *Plato and Milton*; to the Modern

Acknowledgments

Language Association and George Winchester Stone for quotations from Howard Schultz's *Milton and Forbidden Knowledge*; to Harvard University Press for quotations from William Chase Greene's *Moira*, and William B. Hunter's 'Milton's Arianism Reconsidered', *Harvard Theological Review* 52 (1959), 34; to Random House, Inc. for a quotation from *The Complete Works of Tacitus*, tr. Church and Brodribb; to the University of Chicago Press for quotations from Northrop Frye's 'The Typology of *Paradise Regained*', *Modern Philology* 53 (1956), 227–38; to the University of California Press for quotations from *The Sermons of John Donne*, ed. Potter and Simpson (1953–62); and to Chandler B. Beall for a quotation from Stewart A. Baker's 'Sannazaro and Milton's Brief Epic', *Comparative Literature* 20 (1968), 131.

ABBREVIATIONS FOR THE TITLES
OF MILTON'S WRITINGS

Variorum Commentary		*Columbia Works*
Acced	Accedence Commenc't Grammar	G
Animad	Animadversions upon the Remonstrants Defence	A
Apol	An Apology against a Pamphlet	AP
Arc	Arcades	ARC
Areop	Areopagitica	AR
Asclep	'Asclepiads' (called 'Choriambics', *Works* 1, 327)	
BrNotes	Brief Notes upon a late Sermon	BN
Bucer	The Judgement of Martin Bucer, concerning Divorce	M
CarEl	Carmina Elegiaca	CE
Carrier 1, 2	On the University Carrier; Another on the same	UC
CharLP	Milton's Character of the Long Parliament	TC
Circum	Upon the Circumcision	CI
CivP	A Treatise of Civil power	CP
Colas	Colasterion	C
ComBk	Commonplace Book	CB
Comus	Comus	CO
DDD	The Doctrine and Discipline of Divorce	D. and D.
Def 1	Pro Populo Anglicano Defensio (First Defence of the English People)	1D
Def 2	Pro Populo Anglicano Defensio Secunda (Second Defence)	2D
DocCh	De Doctrina Christiana	CD
Educ	Of Education	E
Eikon	Eikonoklastes	K
El 1, &c.	Elegia 1, &c.	EL
Eli	In obitum Praesulis Eliensis	PE
EpDam	Epitaphium Damonis	ED

Epistol	Familiar Letters of Milton	FE
EProl	Early Prolusions by Milton	EP
EpWin	Epitaph on the Marchioness of Winchester	EM
FInf	On the Death of a fair Infant	I
Hirelings	Considerations touching The likeliest means to remove Hirelings out of the church	H
HistBr	History of Britain	B
HistMosc	History of Moscovia	HM
Hor	Fifth Ode of Horace	HOR
Idea	De Idea Platonica	IPA
IlPen	Il Penseroso	IP
L'All	L'Allegro	L'A
Leon 1, &c.	Ad Leonoram Romae canentem	LR
LetMonk	Letter to General Monk	LM
Log	Art of Logic	LO
Lyc	Lycidas	L
Mansus	Mansus	MA
May	Song. On May Morning	MM
Nat	On the Morning of Christ's Nativity	N
Naturam	Naturam non pati senium	NS
NewF	On the new forcers of Conscience	FC
OAP	Observations on the Articles of Peace	O
Passion	The Passion	PA
Patrem	Ad Patrem	ADP
PE	Of Prelatical Episcopacy	P
PhilReg	Philosophus ad Regem	PAR
PL	Paradise Lost	PL
PR	Paradise Regained	PR
Procan	In obitum Procancellarii medici	PM
ProdBom 1, &c.	In Proditionem Bombardicam 1, &c.	PB
Prol 1, &c.	Prolusions 1, &c.	PO
Pro se Def	Pro Se Defensio	SD
Ps 1, &c.	Psalms 1, &c.	PS
QNov	In quintum Novembris	QN
RCG	The Reason of Church-governement Urg'd against Prelaty	CG
Ref	Of Reformation Touching Church-Discipline in England	R

REW	The Readie & Easie Way to Establish a Free Commonwealth	W
Rous	Ad Joannem Rousium	JR
RH	Apologus de Rustico et Hero	RH
SA	Samson Agonistes	SA
Sals	Ad Salsillum poetam Romanum	AS
Shak	On Shakespear. 1630	SH
SolMus	At a solemn Musick	SM
Sonn 1, &c.	Sonnet 1, &c.	S
Tetr	Tetrachordon	T
Time	On Time	TI
TKM	The Tenure of Kings and Magistrates	TE
TR	Of True Religion, Haeresie, Schism, Toleration	TR
Vac	At a Vacation Exercise in the Colledge	V

ABBREVIATIONS FOR TITLES OF PERIODICALS, ETC.

AJP	*American Journal of Philology*
BSUF	*Ball State University Forum*
CL	*Comparative Literature*
ELH	*Journal of English Literary History*
HLQ	*Huntington Library Quarterly*
HTR	*Harvard Theological Review*
JEGP	*Journal of English and Germanic Philology*
LSUSHS	*Louisiana State University Studies, Humanistic Series*
LXX	Septuagint
M&H	*Medievalia et Humanistica*
MLN	*Modern Language Notes*
MP	*Modern Philology*
N&Q	*Notes and Queries*
PLL	*Papers on Language and Literature*
PMASAL	*Papers of the Michigan Academy of Science, Arts, and Letters*
PMLA	*Publications of the Modern Language Association of America*
PQ	*Philological Quarterly*
RES	*Review of English Studies*
RP	*Renaissance Papers*
SAMLA	*South Atlantic Modern Language Association*
SP	*Studies in Philology*
TLS	*[London] Times Literary Supplement*
TSE	*Tulane Studies in English*
TSLL	*Texas Studies in Literature and Language*
UTQ	*University of Toronto Quarterly*
UTSE	*University of Texas Studies in English*

CHRONOLOGICAL TABLE* [D.B.]

I	II	III
Milton born, Bread St., Cheapside, London	9 Dec. 1608	
M. enters St Paul's School		1620? 1615?–20
Ps 114, 136	9 Dec. 1623–8 Dec. 1624	
EProl, CarEl, Asclep, RH		1624–6?
PhilReg		1624–6? 1634? 1642–5?
Mary Powell baptized	24 Jan. 1625	
M. admitted to Christ's College, Cambridge	12 Feb. 1625	
M. matriculates in University	9 April 1625	
Epigrams on Gunpowder Plot		*c.* 1625–6?
M. in London, rusticated from college?	Part of Lent term, 1626	
El 1 (written at home)	April 1626	
M. apparently in Cambridge for Easter term	19 April f.	
Procan (Gostlin d. 21 Oct. 1626)	Oct.–Nov. 1626	
El 2 (Ridding d. between 19 Sept. and 28 Nov.)	Oct.–Nov. 1626	
El 3 (Andrewes d. 25 Sept. 1626; funeral 11 Nov.)	Oct.–Nov. 1626	
QNov	Before 5 Nov. 1626 (early autumn and perhaps summer)	

* Column II lists more or less certain dates, Column III some conjectures.

xvii

I	II	III
Eli (Felton d. 5 Oct. 1626)	Oct.–Nov. 1626	
Prol 1–5		1626–9?
		1631–2?
Hor		1626–9?
El 4 (to T. Young)	March–April 1627	
FInf (on niece buried 22 Jan. 1628?)		22 Jan.–9 April 1628? 1625–6?
El 7		1 May 1628 (or 1627? 1630?)
Sonn 1–6		1628–30
Naturam		June 1628?
Prol 6; *Vac*	July (?), 1628	
M. takes B.A. degree	26 March 1629	
El 5	April–May 1629	
May		1 May 1629?– 31?
Idea		*c.* 1629–31?
M. buys works of G. della Casa	December 1629	
Nat	Christmas 1629	
El 6	Dec. 1629–Jan. 1630	
Epilogue appended to *El* 7		1630–45
Passion	*c.* 26–8 March 1630	
Shak	1630–24 March 1631	
Carrier 1, 2	Jan.–Feb. 1631	
EpWin	April–May 1631	
L'All; IlPen	Summer 1631 (or 1632?)	
Prol 7		1631–2?
Patrem		1631–2? (1634–7?)
Arc		1632? (1629–33?)
M. takes M.A. degree	3 July 1632	
M. at home (Hammersmith)	July 1632–35	

I	II	III
M. begins to record poems in Cambridge MS.		1632? 1637?
Sonn 7 (on 24th birthday)	9 Dec. 1632	
Time		Dec. 1632? (1630?)
Circum		1 Jan. 1633 (1631?)
'Letter to an Unknown Friend'		Jan.–Feb.?, 1633
SolMus		Feb.–Mar. 1633?
A Mask (*Comus*)	Performed 29 Sept. 1634	
Ps cxiv (Greek trans.)	Nov. 1634	
M. at home (Horton)	1635–April 1638	
Milton's mother d.	3 April 1637	
Comus pub. (ed. Lawes)	1637–March 1638	
Important letter to Diodati (*Works* 12, 22–9)	Dated 23 Sept. 1637 (probably should be 23 Nov.)	
Star Chamber decree on censorship	11 July 1637	
Edward King drowned	10 August 1637	
Lyc written	November 1637	
Lyc pub. (*Justa Edouardo King*)	1638	
Sir Henry Wotton's letter to M. (prefixed to *Comus*, 1645)	13 April 1638	
M. in Paris	April?–May 1638	
M. journeys through France to Nice; sails to Genoa	May–June 1638	
M. in Florence (*c.* 2 months)	July?–Aug.–Sept. 1638	
C. Diodati buried	27 Aug. 1638	
M. in Rome (*c.* 2 months)	Oct.–Nov. 1638	
Sals written	Nov. (?), 1638	
M. in Naples	December 1638	

I	II	III
Mansus written	Dec. 1638–Jan. 1639	
M. in Rome again (*c.* 2 months)	Jan.–Feb. 1639	
Leon 1, etc., written	1639?	
M. in Florence again (*c.* 2 months)	March–April 1639	
M. in Venice (a month)	April?–May 1639	
M. in Geneva	June 1639	
M. returns to England	July–Aug. 1639	
M. in lodgings in London, near Fleet Street	1639?–40 (nearly a year)	
EpDam written	Late 1639–early 1640	
EpDam privately printed		1639–45
Long Parliament meets	3 Nov. 1640	
M. living in Aldersgate Street	1640 (autumn?)–1645	
M. sets down list of subjects for tragedies		*c.* 1641
Ref pub.	May 1641	
PE pub.	June–July 1641	
Animad pub.	July (?), 1641	
RCG pub.	Jan.–Feb. 1642	
Apol pub.	April 1642	
M. marries Mary Powell	*c.* 29 May–1 June 1642 (French, *L.R.* 2, 61); 'probably early in July' (Parker, 230, cf. 862–74)	
Mrs Milton returns to parents' home	Probably 'not long before 22 Aug.' (Parker, 873, n. 21)	
Outbreak of Civil War	22 Aug. 1642	
Sonn 8	*c.* 13 Nov. 1642	
Sonn 9–10		1642–5
Parliamentary ordinance on censorship	14 June 1643	

I	II	III
Westminster Assembly convened	1 July 1643	
DDD pub.	*c.* 1 Aug. 1643	
DDD (2nd ed., revised and enlarged)	Jan.–Feb. 1644	
Educ pub.	*c.* 4–5 June 1644	
Bucer pub.	August 1644	
Areop pub.	November 1644	
Attacks on M.'s divorce tracts. Controversy on toleration	1644 f.	
Acced written?		1645?
Tetr and *Colas* pub.	*c.* 4 March 1645	
M. and wife reunited	1645 (before November)	
M. living in Barbican	Sept.–Oct. 1645–Sept. (?), 1647	
Sonn 11 and 12	1645–6	
Poems (dated 1645) pub.	On or before 2 Jan. 1646	
M. working on *HistBr* (bks. 1–4) and *DocCh*	1646–9	Parker, Shawcross, and Carey would include *SA*
Sonn 13 (to Lawes)	9 Feb. 1646	
Daughter Anne b.	29 July 1646	
Sonn 14 (on Mrs Thomason)	December 1646	
NewF		1646–7
Rous	23 Jan. 1647	
J. Milton senior d.	March 1647	
M. living in High Holborn	Aug. (?), 1647–March 1649	
Log and *HistMosc* written?		*c.* 1648? (Parker)
Ps 80–88 versified	April 1648	
Sonn 15 (Fairfax)	14 June–17 Aug. 1648	
Daughter Mary b.	25 Oct. 1648	
King Charles executed	30 Jan. 1649	

I	II	III
Eikon Basilike (by J. Gauden) pub.	1–9 Feb. 1649	
TKM pub.	*c.* 13 Feb. 1649	
M. appointed Secretary for Foreign Tongues to Council of State	15 March 1649 (held office till 1659; as a Latin Secretary, 1654–9)	
OAP pub.	May 1649	
Eikon (reply to *Eikon Basilike*) pub.	*c.* 6 Oct. 1649	Or *c.* 6 Nov. (Parker)
M. living in Scotland Yard	Nov. 1649–Dec. 1651	
Period of the Commonwealth	1649–53	
Def 1 pub.	24 Feb. 1651	
Son John b. (d. June 1652)	16 March 1651	
M. licenser of newspaper *Mercurius Politicus*	23 Jan. 1651–22 Jan. 1652	
M. becomes completely blind	Nov. 1651–Feb. 1652	
M. living in Petty France, Westminster	Dec. 1651–1660	
Sonn 19 ('When I consider')		1652–5
Daughter Deborah b.	2 May 1652	
Mary Powell Milton d.	5 (?) May 1652	
Sonn 16 (Cromwell)	May 1652	
Sonn 17 (Vane)	3 July 1652	
Ps 1–8	August 1653	*Ps* 1 earlier?
Period of Cromwell's Protectorate	1654–8	
Def 2 pub.	*c.* 30 May 1654	
Sonn 18 (Piedmont)	May–June 1655	
Sonn 20–2		1654–6
Pro se Def pub.	*c.* 8 Aug. 1655	
M. marries Katherine Woodcock (b. 1628)	12 Nov. 1656	
Daughter b. (d. 17 March 1658)	19 Oct. 1657	

I	II	III
Katherine M. d.	3 Feb. 1658	
Sonn 23	1658	Before 12 Nov. 1656 (Parker)
Cromwell d.	3 Sept. 1658	
Cromwell's funeral: M. presumably in procession with Marvell and other secretaries	23 Nov. 1658	
M. working on *HistBr*, *DocCh*	1655–60	
PL begun		1658?
CivP pub.	Feb. 1659	
Hirelings pub.	August 1659	
REW pub.	3 March, or slightly earlier, 1660	
LetMonk	March 1660	
BrNotes; *REW* (enlarged)	April 1660	
Charles II enters London	29 May 1660	
M. secluded by friends in Bartholomew Close	Summer 1660	
Parliamentary order for M.'s arrest and burning of *Eikon* and *Def* I	16 June 1660 (public proclamation, concerning books only, 13 Aug.)	
M. not named among those excepted from Act of Pardon	29 Aug. 1660	
M. in custody	Some period between 13 Sept. and release (15–17 Dec. 1660)	
M. living in Holborn		Sept. (?), 1660–early 1661 (Parker)
M. living in Jewin Street		1661–3 (French, *L.R.* 4, 388); till *c.* 1669–70 (Parker, 608, 1125)

I	II	III
M. marries Elizabeth Minshull (b. 1638)	24 Feb. 1663	
PL finished	1663 ?–5	
M. and family at Chalfont St Giles (because of plague)	July 1665–Feb. (?), 1666	
Great Fire in London	2–5 Sept. 1666	
PL (in 10 bks.) pub.	August (?), 1667	
Acced pub. (see under 1645 above)	June 1669	
M. living in Artillery Walk, Bunhill Fields		From *c.* 1669–70 (Parker, 608) or 1663 (French, *L.R.* 4, 388) till 1674
HistBr (6 bks.) pub.	1670	
PR and *SA* pub.	1671	
Log (written *c.* 1648?) pub.	1672	
TR pub.	1673	
Poems (2nd ed., enlarged)	1673	
Epistol and *Prol* pub.	July (?), 1674	
PL (2nd ed., in 12 bks.)	July 1674	
Milton died	8 (?) Nov. 1674	
M. buried in St Giles Cripplegate	12 Nov. 1674	
CharLP (omitted from *HistBr* of 1670) pub.	1681	
HistMosc (written *c.* 1648?) pub.	1682	
Letters of State, ed. E. Phillips (incl. *Sonn* 15, 16, 17, 22)	1694	

Introduction

❦

I

In *The History of the Life of Thomas Ellwood...Written by His Own Hand*,[1] that worthy Quaker, who about 1662 became a friend of Milton, tells the following story:

Some little time before I went to *Alesbury* Prison, I was desired by my quondam Master *Milton* to take an House for him, in the Neighbourhood where I dwelt, that he might get out of the City, for the Safety of himself and his Family, the *Pestilence* then growing hot in *London*. I took a pretty Box for him in *Giles-Chalfont*, a Mile from me; of which I gave him notice: and intended to have waited on him, and seen him well settled in it; but was prevented by that Imprisonment.

But now being released, and returned Home, I soon made a Visit to him, to welcome him into the Country.

After some common Discourses had passed between us, he called for a Manuscript of his; which being brought he delivered to me, bidding me take it home with me, and read it at my Leisure: and when I had so done, return it to him, with my Judgment thereupon.

When I came home, and had set my self to read it, I found it was that Excellent Poem, which he entituled *PARADISE LOST*. After I had, with the best Attention, read it through, I made him another Visit, and returned him his Book, with due Acknowledgement of the Favour he had done me, in Communicating it to me. He asked me how I liked it, and what I thought of it; which I modestly, but freely told him: and after some further Discourse about it, I pleasantly said to him, Thou hast said much here of *Paradise lost*; but what hast thou to say of *Paradise found*? He made me no Answer, but sate some time in a Muse: then brake of[f] that Discourse, and fell upon another Subject.

After the Sickness was over, and the City well cleansed and become safely habitable again, he returned thither. And when afterwards I went to wait on

---

[1] 1st ed., London, 1714, pp. 233–4.

him there (which I seldom failed of doing, whenever my Occasions drew me to *London*) he shewed me his Second POEM, called *PARADISE REGAINED*; and in a pleasant Tone said to me, *This is owing to you: for you put it into my Head, by the Question you put to me at* Chalfont; *which before I had not thought of.*

Although Ellwood gives a greatly condensed account of conversations which must have been of considerable length, there is no reason to doubt that, as far as he goes, he accurately records the facts as he remembered them. He was not a man who would willingly falsify anything; but possessing little humour, he seems to have been too apt to understand literally what was not so intended. An understandable and pardonable pride in the responsibility which Milton apparently reposed in him may also have induced him to take the poet's last statement at face value. The facts, however, which he was able to record leave in uncertainty matters in which certainty is most desirable. What was passing through Milton's mind as he sat in a muse? How far, if at all, is the last statement to be taken seriously?

It is easily conceivable that when Milton finished *Paradise Lost*, he thought that to the 'fit audience' which he expected to find, he had, both by implication and direct statement, made sufficiently clear not only how man had lost, but also how he must recover, Paradise; how 'one greater Man' will 'Restore us, and regain the blissful Seat', will restore what Adam lost when, false to the knowledge he had, and allowing an excess of husbandly devotion to rule his higher, rational nature, he disobeyed God.[2] Yet after reading the poem, Ellwood could ask, 'What hast thou to say of *Paradise found*?' The question must have disappointed Milton. A friend whom he had thought of as belonging to the 'fit audience' which would grasp the full meaning of his great poem had failed to see that it answered his question. What was passing through his mind while he sat in a muse we shall never know; but he may well have thought that as Ellwood had failed to understand, so others might fail; and he may have wondered how he could best ensure their understanding of what he most wanted to say about the greatest truths of human

[2] See *PL* 1. 1–5; 3. 94–5, 107, 203–5; 5. 501, 512–14, 522, 536–7, 541, 611–12; 6. 687, 902, 912; 7. 159; 8. 325; 12. 382–435.

life. That he remained silent and then turned to another subject may mean nothing more than that at the moment he could not think of the most appropriate answer.

The statement 'This is owing to you' and the rest with which Ellwood's story ends cannot mean that Milton had not before thought of the *subject* of *Paradise Regained*. The passages in *Paradise Lost* referred to above, were there nothing else, make that interpretation untenable. Milton, who knew how to pay urbane compliments, was undoubtedly on this occasion, with a touch of characteristic humour, paying one to gratify his gentle friend, who was pleased to take it literally. At most his words can mean only that until Ellwood asked his question, he had not thought of composing a poem on the recovery of Paradise.

In 'To the Reader' prefixed to his Biblical poem, *Davideis*, published in 1712, Ellwood stated (pp. xii–xiii) his intention to abstain from 'the great *Embellishments*' with which celebrated poets adorn their poems, embellishments which 'consist mostly in their *extravagant*, and almost *boundless Fancies*; *Amazing*, and even *Dazeling Flights*; *Luxurious Inventions*; *Wild Hyperble's*; *Lofty Language*'. In 'The Influence of Thomas Ellwood upon Milton's Epics',[3] Max Patrick suggests not only that Ellwood's observations may have led to a revision of *Paradise Lost*, but also that his preference for an unadorned poetical style may have influenced Milton in employing such a style in *Paradise Regained*. However it may or may not be significant that in the passage from the *Life* quoted above, Ellwood says nothing about Milton's style, in which, to be sure, he would not find the 'Dazeling Flights...Wild Hyperble's', and the other features from which he abstained, features characteristic of certain of the metaphysical poets but not of Milton. And there remains the question, to which we have no answer: were Ellwood's stylistic preferences the same in the 1660s, when he first read *Paradise Lost* and *Paradise Regained*, as when he published *Davideis* more than forty years later?[4]

[3] *Essays in History and Literature Presented to Stanley Pargellis* (Chicago, 1965), pp. 119–32.
[4] On the style of *PR*, see below, pp. 17f. and part II of Edward Weismiller's essay at the end of this volume.

According to Ellwood's account *Paradise Regained* was composed between August 1665 and, at the latest, the summer of 1666.[5] But Milton's nephew and biographer Edward Phillips, who appears to have been the chief amanuensis when both *Paradise Lost* and *Paradise Regained* were being dictated,[6] and should therefore have been in the best position to know when the three major poems were produced, confuses the record by stating that *Paradise Regained* 'doubtless was begun and finisht and Printed after the other [*PL*] was publisht, and that in a wonderful short space considering the sublimeness of it.'[7] This means that Milton did not begin work on *Paradise Regained* until after August 1667, more than a year after Ellwood says that he read the poem. However since the word 'doubtless' in Phillips's statement suggests that he was not entirely certain, Ellwood, J. H. Hanford believes, is probably the more reliable witness.[8] But despite the unexplained discrepancy in their testimony, it is significant that both Ellwood and Phillips, who were closest to Milton, agree that *Paradise Regained* was composed after *Paradise Lost* and in a surprisingly short space of time. Thus the long-accepted tradition of the order of the poems was established. Related as they are, it is the logical order which has been generally accepted by modern editors.

The order in which the poems were composed does not, however, tell when they were composed. Although according to Phillips and Aubrey, ten lines of Satan's soliloquy, *Paradise Lost* 4. 32–41, were written as the beginning of a tragedy several years before the epic poem was thought of,[9] it was long agreed, with Milton's own words 'long choosing and beginning late' (*PL* 9. 26) to support the view, that actual work on the poem did not begin until the 1650s, and, in view of his official duties

---

[5] Ellwood gives no dates, but all the evidence now available, which J. Milton French presents in *The Life Records of John Milton* (New Brunswick, N.J., 1949–58), 4. 401–2, 421, indicates that he received the manuscript of *Paradise Lost* in August 1665 and probably returned it later in that month; and that since he was again in prison from 13 March to 25 June 1666, he received the manuscript of *Paradise Regained* before 13 March or soon after 25 June.

[6] See *The Early Lives of Milton*, ed. Darbishire (London, 1932), p. 9.

[7] *Ibid.*, p. 75.

[8] *John Milton, Englishman* (New York, 1949), p. 200.

[9] See *Early Lives*, pp. 13, 72.

as Latin Secretary, his ill health and blindness, probably not until 1655, after the completion of the *Defensio Secunda*, but not later than 1658, and that *Paradise Regained* and *Samson Agonistes* followed.[10]

In recent years, however, there has been an increasing tendency among some scholars to find earlier dates for the inception, if not the final form, of all three of the major poems. This they have to do without the support of any external evidence; and what they adduce as internal evidence, however ingenious, since it is purely conjectural, is quite unconvincing. H. F. Fletcher, who represents this tendency, is persuaded that the composition of *Paradise Lost* was extended over a period of nearly forty years, and that of *Paradise Regained* and *Samson Agonistes* over 'a comparatively lengthy period'.[11] In his unpublished doctoral dissertation, *Milton's Spelling: Its Biographical and Critical Implications*,[12] John T. Shawcross suggests that the first draft of *Paradise Regained* 'could have been written' as early as 1642–4, that the poem was revised between 1646 and the middle of 1651, and that thereafter only incidental changes and additions were made before publication in 1671. The evidence which leads Shawcross to suggest these dates is far too extensive to be reproduced here, or even to be satisfactorily summarized. He admits that it is not conclusive; and since not only Milton's practices in spelling, but also those of his amanuenses and printers are involved—and may never be distinguishable—there remain after all Shawcross's laborious investigations unexplained inconsistencies which make final determination of dates impossible by his method.

A few years later, in 'The Chronology of Milton's Major Poems',[13] attacking the conclusions of Ants Oras in his article 'Milton's Blank Verse',[14] Shawcross, by mechanically applying metrical tests, again arrived at the conclusion that Milton's major poems, or parts of them,

[10] See *Early Lives*, pp. 13, 29, 72, 177–8; David Masson, *The Life of John Milton* (7 vols., London, 1859–94), 5. 405–8; 6. 440–4; E. M. W. Tillyard, *Milton* (London, 1930), pp. 194–5; Hanford, *Englishman*, pp. 172, 200.

[11] See *John Milton's Complete Poetical Works, Reproduced in Photographic Facsimile* (4 vols., Urbana, Ill., 1943–8), 4. 11.

[12] New York University, 1958, pp. 235–40.

[13] *PMLA* 76 (1961), 345–58.

[14] *SAMLA Studies in Milton*, ed. Patrick (Gainesville, Fla., 1953), pp. 128–97.

were composed much earlier than the period after the Restoration. To this article Oras replied in *Blank Verse and Chronology in Milton*,[15] a monograph which subjects the verse 'to a series of consistently applied stylistic tests', includes many graphs and tables of percentages, and more elaborately examines than does his article stylistic features of Milton's verse. Space here permits only a statement of Oras's conclusion, which is that the 'old chronology' in its main outlines seems 'unassailable', and that both *Paradise Regained* and *Samson Agonistes* 'belong to Milton's last period' (p. 40). W. R. Parker, led by 'a feeling about where things do or do not *belong* in [Milton's] artistic and intellectual development', suggests, though he does 'not certainly know', that *Paradise Regained* was begun about 1656-8, and that most of the dialogue and some of the 'almost-choral parts' were composed before *Paradise Lost* was begun as an epic poem.[16] John Carey in his recent edition of the poem (p. 1063) gives as the dates of composition 1667-70.

Since we know from Milton's own statements[17] that as a young man he began to think seriously about composing a great poem, and that as early as 1639-42 he drew up the famous 'Outlines of Tragedies', a list of subjects suitable for such a poem, now preserved in the Cambridge Manuscript,[18] it is reasonable to suppose that if he felt sufficiently mature to attempt a great work—and we do not know that he did—he would begin in the 1640s. But through nearly all of that decade he was conducting a private school and writing pamphlets on the controversies of the time. Through at least the first half of the 1650s his official duties as Latin Secretary to the Council of State, which included writing the two *Defences*, were probably enough fully to occupy his time and thought. He had to recover from private sorrows and the shock of becoming blind, and to learn to work through the eyes of others. Between 1655 and 1660, when his official duties were apparently lightened, he may have found some leisure for his own work; but again

[15] *University of Florida Monographs* 20 (Gainesville, Fla., 1966).
[16] *Milton, a Biography* (2 vols., Oxford, 1968), 2. 1139-40.
[17] See *Mansus* 80-4; *EpDam* 162-8; *RCG* 2 Pref. (*Works* 3. 236).
[18] See Masson, *Life* 2. 117, 121; *Works* 18. 229-45.

for a time after the Restoration, when he had 'fall'n on evil days' and was 'In darkness, and with dangers compast round', when he was in hiding and for a short time in prison in the summer and autumn of 1660, it would be surprising if he could give much of his mind to poetry. All the circumstances of his life, exacting occupations, grief, distractions, blindness, and dangers, for most of the period from 1640 to 1660 were not favourable for the extended and intensive effort which must have gone into the composition of the major poems. If Hanford is right in believing, as I think he is, that the variety of style and mood and the fluctuating inspiration of *Paradise Lost* are reflections of the turbulence and danger in which much of it was composed, so the greater uniformity, the singleness of mood, and the sustained inspiration of *Paradise Regained* and *Samson Agonistes* may be reflections of the security and comfort which Milton recovered after his marriage to Elizabeth Minshull on 24 February 1662/3.[19] Until new evidence definitely pointing to an earlier date can be found, from what we now know, and from the probabilities just stated, we can do no better than assume that *Paradise Regained* was composed at some time between 1665 and 1670.

In the *Stationers' Register* under the date 10 Sept. 1670 there is the following entry: 'Entred...under the hands of Master THO: TOMKYNS and Master Warden ROPER a copie or booke intituled *Paradise regayn'd*; A Poem in 4 Bookes. The Author, **John Milton**. To wch is added *Samson Agonistes*, A drammadic Poem, by the same Author...vjᵈ.' The volume thus registered, which for reasons unknown did not appear until some months later, has a title page, reproduced in facsimile in *Works* 2. 404, and in the editions of Beeching, Bush, Darbishire, and Hughes, which reads: PARADISE / REGAIN'D. / A / POEM. In IV BOOKS. / To which is added / *SAMSON AGONISTES.* / The Author / *JOHN MILTON.* / LONDON. / Printed by *J. M.* for *John Starkey* at the *Mitre* in *Fleetstreet*, near *Temple-Bar.* / MDCLXXI. On the fly leaf facing the title page are the words, 'Licensed July 2, 1670', the date when Thomas Tomkyns, the licenser who had given the imprimatur for

---

[19] See *Englishman*, pp. 172–4; *Early Lives*, p. 29.

Paradise Lost, gave permission for the printing of the two new poems. Nothing is known which explains why *Paradise Regained* was not published by Samuel Simmons, the publisher of *Paradise Lost*, nor why, if it was completed before that poem appeared in 1667, the two were not published together.

The volume, a drab piece of book-making in which the paper is not of the best quality, is a small octavo of 220 pages, of which *Paradise Regained* occupies the first 116, and *Samson Agonistes*, with its own title page and pagination, the remainder. The printing is the work of a careless printer and required a list of errata. In one copy which I have examined the ink has been so unevenly distributed on the type that parts of several pages are quite illegible. The second edition of 1680 made none of the corrections indicated in the errata and introduced many variant readings, listed in *Works* 2. 541–7, for which, even when they are not merely careless misprints, there is no apparent authority. But neither these variants nor the first printer's blunders are significant enough to create textual problems which obscure the meaning of the poem. The first edition of 1671, since it is the only edition which Milton can have supervised before his death in 1674, presumably gives the most reliable text of *Paradise Regained*, and forms the basis of the text of the Columbia Milton which is followed in the present commentary.

In 1688 Randall Taylor published a third edition, a handsome small folio with illustrations, in which the errors of the first edition and most of the variants of the second are repeated. In 1695 Jacob Tonson published *Paradise Regained* together with *Samson Agonistes* and the *Poems on Several Occasions*. At least seven other Tonson reprints of Milton's poems appeared in the first half of the 18th century. Finally in 1752 Tonson brought out Thomas Newton's edition of *Paradise Regained* 'with notes of various authors', with which scholarly annotation of the poem began, which (reissued, 2 vols., 1753 and 1773) remained standard until in 1795 Charles Dunster produced his quarto edition including the bulk of Newton's notes with many additions of his own. In 1801 Henry J. Todd published his elaborate variorum edition of all Milton's poems. To this valuable work, republished in 1809, 1826, 1842, and 1852, all subsequent editors have been indebted. Later editions, either of *Paradise Regained* alone or of all Milton's poems, which deserve mention are those of Edward Hawkins (1824), Thomas Keightley (1859), R. C. Browne (1866 and 1894), David Masson (1874 and 1890), Charles S. Jerram (1877), H. C. Beeching (1900), H. J. C. Grierson (1925), Leonard C. Martin (1925), E. H. Blakeney (1932), Frank A. Patterson (Columbia Milton, 1931–8), James H. Hanford (1936 and 1953), Merritt Y. Hughes (1937 and 1957), Harris F. Fletcher (facsimile edition, 1942–8), Helen Darbishire (1952–5), Jacques Blondel (1955), Douglas Bush (1965), John Carey (1968). In the following commentary these works are referred to by the last names of the editors.

II

In *The Reason of Church-governement* of 1642 occurs Milton's statement about 'that Epick form whereof the two poems of *Homer*, and those other two of *Virgil* and *Tasso* are a diffuse, and the book of *Job* a brief model'.[20] It has been said that the Hebrews produced no epic poetry, but Charles Jones and Barbara Lewalski[21] explain why Milton, influenced by a long-standing tradition that the Book of Job is an epic poem, and by the views of Philo, Josephus, Origen, and especially Jerome on the structure of Hebrew verse, should have thought it to be an epic poem. Although later Hebrew scholarship does not support them, they believed that in Hebrew verse there are the same metres as in Greek and Latin. Jerome even thought that in Job he found hexameter lines consisting of feet which, though they have not the same number of syllables, are quantitatively equivalent to dactyls and spondees. For Milton, then, knowing that internal and external form are inseparable, that the one determines the other, hexameter verse would mean that the Book of Job is an epic poem, since he believed that to be the verse which, in an ancient language, a heroic subject demands, as in English such a subject

---

[20] *Works* 3. 237.
[21] Respectively in 'Milton's "Brief Epic"', *SP* 44 (1947), 209–27; and in *Milton's Brief Epic: the Genre, Meaning and Art of Paradise Regained* (Providence, R.I., 1966), pp. 10–36.

demands blank verse.[22] That the Book of Job meets the requirements of what Milton considered a truly heroic subject—'the better fortitude / Of Patience and Heroic Martyrdom'—the 'suffering for Truths sake' which 'Is fortitude to highest victorie'—needs no more argument to support it than that in this sense the subject of *Paradise Regained* is heroic. In each work there is a struggle between good and evil, between the true and the false; in each a noble man who puts his trust in God is tried by the devil, beset with many temptations to disobey the moral law and be false to God; in each by suffering rather than by doing he maintains his faith, obeys, and wins the victory over evil. But although the two works develop similar themes, Milton did not regard the Book of Job as a stereotyped model, for his poem is more strictly unified, and has a more shapely and balanced structure, and there is no disharmony in it, as there is between the prologue and the epilogue of the Book of Job.[23]

Paradise Regained, as Northrop Frye observes, is

not only a success but a technical experiment that is practically *sui generis*. None of the ordinary literary categories apply to it; its poetic predecessors are nothing like it, and it has left no descendants. If it is a 'brief epic,' it has little resemblance to the epyllion; its closest affinities are with the debate and with the dialectical colloquy of Plato and Boethius, to which most of the Book of Job also belongs. But these forms usually either incorporate one argument into another dialectically or build up two different cases rhetorically; Milton's feat of constructing a double argument on the same words, each highly plausible and yet as different as light from darkness, is, so far as I know, unique in English literature.[24]

Nor is it unique only in English literature. Among numerous Italian and French Biblical poems of the 16th and 17th centuries, I have found none which even remotely resembles *Paradise Regained*. Milton, in short, displays a singular independence of traditional literary forms.

[22] See Ida Langdon, *Milton's Theory of Poetry and Fine Art* (New Haven, 1924), pp. 1–26, 185–8.
[23] See *Encyc. Bibl.* 2. 2465–8.
[24] 'The Typology of *PR*', *MP* 53 (1956), 235. See also E. M. W. Tillyard, *The English Epic and its Background* (London, 1954), p. 447, and Mrs Lewalski, *Brief Epic*, pp. 66–7, 104.

Introduction

There has commonly been too little recognition of the resemblance, which Frye mentions, between *Paradise Regained* and the Platonic dialogues, a resemblance of which Milton must have been fully aware. In its dialectic, its dramatic quality and sharply delineated characters, the poem is very like the dialogues. Socrates, the defender of truth and spiritual values, who has been compared with Christ, and whom Christ mentions with approval (3. 96–7), contends with the Sophists, who, like Satan, make the worse appear the better reason, and exposes the fallacies of their thinking. But one greater than Socrates and one far more dangerous than the Sophists are the agents of Milton's poem, engaged in a far more desperate contest. Christ, the arch-defender of truth, is contending with Satan, the arch-Sophist 'compos'd of Lyes' who has turned all morality upside down.[25]

W. R. Parker has propounded the theory that *Paradise Regained* may originally have been composed in the form of a drama and later converted into its present form. His reasons for so thinking are that three-quarters of the poem (1562 lines) are spoken by the various characters and 'could...have belonged to a projected play, the structure of which can easily be inferred.' Of the speeches three are soliloquies, two by Christ and one by Mary, 'an essentially dramatic device'. Few speeches which might have been choruses have survived, but in some of the non-dramatic passages Parker believes that he sees 'vestiges of choral song' (e.g. 4. 419–25). The final denouement on the pinnacle of the temple, with a Christian *deus ex machina*, which Elizabeth M. Pope found untraditional and 'unorthodox',[26] 'becomes...completely explicable if the poem was first conceived as a drama' and some of the denouement actually composed in that form.[27] Readers may judge for themselves what credence is to be given to this subjective theory.

It is surprising that an episode in the life of Christ so important as the temptation in the wilderness should rarely have been a subject for poetic

[25] See Irene Samuel, *Plato and Milton* (Ithaca, N.Y., 1947), p. 21, and Clifford Davidson, 'The Dialectic of Temptation', *BSUF* 8 (1967), 11–16, which discusses Satan's foolish and sophistical arguments.
[26] See *Paradise Regained: the Tradition and the Poem* (Baltimore, 1947), pp. 8, 95–9.
[27] See *Milton, a Biography*, 2. 1140.

treatment, and never before nor after Milton the subject of a great poem. But as *Paradise Regained* is structurally *sui generis*, so in its treatment of Christ's trial it has no close analogues. The Old English *Christ and Satan*, the mystery plays, *The Temptation* (*Ludus Coventriae* 22) and the *Lokk Smythys Play* (*York Mysteries* 22), if Milton knew them, could have been of very slight use to him. *La vita et passione di Christi* of Antonio Cornozano (Venice, 1518) and *La humanita del Figlivolo di Dio* of Teofilo Folengo (Venice, 1533), which Dunster mentions, again if Milton knew them, apparently suggested only a few minor details. The few resemblances between *Paradise Regained* and Bale's *A Brefe Comedy or Enterlude Concernynge the Tentacyon of Our Lord and Saver Jesus Christ by Satan in the Desert* are only such as a common subject may explain. The *Oratio Prima* of Jacobus Strasburgus's *Orationes Duae Carmine Heroico Scriptae* (Leipzig, 1565), the only brief epic dealing with the temptation which Mrs Lewalski has found, bears little resemblance to Milton's poem. Vida's brief account of the temptation in the *Christiad* (4. 607–55)—too brief to be at all effective—cannot have contributed anything to *Paradise Regained* unless it be the simile in 4. 18–20 comparing Satan to waves dashing against a solid rock, which, however, Milton may have derived directly from Homer or from Fletcher.

In the seventh canto of the second book of *The Faerie Queene*, Milton undoubtedly found suggestions for his treatment of the temptation of the kingdoms.[28] Sir Guyon, the knight of Temperance, in a 'delue' comes upon Mammon, 'An vncouth, saluage, and vnciuile wight', surrounded by heaps of gold, which he makes haste to hide. But when Guyon stays his hand, he says that

> Riches, renowme, and principality,
> Honour, estate, and all this worldes good,
> For which men swinck and sweat incessantly (8. 5–7)

are his, and he offers to give them to Guyon, if he will serve him. Upon Guyon's refusal because these gifts are not in keeping with a 'high heroicke spright', Mammon, arguing like another Satan, and like him

---

[28] See Edwin Greenlaw, 'A Better Teacher than Aquinas', *SP* 14 (1917), 205.

persistent, attempts to persuade Guyon that money will supply him with all things needful, even crowns and kingdoms. After Guyon again rejects his offer, Mammon leads him to the gate of Pluto's realm, where he exposes him to Payne, Strife, Revenge, Despight, and other kindred horrors calculated to terrify him. They then enter the house of Richesse, 'but a litle stride' from the gate of hell, which though the walls are all of gold, is a darksome, dusty place, draped with cobwebs and strewn with dead men's bones. When Guyon once more withstands temptation, Mammon, now angry, conducts him to a sumptuous chamber, where in 'glistring glory' sits his daughter, Philotime, to whom he proposes to marry Guyon, only to have the proposal rejected. Through three days Guyon resists temptation, but at the end, unlike Christ, he emerges from his trial in a state of utter exhaustion, which, however, may be nothing more than the physical effect of a long and trying experience. In another, much more important respect he is unlike Christ: in the 'delue' of Mammon he has to rely for strength upon his habit of temperance, for, unaccompanied by the Palmer, who in the allegory represents right reason, he is deprived of a guide ever-present with Christ. Moreover the ideal to which he strives to be true, as he declares, is to spend his days 'in armes, and in atchieuements braue'; whereas in Milton's view Christ's ideal far transcends brave deeds of arms.

Closest to *Paradise Regained* in subject and in time is Giles Fletcher's *Christs Victorie on Earth*, the second of the four parts of his *Christs Victorie and Triumph in Heaven and Earth* (Cambridge, 1610), which almost certainly provided Milton with details, all, I hope, recorded in my notes. But although Fletcher and Milton treat the same subject, and both represent Christ as a magnanimous Renaissance hero engaged in a spiritualized knightly combat, in other respects the differences between the two poems are more notable than the resemblances. Fletcher's spirited and often noble poem is an allegory in the Spenserian tradition, in a highly ornamented, at times extravagant, style. As Miss M. M. Mahood remarks, it is a work in which 'everything...dances'.[29] The scene becomes even fantastic when, in the third and fourth stanzas,

[29] *Poetry and Humanism* (London, 1950), p. 172.

the wild beasts, tamed in Christ's presence, come kneeling and dancing about him like so many votaries, and the lion licks the dust from his feet while the goat rides upon its back. Milton's poem, in an unadorned style, is only quasi-allegorical; Christ and Satan are fully realized characters, not allegorical symbols, personifications of the right reason and passion which they exemplify. *Paradise Regained* also treats an inner moral struggle, absent from *Christs Victorie*, revealing the greatness of which man is capable. The purpose of the two poems is different: Milton is primarily concerned with righteousness, Fletcher with religious devotion.

Another source of influence upon *Paradise Regained* Merritt Hughes finds in Malory's *Morte d'Arthur*,[30] which he believes contributed more to the poem than appears on the surface. It is the source, he writes, of Satan's banquet, and as evidence he cites the lines:

> Ladies of th' *Hesperides*, that seem'd
> Fairer then feign'd of old, or fabl'd since
> Of Fairy Damsels met in Forest wide
> By Knights of *Logres*, or of *Lyones*,
> *Lancelot* or *Pelleas*, or *Pellenore*. (2. 357–61)

But the Arthurian knights are the only detail in the account of the banquet that may be reminiscent of Malory. For the others, such as the 'Ladies of th' *Hesperides*', as my notes explain, Milton is indebted to classical sources and to Tasso. The banquet cannot be accounted for by any single source but only by many. Other evidence of Malory's influence Hughes finds in the fiend who 'in Likeness of a man of religion' tries to lead Sir Bors into 'error and wanhope'. But Milton did not need to go to Malory to find Satan in disguise. For centuries, indeed ever after his first appearance in the form of a serpent, as I explain in my note on 1. 314, he had assumed many disguises, often that of a venerable old man, as in Fletcher's poem and like Archimago in *The Faerie Queene*.

At most these and a few other resemblances to Malory, which Hughes mentions, are superficial. Although Milton may have seen merits in the

---

[30] See 'The Christ of *PR* and the Renaissance Poetic Tradition', *SP* 35 (1938), 255–7.

Morte d'Arthur which escaped the eye of Roger Ascham, who, in *The Scholemaster*, remarks that 'the whole pleasure' of that 'booke standeth in two speciall poyntes, in open mans slaughter, and bold bawdrye'[31]— and truly there is much of both—he drew from the Arthurian legends nothing more than material for allusions with which to adorn two passages of *Paradise Regained* (2. 357–61; 3. 337–43). After finding in the poetry of Spenser the image of his own ethical ideal and his own conception of the poet as a moral teacher, would he have felt any need, Jacques Blondel asks (p. 25), to have recourse to Malory? Though the chivalric ideal expressed by Malory's Lord Balin in the following words, 'Manhood and worship is hyd within mans persone and many a worshipful knyghte is not knowne unto all people', might serve as epigraph to *Paradise Regained*, nevertheless, as Blondel observes, there is a profound difference between that poem and the *Morte d'Arthur*. The deeds 'Above Heroic' which Christ exemplifies do not relate him to Galahad and Percivale and the other Arthurian knights.[32]

In '*PR*: the Meditative Combat',[33] Louis Martz attempts to prove that there is a close similarity between Milton's poem and the *Georgics* of Virgil; that both are 'meditative' poems, in a 'middle style', and develop a common ethical theme: the temperate, frugal life as opposed to luxury, grandeur, and the vice of empires. The *Georgics* is unquestionably a *didactic* poem, like the *Works and Days* of Hesiod, but by no generally accepted meaning of the term can it be called meditative. *Paradise Regained*, in which the agents are presented dramatically, engaged in a mortal combat, is a poem of action; and that the stage is set in the souls of Christ and Satan in no wise alters that fact. The two poems are not stylistically alike. In the *Georgics* there is a profusion of pictorial imagery and mythological allusions, both of which are conspicuously absent from the unadorned but noble style of *Paradise Regained*. Nor do the poems develop a common theme. At the end of the

---

[31] *English Works*, ed. Wright (Cambridge, 1904), p. 231.
[32] By the time he composed *PR*, if not long before, Milton had evidently come to believe that the model of the Christian hero which he was concerned to depict, if it was to carry conviction, must be true; it could not be a fiction, however edifying that might be.
[33] *ELH* 27 (1960), 223–47.

second book of the *Georgics* there is a passage in praise of the frugal, temperate life of the Italian peasants; but the poem as a whole is a gospel, a glorification, of work; and the moral of it all is that both men and beasts, even the bees, according to the law of their being, ought to work with all their might. It need hardly be remarked that *Paradise Regained* means much more than this.

Prior to Milton the stylist and innovator most successful in the creation of a brief epic, Stewart A. Baker believes, was Jacopo Sannazaro, who in the *De partu virginis*, his brief epic on the nativity, produced a model for the use of 'pastoral motifs and the pastoral point of view to adapt Virgilian epic to a Christian subject and theme' (p. 116), and so treated his subject that it made possible a form of epic poetry wherein greatness consists in humility and heroism in a willingness to suffer. 'In both Sannazaro and Milton...', Baker writes (p. 131),[34]

we find genre used functionally to create both theme and implicit metaphor. In both poets we find the pastoral landscape developed as a symbol for the meditative spirit in its natural place, a state of mind which reveals the emanation of the future from the typological past. In this special milieu, epic motifs and values are introduced to be modified, inverted or redefined by speakers assuming the pastoral point of view. This interplay of genres, of epic and pastoral motifs and vocabularies, becomes one of the chief means of redefining heroism in the context of the Christian epic.

If Sannazaro left a model of a new type of epic poem, Milton greatly improved upon that model, and it is to him that John M. Steadman attributes the achievement of a 'Copernican revolution' in epic poetry. In his invaluable book *Milton and the Renaissance Hero*,[35] which, more thoroughly and perceptively than had been done before, examines and elucidates Milton's conception of the true epic subject and the true epic hero, Steadman says (p. 177):

Milton found the heroic poem brick and left it marble. For the praise of men he substituted the glory of God. Instead of human strength, he depicted mortal frailty—accentuating this contrast by juxtaposing divine and human virtues.

[34] 'Sannazaro and Milton's Brief Epic', *CL* 20 (1968), 116–32.
[35] Oxford, 1967.

Instead of the physical warfare of secular polities, he described the moral conflict of spiritual societies. Instead of celebrating heroic exploits, he stressed their imperfections, weighing man's sins against the truly 'magnific' works of God. By this radical reorientation of epic tradition, he based the heroic poem on the cornerstone of Protestant ethics, the 'vanity of human merits'.

From its time of publication, as Edward Phillips informs us,[36] *Paradise Regained* was 'generally censur'd to be much inferiour' to *Paradise Lost*, though Milton 'could not hear with patience any such thing when related to him; possibly the Subject may not afford such variety of Invention, but it is thought by the most judicious to be little or nothing inferiour to the other for stile and decorum.' The latter part of this statement, in which Phillips may be repeating what Milton himself had said—and he was a more competent judge than many of his critics either then or now—implies all that need be said in answer to the disparaging criticism. In the present century, as in the seventeenth, such criticism still often arises from a mistaken comparison of the two poems, as when J. W. Mackail regrets that in *Paradise Regained* there is 'not the organ-music that we knew'.[37] Milton never intended that there should be. With a sense of style and decorum as nice and as unerring as that of Mozart, he knew that the subject of *Paradise Regained* demanded a very different kind of music. As Douglas Bush has said, 'In interior drama— almost interior monologue with an objectified tempter—everything, including rhythm, must be pitched in a more subdued key.'[38] We should not, then, expect to find in *Paradise Regained* the splendours of *Paradise Lost*, though where they serve a necessary purpose, there are splendours, as in the descriptions of the Parthian and Roman empires, the eulogy of Greek culture, and the description of the magical banquet with its lovely evocation of myth and romance. But as a whole *Paradise Regained* is one of the most unadorned poems in the English language. Except for Belial's lewd proposal it is nearly devoid of the usual epic machinery. In the first three books there are no epic similes, and the few in the

[36] *Early Lives*, pp. 75-6.
[37] *The Springs of Helicon* (New York, 1909), p. 187.
[38] *English Literature in the Earlier Seventeenth Century* (2nd ed., Oxford, 1962), p. 413.

fourth book, notably the three near the beginning, though most apt and effective, are not elaborated as epic similes commonly are. There is a general avoidance of the elaborate, periodic sentences and the highly complex syntax of *Paradise Lost*. The rhythm for the most part is very close to the rhythm of the normal speech of cultivated men. The language, which Wordsworth considered 'almost faultless',[39] is simple and direct, even when Milton is being most learned; but like the language of the King James Version of the Bible, which it often almost reproduces, its simple directness never becomes meanness. It is rather a noble simplicity, animated and made deeply moving by Milton's lofty moral idealism and by the passionate but restrained intensity of Christ's spiritual struggle with Satan. Thus what might seem necessarily flatly prosaic becomes transmuted into great poetry.

When Milton chose the temptation of Christ as the subject of *Paradise Regained*, he chose that episode in all history which has traditionally been regarded as the antithesis and the corollary of the temptation of Adam; it was therefore the only subject for a poem which should be the counterpart of *Paradise Lost*. And in view of his purpose both subjects were for him the natural choices, since in *Areopagitica* he had said: 'I cannot praise a fugitive and cloister'd vertue, unexercis'd & unbreath'd, that never sallies out and sees her adversary, but slinks out of the race, where that immortall garland is to be run for, not without dust and heat.'[40] The first Adam by disobedience lost Paradise, Christ, the second Adam, by obedience regained it. To reproach Milton, as does Malcolm Ross, because he did not choose Christ's death and resurrection, 'the Eucharistic sacrifice of the cross',[41] is to misunderstand his purpose. To the question why he did not write a poem on the crucifixion, C. S. Lewis answers, because he had 'more sense'.[42] It is too far removed from

---

[39] *The Prose Works of William Wordsworth*, ed. Grosart (3 vols., London, 1897), 3. 430.

[40] *Works* 4. 311.

[41] *Poetry and Dogma* (New Brunswick, N.J., 1954), pp. 221–2.

[42] *A Preface to Paradise Lost* (London and New York, 1942), p. 89. Although Milton's early attempt to compose a poem on the passion was a failure, 'Christ Crucifi'd' appears in the 'Outlines for Tragedies' (*Works* 18. 241); but, as he must later have seen, in neither the temptation nor the crucifixion is Christ a tragic character; and he probably knew that the *Christus Patiens* of Grotius is somewhat less than a success as a tragedy.

ordinary experience, and it would not answer Ellwood's question, 'What hast thou to say of *Paradise found*?' He never meant *Paradise Regained*, any more than *Paradise Lost*, to be *primarily* a *religious*—much less a theological—poem;[43] nor in it is he concerned with man's final redemption, the 'glorious work' which Christ only at the end, after his victory over Satan, is about to begin. He did intend it to be a moral poem, which, by showing the example of Christ resisting temptation, might teach men how to restore right reason and faith to their proper place and remain obedient to the moral law of God, become free men, and thus realize the best that is possible in human nature. Therein lies the merit of which man is capable; and therein is Paradise regained, the 'paradise within thee, happier farr' which was promised to Adam.

The threefold temptation of Christ in the wilderness is related in Matt. 4. 1–11 and in Luke 4. 1–13. In Mark 1. 13 we read merely that Christ 'was there in the wilderness forty days, tempted of Satan'; Mark, however, adds 'and was with the wild beasts', a detail, not mentioned by the other two, which Milton uses in 1. 310–13. Matthew and Luke agree that the temptations were: (1) to turn a stone into bread; (2) to accept all the kingdoms of the world and the glory of them—and the power, Luke adds—as gifts which Satan would bestow, upon condition that Christ worship him; and (3) to cast himself down from the pinnacle of the temple in Jerusalem. This is the order of the temptations in Luke; but Matthew, reversing the order of the second and third, has the

[43] Nevertheless some commentators believe that they find in the poem much more theology than I think Milton intended us to find there. For his purpose in representing the morally exemplary hero, theology as it is elaborated in *De Doctrina Christiana* simply is not necessary. Mrs Lewalski, for example (*Brief Epic*, pp. 182–92) maintains that in *PR* Milton deals in turn with each aspect of Christ's threefold mission as prophet, priest, and king, and that these aspects are basic to its structure. In the first temptation she, as had certain Biblical commentators, sees the true prophet defeating Satan, the father of lies; in the temptation of the kingdoms, the true king of the church and the world dethroning Satan, the prince of this world; and on the pinnacle of the temple, the suffering priest overthrowing the prince of darkness and prince of the air (p. 330). From Mrs Lewalski's interpretation of the structure of *PR* John Carey (p. 1066) dissents, as do I, on the ground that it introduces an imbalance into the poem, the roles of prophet and king being elaborately treated but the role of priest 'hardly introduced except in the storm-tower sequence'.

On the so-called 'triple equation', which both Miss Pope and Mrs Lewalski accept, see my comments below, p. 32.

temptation of the kingdoms come last, and at the end, like Mark, has ministering angels come to Christ, another detail of which Milton makes significant use (in 4. 581–635). Like Matthew, Milton has all the temptations come after the forty days of fasting, and thus produces the effect of highly concentrated action, and suggests the urgent haste which Satan, fearing the end of his dominion, believes that the occasion demands. Milton, however, follows the order in Luke, and thus, with the temptation on the pinnacle of the temple coming last, brings the contest between Christ and Satan to a more dramatic and decisive conclusion than would be possible with Matthew's order.[44] That order also gives the poem the symmetrical structure which is characteristic of Milton's work. The first temptation to distrust God's providence, told with almost Scriptural brevity, is followed by the elaborate, and also symmetrical, composite temptation of the kingdoms, and is balanced by the brief third temptation which invites presumption upon God's providence. With these proportions maintained, Matthew's order would then result in an imbalance; for the first two temptations would appear to be little more than a prelude to the third, and relatively less important. The temptation on the pinnacle of the temple in the economy of Milton's poem cannot come anywhere but at the end.

Why *Paradise Regained* was divided into four books long remained a problem for which no satisfactory solution was offered. Why was it divided at all, since it is short enough to be read at one sitting? The divisions do not coincide with significant breaks in the action. The first book ends with nightfall after the first temptation, but the description of night and the dawn of another day is deferred until the middle of the second book. The elaborate second temptation occupies the remainder of the second, all of the third, and about two-thirds of the fourth books. That Milton, who had carefully divided *Paradise Lost* into books which mark stages in the action, should have been responsible for this seemingly arbitrary, even capricious, division, did not seem credible. A. S. P.

---

[44] Before Milton's time, authors of works of any kind dealing with the life of Christ, when they were free to choose, usually followed the order in Matthew. See E. M. Pope, *PR, Tradition and Poem*, p. 8.

Woodhouse, however, has perceived why he should have been responsible for it.[45] As he points out, the temptations are so balanced that if we were to rely upon the structural pattern of the poem, the effect of the symmetry might be too emphatic and mechanical. This danger Milton has offset by the device, simple once it is seen, of *not* making the divisions coincide with breaks in the action. This 'staggered effect', as Woodhouse aptly calls it, partly conceals but does not break the symmetry of the poem which then gradually impresses itself upon the reader.

By drawing upon his wide and varied reading, and by one of the great feats of the imagination, Milton has amplified thirteen verses of Luke's Gospel, and a few details from Matthew and Mark, into a poem of 2,070 lines; but though he has amplified, he has not in any essential way modified what he found in Scripture.[46]

Paradise Regained also amplifies the following lines in *Paradise Lost*:

> Henceforth I learne, that to obey is best,
> And love with fear the onely God, to walk
> As in his presence, ever to observe
> His providence, and on him sole depend,
> Mercifull over all his works, with good
> Still overcoming evil, and by small
> Accomplishing great things, by things deemd weak
> Subverting worldly strong, and worldly wise
> By simply meek; that suffering for Truths sake
> Is fortitude to highest victorie,
> And to the faithful Death the Gate of Life;
> Taught this by his example whom I now
> Acknowledge my Redeemer ever blest (12. 561–73).

Adam, now repentant, is making his great profession of faith. From the bitter experience of temptation and disobedience, and from the example

---

[45] See 'Theme and Pattern in *PR*', *UTQ* 25 (1955–6), 170–1.

[46] Allan Gilbert is correct in setting up as a principle necessary for understanding a poem by Milton that he is unlikely to modify a Biblical story. See 'Temptation in *PR*', *JEGP* 15 (1916), 600. In this respect he is unlike the French writers of Biblical epic poems in the 17th century who both materially and morally deformed and distorted the Bible. See Richard Sayce, *The French Biblical Epic in the Seventeenth Century* (Oxford, 1955), pp. 151–61.

of Christ revealed to him by the angel Michael, he has learned that the cardinal principles by which the true Christian must rule his life are humble, faithful obedience to God, and patient endurance, 'suffering for Truths sake', which is Christian heroism. These principles are the two themes announced in the opening lines of *Paradise Regained*; and as the poem advances we see Christ perfectly translating them into action. The one is an unchanging and constantly active principle; the other gradually develops. From the experience of trial Christ gains a fuller and fuller revelation of his own nature and mission, which becomes complete on the pinnacle of the temple, where at last by merit he proves himself to be the heroic Son of God; his divinity asserts itself, and the two themes are united.

Although Milton nowhere says in so many words that he means his readers, like Adam, to be taught by Christ's example, that, I am persuaded, was his object in composing *Paradise Regained*.[47] It is significant that even Satan, though with evil intent, admits that Christ is 'of good, wise, just, the perfect shape' (3. 11), that is, he is the perfect pattern of virtue. The Christ of *Paradise Regained* is the Christ of the New Testament, who was 'in all points tempted like as we are, yet without sin'.[48] His virtue, if it be of a higher degree, is not in kind beyond what the ordinary man, employing the same spiritual resources, may achieve. In Milton's time, when there was more stress than there now is upon the moral importance of example, that Christ is the great moral exemplar was a point of orthodox belief, which for centuries religious writers, especially when they were explaining the significance of the temptation, had so often emphasized that Milton could assume that it would be understood.[49] In an age when the *De Imitatione Christi* of Thomas à

[47] See Blondel, pp. 72, 75; Bush, *English Literature in the Earlier Seventeenth Century*, p. 413.

[48] Heb. 4. 15; 2. 18.

[49] See Augustine, *Ioan. Evang.* 52 (Migne, *Pat. Lat.* 35. 1770); *Civ. D.* 7. 33; Aquinas, *Sum. Th.* 3. 41. 1; Bonaventure, *De Sex Alis Seraphim* 5 (*Opera Omnia*, Quaracchi, 1898, 8. 140–1); Bernard of Clairvaux, *Instructio Sacerdotis* 6 (*Opera*, Paris, 1690, 2. 526–7); Marsilio Ficino, *De Christiana Religione* (*Opuscula*, Venice, 1503, sig. h2); Luther, *Predigten* (*Sämtliche Werke*, Frankfurt-am-M.–Erlangen, 1862, 1. 250, 578); Martin Bucer, *Enarrat. in Evang.* (Strasbourg, 1537, sig. 4m); Erasmus, *Institutio Principis* (*Opera Omnia*, Leyden,

Kempis, both in the original Latin and translation, was pouring by the thousand from printing presses all over Europe, readers of *Paradise Regained* would not need to be told that in Christ they should see the great moral exemplar who, because his will is controlled by faith and directed by right reason, can obey God, and so preserve the hierarchical order of Nature; and who sees that it is his first duty to seek his own moral perfection before he attempts to save others.

Douglas Bush's excellent statement of Milton's ethical and religious principles[50] does not dispose one to agree with Tillyard that Milton has deliberately divested *Paradise Regained* 'of all relation to ordinary life', because he meant to say 'that the business of the human mind with itself' and with God is more important 'than all its relations with human beings'.[51] But the business of the mind with itself and with God is the condition of the possibility of its right relations with other human beings. Tillyard is ascribing an oddly withdrawn attitude to Milton, who in *An Apology for Smectymnuus* writes that 'he who would not be frustrate of his hope to write well hereafter in laudable things, ought him selfe to bee a true Poem, that is, a composition, and patterne of the best and honourablest things'.[52] Milton was one of the poets least likely ever to divorce poetry from what we call life, that is our life as responsible moral agents. If ever a poet intended his poetry to be practical, in the best sense of that much abused word, it was Milton, who would have agreed with Archi-

1703–6, 4. 578); Calvin, *Harm. Evang.*, Matt. 4. 6 (*Opera Omnia*, Brunswick, 1864–1900, 45. 134); Montaigne, *Essays* 1. 20 (tr. E. J. Trechmann, London, 1927, 1. 78); Pierre Bardin, *Le Lycée du Sr Bardin* . . . (2 vols., Paris, 1632–4, 2. 890–1); François de Grenaille, *L'Honneste Garçon* (2 vols., Paris, 1642, 1. 154, 177–8); William Ames, *The Marrow of Sacred Divinity* (London, 1643), p. 98; Joseph Hall, *Contemplations* 2. 3 (*Works*, Oxford, 1837, 2. 344); Lancelot Andrewes, *Ninety-Six Sermons* (Oxford, 1843), 5. 480, 503; Amandus Polanus, *Syntagma Theologiae Christianae* (Hanover, 1675), p. 387; Jeremy Taylor, *Ductor Dubitantium* (*Works*, ed. Heber and Eden, London, 1854–5, 9. 488–91). Taylor's life of Christ is entitled *The Great Exemplar of Sanctity and Holy Life According to the Christian Institution in the History of the Life and Death of the Ever-Blessed Jesus Christ, the Saviour of the World* (London, 1649). The tradition of Christ as exemplary appears again in the recent novel of Nikos Kazantzakis, *The Last Temptation of Christ*, tr. Bien (New York, 1960), p. 3.

[50] See *Paradise Lost in Our Time* (Ithaca, N.Y., 1945), pp. 29–57.
[51] *Milton*, p. 319.
[52] *Works* 3. 303.

bald MacLeish that poetry is one of the best means by which we can make sense of our lives.[53]

III

The first temptation, to turn a stone into bread, has often, as by many of the Church Fathers, been interpreted as an appeal to bodily appetite, an inducement to commit the sin of gluttony. But Christ's question 'Why dost thou then suggest to me distrust?' leaves no doubt that Milton, agreeing with Calvin and several other Renaissance commentators, saw in it the temptation to commit the more fundamental sin of distrusting God's providence, a meaning further to be inferred from Satan's words, 'If thou be the Son of God' (Matt. 4. 3; Luke 4. 3). Milton is thus at the beginning emphasizing the right reason and humble faith which are Christ's guiding principles and strength throughout his trial. The first temptation, therefore, is not less important than those which follow. Satan does appeal to Christ's bodily appetite, but that, as when he tempted Eve, is only a means to an end, which he cunningly though vainly attempts to conceal and misrepresent by suggesting to Christ a charitable motive for miraculously creating bread. Like the apple which tempted Eve, bread has in itself no significance; anything else which might induce Christ to doubt that God, in his own time and in his own way, will provide whatever is needful would serve Satan's purpose equally well.

The long second temptation may seem, on casual reading, to modify the Scriptural accounts; but actually Milton does nothing more than state in concrete terms and with many details what Luke states generally and with the fewest possible details. The banquet, riches, fame, the kingdom of David, and the might of Parthia and Rome, and the learning of the Greeks are only particular forms of the kingdoms of the world and their power and glory, Luke's terms. That they are treated at far greater length than the other two temptations need raise no problem. The temptations to distrust and presumption and their decisive rejection

[53] See *Poetry and Experience* (Boston, 1961), p. 149.

can most effectively be illustrated by single acts committed in a moment of time; and any attempt to amplify the accounts of such acts would result only in diffuseness and weakened effect. Moreover on offering the first and third temptations, both because he is greatly alarmed, and because he wishes to take Christ off guard, and rush him into ill-considered acts, Satan is using haste as an important part of his strategy. The worldly values, however, presented in an ascending scale, which are the materials of the second temptation, can appear with all their enticing power only if their most alluring aspects are presented in rich detail, as they present themselves in daily life. And there are yet other reasons for the elaboration of this part of the poem. Since the other two, because of their nature, could not reasonably and artistically be expanded, the elaborated second temptation afforded Milton the only means of fully revealing the *ethos* and *dianoia* of Christ and Satan, without which the poem would fail of its purpose. And it was the only way of producing a poem of the 'adequate magnitude', one of the two qualities, order in the parts being the other, on which, according to Aristotle, beauty depends.[54]

The banquet is not, as some have argued, an awkward and pointless repetition of the first temptation. If it were, it would destroy the symmetry of this part of the poem, which is as carefully maintained as the symmetry of the poem as a whole. The banquet is a temptation contemplative in character, as is the learning of the Greeks; and with four temptations coming between them which are active, they are so placed that they balance each other.[55] The cumulative effect of the details of the banquet scene, if they are read with due attention, is aesthetic rather than gustatory. Many of them, the pleasant grove, the song of birds, the table 'richly spred, in regal mode', a 'stately side-board', 'stripling youths rich clad', Nymphs and Naiades, flowers, music, and perfumes have nothing to do with satisfying hunger, except as they are the decorative accompaniments of food. Even the food with which the table is overloaded, as at a Lucullan feast, is so described as to appeal as much

[54] *Poet.* 7.
[55] See Woodhouse, 'Theme', *UTQ* 25 (1955–6), 170.

to the eye as to the palate. The clue to the meaning of all this rich array comes near the end in the one word 'Splendour'. With this lavish and pompous parade of luxurious things, which would appeal to a Mammon or a Heliogabalus, Satan hopes to induce Christ to seek the glory of worldly splendour, and to seek it as a final end. His misunderstanding of what will appeal to Christ's noble nature, which continues throughout the second temptation, is ironical, and would be comical if the issue were not so deadly serious. All splendid things are already Christ's by right, as Satan admits. If Christ were to accept them thus impudently offered by one who has usurped them, he would be surrendering his right to them, and submitting both himself and them to Satan.

The next temptations, to seek riches, fame, political and military power, are all active in their nature. Satan, making the ethical appeal, represents them as noble ends because they will enable Christ to deliver his people from their Roman conquerors and to sit upon his 'Father David's Throne', which is his right. Satan anxiously endeavours to persuade Christ to become a hero like Alexander the Great, Scipio, Pompey, and Julius Caesar; but as Christ retorts, heroes such as these do nothing

> But rob and spoil, burn, slaughter, and enslave
> Peaceable Nations...
>   [and] leave behind
> Nothing but ruin wheresoe're they rove (3. 75–9).

Compared with the heroism which Christ must exemplify, theirs is but a ludicrous parody. It is not his duty, Christ declares, to liberate those who are not worthy, and hence not capable, of liberty. And he reminds Satan of Job (an embarrassing reminder) and of Socrates, who suffered for truth's sake, who became heroes in the sense which Christ is at once expounding and exemplifying. But heroism in this sense Satan, who has learned nothing from encounters with Abdiel and Job, is incapable of understanding. In rejecting all these proffered gifts and exposing the sophistry of the rhetoric with which Satan attempts to persuade him that he must use doubtful means to attain good ends, Christ is not rejecting action as such. His answer (3. 182–7) when Satan reproaches him for inaction leaves that in no doubt. As Woodhouse explains,[56] the prevailing note throughout all the temptations is passion in the original sense of suffering (*passio*); and it is passion, not contemplation, which is opposed to action. Christ says nothing at any time which in any way implies that he never will act. He, like Adam, Milton, everyman, is made for both contemplation and action. He does, however, insist that it is his *present* duty to await God's time for action. Nothing could better demonstrate the humility, unselfishness, and trust in God, the strength made perfect in weakness, which enables Christ to withstand all the wiles of Satan and to win the 'highest victorie'.

Of all the temptations none has so commonly been misunderstood as Satan's offer of Greek learning, the highest, contemplative form of worldly power and glory. Christ's answer has been read as an utter and amazing repudiation of that learning both by Christ and by Milton himself, even though neither is in the least unwilling to let it be known that he is deeply versed in Greek philosophy and literature. Milton had not in old age become an anti-intellectual, nor a quietist who relied upon moments of mystical illumination. If he had, *Paradise Lost*, *Paradise Regained*, and *Samson Agonistes* would be very different poems from what they are—if they could ever have been composed. As I explain in my note on 4. 286–384, he is asserting his life-long hierarchy of values in which the religious and ethical were always supreme. Like many other Christian humanists, he never thought the Greek classics the most important branch of learning nor the best of all literature. Religion and ethics are the one and the Bible the other. Christ's charge against the Greek philosophers is not that they teach *evil* doctrines, but doctrines that are insufficient for man's deepest needs. The best of their wisdom is natural wisdom, which always falls short of revealed wisdom. They cannot teach the highest truths which are necessary for man's salvation. These only the Bible and Christianity can teach. Nor, severely as he criticizes Greek poetry and oratory, does he condemn them as utterly worthless; he does explain wherein he finds them inferior to the poetry and oratory of the Hebrews. Greek learning still has its place, and can

[56] 'Theme', *UTQ* 25 (1955–6), 168.

be useful to one who knows how to use it aright, as it is to Christ in answering Satan, and as it was to Augustine and to Milton himself, to say nothing of many other good Christians before and after his time. On this point we need only consider the prominent place which he gives to classical studies in *Of Education*. Christ rejects Greek learning not only because it is inferior to Hebrew and Christian learning, but also because it is offered as a means to securing regal power and glory; whereas 'The end...of Learning', Milton declares in *Of Education*, 'is to repair the ruines of our first Parents by regaining to know God aright, and out of that knowledge to love him, to imitate him, to be like him, as we may the neerest by possessing our souls of true vertue, which being united to the heavenly grace of faith makes up the highest perfection.'[57] Furthermore, in the logic of the poem, as is more fully explained in the note on 4. 225–8, Christ *must* refuse to accept Greek learning in order to declare his own nature as the historic Christ, who is to introduce into history a power of grace which the light of nature cannot bestow.

Splendour, riches, fame, political and military power, and learning are not in themselves evil. For those who can keep them in their proper place and use them aright, they are goods; but when they are accepted as ultimate values, they displace the really ultimate values and become evils. If Christ were to accept them on Satan's terms, he would be violating true order, and accepting the kingdom of the devil, which is the kingdom of disorder. The result of all Satan's most anxious and ingenious efforts to present his kingdom in its most glowingly attractive colours, a result the irony of which he never sees, is that he provides Christ with the occasion for unanswerably condemning that kingdom. Thus Christ rejects the kingdoms of the world *only* as they are offered to him on Satan's terms. And thus, as I explain in my note on 3. 47–8, Stein is entirely right in denying that the rejection implies *contemptus mundi*.

Like the banquet, the night of storm which follows the temptation of learning appears to some commentators to present a problem. Is it part of the temptation of the kingdoms, or merely a prelude to the temptation

[57] *Works* 4. 277.

on the pinnacle of the temple, as the earlier dream of food is a prelude
to the temptation of bread? Dick Taylor, whose arguments are summarized in my note on 4. 368–540, sees in it a shrewdly conceived and
powerfully executed temptation; but I can regard it only as a necessary
psychological preliminary to the last temptation.[58] After Christ's rejection of learning, Satan, in a panic of fear because of his repeated failures,
is convinced that 'all his darts are spent'; he has nothing more to offer,
and further guileful argument would be futile. Rationalizing his failure
on the ground that power and glory 'have been before contemn'd, and
may agen', to discover what more Christ is 'then man, / Worth naming
Son of God', he admits that he must adopt another method. The only
method now left to him is physical violence, and hence the storm. By
making Christ feel deserted and helpless in a hostile natural world, and
again displaying his power, he hopes to terrify Christ, and thus predis-
pose him to yield when in the morning immediately after the night of
storm, he is suddenly faced with another temptation. A further objection
to regarding the storm as the last of the temptations of the kingdoms is
that, if it were that, it would destroy the symmetrical pattern: two
temptations of a contemplative nature would not balance each other;
nor would night, as after the first temptation, mark an important break
in the action.

On the following morning, in a calm that is in striking contrast with
the tempest of the night, and symbolic of the divine power to restore
order, Satan, dismayed, learns that again he has failed. Not only is
Christ completely unmoved by the storm and the fearsome dreams, but
he has detected Satan's evil intent, and tells him that he is toiling in vain.
Enraged by yet another failure, like a cornered beast, he proceeds to his
last desperate act. Hoping by a sudden assault to allow Christ no time
to consider what is proposed to him, Satan in the greatest haste, with
which Milton's rapid narrative corresponds, bears him away to Jerusalem, and, setting him on the highest pinnacle of the temple, says in
scorn:

[58] 'Storm Scene', *UTQ* 24 (1954–5), 360; and see also Blondel, pp. 55–6; Northrop Frye,
'Typology', *MP* 53 (1956), 236.

There stand, if thou wilt stand; to stand upright
Will ask thee skill; I to thy Fathers house
Have brought thee, and highest plac't, highest is best,
Now shew thy Progeny; if not to stand,
Cast thy self down; safely if Son of God...(4. 551–5).

Thus he tempts Christ to commit the sin of presumption; that is, need-lessly and unreasonably to expose himself to danger to see whether God will deliver him. But this is not Satan's whole purpose. He intends that Christ shall fall and be killed—it is an ill-concealed attempt at murder—and his death will for ever free Satan from the doubt and fear that tor-ment him. His injunction to stand, as Woodhouse observes,[59] is purely ironical; he never for a moment believes that it is possible. But if he can be ironical, so can Christ and the event. For the first and only time Christ complies with Satan's suggestion; but he does so *not* in surrender to Satan, not as finding his motive in the suggestion, but in obedience to God, like Samson going to the festival of Dagon. In so doing he performs his supreme act of humble trust and obedience; and with that act, as Satan is appalled to see, his divinity asserts itself. When Christ says, 'It is written, / Tempt not the Lord thy God', he is expressing a double meaning. As in all the earlier temptations, he is maintaining his exemplary character;[60] he will not put God to the test; and he is making his first claim to active participation in the godhead. Obedience and Christian heroism, the themes which Milton has been developing throughout the poem, are now united. In the instant that Christ stands, Satan knows that he is defeated, for he falls. To his crew of fallen angels he returns with 'Joyless triumphals...Ruin, and desperation, and dismay'. Like another Macbeth he has brought about his own ruin and the triumph of what he sought to destroy.[61]

Before the appearance of Woodhouse's essay to which I have just referred, too little attention was given to the last forty-four lines of *Paradise Regained*, in which ministering angels in a hymn of triumph

[59] 'Theme', *UTQ* 25 (1955–6), 181.
[60] See Blondel, p. 57.
[61] For comments on Arnold Stein's interpretation of the last temptation and his disagreement with Woodhouse, see my note on 4. 551–9.

explain the significance of Christ's victory and provide for him a heavenly feast, after which 'hee unobserv'd / Home to his Mothers house private return'd.' The poem, Woodhouse explains,[62] had it been written by a poet who lacked Milton's appreciation of classical form and effect, might have ended with Christ's victory; but that ending would have left the pattern incomplete. Therefore in the closing lines Milton achieves the quiet ending which both the pattern and the parallel with *Paradise Lost* demand. The heavenly feast balances the banquet of the temptation; and to its contrast between Satanic and natural beauty adds, as a third element, heavenly beauty. As the angels proclaim Christ's age-old but newly apprehended divinity, they also are confirming it. By overcoming all temptations Christ has again defeated Satan, 'aveng'd / Supplanted *Adam*' and 'regain'd lost Paradise'. Fully understanding his own nature and his mission as the redeemer, and at peace within himself, he is now prepared to enter upon his 'glorious work' of salvation.

Why does he return to his *mother's* house? Because this also is the completion of a pattern. Again, as at the beginning of the poem, Milton is emphasizing Christ's humanity. Moreover, as he has explained in his soliloquy (1. 227–58), it was from Mary that he gained his first though imperfect conception of his nature and mission; and now, with the complete revelation of both, to Mary he returns, Mary who has said of herself in words to be remembered here:

> this is my favour'd lot,
> My Exaltation to Afflictions high;
> Afflicted I may be, it seems, and blest;
> I will not argue that, nor will repine (2. 91–4).

In her own person Mary realizes the patient endurance which is the Christian heroism exemplified to a supreme degree by Christ.

[62] 'Theme', *UTQ* 25 (1955–6), 180–2.

IV

One of the interpretations upon which Biblical commentators, for centuries before Milton's time, had expended much misguided ingenuity is that the Gospels imply a parallelism between the temptations of Christ, Adam, and all men. This is the so-called 'triple equation'.[63] Much more space than this introduction allows would be required to recapitulate all the arguments that were employed to prove wherein the parallelism consists. Although commentators did not all agree, most of them believed that the temptations were, in an ascending scale, gluttony, vainglory, and avarice; that is the flesh, the world, and the devil. But if this scale is to be maintained, how it is to be made to fit the different order of the temptations in Matthew and Luke does not appear. As far as Milton is concerned, I cannot see that the matter has any importance.[64] He was content with the simple contrast between Adam's disobedience and Christ's obedience without anatomizing them into a scheme of corresponding sins and virtues. The traditional 'triple equation' entirely fails to account for Milton's interpretation of Christ's three temptations, which plainly are distrust, worldly power and glory, and presumption.

All through the action of *Paradise Regained*, until the moment of Christ's final victory, many commentators have believed that Satan, having heard Christ after his baptism proclaimed as the Son of God, fears yet doubts that he is the Messiah who drove him and his followers from heaven; and that in all the temptations he is persistently endeavouring to discover Christ's identity, which Christ as persistently conceals from him. The principal support for this interpretation is found in Satan's address in his first demonic council, in which he says:

> His first-begot we know, and sore have felt,
> When his fierce thunder drove us to the deep;
> Who this is we must learn, for man he seems
> In all his lineaments, though in his face
> The glimpses of his Fathers glory shine (1. 89–93);

[63] See E. M. Pope, *PR, Tradition and Poem*, pp. 51–69.   [64] See Blondel, p. 51.

. and in his angry, scornful speech before the final temptation, beginning

> Then hear, O son of *David*, Virgin-born;
> For Son of God to me is yet in doubt (4. 500–1).

To accept at face value such statements as these and a few others like them is to place naive confidence in the father of lies, and to ignore much else in the poem which clearly does not point to any uncertainty about Christ's identity, notably his own words immediately after the first temptation:

> Why dost thou then suggest to me distrust,
> Knowing who I am, as I know who thou art? (1. 355–6)

After these most unequivocal words Satan can have no slightest reason to doubt Christ's identity, nor Christ to conceal it. But if Satan is to maintain his evil power, which he is desperately afraid that he is about to lose, he has every reason to induce Christ to doubt that he is the only begotten Son of God, and so never to attempt the fulfilment of his Messianic mission. Woodhouse[65] is unquestionably right in pointing out that the 'identity motive', as it is called, neither does justice to the character of Satan, nor explains the nature of his doubt. He is still the incurable romantic that he himself characterized, and that he deliberately chose to be, in his most significant and most damning soliloquy in *Paradise Lost* 4. 32–113, which, if it had more often been correctly read, would have prevented much of the nonsense which has been written about him as the courageous hero resisting a tyrannical God. He rebels against God and against admitted facts; he refuses to accept his place in the great chain of being, and to act upon what he admits to be true. Because he refuses to accept the truth, his doubt about Christ's identity, to quote Woodhouse, 'is at once real and unreal...He would give anything to have it confirmed, or (failing that) to receive proof so categorical as to destroy it forever.' But cling as he will to his doubt, he does so 'patently with diminishing conviction and mounting despair'. Until his persistent assaults upon Christ's virtue become nothing but acts of spite, Satan, the great egoist, has abated none of the insensate pride which

[65] See 'Theme', *UTQ* 25 (1955–6), 172; Blondel, pp. 47–8.

caused his fall. To be supreme is still as much his object as when he
revolted in heaven. Base passions, hate, revenge, lust for power, still
rule his reason. Lorenzo's words about 'The man that hath no music
in himself', who 'Is fit for treasons, stratagems, and spoils...Let no
such man be trusted', perfectly apply to Satan, the 'motions' of whose
'spirit are dull as night, / And his affections dark as Erebus'—whose
soul is a great disharmony.[66] With an active but always misdirected
mind, he is an example of 'stupid intelligence', to use Albert Camus's
term.[67] Not only does he refuse to accept facts, but he is so shut up
within himself that he can conceive no motives, no values higher than
his own, nor ever understand a noble nature such as Christ's. As in
Paradise Lost he is an ugly parody of God and of divine goodness, so in
Paradise Regained is he a parody of the epic hero, and so by contrast
accentuates true heroism. His unreason and his conception of heroism
as only selfishly ambitious are parodies of Christ's right reason and
heroic virtue. So literal is his mind that spiritual meanings and metaphors, even Christ's clear statements, are beyond his comprehension,
and are distorted into meanings of his own. Adroit as he is in finding
arguments which he hopes will persuade Christ to do his will, his
reasoning, as when he first led the angels astray and when he tempted
Eve, is always sophistical, a mixture of falsehood, misrepresentation, and
suppression of whatever is counter to his purpose. Like a cunning
bargainer determined to secure what he wants, and prepared, if he must,
to raise his price, he has no scruples. If no other means are effective, he
will by psychological attrition overcome Christ's resistance. But as
arguments and stratagems one after another completely fail to move
Christ, Satan's fear of the threat to his continued power, which he
betrays in the demonic councils, mounts until it becomes such a panic
of rage and despair that it drives him to his final act of violence and his
second great defeat and fall. Other great evil-doers there are in literature,
Medea, Mephistopheles, Iago, Macbeth, Captain Ahab, but in destruc-

---

[66] Shakespeare, *Merch.* 5. 1. 83–8; see James Hutton, 'Some English Poems in Praise of
  Music', *English Miscellany*, ed. Praz, 2 (Rome, 1951), 3–28.
[67] *Resistance, Rebellion, and Death*, tr. O'Brien (New York, 1961), p. 254.

tive malignity none of them equals Satan. He is faultlessly and dramatically represented for what he is, a soul self-damned. He is only what he has deliberately chosen to be, and will as deliberately persist in being, even though through ages of evil-doing he has found no peace, no satisfaction, no slightest happiness, but, like certain dictators of our time, only fear and despair.

Since Christ in his divine nature cannot be tempted, Milton (as a directive to the reader) has been careful to announce in the fourth line of *Paradise Regained*—an echo of the fourth line of *Paradise Lost*—and three times in God's address to Gabriel (1. 140, 150, 166) that it is Christ the *man*, meeting trials on a strictly human level, whom we are to witness. But this emphasis upon his humanity must not be taken as a denial of his divine nature,[68] although Milton has often been charged,

---

[68] See William B. Hunter, 'Milton's Arianism Reconsidered', *HTR* 52 (1959), 13; Arthur Sewell, *A Study in Milton's Christian Doctrine* (London, 1939), p. 149. Although in *DocCh* 1. 5 (*Works* 14. 227, 259) there are statements which may seem to mean that Christ was not divine, there is much more evidence in that work, as in *Paradise Lost*, that Milton, though he did not believe Christ to be co-essential and co-equal with the Father (1. 5, *Works* 14. 211, 215, 329), nevertheless did believe in his dual nature (1. 14, *Works* 14. 207, 229, 331) and regarded him as the divine mediator and redeemer (1. 14, *Works* 15. 257, 279, 287–9). Hunter, who maintains that Milton was not an Arian, writes (p. 34): 'Subordinationism as such has not been branded as heretical, although it is not the view of the Trinity found most widely today—nor in the seventeenth century for that matter. As Milton himself observes [1. 5, *Works* 14. 357], his view of the Son agrees with the faith expressed in the Apostles' Creed; and he might have added the Nicene Creed. The equality of the persons of the Trinity was not officially affirmed at Nicaea and never has been; neither was the eternal generation of the Logos.' See Roland M. Frye, *God, Man, and Satan* (Princeton, N.J., 1960), pp. 269–76; C. A. Patrides, *Milton and the Christian Tradition* (Oxford, 1966), pp. 15–25, which support Hunter. Although commentators have generally agreed that Milton's tenets on the Trinity are unorthodox and Arian, Hunter's belief is not new. But is it a tenable belief? In 'Milton's Arianism Again Considered', *HTR* 54 (1961), 195–205, Maurice Kelley argues that it is not, because Hunter has paid too little attention to the one most important term in the Nicene Creed and to the anathemas with which that Creed ends, anathemas dealing point by point with what were regarded as the heresies raised in the *Thalia* of Arius. The term is ὁμοούσιος, 'of the same essence'. The Creed asserts that God the Son is 'of the same essence' with the Father, and anathematizes those who insist that he is of a different essence, as do Arius and Milton. The second anathema is pronounced against those who deny the eternity of the Son, and insist, again as do Arius and Milton, that the Father's generation of the Son was a temporal act, saying, 'There was when he was not, and before being born he was not'. See *TR, Works* 6. 169; *DocCh* 1. 5, *Works* 14. 189, 193, 203, 231; J. N. D. Kelly, *Early Christian Creeds*, 2nd ed. (New York, 1961), pp. 215–16. However, as Maurice Kelley further explains, quoting from

among other heresies, with Socinianism and Unitarianism.[69] For Coleridge the 'sceptical Socinian' of the poem is Satan, whom even those who persist in admiring him in *Paradise Lost* do not seem to have mistaken as the mouthpiece for Milton's beliefs.[70]

Although there is virtually no theological speculation and dogma in *Paradise Regained*, there is clear evidence that Christ is the θεάνθρωπος of *De Doctrina Christiana* 1. 14 (*Works* 15. 279). Satan, who would give anything to be able to believe Christ is not the 'first-begot' of Him whose 'fierce thunder drove us to the deep' (1. 89–90), admits that in Christ's face 'The glimpses of his Fathers glory shine' (1. 89–93). In addressing Gabriel, God acknowledges Christ as 'by merit call'd my Son' who will 'earn Salvation for the Sons of men' (1. 166–7). Nothing could be less equivocal than Christ's own statements in his first soliloquy declaring that he is the Messiah born to attain 'the promis'd Kingdom' and 'work Redemption for mankind' (1. 259–67). He himself is acknowledging his identity as the Son of God when, in rebuking Satan after the first temptation, he says 'Knowing who I am, as I know who thou art' (1. 356). His ability to see through Satan's disguise and to detect his hypocrisy is itself evidence that he is no mere man. Again after the banquet when he informs Satan that

> I can at will, doubt not, as soon as thou,
> Command a Table in this Wilderness,

Schaff-Herzog (s.v. Arianism), although Milton and Isaac Newton approach the Arian view of the relation of the Son to the Father, they widely differ from Arianism in spirit and aim. How widely may most readily be learned from the summary statement of Arian doctrine in the *Dict. de théol. cath.*, ed. Vacant, 1. 1784–91. By their time the term 'Arian', having taken on a broader meaning than that originally belonging to it, had come to denote theologians who, though rejecting orthodox dogmas concerning the Trinity, stressed the divinity, as opposed to the mere humanity, of Christ. Those who most nearly approached orthodox dogma and were farthest from Socinian and Unitarian views were known as 'high Arians'; 'antitrinitarians' would more precisely describe them. Milton, as Kelley believes, was one of these.

[69] See Legouis and Cazamian, *History of English Literature*, tr. Irvine (New York, 1926), p. 292; Herbert McLachlan, *The Religious Opinions of Milton, Locke, and Newton* (Manchester, 1941), p. 66.

[70] See Roberta F. Brinkley, *Coleridge on the Seventeenth Century* (Durham, N.C., 1955), p. 604. Blondel (p. 68) finds in *PR* only very slight traces of Socinian doctrine.

And call swift flights of Angels ministrant
Array'd in Glory on my cup to attend (2. 383–6),

he is declaring the miraculous power which he possesses only as he is
divine. All his references to his kingdom are clearly to the kingdom of
the Messiah. On the pinnacle of the temple, when, as Satan is forced
to realize, his divinity at last asserts itself, it is that divinity which defeats
Satan. And finally the angelic hymn (4. 596–635) which celebrates
Christ's triumph is such as can properly be addressed only to the divine
Son of God.

Until the present century, for the most part critics of *Paradise
Regained* and readers generally seem to have found in the person of
Christ little to which they thought it necessary to take exception. They
were able to accept him as a credible character in no way essentially
different from the Christ of the synoptic Gospels. Nor did many of
them see in him the self-portrait of an ageing Milton who had retreated
into Stoicism. But in the past fifty years, as *Paradise Regained* has
attracted more attention, some critics, although most of the more
eminent are not of their number, have thought Christ an artistic failure,
a cold, repellent, impossibly perfect and stoical superman, or an all too
human and pharisaical prig. And they stress what they take to be the
autobiographical element in the poem, and deplore it as a serious
mistake.[71] Others who do not go so far as to identify Christ and Milton
emphasize their resemblance, without, however, explaining precisely
wherein they are alike.[72]

To find autobiography in the poem is easy—too easy. One of the
passages most often cited as evidence for it is the following from Christ's
first soliloquy:

[71] See J. Bailey, *Milton* (London, 1915), p. 202; D. Saurat, *Milton: Man and Thinker* (New
York, 1925), p. 234; P. Phelps-Morand, *De Comus à Satan* (Paris, 1939), p. 232; *The
Oxford Book of English Verse*, ed. Lord David Cecil (Oxford, 1940), p. xxii; Northrop
Frye, 'Typology', *MP* 53 (1956), 234; W. W. Robson, 'The Better Fortitude', *The Living
Milton*, ed. Kermode (London, 1960), pp. 128, 134, 136; A. E. Dyson, 'The Meaning of
PR', *TSLL* 3 (1961), 200–8.
[72] See Legouis and Cazamian, *History of English Literature*, tr. Irvine, p. 376; Tillyard,
Milton, pp. 305–6.

> When I was yet a child, no childish play
> To me was pleasing, all my mind was set
> Serious to learn and know, and thence to do
> What might be publick good; my self I thought
> Born to that end, born to promote all truth,
> All righteous things (1. 201–6).

Between these lines and much else in the soliloquy and Milton's auto-biographical statements in the sixth Latin Elegy and in the prose works in which he describes his serious and studious youth there is resemblance.[73] But resemblance is not identity, and in this instance identification is not only unnecessary, but it fails to explain why Christ is as he is and not otherwise.[74] Furthermore it seems not to have occurred to those who accept the identification, nor to those who oppose it, that for Milton, or any other devout Christian, to identify himself with Christ, our Lord and Saviour, even in his human nature, would be the greatest violation of decorum. Imitation of Christ is one thing, but identification with him is quite another.

As Frank Kermode explains,

It is essential, to begin with, that we should not hesitate to accept Milton as a hero. He clearly aspired, in a remarkably unaffected way, to heroism, and thought it necessary to his day labour, 'not presuming to sing high praises of heroick men...unlesse he have in himselfe the experience and the practice of all which is praise-worthy'. This is not merely to say that Milton was in love with the breathed and exercised virtue of Guyon; that in his life and work he honoured the virtue which heroically rejects. He had in mind a more sharply defined heroic pattern. He cast himself as well as his Christ in this heroic mould;

---

[73] See *El* 6. 49–90; *RCG* (*Works* 3. 241); *Apol* (3. 304); *Def 2* (8. 119–21). But from the first and seventh Latin Elegies and *L'All* it appears that as a young man Milton was not so wholly serious that he could not, and on occasion did not, enjoy a gaudy day. He may have been a Puritan, and *PR* may be a poem of Miltonic Puritanism; but that was not the grim Puritanism of Cromwell, Bunyan, and the extremists. See H. J. C. Grierson, 'John Milton', *The Criterion* 8 (1928), 254. On the fallacies of the autobiographical interpretation of Milton's poems, see Bush, *Our Time*, pp. 58–87, and 'John Milton', *English Institute Essays: 1946* (New York, 1947), pp. 5–19.

[74] See Blondel, pp. 57–62; K. Muir, *John Milton* (London, 1955), p. 170. Muir finds in *PR* a credible picture of the historical Christ, in whom are both the limitations and the virtues of a Jew living in the time of Tiberius.

hence a degree of resemblance between them which has dangerously and un-necessarily been called identity.[75]

He found in himself a partial image of the heroism, of the moral attitude to the world, which he recognized in Christ, whom he accepted as his great moral exemplar. And, since his purpose is didactic, as Kermode further explains (p. 321), 'To make Christ unchallengeably exemplary Milton shaped *Paradise Regain'd* to contain a hero who completes and transcends the heroic data, not merely in his patience and heroic martyr-dom, but gaining exemplary rewards, which transcend the rewards of pagan heroism—sensual satisfaction, glory, power, even secular know-ledge.' Milton, then, does in the poem what the dramatic situation and his didactic purpose demand of him as an artist; and it is not autobio-graphical but poetic facts which need concern us.

Identification is further unnecessary because, as I explain in my notes on the lines quoted above, Milton is there merely following the tradition that Christ as a boy was precocious and unusually serious. And although as a man he is commonly thought of as meek and mild, full of charity and mercy, the Gospels do not represent him as displaying those qualities to Satan, or to the money-changers in the temple, or to the Pharisees, or on one occasion even to Peter. 'Our Saviour who had all gifts in him was Lord to express his indoctrinating power in what sort him best seem'd; sometimes by a milde and familiar converse...otherwhiles with bitter and irefull rebukes if not teaching yet leaving excuselesse those his wilfull impugners.'[76]

Satan, the great impugner, in deliberately choosing evil as his good, and as deliberately adhering to his choice, has forfeited all claim to mercy.[77] It is therefore no part of Christ's duty, out of charity and mercy, to attempt to convert him, for he cannot, he will not, be con-

---

[75] 'Milton's Hero', *RES* n.s. 4 (1953), 317.   [76] *Apol, Works* 3. 312–13.
[77] He is under the condemnation pronounced by God in *PL* 3. 198–202:

> This my long sufferance and my day of grace
> They who neglect and scorn, shall never taste;
> But hard be hard'nd, blind be blinded more,
> That they may stumble on, and deeper fall;
> And none but such from mercy I exclude.

verted. It is his duty, out of obedience to God and good will to man, whom he must save, to leave Satan 'excuselesse' and to confound him. He can fulfil his duty only by the adamant resistance which he maintains in all the temptations. And it is not merely a resistance of negation, for in rejecting each of Satan's gifts, he vigorously affirms the positive moral reason for rejecting it.[78]

Although, as Kermode believes, *Paradise Regained* is self-contained, and the main lines of Christ's character and the lesson which, as the exemplary hero, he is intended to teach may be clearly discerned without looking beyond the poem itself, his character, though it will not be altered, may be further explained if it is viewed in the light of the historically developed heroic tradition. Epic heroes have always been depicted as ideal characters, according to what the societies which produced them conceived as ideal. Achilles, Agamemnon, and Odysseus, as they are men of the greatest physical courage, engaged in deeds of war, exemplify the ideal of the active virtues. In the Middle Ages the influence of the Church, which had long been teaching the superior importance of the contemplative over the active virtues, begins to be evident in the sinless Galahad and the penitent and ascetic Percivale. In the 16th century, especially in Italy, both moralists and poets were much concerned with the question of the relative importance of the two ideals. Tasso professed that in Godfrey and Rinaldo of the *Jerusalem Delivered* he had embodied the two; and, although in his Discourse, *Della Virtù Eroica e della Carità*, he doubtfully inclined in favour of the active type, in theory at least he believed heroic virtue to be the perfect union and balance of the active and the contemplative virtues. Others argued that in Aeneas Virgil had achieved that balance. Finally in the Arthur of *The Faerie Queene*, heroic virtue becomes 'magnificence', that is magnanimity, which, as Spenser explains in his letter to Ralegh, is the perfection of the active and the contemplative, and, as he calls them, the Aristotelian virtues, and 'conteineth in it them all'. Spenser, then, intends Arthur to be the perfect magnanimous hero of the Renaissance tradition.[79]

[78] See Blondel, pp. 62–3.
[79] For much of the foregoing explanation of the heroic tradition I am indebted to Hughes's

Introduction

But Christ, not Arthur, is the last great figure in the long heroic succession, and the most perfect, because his strength lies in right reason supported by humble and obedient trust in God—right reason, which, to quote Richard Hooker, is 'that light of Reason, whereby good may be known from evil, and which discovering the same rightly is termed right';[80] it is what the Cambridge Platonists called 'the candle of the Lord'. It is not ratiocination, but a faculty which not only distinguishes between good and evil, but also controls 'many lesser faculties that serve / Reason as chief', among them the will. It is, then, as Hoopes writes, 'the principle and means of moral control in the daily life of man'. Thus in the Christian and the Miltonic sense Christ is more magnanimous than any of the heroes who came before him. To use a Platonic term, he possesses σωφροσύνη. The word has no exact English equivalent, but for Plato it meant the health, order, harmony of the soul, and is closely related to justice in his sense, that is knowing one's station and one's duties, and acting accordingly. Although it is not itself a virtue, it is a condition of the possibility of virtue.[81]

By a long and extremely complex process in which medieval philosophers and theologians, notably Thomas Aquinas, had a large part, the conception of magnanimity set forth in the *Nicomachean Ethics* (4. 7)[82] was transformed in order to reconcile it with Christian humility.[83] What it became in its Christianized form may best be understood from Aquinas, who defines it as a virtue which is concerned with honours, which in turn are the reward of virtue,

article 'Christ of *PR*', *SP* 35 (1938), 254–77, though I have necessarily greatly abbreviated the evidence which he presents.

[80] *Eccles. Pol.* 1. 7. 4. See Bush, *Our Time*, p. 37; William Madsen, 'The Idea of Nature in Milton's Poetry', Young *et al.*, *Three Studies in the Renaissance* (New Haven, 1958), pp. 239–40; Robert Hoopes, *Right Reason in the English Renaissance* (Cambridge, Mass., 1962), pp. 190–1, 197, 199.

[81] See *Gorgias* 504, 507–8; *Rep.* 4. 430, 441E, 442D; 9. 591D; *Laws* 2. 653B; 3. 696–7A; 4. 710A; Helen North, *Sophrosyne: Self-Knowledge and Self-Restraint in Greek Literature* (Ithaca, N.Y., 1966), pp. 150–96.

[82] See W. D. Ross, *Aristotle* (New York, 1924), p. 208.

[83] See R.-A. Gauthier, *Magnanimité: l'idéal de la grandeur dans la philosophie païenne et dans la théologie chrétienne* (Paris, 1951), pp. 295–371; Françoise Jukovsky, *La Gloire dans la poésie française et néolatine du XVIᵉ siècle* (Geneva, 1969), pp. 125–7.

in the sense that a man strives to do what deserves honor, but not so as to think much of honor accorded by man....On the other hand, humility leads a man to think little of himself as he considers his own deficiency, while magnanimity leads him to despise others in so far as they fall away from God's gifts; since he does not think so much of others that he will do anything wrong for their sake. But humility makes us honor others and esteem them better than ourselves, in so far as we see in them some of God's gifts. Therefore it is written of the just man (Ps. 15. 4): 'In whose eyes a vile person is contemned', which signifies the contempt of magnanimity; 'but he honoreth them that fear the Lord', which points to the reverential attitude of humility. Therefore it is evident that magnanimity and humility are not opposed to each other, although they seem to tend in opposite directions, because they proceed according to different considerations.[84]

As far as I am able to learn, it has not been noticed that in the *De Doctrina Christiana* 2. 9 Milton's views of humility and magnanimity are substantially the same as those of Aquinas, and that he accepts what had long been the orthodox teaching of the Church. 'Lowliness of mind and magnanimity', he says, are 'virtues more peculiarly appropriate to a high station', although unlike Aquinas he does not limit them to those of high estate. The former, he explains,

consists in thinking humbly of ourselves, and in abstaining from self-commendation, except where occasion requires it....Allied to lowliness is the love of an unspotted reputation, and of the praises of good men, with a proportionate contempt for those of the wicked....MAGNANIMITY is shown, when in the seeking or avoiding, the acceptance or refusal of riches, advantages, or honours, we are actuated by a regard to our own dignity, rightly understood.... Allied to this is indignation at the unfounded praises or undeserved prosperity of the wicked....Such, finally, is the spirit by which every true Christian is guided in his estimate of himself.

Milton's list of Biblical examples of magnanimity, which includes Job, ends with Christ 'rejecting the empire of the world'. And he names Christ as 'the great pattern of fortitude', which is closely related to magnanimity, and 'is chiefly conspicuous in repelling evil, or in regarding its approach with equanimity.'[85]

[84] *Sum. Th.* 2. 2. 129. 1, 3.   [85] *Works* 17. 235–45, 249, 247.

Introduction

Taking issue especially with Hughes, Arnold Stein[86] denies that magnanimity, 'however aggrandized', can fully support the weight of Milton's theme in *Paradise Regained*. That it does not *fully* support it may be granted, since humility is also a part and an important part of its support. The poem, Stein insists, is a 'drama of knowledge', and hence knowledge is the 'ultimate cause', and knowledge of God the 'ultimate knowledge'. He also calls it a 'drama of salvation', which plainly it is not, since moral perfection is never what Milton, or Christians generally, understand as salvation. But even if knowledge of God is the ultimate cause of virtue,[87] I can find nothing in the text of the *Paradise Regained* to indicate that Milton is there much concerned with the ultimate cause of virtue; I do find much evidence that he is greatly concerned with the effect which virtue has upon man's life. Since he says that a humble and magnanimous spirit is that 'by which every true Christian is guided in his estimate of himself';[88] since Christ is the great exemplar for every Christian; and since his conduct throughout the temptations perfectly conforms to the principles of Aquinas and Milton, there ought to be no doubt that he stands as 'the great pattern' of humility and magnanimity, a pattern made all the more impressive by the contrast with Satan, who in his pride is utterly incapable of any humble or magnanimous impulse.

[86] See *Heroic Knowledge: an Interpretation of Paradise Regained and Samson Agonistes* (Minneapolis, Minn., 1957), pp. 29–34.

[87] Stein maintains (p. 30) that Milton's attitude to the virtues in *PR* is not the same as that in *DocCh*, where they are 'splintered', as he says, in order to make them apply to all cases. But the only real difference is that in *DocCh* the virtues, as they should be in a *treatise*, are discussed, defined in rational terms, and hence must be isolated; whereas in the *poem*, again as they should be, they are presented poetically: that is by means of an example of their decisive function in human life. However they are treated, they are the same virtues, interrelated and interacting.

[88] Stein denies that the mention in *DocCh* of Christ's rejection of empire as an example of magnanimity gives any complete interpretation of the poem. He also denies that Christ is 'openly defining his central moral position' when he informs Satan that it is 'Far more magnanimous' to lay down a kingdom than to 'assume' it (2. 483). In *Milton and the Renaissance Hero* (p. 152) J. M. Steadman, however, writes that Christ's ordeal in the desert, while it tests a variety of virtues, is primarily a demonstration of his magnanimity. In so far as humility also determines Christ's moral position, Stein is correct; but to deny the part which magnanimity plays is to reject plain evidence from Milton, the principal witness in the case.

The best commentaries on the Christ of *Paradise Regained*, as Hughes observed years ago,[89] are to be found in the *Defence of Poesie* where Sidney refers to the 'saying of *Plato* and *Tully*...that who could see vertue, woulde bee woonderfullie ravished with the love of her bewtie';[90] and in *The Reason of Church-governement*, where Milton speaks of 'the very visible shape and image of vertue, whereby she is not only seene in the regular gestures and motions of her heavenly paces as she walkes, but also makes the harmony of her voice audible to mortall eares.'[91] And the Christ who 'himselfe came downe amongst us to be a teacher' is the Christ whose heart 'Contains of good, wise, just, the perfect shape' (3. 11). The great central purpose and value of heroic poetry for Sidney, Spenser, and Milton was the evocation of the vision of virtue, the vision which they themselves had seen, and which Milton embodies in Christ, the purely exemplary hero. If we today, content with lesser ideals, no longer see the beauty of moral perfection, desperately as we need to see and be 'ravished with the love' of it, the exalted and inspired didacticism of Milton's poem can yet help us to see the vision, and having seen it to create a happier world.

[89] 'Christ of *PR*', *SP* 35 (1938), 276.
[90] *Works*, ed. Feuillerat (Cambridge, 1912–26), 3. 25.
[91] *Works* 3. 185.

Notes

EDITIONS OF MILTON CITED

Beeching, H. C., ed., *Poetical Works*. Oxford, Clarendon, 1900

Blakeney, E. H., ed., *Paradise Regained*. London, E. Partridge, 1932

Blondel, Jacques, ed., *Le Paradis reconquis*. Paris, Aubier, [1955]

Browne, R. C., ed., *English Poems*. 2 vols., Oxford, Clarendon, 1894

Bush, Douglas, ed., *Complete Poetical Works*. Boston, Houghton Mifflin, 1965; London, Oxford Univ. Press, 1966, 1969

Carey, John, and Alistair Fowler, eds., *Poems*. London, Longmans Green/New York, Atheneum, 1968

Darbishire, Helen, ed., *Poetical Works*. 2 vols., Oxford, Clarendon, 1952–5

Dunster, Charles, ed., *Paradise Regained*. London, 1795

Fletcher, Harris F., ed., *Complete Poetical Works Reproduced in Photographic Facsimile*. 4 vols., Urbana, Univ. of Illinois Press, 1943–8

Fowler, Alistair, *see* Carey, John, and Alistair Fowler

Grierson, H. J. C., ed., *Poems*. 2 vols., London, Chatto & Windus, 1925

Hanford, James Holly, ed., *Poems*. New York, Nelson, 1936; rev. ed., New York, Ronald, 1953

Hawkins, Edward, ed., *Poetical Works*. 4 vols., Oxford, 1824

Hughes, Merritt Y., ed., *Complete Poems and Major Prose* [Hughes, 2nd ed.]. New York, Odyssey, 1957

Hughes, Merritt Y., ed., *Paradise Regained, the Minor Poems, and Samson Agonistes* [Hughes, 1st ed.]. New York, Odyssey, 1937

Jerram, Charles S., ed., *Paradise Regained*. London, 1877

Keightley, Thomas, ed., *Poems*. 2 vols., London, 1859

Martin, Leonard C., ed., *Paradise Regained*. Oxford, Clarendon, 1925

Masson, David, ed., *Poetical Works*. 3 vols., London and New York, Macmillan, 1890

Newton, Thomas, ed., *Paradise Regain'd...Samson Agonistes...and Poems upon Several Occasions*. 2 vols., London, 1773

Patterson, Frank A., ed., *Works* [Columbia Milton]. 18 vols., New York, Columbia Univ. Press, 1931–8

Todd, Henry J., ed., *Poetical Works*. 2nd ed., 7 vols., London, 1809

Book I

❦

1–7 Editors note the imitation of the possibly spurious opening lines of the *Aeneid* 1ª–1ᵈ: 'I am he who once tuned my song on a slender reed, then, leaving the woodland, constrained the neighbouring fields to serve the husbandmen, however grasping—a work welcome to farmers: but now bristling Mars...I sing';[1] and of Ovid, *Tr.* 4. 10. 1: 'I am he who once wrote of tender loves';[2] and of the first lines of *The Faerie Queene*:

> Lo I the man, whose Muse whilome did maske,
> As time her taught, in lowly Shepheards weeds,
> Am now enforst a far vnfitter taske,
> For trumpets sterne to chaunge mine Oaten reeds.

While linking *PR* and *PL*, Milton, following epic convention, announces his subject, which is the counterpart of that of *PL*: a great temptation *resisted* and Satan *defeated*. The crucial words in the passage are 'disobedience' and 'obedience', as in Rom. 5. 19: 'For as by one man's disobedience many were made sinners, so by the obedience of one shall many be made righteous.' Cf. 1 Cor. 15. 22. In *DocCh* 2. 3 (*Works* 17. 69) Milton defines obedience as 'that virtue whereby we propose to ourselves the will of God as the paramount rule of our conduct, and serve him alone.'

3 *Recover'd Paradise.* By Christ's successful resistance of Satan man, following the example of Christ, may regain the state of obedience which by Adam's sin was lost. Man will finally be saved by the grace of God and by Christ's death and resurrection, as we are to understand from the words of the angels in 4. 634–5: 'On thy glorious work / Now enter, and begin to save mankind.'

---

[1] Ille ego, qui quondam gracili modulatus avena
 carmen, et egressus silvis vicina coegi
 ut quamvis avido parerent arva colono,
 gratum opus agricolis; at nunc horrentia Martis
 ...cano.

[2] Ille ego qui fuerim, tenerorum lusor amorum.

4 *mans.* Cf. *PL* 1. 4–5: 'till one greater Man / Restore us, and regain the blissful Seat'. God, addressing Gabriel in 130–67 below, three times, in 140, 150, 166, speaks of Christ as man. In 'Paradise Regained', *PMASAL* 22 (1936), 496, Warner Rice observes that much of our feeling about the events narrated in *PR* is determined by our grasp of Milton's conception of the character and being of Christ. He is not here much concerned with the theological speculations of *DocCh* 1. 5–6, 14–15; but he is concerned to emphasize Christ's humanity, and to the last to show him tried on a strictly human level, as any man may be tried, and resisting temptation as any man may resist it. See note on 4. 560–1.

5–6 The fulfilment of the curse pronounced upon the serpent in Gen. 3. 15: 'It shall bruise thy head, and thou shalt bruise his heel.' Cf. *PL* 10. 181.

7 In pronouncing judgment on Adam, God said (Gen. 3. 17–18): 'Cursed is the ground for thy sake...Thorns also and thistles shall it bring forth to thee'. But Isa. 51. 3 reads: 'The Lord shall comfort Zion: he will comfort all her waste places; and he will make her wilderness like Eden, and her desert like the garden of the Lord.' In *DocCh* 1. 13 (*Works* 15. 217) Milton says: 'All nature is likewise subject to mortality and a curse on account of man.' The same idea is treated at some length in *PL* 10. 651 ff. But cf. *DocCh* 1. 3 (14. 63): 'The creation of the world, and the removal of the curse from the ground, Gen. viii. 21. are among his sole decrees.'

wast wilderness. Cf. 'waste...wilderness' in Deut. 32. 10 and 'wasteful Wilderness' in Spenser, *F.Q.* 1. 1. 32. 1. As in 4. 532 below; *PL* 1. 60; 3. 424; 10. 282 'wast' is used in the sense of Lat. *vastus*, desolate, dreary.

8–12 Cf. Luke 4. 1: 'And Jesus being full of the Holy Ghost returned from Jordan, and was led by the Spirit into the wilderness.' Cf. Matt. 4. 1.

In *RCG* 2, Introd. (*Works* 3. 241) Milton expresses the conviction that a lofty poem can be accomplished only 'by devout prayer to that eternall Spirit who can enrich with all utterance and knowledge'; and in *PL* 1. 1–49; 9. 13–47 he invokes the 'Heav'nly Muse', the Urania of *PL* 7. 1. The Muse has traditionally been identified with the Third Person of the Trinity; but in *This Great Argument* (Princeton, N.J., 1941), pp. 109–18, Maurice Kelley rejects this identification, because he finds it unsupported by *DocCh* 1. 6 (*Works* 14. 356–403) where Milton's unorthodox views concerning the Holy Ghost are most elaborately explained, and where, moreover (14. 394–5) he emphatically says that the Holy Spirit, 'who is sought from the Father, and given by him, not by himself, can neither be God, nor an object of invocation.' Kelley (pp. 117–18) concludes that, because of his 'anti-Trinitarianism', Milton invoked as his Muse 'a personification of the various attributes of God the Father, and thus turned for inspiration and knowledge not to what he considered a subordinate figure but rather to the Father himself—the very fountain-head of all wisdom and enlightenment.'

In 'The Mystery of Milton's Muse' (*RP* 1967, pp. 69–83) N. H. Henry argues that the prohibition in *DocCh* against invoking the Holy Spirit, which has no mediatorial functions, applies to ecclesiastical and theological matters but not to literary invocations. As ancient and Renaissance poets were indefinite in their invocations of the muses, so Milton, he believes, has deliberately and painstakingly fashioned a literary conceit or a 'mystery' analogous to the mystery of the Trinity, which allows varying interpretations or identifications of his source of inspiration. Since in *PL* 7. 5 Milton says 'The meaning, not the Name I call', and since in the Judaeo-Christian Godhead many names are involved, Milton seems to be invoking as many as all Christian readers will find appropriate. Henry's conclusion, not greatly different from Kelley's, is that the overall appeal is to the Christian Godhead, and that whether it be to the Father, the Son, or the Holy Spirit is relatively unimportant. All three are reflected, and 'neither Trinitarian nor anti-Trinitarian will find sure evidence to disabuse him of a conviction that Urania is a Christian muse reflecting three parts of the Godhead' (p. 80.).

If Milton needed a precedent for invoking God the Father as his Muse, he could find it at the beginning of the several parts of Du Bartas' *Semaines*.

8 *Eremite*. A recluse, a hermit, from ἐρημίτης, of the desert, ἐρημία; but Milton here uses the word 'with allusion to the lit. sense "desert dweller"' (*OED*).

11 *By proof*. By trial and testing. Here and in 130 there is an allusion to trial by combat, a knightly ordeal such as Giles Fletcher describes in *C.V.* 2. In 174 below Milton uses the word 'duel'. To think thus of the temptation seems to have been something of a commonplace in the 17th century, for John Udall and William Perkins use as titles *The combate betwixt Christ and the Deuill* and *The Combate betweene Christ and the Deuill expounded*; seven of Lancelot Andrewes' *Ninety-Six Sermons* are on *The Wonderful Combat for God's Glory and Man's Salvation between Christ and Satan*; and in *Contemp.* (*Works*, ed. Wynter, Oxford, 1863, 2. 340) Joseph Hall calls the temptation a duel and Christ 'our Almighty Champion'. See E. M. Pope, *PR, Tradition and Poem*, pp. 115–20.

51

13 *natures bounds.* Nature, 'a difficult word; often impossible to discriminate with any certainty between meanings' (Laura E. Lockwood, *Lexicon to the English Poetical Works of John Milton*, New York, 1907), but here presumably 'the created universe' (as in *PL* 8. 153; 10. 892), to which the action of *PR* is confined, unlike that of *PL* which ranges over hell, heaven, chaos, and the world.

14 *full summ'd.* A hawk is 'full summ'd' when fully feathered; it lacks nothing of the sum of its feathers, and hence is ready for hunting (*OED*). Cf. *PL* 7. 421: 'They summ'd thir Penns'.

14–15 *deeds | Above Heroic. PR* will treat more serious matters, heroism of a nobler order, than that commonly treated in epic poetry. These words recall Milton's statements in *PL* that his 'adventrous Song | ...intends to soar | Above th'*Aonian* Mount' (1, 13–15), and that his argument is 'Not less but more Heroic then the wrauth | Of stern *Achilles*... | ...or rage | Of *Turnus*... | Or *Neptun*'s ire or *Juno*'s' (9. 13–18); and his regret that wars and knightly combats have been deemed the only heroic argument, while 'the better fortitude| Of Patience and Heroic Martyrdom' has been 'Unsung' (9. 31–3). Milton not only rejects the classical and pagan heroic ideal and presents a *Christian* hero, but he also gives central position to the theme of human depravity and divine mercy. See J. M. Steadman, *Milton and the Renaissance Hero*, pp. vi–vii, xiii–xx.

16 *unrecorded.* The Gospels (Matt. 4. 1–11; Mark 1. 12–13; Luke 4. 1–13) give only summary accounts of the temptation. *PR* will give a detailed account, telling what Milton believes to be ideally true.

18–32 There are in *PR* three accounts of the baptism, which, although superficially repetitive, reveal three dramatically different points of view, each successively more comprehensive. The present, brief, objective account leaves the impression of an audience witnessing an unusual event with neither belief nor unbelief, but with only incomplete comprehension. The next account, Satan's (70–85), shows that he grasps the physical reality and worldly aspect of the miracle and is alarmed by it; but he tries to destroy its significance with scorn and cynicism. The third, Christ's (269–89), goes beyond the other two. Christ, with deep, personal, human feeling, as well as divine understanding, gives the scene its real significance. With humble faith he interprets the scene as meaning that he is approved of God, and that the time has come when

> I no more should live obscure,
> But openly begin, as best becomes
> The Authority which I deriv'd from Heaven (287–9).

Book I

See A. H. Sackton, 'Architectonic Structure in *PR*', *UTSE* 33 (1954), 34–5.

18–22 These lines summarize the accounts of John the Baptist in Matt. 3; Mark 1. 2–11; Luke 3. 1–20. Cf. Josephus, *A.J.* 18. 5.

18 *Proclaimer.* 'Proclaimer represents the secondary sense of προφήτης, originally one who "speaks *for*," i.e. "interprets the will of" a god....Hence in the New Test. προφητεύειν is "to preach," and nearly = κηρύσσειν (from κῆρυξ "a herald")' (Jerram, p. 65). The Geneva Bible on Matt. 3. 1 explains that 'John, who through his singular holiness and austereness of life, caused all men to cast their eyes upon him, prepareth the way for Christ...and delivereth the sum of the Gospel, which in short space after should be delivered more fully.'

19 *the sound of Trumpet.* Editors cite Isa. 58. 1 : 'Lift up thy voice like a trumpet, and shew my people their transgression.' Cf. Heb. 12. 19; Rev. 1. 10; 4. 1.

20–1 John's function as a forerunner of Christ was to call men to repentance in preparation for the coming of the kingdom of heaven. The baptism which he administered was a rite signifying the remission of sins for those who repented, and hence their worthiness to enter the kingdom of heaven (Matt. 3. 2, 11; Mark 1. 3–4; Luke 3. 3; cf. Isa. 1. 16–18). In *DocCh* 1. 28 (*Works* 16. 185) Milton explains that 'The baptism of John was essentially the same as the baptism of Christ; but it differed in the form of words used in its administration, and in the comparative remoteness of its efficacy.'

20 *Heavens Kingdom.* See also 241, 265; 2. 36, 481; 3. 152, 171, 199, 242, 351; 4. 151, 282, 369, 389. As Howard Schultz explains in *Milton and Forbidden Knowledge* (New York, 1955, pp. 228–36), the 'Kingdom' is the Invisible Church. On pp. 218–27, and in 'Christ and Antichrist in *PR*', *PMLA* 67 (1952), 790–808, he holds that in *PR* Milton meant to define the kingdom of Christ, that he was presenting Christ as setting a pattern for the Church and its ministers, *not* primarily a pattern for the Christian layman, and that the poem is, then, an allegory of the Church. If so, it is a very dark allegory. I do not find it possible to make Schultz's interpretation fit what we find in the text of *PR*; nor has he taken sufficiently into account what Milton says in *DocCh* 1. 24 (*Works* 16. 61)—in a chapter on the Invisible Church—namely, that 'from this union and fellowship of the *regenerate* with the Father and Christ, and of the members of Christ's body among themselves, *results* the mystical body called The Invisible Church, whereof Christ is the head' (italics mine). What the 'union and fellowship' are Milton has explained, with many supporting quotations from Scripture, just before the statement here quoted. Simply expressed they mean loving God and humbly trusting and obeying him. What Milton says means that before there can be an Invisible Church, the individual Christians (see Blondel, p. 40) who will constitute it must by loving, trusting, and obeying God become regenerate, must be spiritually qualified to become members. Christ, whose earthly ministry is but a beginning (Blondel, pp. 84–5), is, as we see him in *PR*, laying down 'the rudiments / Of his great warfare' (157–8, below); he is spiritually qualifying himself to become the head of the Church; at the same time he is the great exemplar showing every man how he may achieve the spiritual qualifications. See note on 4. 540–95 below.

E. L. Marilla (*Milton and Modern Man*, University, Ala., 1968, pp. 131, 56–7) finds this interpretation unacceptable because it denies what he 'conceives to be a significant relationship' between *PR* and *PL*, namely: that as in *PL* Milton shows how man, by yielding to evil, can sacrifice 'a just and peaceful order of society', so in *PR*, the companion poem, he is setting forth the requirements for the establishment 'of a near-ideal society'. Furthermore, within *PR* Christ's kingdom does not come into existence, and even Christ himself does not know how or when it is to be established.

21–2 Cf. Matt. 3. 5: 'Then went out to him Jerusalem, and all Judæa, and all the region round about Jordan'.

24–37 As Dick Taylor observes, prophecies, signs, and portents have 'a noteworthy role in *Paradise Regained*. Throughout Milton has treated with great prominence the various true prophecies and revelations concerning the Messiah.' See 'The Storm Scene in *PR*', *UTQ* 24 (1954–5), 364–5. He has especially called attention to the prophecy concerning Christ's accession to the throne of David. See 1. 55–9, 81–5, 126–8, 132–6, 238–41 and note, 253–4, 260–5, 276, 281–6, 293, 385, 393–6, 455–9; 2. 4–5, 32–6, 50–1, 83–92, 440–2; 3. 15–16, 60–3, 152–3, 177–8, 184–5, 351–2; 4. 108, 288–90, 380–93, 469–83, 489–91, 502–7, 512–13, 556–9. From such emphasis on prophecies and signs, 'against the perspective of true and false revelation', Taylor believes, 'it seems almost a certainty that the contemporary interest in prodigies and portents has a significant bearing on this aspect of the poem', and would be so understood by Milton's contemporaries. See note on 430, below. On Satan's use of portents see 3. 393–6, and especially 4. 368–540 below and notes.

In 'The Purpose of Dryden's *Annus Mirabilis*', *HLQ* 10 (1946), 46–7, E. N. Hooker points out that there was in England in the 1660s an excited controversy over prodigies and heavenly signs, as for example mystical significance in the number of the year 1666, warnings from God of his wrath in the comet of 1664, and in the plague and fire in London, and whatever else to which terrible meaning could be attached. Although, as Taylor also observes, Milton strongly disapproved of the vulgar and hysterical sign-reading prevalent about him, as appears from *Ref* 1 (*Works* 3. 50), he believed that at proper times God revealed his mind and will to man, as is stated in *Areop* (*Works* 4. 340), but that man must by his reason distinguish the true from the false. See notes on 4. 382–93, below.

24 *as then.* For the time being. Then is 'strengthened by *as* preceding, which with adverbs and advb. phrases...has a restrictive force' (*OED*).

obscure. Cf. John 1. 26: 'There standeth one among you, whom ye know not.'

25–6 Cf. Matt. 3. 14: 'John forbad him, saying, I have need to be baptized of thee, and comest thou to me?' Cf. also John 1. 29.

divinely warn'd. The verse just quoted, while it does not state that John had been divinely informed that Jesus was the Messiah, implies that he had been. But according to John 1. 33, John said: 'I knew him not: but he that sent me to baptize with water, the same said unto me, Upon whom thou shalt see the Spirit descending, and remaining on him, the same is he which baptizeth with the Holy Ghost.'

26–8 See the preceding note and cf. Matt. 3. 11; 'He that cometh after me is mightier than I, whose shoes I am not worthy to bear.' Cf. also Mark 1. 7; Luke 3. 16; John 1. 26–7.

worthier. In *A Shakespearian Grammar* (London, 1872), 5, E. A. Abbott gives many examples from Shakespeare of adjectives used as nouns, a usage common in Milton's poetry, as in 2. 159–60 below; *PL* 1. 71; 2. 97, 980; 11. 4.

28–32 Cf. Matt. 3. 16–17: 'and, lo, the heavens were opened unto him, and he saw the Spirit of God descending like a dove, and lighting upon him: And lo a voice from heaven, saying, This is my beloved Son, in whom I am well pleased.' Cf. also Mark 1. 10–11; Luke 3. 21–2; John 1. 32. See also 83 and 282 below.

33 *Adversary.* A term often meaning the devil (*OED*). The name 'Satan' in Hebrew means 'adversary', one who plots against another. Διάβολος, whence devil, the slanderer or false accuser, is another equivalent. Cf. *PL* 1. 81–2; 2. 629; 3. 156.

33–4 Cf. Job 1. 7: 'And the Lord said unto Satan, Whence comest thou? Then Satan answered the Lord, and said, From going to and fro in the earth, and from walking up and down in it'; and 1 Pet. 5. 8: 'your adversary the devil, as a roaring lion, walketh about, seeking whom he may devour.'

34 *that assembly fam'd.* The multitude that came to John to be baptized. See note on 21–2 above.

35 *the voice divine.* See note on 28–32 above.

36 *th' exalted man.* See note on 4 above.

37–43 In 'Storm Scene', *UTQ* 24 (1954–5), 372, Dick Taylor writes: 'throughout the poem up to the storm episode, it has been Milton's consistent practice to describe Satan, almost incident by incident, as at a loss, or confounded, or speechless, at the failure of each stratagem, but nevertheless quickly producing another still more forceful. Rage and despair are the first emotions which he ascribes to Satan and they are notable—particularly despair—from then on.' See 2. 119–20, 140–7, 392; 3. 2–6, 145–9, 203; 4. 1–6, 10–24, 195, 365–7 below. Important as are rage and despair, *fear*, I think, is even more important in motivating Satan's thoughts and actions. See note on 44–105 below. Taylor believes that the consistent representation of Satan as confounded and then immediately and energetically pursuing a new and forceful stratagem involves a considerable discrepancy, which in 4. 10–24 Milton endeavours to correct. But is there really a discrepancy? Since Milton has been consistent, we may well look for a reason for the consistency. That, I think, is to be found in 4. 10–14 below:

> But as a man who had been matchless held
> In cunning, over-reach't where least he thought,
> To salve his credit, and for very spight
> Still will be tempting him who foyls him still,
> And never cease, though to his shame the more.

Each repulse by Christ so deeply wounds Satan's pride and so greatly increases his fear that he is for the moment confounded by rage and despair. But because of his persistent refusal to accept facts (see note on 91 below) and 'for very spight', and in defiance of reason, which, with all other good, he has utterly renounced (see *PL* 4. 32–113), he rallies his power, for power he still has (see 4. 394–5 below), to devise new stratagems, however futile they may be. Milton with consummate art is depicting a damned soul, one so inveterate in evil that, though he knows that his evil acts can bring him no satisfaction (*PL* 4. 73–113), he spitefully persists, and can now only persist in doing evil.

37 *high attest.* See note on 28–32 above.

39–42 The demonic councils in *PR*, Hughes observes in his first edition (p. 447), are more like those in the first book of Vida's *Christiad*, the fourth canto of Tasso's *Jerusalem Delivered*, and Milton's own *QNov* than those more fully recounted in *PL*; but, as he remarks, 'They were a conventional part of the Christian epic which could hardly be altogether eliminated from *P.R.*'

39 *his place...in mid air.* In *PL* 1. 516–17 the fallen angels, now become the gods of the heathen, rule 'the middle Air / Thir highest Heav'n'; in 10. 399–400 Satan bids Sin and Death to exercise dominion on earth 'and in the Aire', and in 10. 188–9 the air is 'The Realm it self of Satan long usurpt'. Other references to the air or mid air as the habitation of Satan and his followers occur in *QNov* 12; *IlPen* 93–4; *PL* 4. 940; 12. 454; *PR* 1. 44–5, 63, 115–18, 366; 2. 117, 124, 374; 4. 201.

The term 'mid air' implies an old theory, commonly accepted in the 17th century, that the air is divided into three regions, the middle one of which, the *media regio*, reaching to the tops of the highest mountains, is a cold region of thick clouds and mist, as it is represented in Palingenius, *Zodiake*, tr. Googe (New York, 1947), p. 222, and in line 41 below.

That the air is the natural habitation of demons is a very old and widely accepted belief, probably arrived at by reasoning that as there are living beings whose natural habitations are earth and water, so there must be those which live in air and fire (Aristotle, *Hist. An.* 5. 19–20; Ocellus Lucanus, *Univ. Nat.* 3. 3; Philo, *Gigant.* 2; Chalcidius, *In Platonis Timaeum Commentarius* 131, 134). The Pythagoreans believed that the whole air is full of souls which they thought of as demons and heroes, as appears from Diogenes Laertius 8. 1. 32; Eusebius, *P.E.* 4. 23 (Migne, *Pat. Gr.* 21. 305–6); Psellus, *Op. Daem.* (Migne, *Pat. Gr.* 122. 841). The expression 'prince of the power of the air' in Eph. 2. 2 implies the same belief, to which Christian writers from the patristic period onward often advert, e.g. Augustine, *Civ. D.* 8. 15, 21; *De Agone* 3–5 (Migne, *Pat. Lat.* 40. 292–4); Tasso, *Jerusalem* 13. 11. 1–2; Richard Hooker, *Eccles. Pol.* 1. 4. 3; Robert Burton, *Anat.* 1. 2. 1. 2; Sir Thomas Browne, *Pseud.* 1. 11.

On the identification of the fallen angels and the gods of the heathen with demons, see notes on 117 and 2. 122–4 below.

40 *his mighty Peers.* In *PL* the term 'peers' occurs nine times (1. 39, 618, 757; 2. 119, 445, 507; 5. 812; 6. 127; 10. 456) with reference, as here, to the followers of Satan. In repeatedly calling them his peers Milton is emphasizing their natural equality with Satan. But as his acts prove, and as Abdiel states in *PL* 5. 809–48 and 6. 171–88, he always aspired 'To set himself in Glory above his Peers', and 'trusted to have equal'd the most High'; thus he is both a tyrant and a rebel, a destroyer of justice and order, since tyranny consists in ruling one's natural equals, and rebellion in making oneself equal to one's natural superiors (Aristotle, *Pol.* 2. 9. 6–7; 4. 10). On Satan as the archetypal tyrant, see M. Y. Hughes, 'Satan and the "Myth" of the Tyrant', *Essays in English Literature…Presented to A. S. P. Woodhouse*, ed. MacLure and Watt (Toronto, 1964), pp. 125–48.

42   *A gloomy Consistory.* Cf. Virgil, *A.* 3. 679: *concilium horrendum.* The gloom of the present council is in marked contrast with the confident tone of the infernal councils in *PL*.

A consistory is a council, but the term commonly means an ecclesiastical court or the Papal Senate (*OED*). In *PL* 1. 795 Satan and his followers are said to have sat in 'secret conclave'; in 2. 391 Satan addresses them as a 'Synod of Gods'; and in 10. 312–13 Sin and Death 'by wondrous Art / Pontifical' build a bridge from hell to the world. In the light of Milton's many severe criticisms of the Church, both Roman and Anglican, in his prose works, and of the burlesque treatment of many of its institutions in the description of the limbo of vanities in *PL* 3. 444–97, application of ecclesiastical terms to the acts of Satan and his host is probably meant to express disapproval of both them and the Church of Rome.

43   *bespake.* Here used intransitively, meaning 'spoke' (*OED*), as often in Spenser, e.g. *S.C.*, Feb. 97; *D.* 262; *F.Q.* 1. 2. 32. 4. Cf. *Lyc* 112; *Nat* 76.

44–105   Having summoned his 'peers' to a council—a traditional feature of Biblical epic poems—Satan addresses them in a gloomy speech strikingly different from his proud, arrogant utterances in *PL*. Having heard the voice from heaven proclaim the son of God, he is tortured, and throughout the poem will continue to be tortured, by the fear of what that proclamation may mean. Although he foresees some horrible doom—he is not sure what—awaiting him and his followers, he will not, he dares not, admit so much to them. But neither does he dare not to warn them of their danger; and he must try to encourage them. To do so he resorts to the pretence of doubting who Christ is (see note on 91 below). But the predominant note in his speech is the foreboding of danger, danger so great, he says, that it admits no long debate. Thus he precludes any debate; and his followers in dismay, like dumb, driven cattle, without question accept the announcement of their 'great Dictator' that as he undertook to ruin Adam, and succeeded, so will he undertake to avert the 'fatal wound' which now threatens from the seed of Eve, the wound at which he sneered in *PL* 10. 498–501. See D. C. Allen, *The Harmonious Vision* (Baltimore, 1954), pp. 112–14.

44–6 See note on 39 above. Contrast the noble, heavenly titles with which Satan addresses his followers in *PL* 2. 11, 430; 5. 772; 10. 460, titles of which, in their present condition, it would not be politic to remind them.

46–7 *Hell | Our hated habitation.* In 362–4 below Satan calls hell 'that hideous place…my dolorous Prison'. Although in *PL* 1. 263 he declared that it was 'Better to reign in Hell, then serve in Heav'n', in 2. 58 he called hell 'this dark opprobrious Den of shame'. From the first neither he nor his followers were in doubt, or ever could be, that hell was a place of horror and misery.

48 *as the years of men.* As the years of men are recorded or counted.

50 *In manner at our will.* As if earthly affairs were in our power (instead of God's).

51 *facil.* 'Easily led', 'compliant' (*OED*), as in *PL* 9. 1158.

52 *deceiv'd by me.* See *PL* 9. 532 ff.

53 *attending.* Awaiting, expecting (*OED*), like Fr. *attendre*. Cf. *PL* 3. 270–1; 11. 551–2.

53–5 After Satan had seduced Adam and Eve, God cursed the serpent, saying (Gen. 3. 15): 'And I will put enmity between thee and the woman, and between thy seed and her seed; it shall bruise thy head, and thou shalt bruise his heel.' In thus pronouncing the punishment of the serpent, God 'anticipated the condemnation of mankind by a gratuitous redemption' (*DocCh* 1. 14, *Works* 15. 253).

55–9 See note on 24–37 above.

55–6 *long the decrees of Heav'n | Delay.* The meaning is close to that of the old proverb: 'The mills of God grind slow', which in varying forms is found in *Orac. Sib.* 8. 14; Plutarch, *On the Delay of Divine Vengeance* 549; Origen, *Cels.* 8. 40 (Migne, *Pat. Gr.* 11. 1575); George Herbert, *Outlandish Proverbs* 747. Cf. also Ps. 90. 4.

57 *the circling hours.* The same expression occurs in *PL* 6. 3. Here it is nearly equivalent to *volventibus annis* in Virgil, *A.* 1. 234. In Greek ὥρα (Ion. ὥρη) commonly means a part of the year, a season, as in Homer, *Od.* 2. 107; 10. 469; Hesiod, *Theog.* 58; Sophocles, *O.T.* 156. Milton is also alluding to the Hours, ῏Ωραι, the daughters of Zeus and Themis (Hesiod, *Theog.* 901–2), whose dance symbolizes the course of the seasons (*Homeric Hy. to Apollo* 194; Pindar, *Ol.* 4. 2; Xenophon, *Sym.* 7. 5). 'The epithet "circling" is a translation of κυκλάδες, which occurs frequently in this connection (cf. *Orph. Hy.* 60. 10; Euripides, *Alc.* 449)' (Charles G. Osgood, *The Classical Mythology of Milton's English Poems*, New York, 1900, p. 44).

58 *compast.* 'The metaphor [the dance of the Hours] is continued in "compassed," i.e. "brought round"' (Jerram, p. 68). Cf. Gal. 4. 4–5: 'But when the fulness of the time was come, God sent forth his Son...To redeem them that were under the law.' See also 286–7 below.

59 See note on 53–5 above.

60–1 The meaning is: if by the breaking of the *head* is not intended the breaking of *all* our power. It is to be noted that Satan substitutes 'broken' for 'bruise', the term used in the curse to which he refers. See note on 53–5 above. He does not understand the meaning of the curse, because the literalness of his mind always prevents his grasping the meaning of a metaphor.

62 *infring'd.* Broken, defeated, like Lat. *infringere*, a meaning now obsolete but common in the 17th century (*OED*).

65 *Destin'd to this.* Divinely appointed to wound our head.
   late. An adverb, 'lately', as in 133, 327; *PL* 1. 113; 3. 151; 5. 240; *Sonn* 23. 1. See also 89–93 below and notes.

68 Cf. Luke 2. 52: 'And Jesus increased in wisdom and stature, and in favour with God and man.'

69 *multiplies.* Increases, augments, like Lat. *multiplicare.*

70–85 See note on 18–32 above.

70 *Prophet.* See note on 18–22 above.

71–8 As Marilla observes in *Milton and Modern Man* (p. 58), Satan distinguishes between the motivation of the crowd, the 'all' of line 75, who came to be baptized, and the motivation of Christ. The 'all' hoped by baptism to be cleansed of their sins, and thus 'to enter into the good graces of Christ' when he should finally become the 'King' of men. These, Satan assumes, offer no threat to defeat his plan to overcome the forces of righteousness. Christ, however, came to be baptized not in order to cleanse himself, but rather in order that by 'the testimony of Heaven...thenceforth the Nations may not doubt' who he is.

71 *Harbinger.* A harbinger (O.F. *herbergere, herbergeour*) originally was one who provided lodging, but as early as 1550 the word had come to mean one who goes before to announce the coming of another (*OED*).

72 *the Consecrated stream.* Cf. Matt. 3. 6; Mark 1. 5. The Jordan is called 'consecrated' probably because in Biblical history it was the scene of several miracles and of the baptism of Christ. See Joshua 3. 15–17; 22. 10; 2 Kings 2. 7, 14. In his Greek version of Ps. 114. 7 Milton has Ἱρὸς Ἰορδάνης, 'Holy Jordan'.

73–5 Cf. Mark 1. 4: 'John did baptize in the wilderness, and preach the baptism of repentance for the remission of sins.' Cf. also Luke 3. 3. Satan, suspecting that John's real object is to establish the kingdom of Christ, ridicules and attempts to discredit him as a pretender.

Jerram (p. 69) believes it possible that Milton 'puts into the mouth of Satan his own views on the doctrine of the cleansing away of original sin in Christian baptism.' From *DocCh* 1. 28 (*Works* 16. 169–71), where his views are most fully presented, it is clear that Milton believed baptism, or any other sacrament, to be merely an outward symbol of a spiritual change effected by the Holy Spirit, a rite which in itself is not efficacious. In effect he means that in the act of baptism one is not preparing oneself for heaven, but rather publicly avowing one's intention to live a righteous life in this world.

As Marilla (*Milton and Modern Man*, p. 132) remarks, at the time when *PR* was published, Milton, as for years before, was not in a position in which he could safely publish his unorthodox opinions. And what he said of baptism would certainly have been regarded as heretical. But he could trust that casual readers would see in the present passage nothing more than a repetition of a very old story; and that only most unfriendly readers would look for blasphemy, and for them there would be the fact that it was Satan who uttered the blasphemy.

74 Cf. 1 John 3. 3: 'And every man that hath this hope in him purifieth himself, even as he is pure.'

77–9 To discredit Christ, Satan gratuitously misinterprets his motives, as in *PL* 1. 95, 260; 2. 144 and elsewhere he attributes unworthy motives to God.

Thus, as the term 'devil', often applied to him (see note on 33 above), signifies, he is the false accuser or slanderer who speaks evil of God to men and of men to God.

77–85 See note on 24–37.

82 *her Crystal Dores.* Instead of 'her', present usage requires 'its', a form which began to appear about 1600, but which occurs only three times in Milton's poetry: *Nat* 106; *PL* 1. 254; 4. 813. 'Crystal' here probably means 'clear', 'shining', as in Spenser, *T.M.* 506; *Mui.* 44; *F.Q.* 2. 12. 64. 7. Cf. Rev. 21. 11; 22. 1. The spelling 'dores' prevailed in the 17th century and is found as late as 1684 (*OED*).

83 *A perfect Dove.* According to Luke 3. 22 'the Holy Ghost descended in bodily shape like a dove' (σωματικῷ εἴδει ὡσεὶ περιστεράν); according to Matt. 3. 16: ὡσεὶ περιστεράν; and Mark 1. 10: ὡς περιστεράν, 'like a dove'. Erasmus (*Nov. Test.*, Matt. 3. 16) comments on the obscurity of the meaning. In 30 above Milton speaking in his own person says 'in likeness of a Dove', and Christ in 282 below, even more closely following Scripture, says 'like a Dove'. But Satan, characteristically substituting a material for a spiritual meaning, says 'a perfect', that is a *real* dove. In *DocCh* 1. 6 (*Works* 14. 367) Milton writes: 'The descent...and appearance of the Holy Spirit in the likeness of a dove, seems to have been nothing more than a representation of the ineffable affection of the Father for the Son, communicated by the Holy Spirit under the appropriate image of a dove, and accompanied by a voice from heaven declaratory of that affection.' The image is appropriate because, as John Diodati explains in *Pious Annotations upon the Holy Bible* (London, 1643, Matt. 3. 16), in Scripture the dove is the symbol of 'perfect innocency, purity, simplicitie, grace, and mildnesse...opposite to the deceits, and dammages of the spirit of Satan who seduced *Eve* under the shape of the Serpent which is cunning, impure, and venemous.'

Milton evidently preferred the spelling 'perfet', still common in the 17th century (*OED*), since in his poetry he uses it in twenty-two of the thirty-one occurrences of the word.

84 *Sov'raign.* In *Ref* 2 (*Works* 3. 63) the spelling 'soveraigne' occurs, but elsewhere Milton uses 'sovran', 'sov'ran', or 'soveran'.

85 See note on 28–32 above. The omission of the pronominal subject, as here and in 137, 221, and in *PL* 2. 730, is fairly common in Spenser, as in *F.Q.* 1. 1.

42. 6; 1. 11. 28. 6, and in Shakespeare, as in *Merch.* 1. 1. 175; *R. II* 2. 2. 127; *W.T.* 5. 1. 23 (Abbott, *Shakes. Gram.* 244).

86–7 There are many ancient stories of the unions of immortals and mortals, as notably those of the angels and 'the daughters of men' (see note on 117 below); that of Zeus and Alcmena (Hesiod, *Theog.* 950–1; *Shield* 27–56; Apollodorus 2. 4. 8); that of Aphrodite and Anchises (Hesiod, *Theog.* 1008–10; Homer, *Il.* 5. 247–8; Virgil, *A.* 1. 617); and that of Jupiter and Pomponia (Silius Italicus 13. 615–46; 17. 653–4).

87 *obtains.* Holds, possesses, like Lat. *obtinere* (*OED*), as in *PL* 3. 546, Milton's only other use of the word in this sense.

89–90 For the account of Messiah's triumph over Satan and his host, see *PL* 6. 80 ff.

91 *Who this is we must learn.* Cf. 4. 501 below: 'For Son of God to me is yet in doubt'; also 4. 514–21 and Joseph Beaumont, *Psyche* 9. 165. Commentators have usually assumed that Milton represents Satan as in doubt about Christ's identity and whether he is the 'son of God by nature' or merely a perfect man and God's 'adopted son by grace'; and that he makes Christ fence with Satan and deny him the proof which he seeks. But in 'Theme', *UTQ* 25 (1955–6), 171–3, Woodhouse observes that 'this leaves much in the text unexplained—Christ's reply, for example, to the first temptation:

> Why dost thou then suggest to me distrust,
> *Knowing who I am*, as I know who thou art?

It also does too little justice to the characterization; and it fails to fathom the nature of a Satanic doubt.

'Though shorn of his grandeur...the Satan of *Paradise Regained* is the same character as the Satan of *Paradise Lost*. He is the great romantic, the rebel not only against God, but against fact, who cannot bring himself to accept his place in the scale of being or to act upon what in his heart he knows to be the truth (that is the whole purport of the great soliloquy in Book IV of *Paradise Lost*...). And in *Paradise Regained* Satan's doubt respecting Christ is at once real and unreal. It is an assiduously fostered doubt because he will not let himself acknowledge the truth; and yet the doubt torments him. He would give anything to have it confirmed, or (failing that) to receive proof so categorical as to destroy it for ever....He clings to the doubt, but patently with diminishing conviction and mounting despair....Nor do I find any reliable evidence that the Christ of *Paradise Regained* tries to conceal his own identity.' See 3. 201–2 below. Satan's doubt, Allen (*Vision*, p. 111) writes, is not about Christ's identity but about his own failing powers as a corrupter. He uses his pretended uncertainty about Christ both as a means of encouraging his followers and as an implement of seduction. Throughout *PR* he pretends to doubt who Christ is so that he may induce the 'exalted man' to distrust himself. See Matthew Poole, *Annotations upon the Holy Bible*, Matt. 4. 3 (London, 1683–5). In 'An Irony in *PR*', *PLL* 3 (1967), 377–80, G. M. Muldrow finds in the interplay between Satan's *conceptual* knowledge of Christ's identity as the Messiah, who had driven him from heaven, and his *experiential* knowledge of him as the incarnate Son of God, a knowledge completed only with his defeat at the end of the poem. This interplay constitutes one of the principal ironies of the poem, and 'provides much of the dramatic interest and suspense'. And in gaining experiential knowledge of Christ, Satan is paid in the same coin in which he had paid Adam, who in eating the apple gained experiential knowledge of the evil of which he already had conceptual knowledge.

94–5 *edge | Of hazard.* The expression, meaning 'extreme peril', used also by Shakespeare in *All's W.* 3. 3. 6 (cf. *PL* 1. 276–7: 'perilous edge | Of battle'), is probably derived from the game of tennis, in which the hazard is the side of the court into which the ball is served. But Browne (2. 300) quotes Homer, *Il.* 10. 173–4: 'death or life is balanced on a razor's edge' (ἐπὶ ξυροῦ ἵσταται | …ὄλεθρος…ἠὲ βιῶναι), which was a proverbial expression frequently used by Greek writers 'to express a delicately balanced likelihood of failure or success' (Liddell and Scott, s.v. ξυρόν).

95 *no long debate.* See note on 44–105 above.

96–7 Although in *PL* 1. 645–7 Satan recommended the use of guile, he had earlier and again later in 2. 40–2 presented a choice—or so pretended—between guile, 'our better part', and force. In the present council he admits no choice, but explicitly rejects force, and announces that he must use guile, which not only has succeeded once, but is more congenial to his nature.

99 Of Christ's three functions—as prophet, as priest, and as king—Satan fixes upon that of the king to the exclusion of the others; and, because of the constricting literalness of his mind, failing as usual to understand a metaphorical meaning, he can think of Christ only as an earthly king.

100–3 At the close of the council in Pandemonium (*PL* 2. 1–416), of all the fallen angels only Satan had volunteered to seek their deliverance by going to the world to corrupt man, the plan which a few minutes before all had eagerly approved.

103 *a calmer voyage.* Upon his first journey to the world, Satan had to pass from hell through chaos, the 'dark / Illimitable Ocean', a perilous course. See W. C. Curry, *Milton's Ontology, Cosmogony, and Physics* (Lexington, Ky., 1957), pp. 149–51. Now he need descend only from mid air (see note on 39 above). Although he has been emphasizing the present danger, to protect himself in the event of failure, Satan wishes to give his followers some assurance of success if they entrust the new undertaking to him.

104 That guile was once successful is the best reason to hope that it will again succeed. Satan's reasoning might be valid if he had again to seduce only an Adam and an Eve, but he has just admitted that he has to deal with a far more formidable opponent.

106–10 Contrast the exultant mood of the fallen angels at the close of the council in Pandemonium (*PL* 2. 386–8).

107 *amazement.* 'Bewilderment, perplexity', as in *PL* 2. 758, a meaning common in the 17th century (*OED*).

111 *Unanimous.* So were they unanimous in deciding to ruin man (*PL* 2. 388–9).

112 *main.* 'Highly important', 'momentous' (*OED*), as in *PL* 6. 471.

113 *Dictator.* In ancient Rome, in time of danger to the state, the law, in the interest of public safety, provided for the appointment of a *dictator* or *magister populi*, who for the period of his appointment had absolute power, and from whose decisions there was no appeal (Polybius 3. 87. 7–8; Livy 2. 18. 5–8; 3. 20. 8; 9. 22. 1; 24. 1; Cicero, *Rep.* 1. 40; *Fin.* 3. 75; *Leg.* 3. 3. 9; Silius Italicus 6. 590–618; Mommsen, *History of Rome*, tr. Dickson, New York, 1887, 1. 262). Among other moderns Machiavelli (*Discourses on Livy* 1. 34) and James Harrington (*Oceana*, ed. Liljegren, Heidelberg, 1924, p. 112) held that in a national crisis a constitutional dictator is necessary. Because of the crisis in which Satan and his followers now find themselves, they appoint him dictator. That his powers are extraordinary and temporary, Zera Fink, in *The Classical Republicans* (Evanston, Ill., 1945, pp. 195–6), believes, is to be inferred from the second council (2. 105–96) and 'from his care to have them renewed' at that council. But, as Fink observes: 'The career of Satan as a dictator is a career of unrelieved failure. The theme required that Satan should fail; it did not require that he should be represented in failure as a dictator.' The implication then seems clear that Milton had no faith in the efficacy of a dictatorship when the ordinary constitutional machinery breaks down. 'Thus there emerges out of the poem a point of view', Fink concludes, 'thoroughly consistent with that in *The ready and easy way*, in which Milton had put his full faith in the adequacy of perfectly-contrived institutions to meet all situations whether of peace or crisis.'

In securing authority to act as a constitutional dictator, Satan, however, is securing confirmation of powers which actually he has exercised ever since his revolt in heaven. He was equally careful, and for the same reason, to secure authority from the council in Pandemonium in *PL* 2. The reason is that a shrewd dictator, as in a way Satan is, well knows that when he faces possible disaster for which he may be held accountable, the only course that promises some measure of safety for himself lies in convincing his followers of the difficulty and danger which confront them, and in being authorized to act in the crisis.

115 *Thir.* It seems best, in view of the overall plan of the Variorum, for this and other such now unusual spellings as *strook* for *struck* and *hunderd* for *hundred* to be discussed in the volume devoted to prosody and related problems of language.

117 The belief that the fallen angels became the gods of the heathen, as Milton represents them in *PL* 1. 361 ff., and that they had subdued and were ruling the world, as Plato (*Critias* 109; cf. *States.* 271 ff.) represents the gods ruling their allotted districts or kingdoms, appeared early in the Christian era, as witness Justin Martyr, 2 *Apol.* 5; *Dial. Tryph.* 79 (Migne, *Pat. Gr.* 6. 452, 661–3); Lactantius, *Epit.* 28 (Migne, *Pat. Lat.* 6. 1035–6); *Vita B. Martini*, ed. Dubner (Paris, 1877), pp. 34–6. The first step toward their identification was probably the older identification of gods and demons which began as early as Democritus, who, according to Eduard Zeller (*Greek Philosophy to the Time of Socrates*, tr. Alleyne, London, 1881, 2. 290), 'mediating between the philosophers and the popular religion, entered upon the course so often pursued in after times, viz. that of degrading the gods of polytheism into demons.' In 1 Cor. 10. 20 Paul writes: 'The things which the Gentiles sacrifice, they sacrifice to devils' (δαιμονίοις); and in LXX Ps. 95. 5 the gods of the heathen are called δαιμόνια. The same idea appears in Clement of Alexandria, *Cohort. ad Gr.* 4. 49 (Migne, *Pat. Gr.* 8. 143–6); Lactantius, *D.I.* 2. 15; 4. 27 (Migne, *Pat. Lat.* 6. 330–3, 531–5); Tertullian, *Apol.* 22 (*Pat. Lat.* 1. 405–6); Augustine, *Civ. D.* 9. 23. The second step seems to have been the belief that the fallen angels and demons were related, a belief which arose among Jewish writers as early as the author of *Enoch*, who in chapters 6–8 relates, as does Satan in 2. 178–81 below, that the angels of God married the daughters of men, and thus became the parents of demons—or of giants, as some believed. See *Book of Jubilees* 5. 1; *Test. XII Patr.*, *Reuben* 5. 6–7; Josephus, *A.J.* 1. 3. 1; Philo, *Gigant.* 2. 6; Lactantius, *Epit.* 27–8 (Migne, *Pat. Lat.* 6. 1034–6). The story, repeated, though not with approval, in Justin Martyr, *2 Apol.* 5 (Migne, *Pat. Gr.* 6. 452–3), and in Augustine, *Civ. D.* 15. 22–3, comes from Gen. 6. 2: 'The sons of God saw the daughters of men that they were fair; and they took them wives of all which they chose', which, however, in the LXX *Codex Alexandrinus* reads, not 'the *sons* of God' but 'the *angels* of God' (οἱ ἄγγελοι τοῦ θεοῦ). Having thus become related, the fallen angels and demons were actually identified, as they are by Philo, who regarded demons as messengers (ἄγγελοι) between God and the world, and explained that what other philosophers called demons, Moses called angels (*Gigant.* 2. 6).

Once demons had been identified with the heathen gods, it logically followed that the fallen angels and the heathen gods were one and the same. See Justin Martyr, *2 Apol.* 5 (Migne, *Pat. Gr.* 6. 452–3); Jerome, *Comment. in Dan.* 4. 92 (Migne, *Pat. Lat.* 25. 511). Hooker (*Eccles. Pol.* 1. 4. 3) writes: 'These wicked spirits [the fallen angels] the heathens honoured instead of gods, both generally under the name of *Dii inferi*, "gods infernal;" and particularly, some in oracles, some in idols, some as household gods'. Thomas Heywood in *The Hierarchie of the Blessed Angells* (London, 1635, p. 436) repeats the belief in the following lines:

> Of the Rebellious there be Orders nine,
> As corresponding with the Spirits Diuine.
> In the first eminent place are those install'd
> As would on earth be worship, and gods call'd.
> As he that did his Oracles proclaime
> In Delphos, Shadow'd by *Apollo*'s name.

119 *Coast*. In the sense of border, district, or environs near a frontier (*OED*), 'coast' (Lat. *costa*), often in the plural, frequently occurs in the A.V., as in Num. 13. 29; Deut. 3. 17; Exod. 10. 4; Joshua 15. 21; Matt. 15. 39; Mark 5. 17. In *Theatrum Terrae Sanctae* (Cologne, 1613), p. 19, Christianus Adrichomius places the temptation of Christ in the Desert of Quarentana between Jerusalem and Jericho.

120 *His easie steps*. An allusion to 103–4 above, in contrast with *PL* 1. 295–6: 'to support uneasie steps / Over the burning Marle.'

girded with snaky wiles. 'An ironic allusion to Isaiah's prophecy (xi, 5) that righteousness should be the girdle of the loins of the restorer of Israel' (Hughes, p. 485). 'Girded' here means invested or indued with attributes, i.e. wiles (*OED*). Cf. *PL* 7. 194. Milton may have remembered κακοῖσι δόλοισι κεκασμένε in Homer, *Il.* 4. 339 and *dolis instructis* in Virgil, *A.* 2. 152.

122 *This man of men.* Analogous to such expressions as 'heaven of heavens' and 'god of gods' which signify that the subject is supreme in its kind. Milton's views of Christ's nature, stated in *DocCh* 1. 5, 14 (*Works* 14. 176–357; 15. 250–83), are that Christ, the only begotten Son of God, is not of one essence with the Father, but subordinate to him and not eternal. His nature, however, is twofold, divine and human. In *DocCh* 1. 14 (*Works* 15. 263) Milton says that the incarnation of Christ 'is generally considered by theologians as, next to the Trinity in Unity, the greatest mystery of our religion.'

126–8 The 'Counsel pre-ordain'd' is the curse pronounced in Gen. 3. 15. See note on 24–37 above.

128 *frequence.* Assembly, attendance in great numbers (*OED*), like Lat. *frequentia.* Jerram (p. 72) gives examples of 'frequency' and 'frequent' in this sense from Jonson, *Cat.* 4. 2 and Chapman, *Il.* 2. 71.

129 *Gabriel.* The only appearances of Gabriel in the Bible, in each of which he is the messenger of God, are in Dan. 8. 16; 9. 21, and Luke 1. 19, 26, in the last of which he is the angel of the annunciation, to which line 134 refers. Michael, Uriel, Raphael, and Gabriel are the four angels or 'presences' who stand about the throne of God (*Enoch* 9. 1). It is Gabriel's function to 'pray and intercede for those who dwell on the earth' (*Enoch* 40. 6, 9), probably because he is 'the strong one of God'. See Edmund Castell, *Lexicon Hepta-glotton* (London, 1669), col. 478, and Johann Buxtorf, *Lexicon Hebraicum et Chaldaicum* (Basle, 1676), s.v. Uriel.

Thus it is appropriate that he is the angel here addressed, as it is in *PL* 4 that he is the guardian of the gate of Paradise and confronts Satan, and that in Book 6 he is one of the leaders of the celestial armies.

130–1 As Allen (*Vision*, pp. 117–18) observes, Milton, to turn the imaginations of his readers in a new direction, early in *PR* takes them to heaven and shows them a scene quite detached from that of *PL*. God's speech to Gabriel contains no reference to earlier events in heaven. The purpose of the scene is to help readers to start afresh, helped by a set of conditions different from those in *PL*. We are told that a duel is about to begin that will be worth watching; but since we must watch it as men, it is a man whom we shall see.

God's speech is in striking contrast with Satan's earlier one (44–105). The latter is marked by doubts and fears, God's by serenity and confidence in the Son. The contrast becomes even more striking when we hear Christ's soliloquy (196–293), which reveals both his humanity and his divine perfection. He awaits an event which, as a human being, he cannot foresee; but he awaits it with perfect faith, reflecting God's confidence in him, and with no shadow of fear. Thus in these three speeches Milton introduces, in three significant variations, the theme of doubt versus faith which is to have a large part in *PR*. See A. H. Sackton, 'Architectonic Structure', *UTSE* 33 (1954), 36–7.

130 *proof.* See note on 11 above.

131–2 Editors have suggested various sources for these lines, but the conception of angels as God's messengers and ministers upon earth is so old and widespread that it is futile to look for a particular source. See *DocCh* 1. 9 (*Works* 15. 97–105); Heywood, *Hierarchie*, pp. 194–5; *Cath. Encyc.* 1. 477–8.

133–40 See Luke 1. 26–37 for the account of the annunciation, which Milton closely follows.

133–6 See note on 24–37 above.

133 *verifie.* 'To fulfil' (Lockwood, *Lexicon*), but probably more correctly 'to show to be true by demonstration' (*OED*).
   solemn message late. Recent solemn message. Todd (5. 23) places a comma after 'message', evidently taking 'late' as an adverb modifying 'sent', for which there is little defence. Milton often uses nouns preceded and followed by adjectives, as in *Lyc.* 6; *PL* 1. 733; 2. 615, 616; 3. 44, 396, 439, 692; 5. 5; *PR* 2. 352; 4. 411; *SA* 320–1.

137 *Then.* Some editors suggest that 'then' may be a misprint for 'thou', but as in 85 above (see note) the pronominal subject may be omitted.

140 *man.* See note on 4 above.

142–3 *I expose | To Satan.* See Job 1–2. 'Expose' may be used with a double meaning—'to lay open' to danger and 'to make known, disclose' (*OED*).

143 *assay.* 'To practise by way of trial' (*OED*).

144–6 See Satan's speech above, and especially lines 47–52 and 100–3.

146 *Apostasie.* Cf. 'appetite' in 2. 264 below and 'servitude' in *PL* 12. 132. Blakeney (p. 98) notes Shakespeare's not uncommon use of abstract for concrete nouns, e.g. 'baseness' for base fellows in *Wives* 2. 2. 21. Cf. *servitus* and *servitium* in Latin. Milton's abstract terms are often more suggestive and hence more poetic than the corresponding concrete terms.

147 *Less over-weening.* That is, he might have learned to be less arrogant and presumptuous. But the ellipsis is slightly awkward.

147-9 See Job 1-2 and cf. 369, 425-6 and notes, and 3. 64-8 below.

150 *man.* See note on 4 above.

155-6 *I mean | To exercise him.* In *DocCh* 1. 2 (*Works* 15. 87) Milton writes: 'Temptation is either for evil or for good....A good temptation is that whereby God tempts even the righteous for the purpose of proving them, not as though he were ignorant of the disposition of their hearts, but for the purpose of exercising or manifesting their faith or patience, as in the case of Abraham and Job.'

157-8 *rudiments | Of his great warfare.* Editors note the borrowing from Virgil, *A.* 11. 156-7: *bellique propinqui | dura rudimenta.*

159 See *PL* 2. 648-889; 10. 585-609, and cf. Rom. 6. 23: 'For the wages of sin is death; but the gift of God is eternal life through Jesus Christ our Lord.'

161 *weakness.* Cf. 1 Cor. 1. 27: 'God hath chosen the weak things of the world to confound the things which are mighty.' Cf. also Ps. 8. 2.

162 'Mass', Jerram (p. 73) observes, 'forcibly brings out the idea of inert passive resistance, which is harder to subdue than even the active opposition of "Satanic strength."'

163 *Angels and Ætherial Powers.* If 'Ætherial Powers' means only angels in the generic sense, as it does in *PL* 3. 100, Milton's expression is redundant, since he has just mentioned angels. But he may be referring, with greater precision than is usual with him, to two of the nine orders in the heavenly hierarchy as that is elaborated in Dionysius, *Hierarchia* 6. 2 (Migne, *Pat. Gr.* 3. 200-5). Aquinas, who adopted the angelology of Dionysius, and in *Sum. Th.* 1. 108. 6 explains the functions of the several orders of Angels, states that it is the duty of the Powers 'to order the manner of carrying out what has been commanded or decided';[3] that of angels is 'to execute what is to be done'.[4] Since Angels and Powers are concerned with the execution of the government of God,

---

[3] ordinare qualiter ea quae praecepta vel definita sunt.
[4] alii vero sunt qui simpliciter exequuntur.

they must be concerned with the affairs of men. Milton might then appropriately mention them here, because they especially should understand the great action about to take place and should know the consummate virtue of the chief actor therein.

165 *From*. Because of, like Lat. *ex* and *prae*, as in *PL* 1. 98, 113; 9. 333.

166 *This perfect man*. See notes on 4. 535–7 below and 122 above.
 by merit call'd my Son. For Milton virtue constitutes the only real merit; hence God, addressing the Son in *PL* 3. 308–11, says that he has been found

> By Merit more then Birthright son of God,
> Found worthiest to be so by being Good,
> Farr more then Great or High.

It is merit which entitles him to reign over all 'In Heaven, or Earth, or under Earth in Hell' (*PL* 3. 322); and it is only merit in the same sense which entitles earthly rulers to reign over their fellow men; Satan's reign in hell shows the same principle inverted, for in the topsy-turvy morality of hell, where evil is taken for good (*PL* 4. 110), there can be no pre-eminence except in evil; and so, because of his pre-eminent wickedness, Satan by merit reigns.

168–9 Note the contrast with 106–9 above.

170–1 According to Dionysius, *Div. Nom.* 4. 8–9 (Migne, *Pat. Gr.* 3. 704–5), and Aquinas, *Sum. Th.* 2. 2. 180. 6, there are three symbolic movements of the angels, the circular, the straight, and the oblique (*circularis, et rectus, et obliquus*). In *Conv.* 2. 6 and *Parad.* 28. 96–137 Dante represents the several choirs of angels as circling the throne of God and singing. Cf. *Lyc* 180; *PL* 5. 618–22.

171–2 *the hand | Sung with the voice*. For other occurrences of 'hand' used to distinguish instrumental from vocal music, see 4. 254–6 below and *Arc* 77. 'Sing' meaning 'to play on a musical instrument' (Lockwood, *Lexicon*) does not appear in *OED*. Editors quote Tibullus 3. 4. 41: 'when the fingers had spoken (*locuti*) along with the voice'. Milton must have known that Lat. *canere*, 'to sing', also frequently means 'to play upon a musical instrument', as in Catullus 63. 23; Lucretius 4. 585; Cicero, *Div.* 1. 17. 30; Ovid, *M.* 1. 683; Quintilian 1. 10. 14.
 The hymns mentioned here, like those mentioned or given in full in *Nat* 100, 114–16; *PL* 3. 347–9, 372–415; 7. 557–73, 602–32; Dante, *Parad.* 28. 94; Fletcher, *C.V.* 2. 61. 6–8; 3. 32. 13; 4. 15–16, belong to a tradition which may

have been established by the song of the angels at the nativity in Luke 2. 14, and the heavenly host's singing and playing upon harps in Rev. 5. 8–9; 14. 2–3; 15. 2–3.

172 *argument*. The theme or subject, as in *PL* 1. 24 and Spenser, *F.Q.* 2. 10. 3. 1.

173–81 This hymn, briefer and in a plainer style than those in *PL* 3. 372–415 and 7. 602–32, is suited to the narrower scope and greater austerity of *PR*.

173 *Victory and Triumph*. Perhaps reminiscent of Fletcher's title, *Christs Victorie and Triumph*.

174 *duel*. In *PL* 12. 386–7 Michael, speaking to Adam of Christ's struggle with Satan, says: 'Dream not of thir fight, / As of a duel.' Some editors have complained of the meanness in the usual sense of the word 'duel' which is unworthy of the speakers and the occasion. But in using it Milton may have thought of Lat. *duellum*, an early and poetical form of *bellum*. At all events Milton is continuing from lines 11 and 130 above the figure of a single combat, which aptly suits what happens in *PR*.

176 Cf. John 10. 15: 'As the Father knoweth me, even so know I the Father.'
   secure. Free from care or anxiety, like Lat. *securus*, as in *PL* 1. 261; 5. 238; 9. 1175, a meaning common in the 17th century (*OED*).

177 *though untri'd*. Christ *as Messiah* has already proved himself in the war in heaven; but *as man*, although his soliloquy in lines 196–293 reveals that his virtue is not entirely untried, he has not thus far met any great moral test. For the belief that the incarnation was a mystery even to the angels, see Irenaeus, *Con. Haer.* 3. 16 (Migne, *Pat. Gr.* 7. 920); Ambrose, *Fid.* 1. 10; 4. 1 (Migne, *Pat. Lat.* 16. 543–4, 617–20). See note on 122 above.

180 *frustrate*. In the 16th and 17th centuries the suffix *-ed* was often dropped from the past tense and the past participle of verbs ending in *-t* or *-d* (Abbott, *Shakes. Gram.* 341–2).

182 *Odes*. Hymns in noble style upon lofty themes (cf. 4. 257 below; *Nat* 24; and *RCG* 2. pref., *Works* 3. 238), such poems as those of which Sidney, in the *Defence of Poesie* (*Works*, ed. Feuillerat, 3. 9) said: 'The chiefe [of the three general kinds of poetry]...were they that did imitate the unconceiveable excellencies of God.'
   Vigils. Equivalent to Lat. *vigiliae*, which Du Cange defines as *nocturnae*

preces, prayers said or sung at a nocturnal service, in which sense *OED* cites the present use of 'vigils'. Cf. *PL* 3. 416–17.

184   *Bethabara*. According to John 1. 28 Jesus was baptized in the River Jordan at Bethabara, which by tradition was the ford of Makhadet Hajla. Adrichomius (*Theatrum*, pp. 126–7) says the name means 'house of crossing... either because...there the Israelites crossed over into Canaan, or because there was a ford of Jordan'. Milton apparently takes the latter interpretation, since in 328 and 4. 510 below he mentions John's baptizing at the 'Ford of Jordan' (A. H. Gilbert, *A Geographical Dictionary of Milton*, New Haven, 1919, p. 54).

185   *much revolving*. The expression is reminiscent of such uses of *volvere* and *revolvere* as occur in Virgil, *A.* 1. 305: 'Aeneas through the night revolving (*volvens*) many things'; and 2. 10: 'but why do I vainly unfold (*revolvo*) these unwelcome things?'; and Ovid, *F.* 4. 667: 'Numa pondered (*revolvit*) the vision.' Cf. *PL* 4. 31; *SA* 1638.

189   *the Spirit leading*. Cf. Matt. 4. 1: 'Then was Jesus led up of the Spirit into the wilderness'. Cf. Mark 1. 12; Luke 4. 1. 'Christ wished to be tempted,' says Aquinas (*Sum. Th.* 3. 41. 1), 'first so that he might help us to resist temptation.' The leading of the Spirit, William Perkins explains in *The Combate betweene Christ and the Deuill expounded* (*Works*, London, 1616–18, 3. 373), was 'a motion of the holy Ghost, wherewith Christ was...made willing to encounter with Sathan in that combate...[It] was a peculiar motion, not forced or constrained, but voluntarie.'

190–1   See 302 below and note.

193   *Desert wild*. See note on 119 above.

196–293   In *Heroic Knowledge*, pp. 104–5, Stein interprets the significance of Christ's soliloquy thus: Christ's autobiographical soliloquy, which is without Scriptural authority, is an extremely important 'personal revelation' of the development that has taken place within his own consciousness before his 'first encounter with Satan'; and it will provide an 'evolving commentary on all the temptations'. Christ's 'first response' as a child 'was intuitive', a 'desire to learn, to know, and to do'. This was his 'first recognition' of the 'Light from above' (4. 289), a recognition 'accompanied by the inseparable intuition' that 'by endeavour' he must better understand the light, 'and that the understanding must' be expressed 'in action'. 'The second stage of consciousness', which 'evolved from the first', was '*discursive* and disciplined, the study of the law, in which' Christ found 'the intuitive verified and strengthened'. 'The third stage', aspiring to heroic deeds, was 'a kind of *human intuition*, an earthly interpretation of the divinely inspired need of the understanding to express itself in action.' The child was 'innocent of any evil in his heroic ideal', but he 'recognized for himself' the fundamental discrepancy 'between the human and the divine represented by the use of force'. 'The fourth stage', with 'persuasion' as 'the key', defined anew what may 'be public good in terms of knowledge'. For the expression of the understanding 'in action' 'persuasion' is 'the proper means'. 'The fourth stage' is, 'then', a 'return to the original intuition', now proved by intellectual experience, including the course 'of action' which Christ has rejected. The fourth stage will continue throughout *PR*, while Christ improves his gifts, becomes what he is, and still wrestles with the problem of using 'his "knowledge and illumination"'.

196–7 Cf. *SA* 19–21:

> restless thoughts, that like a deadly swarm
> Of Hornets arm'd, no sooner found alone,
> But rush upon me thronging.

198–9 In the famous defence of himself in *Apol* (*Works* 3. 302), Milton speaks of 'every instinct and presage of nature which is not wont to be false'; and in *RCG* 2 (3. 236) he says: 'I began thus farre to assent both to them and divers of my friends here at home, and not lesse to an inward prompting which now grew daily upon me.'

200 *sorting.* 'That corresponds, agrees, or suits (with others of the same class or kind)' (*OED*).

201–6 These lines, printed in 1760 below Cipriani's etching of the portrait of Milton at the age of ten, have often been read as a reflection of Milton's own childhood. But as H. F. Fletcher (*Intellectual Development of John Milton* 1, Urbana, Ill., 1956, 385) does well to point out, there are in the present passage nothing but accidental resemblances, not to established facts about Milton's childhood, but to traditions that have grown up about it. The lines concern not the boy Milton, but the boy Jesus. On autobiographical interpretations of *PR*, see introduction, pp. 37f.

Authority for the view of Christ's childhood here presented is the incident mentioned in lines 209–13 below, his discussion with the doctors of the law in the temple, and the statement in Luke 2. 40: 'And the child grew, and waxed strong in spirit, filled with wisdom: and the grace of God was upon him.' The whole tradition concerning Christ's childhood represents it as highly unusual. This is especially evident in apocryphal accounts, as in the *Gospel of Pseudo-Matthew*, the *Gospel of the Infancy*, and the *Gospel of Thomas*, which show him mainly as a worker of miracles, some of them grotesque, even malevolent.

203 *Serious.* An adverb, earlier 'seriouse'. In M.E. adverbs in -*e* are common, but in the 15th century when the unstressed -*e* disappeared, these adverbs became indistinguishable from adjectives (H. C. Wyld, *Short History of English*, London, 1914, p. 326).

204-5 When brought before Pilate, Jesus said (John 18. 37): 'To this end was I born, and for this cause came I into the world, that I should bear witness unto the truth.'

206-7 Editors note the resemblance to Virgil, *A.* 9. 311: 'endowed beyond his years with the spirit and thought of a man';[5] and Spenser, *F.Q.* 2. 2. 15. 5-6: 'grauitie, / Aboue the reason of her youthly yeares'.

207 Cf. Ps. 119. 103: 'How sweet are thy words unto my taste! yea, sweeter than honey to my mouth!'

208 In Ps. 1. 2 it is said of the righteous man, 'But his delight is in the law of the Lord; and in his law doth he meditate day and night.'

209-14 These lines summarize the account in Luke 2. 46-50 of Christ's discussion with the doctors of the law in the temple when he was twelve years old. Satan summarizes the same account in 4. 215-20 below. 'Milton does not imply that Jesus acted the part of a teacher,' says Jerram (p. 78); but the words 'propose / What might improve my knowledge or their own' and 'Teaching not taught' in 4. 220 can have no other meaning, although it is without Scriptural authority. The two statements, as S. H. Stedman suggests ('Milton and a School Prayer', *TLS*, 11 Aug. 1927, p. 584), may be a reminiscence of Milton's days at St Paul's School, where, every Monday and Wednesday, in two prayers, still in use, which speak of Christ among the doctors, he heard the words *inter doctores illos disputasti* and *docuisti ipsos doctores*.

210 *Feast.* The Passover. See Luke 2. 41.

214 *admir'd.* Wondered or marvelled at, like Lat. *admirari*, as in *PL* 1. 690; 2. 677; 6. 498, a meaning common in the 17th century.

---

[5] ante annos animumque gerens curamque virilem.

217 So great was Jewish hatred of Roman rule that it had led to such revolts as that against Sabinus, the Roman procurator, in 4 B.C. (Josephus, *A.J.* 17. 10. 1–7; *B.J.* 2. 3. 1–4), and that of Judas of Galilee in A.D. 6–7 (*A.J.* 18. 1. 1–6; *B.J.* 2. 8. 1). In the time of Christ the strongest opposition to the Romans came from the Zealots, an organized and fanatically active party from the time of Herod to the capture of Jerusalem by Titus in A.D. 70.

218–23 The thought expressed here is close to that of Erasmus in the *Institutio Principis Christiani* that if those who call themselves Christians will but live in accord with the lessons of the Sermon on the Mount, there will be no occasion to use force among them, for force will be replaced by reason and brotherly love, and they will live together in peace.

218–20 Hughes (p. 487) notes the contrast with the prophecy of Anchises, in Virgil (*A.* 6. 851–3), that Rome was destined to rule and bring peace to the nations of the world and to quell the proud.[6]

219 *Brute violence.* Milton's many statements concerning force and violence are almost all condemnatory, because he believed that in the hierarchical order of all things, reason is superior to them and should prevail. See 2. 479 below; *Comus* 450–1; *Sonn* 15. 9–11; *PL* 1. 648–9; 6. 40–1, 124–6; 9. 1171–4; 11. 671–3; *CivP* (*Works* 6. 22).

proud Tyrannick pow'r. Of tyrants and tyranny Milton speaks even more often than of force and violence, and with equal abhorrence, because tyranny, which, through pride, uses force and violence, is the rule of equals by their equals, and thus violates the hierarchical order in which only natural superiors must rule their inferiors. See *PL* 5. 809–12, 831–5; 6. 174–87; 12. 90–6; *Eikon* (*Works* 5. 241–2); *TKM* (5. 7); *Def 2* (8. 25); C. S. Lewis, *Preface*, pp. 72–80. See also the note on 40 above.

220 Although from childhood Christ must have known that the Jews looked for a Messiah who, as a temporal king, would deliver them from their Roman conquerors (Josephus, *B.J.* 6. 5. 4; *Encyc. Bibl.* 3. 3057–64), nothing in the Gospels suggests that he ever desired temporal power. Milton, however, represents him as having desired it, not for his own sake but for the good end which he states. The desire, however, is now transformed into a higher purpose which he goes on to explain. He has faced and rejected worldly ambition; and

---

[6] tu regere imperio populos, Romane, memento
(hae tibi erunt artes), pacisque imponere morem,
parcere subiectis et debellare superbos.

his is already no wholly untried, cloistered virtue. He has learned humility and now relies upon the guidance of divine providence.

222 John Jortin (*Tracts*, London, 1790, 1. 318) suggests as a parallel to this line, Virgil, *G*. 4. 561–2: 'And a victor gives laws to willing nations';[7] and Blakeney (p. 101) suggests also Euripides, *Hec*. 816: 'Persuasion, the supreme ruler of men.'[8] Milton may have remembered Spenser, *F.Q*. 3. 2. 13. 3–4:

> Ah, but if reason faire might you perswade,
> To slake your wrath, and mollifie your mind;

and 4. 9. 32. 8–9:

> And would them faine from battell to surceasse,
> With gentle words perswading them to friendly peace.

223 *perswasion*. Cf. *RCG* (*Works* 3. 181): 'Persuasion certainly is a more winning, and more manlike way to keepe men in obedience then feare.'

224–6 The same distinction between those who wilfully do evil and those who are 'unware misled' is made between the fallen angels and man in *PL* 3. 129–32.

226 *the stubborn only to subdue*. Possibly reminiscent of Virgil, *A*. 6. 853: 'to subdue (*debellare*) the proud'. Against those who, like Pharaoh of the stubborn heart, will not be moved by reason, the highest faculty of the soul, force must be used. God, addressing Messiah in *PL* 6. 37–41, says:

> the easier conquest now
> Remains thee...to subdue
> By force, who reason for thir Law refuse.

subdue. The first edition reads 'destroy', which in the Errata is changed to 'subdue', perhaps, as Newton (1. 25) suggests, because Milton recalled Luke 9. 56: 'For the Son of man is not come to destroy men's lives, but to save them.'

228 *inly*. 'Inwardly', but possibly also 'heartily' —or 'entirely', the gloss on Spenser, *S.C.*, May 38. Cf. 3. 203 below and *PL* 11. 444.

231–2 Milton's profound conviction concerning the power of virtue is most memorably expressed in *Comus* 372–4:

[7] victorque volentis
per populos dat iura.
[8] πειθὼ δὲ τὴν τύραννον ἀνθρώποις μόνην.

> Vertue could see to do what vertue would
> By her own radiant light, though Sun and Moon
> Were in the flat Sea sunk;

and in 588–9:

> Vertue may be assail'd, but never hurt,
> Surpriz'd by unjust force, but not enthrall'd.

Of such virtue the Lady in *Comus* and Abdiel in *PL* are vivid examples, but Christ is the supreme example. This is his chief significance in *PR*.

233 *express.* 'Manifest', 'reveal by external tokens' (*OED*), like Lat. *exprimere*, as in *PL* 3. 140; 5. 574; 6. 720.

234–41 Although the Gospels nowhere represent Mary as informing Jesus of his divine mission, and although his question (Luke 2. 49) 'Wist ye not that I must be about my Father's business?' may imply that she did not understand that mission, yet Gabriel's announcement to her (Luke 1. 30–5), the prophecy of Elizabeth (Luke 1. 42–5) and her own words, the Magnificat (Luke 1. 46–55), and the extraordinary circumstances of the conception and birth of Christ give credibility to her statements here.

238–58 The autobiographical details in these lines are taken from Matt. 1 and Luke 1–2.

238–9 Cf. Luke 1. 26–31: 'And in the sixth month the angel Gabriel was sent from God unto a city of Galilee, named Nazareth, To a virgin espoused to a man whose name was Joseph, of the house of David; and the virgin's name was Mary....And the angel said unto her, Fear not, Mary: for thou hast found favour with God. And, behold, thou shalt conceive in thy womb, and bring forth a son, and shalt call his name Jesus.'

240–1 Cf. Luke 1. 32–3: 'He shall be great, and shall be called the Son of the Highest: and the Lord God shall give unto him the throne of his father David: And he shall reign over the house of Jacob for ever; and of his kingdom there shall be no end.' Cf. also Heb. 1. 8 and *PL* 12. 369–71. Line 241 is repeated in 4. 151 below. Among the many references in *PR* to prophecies and revelations concerning Messiah (see note on 24–37 above), Milton calls special attention to the prophecy of Christ's accession to the throne of David. Later, in tempting Christ with his aid prematurely to gain control of the kingdoms of the world, Satan will skilfully though vainly endeavour to persuade him that in so doing he will be fulfilling the prophecy. See 3. 152–80, 351–85; 4. 105–8, 374–81, 467–83 below.

242–3 Cf. Luke 2. 13–14: 'And suddenly there was with the angel a multitude of the heavenly host praising God, and saying, Glory to God in the highest, and on earth peace, good will toward men.' See also *Nat* 93–100, 117–24; *PL* 12. 366–7.

242 *Quire*. Since the end of the 17th century the word has been 'fictitiously spelt *choir*, app. as a partial assimilation to Gr.-L. *chorus* or F. *chœur*' (*OED*).

244 Cf. Luke 2. 8: 'And there were in the same country shepherds abiding in the field, keeping watch over their flock by night.' Cf. also *Nat* 85–7; *PL* 12. 365.

245 *Messiah*. See Luke 2. 11: 'For unto you is born this day in the city of David a Saviour, which is Christ the Lord.' Cf. also *Nat* 116; *PL* 12. 358–9. Milton's conception of Christ, the Messiah, as the spiritual redeemer of man, is briefly stated in *PL* 3. 274–343 and much more elaborately in *DocCh* 1. 14–16 (*Works* 15. 250–341). See Maurice Kelley, *Argument*, pp. 156–84. His doctrine is very similar to that of Heb. 1–10, the author of which, like Milton in *PR*, writes with practical rather than theoretical intent, and regards Christ as the great and abiding exemplar for all men.

The principal elements of the doctrine are that to his divine nature Christ has joined human nature, and become the 'Head of all mankind' who has raised man 'to a far more excellent state of grace and glory than that from which he had fallen' (*DocCh* 1. 14, *Works* 15. 251). To satisfy divine justice, Christ, as man, outdoing hellish hate with heavenly love, was judged and put to death. But in his resurrection he raised with him his brethren ransomed with his life, and became the universal, spiritual king.

Christ, then, is the great high priest and mediator between God and fallen man, a mediator superior to all those under the old dispensation, because by the sacrifice of himself he performed in actuality what the old high priests performed only typically and figuratively. But in order to be such a supreme mediator, to become 'the author and finisher of our faith' to whom we must look, he had to assume human nature, had fully to partake of the common lot of men, to suffer, and willingly to die, and thus to show divine love active in human life.

247 Cf. Luke 2. 12: 'Ye shall find the babe wrapped in swaddling clothes, lying in a manger.' Cf. also *Nat* 31; *PL* 12. 364.

248 Cf. Luke 2. 7: 'There was no room for them in the inn.' Cf. also 254 below and *PL* 12. 360–1.

249–50 Cf. Matt. 2. 1–2: 'Behold, there came wise men from the east to Jerusalem, Saying...we have seen his star in the east, and are come to worship him.' Cf. also *Nat* 240–1; *PL* 12. 360–3. The belief that new stars appeared at the time of important events, as at the birth of a great man, was common in antiquity, as J. G. Frazer amply shows in *The Golden Bough*, 2nd ed. (London, 1963), 4. 59–68. There are traditions that when Alexander Severus was born, a great new star was seen (*Scrip. Hist. Aug., Alex. Sev.* 13); that when Augustus entered Rome to become emperor, several new stars appeared (Pliny, *N.H.* 2. 28. 98); and that at the time of the games in honour of the apotheosis of Julius Caesar, a comet, believed to be the soul of Caesar, shone for several days (Suetonius, *Caes.* 1. 88). Since it is a matter of common knowledge that new stars appear on important occasions, why, asks Origen in *Cels.* 1. 59 (Migne, *Pat. Gr.* 11. 769), should there be any wonder that one arose when Christ was born?

In *Nat* 23 the 'Wise Men' are called 'Wizards' and in *PL* 12. 363 the 'Eastern Sages'. The original word of which 'Wise Men' and 'Wizards' are translations is μάγοι, in the Vulgate, *magi*, i.e. Persian priests and wise men (Herodotus 1. 101; Cicero, *Div.* 1. 23. 46; 1. 41. 90).

251 Cf. Matt. 2. 11: 'And when they had opened their treasures, they presented unto him gifts; gold, and frankincense, and myrrh.' Cf. *PL* 12. 363.

252–4 See note on 24–37 above.

253 *new grav'n.* This expression, as Jerram (p. 79) observes, 'recals the ancient belief that the sky was a solid dome in which the stars were set....Hence "coelum stellis fulgentibus *aptum*," Virgil, *A.* 11. 202.' Cf. Shakespeare, *Merch.* 5. 1. 58–9: 'The floor of heaven / Is thick inlaid with patines of bright gold.'

255–8 According to Luke 2. 22–38, when Joseph and Mary brought the infant Jesus into the temple to offer sacrifices required by the Mosaic law, Simeon, by the revelation of the Holy Ghost, recognized Jesus as 'the Lord's Christ', and gave thanks to God, and said to Mary: 'Behold, this child is set for the fall and rising again of many in Israel; and for a sign which shall be spoken against ...that the thoughts of many hearts may be revealed.' And 'in that instant' Anna, an aged prophetess, coming into the temple, 'gave thanks likewise unto the Lord, and spake of him to all them that looked for redemption in Jerusalem.'

257 *vested Priest.* The design and the materials of the holy garments, the breastplate, and the ephod of the Hebrew priests are specified in detail in Exod. 28.

259 *revolv'd.* Turned over, searched through, studied ('a book, or the works of an author') (*OED*). Cf. Lat. *revolvere* and see note on 185 above.

261 Passages in the O.T. which have been interpreted as Messianic prophecies are numerous: e.g. Deut. 18. 15–19; Isa. 7. 14–17; 9. 6–7; 33. 14–24; 53; Jer. 33. 14–16. Consult Hastings, *Encyc. Rel. Eth.* 8. 571–5. See also the following note and the notes on 24–37 and 245 above.

262–3 Newton (1. 26), Todd (5. 40), and Hawkins (3. 31) quote what purports to be a passage from Justin Martyr to the effect that 'the Jews thought that the Messiah, when he came, would be without all power and distinction, and *unknown even to himself*, till Elias had anointed and declared him.' I can discover nothing in the works of Justin exactly corresponding to their quotation.[9]

That Jesus believed himself to be the Messiah (see note on 245 above) seems to be sufficiently attested by his answers to John the Baptist in Matt. 11. 2–10 and to the high priest in Mark 14. 61–2. The confession of faith, 'Thou art the Christ, the Son of the living God', in Matt. 16. 16 (cf. Mark 8. 27–30; Luke 9. 18–20; John 1. 41), which he elicited from Peter is further indication of his own belief as well as that of his disciples. Cf. 2. 3–4 below and note.

264 *many a hard assay.* See note on 143 above and cf. 4. 478 below and *Comus* 971. Spenser uses the same expression in *F.Q.* 2. 3. 15. 7; 2. 8. 7. 4; 2. 12. 38. 8.
even to the death. Cf. Isa. 53. 8: 'for he was cut off out of the land of the living.' Cf. also *PL* 12. 404–6, 411–16.

266–7 In discussing Christ as the redeemer in *DocCh* 1. 14 (*Works* 15. 253), Milton defines redemption as 'that act whereby Christ, being sent in the fulness of time, redeemed all believers at the price of his own blood, by his own voluntary act, conformably to the eternal counsel and grace of God the Father.'
whose sins. Cf. Isa. 53. 6: 'The Lord hath laid on him the iniquity of us all.' Cf. also *PL* 3. 203–12; 12. 402–10; *DocCh* 1. 15 (*Works* 15. 285–303).

---

[9] The following from *Dial. Tryph.* 49 (Migne, *Pat. Gr.* 6. 581) must be the passage which they meant to quote, although it lacks the important idea 'without all power and distinction, and unknown even to himself': Καὶ γὰρ πάντες ἡμεῖς τὸν Χριστὸν ἄνθρωπον ἐξ ἀνθρώπων προσδοκῶμεν γενήσεσθαι, καὶ τὸν Ἡλίαν χρῖσαι αὐτὸν ἐλθόντα. Ἐὰν δὲ αὐτὸς φαίνηται ὢν ὁ Χριστός, ἄνθρωπον μὲν ἐξ ἀνθρώπων γενόμενον ἐκ παντὸς ἐπίστασθαι δεῖ· ἐκ δὲ τοῦ μηδὲ Ἡλίαν ἐληλυθέναι, οὐδὲ τοῦτον ἀποφαίνομαι εἶναι.

268 *neither...or.* Like Lat. *neque...aut*, although not the usual English expression. *OED* gives several examples.

269–89 See notes on 18–32 above.

269 *waited.* Awaited, as in *PL* 3. 485; 9. 839.

270 *The Baptist.* See note on 18–22 above.
of whose birth. See Luke 1. 5–25, 57–66.

271 *Not knew by sight.* Although their mothers were cousins (Luke 1. 36), Jesus and John the Baptist had not met before Jesus came to the latter to be baptized, for John said, 'I knew him not' (John 1. 33).

271–3 See note on 20–1 above.

275–9 See notes on 25–6, 26–8 above.

277 *Harbinger.* See note on 71 above.

280 *laving stream.* Editors suggest an allusion to the phrase 'laver of regeneration', frequently applied to baptism.

281 *eternal doors.* The 'everlasting doors' of Ps. 24. 7.

286–7 See 58 above and note.

289 See note on 28–32 above.

290–3 Cf. 4. 116 below. Since in Christ divine and human natures are united, the question of the nature and extent of his knowledge was much debated by theologians from the patristic period onward. Many of their arguments are discussed by Aquinas in *Sum. Th.* 3. 9–12. Milton makes his position clear in *DocCh* 1. 5 (*Works* 14. 227) where he writes: 'The Son likewise teaches that the attributes of divinity belong to the Father alone, to the exclusion even of himself. With regard to omniscience Matt. xxiv. 36. "of that day and hour knoweth no man, no not the angels of heaven, but my Father only"; and still more explicitly, Mark xiii. 32. "not the angels which are in heaven, neither the Son, but the Father."' Later (14. 317), after quoting many supporting passages of Scripture, Milton concludes that 'Even the Son...knows not all things absolutely; there being some secret purposes, the knowledge of which the Father has reserved to himself alone.'

Keightley's note (2. 231) reads: 'Milton seems to have agreed with those who, with Beza and Grotius, held that the divine knowledge was gradually communicated to the human nature of Jesus...and...that he was not omniscient'.

The concluding words of Christ's soliloquy, Woodhouse observes ('Theme', *UTQ* 25, 1955–6, 174), 'are surely a directive how to read the experience on which the hero is about to enter: its purpose is revelation. The words also epitomize what is to be Christ's unshakable position throughout the ordeal: a position of absolute obedience and complete trust. And the two things taken together bring into relief an essential feature of the pattern of *Paradise Regained*, namely, the combination of two elements, the one static, the other progressive, and the dependence of pattern at this point wholly upon theme. But this does not exhaust the significance of the soliloquy. For it presently appears that Satan, like Christ's followers, assumes the common conception of the Messianic mission, which Christ has already outgrown, but that, when he seeks to utilize it in the temptations, he is at least appealing to motives and emotions which Christ once entertained. This is typical of the close integration and artistic economy which mark the whole poem.'

294   *Morning Star.* In Rev. 22. 16 Jesus says: 'I am...the bright and morning star', whence Spenser (*H.H.L.* 170), Fletcher (*C.V.* 4. 12. 1), and Milton have adopted the expression. Blakeney (p. 102) quotes Prudentius, *Cath.* 2. 67: *Tu, rex, Eoi sideris.*

296   *horrid.* Causing horror or aversion (*OED*), like Lat. *horridus*, as in 4. 94 below; *Comus* 428; *PL* 1. 83. The line may be reminiscent of Virgil, *A.* 1. 165: 'an overhanging grove dark with horrid (*horrenti*) shades'; and 9. 382: 'The forest spread far and wide with horrid (*horrida*) thickets.'

It is symbolically significant that what is most emphasized about the desert is its pathlessness. Through a pathless waste Christ is wandering in order to find 'the way of truth', while Satan endeavours to mislead him. When at the end the angels, after celebrating the victory, bring him 'in his way with joy', the reader feels the metaphor in 'way' and the contrast with the pathless wilderness through which he has been moving.

297–8   Masson (3. 565) and Blakeney (pp. 102–3) would change the original and generally accepted punctuation, and read: 'The way he came, not having mark'd, return was difficult.' But the comma after 'came' would indicate a non-essential modifier which makes nonsense of the lines.

299–301   The syntax is slightly involved, since 'accompanied', which modifies 'he', intervenes between 'thoughts' and its modifier 'lodg'd'.

302 The thought, much like that in *PL* 8. 427–9 and 9. 249 and Sylvester's Du Bartas, *D.W.W.*, *The First Day* 66, is reminiscent of Scipio's aphorism, quoted in Cicero, *Off.* 3. 1: 'never less alone than when alone'.[10] Hughes (p. 489) refers to Cowley's essay *Of Solitude*, which opens with the remark that this aphorism 'is now become a very vulgar saying'. 'It was defended', Hughes adds, 'by Sir George MacKenzie in *A Moral Essay, preferring Solitude to Publick Employment and all its Appanages*...(Edinburgh, 1665).' John Evelyn replied with *Public Employment...preferred to Solitude* (London, 1667).

303 *forty days.* According to Luke 4. 2 Christ was 'forty days tempted of the devil', but according to Matt. 4. 2–3 the temptations came at the end of the forty days. Milton follows Matthew, probably for the sake of greater intensity and unity secured by compressing the incidents within a brief space of time.

306 Editors suggest that frequent Biblical references to dew, as in Judges 6. 37–40; Ps. 133. 3; Dan. 4. 15, may explain this line; but in *Milton and Science* (Cambridge, Mass., 1956, p. 102) Kester Svendsen points out that 'bitter, blasting dew' was commonly believed to be harmful, and that in finding shelter in a cave Christ was protecting himself.

307 *one.* The use of 'one' as equivalent to the indefinite article was already obsolete in Milton's time (*OED*).

Cave. This detail may have been suggested by the account in 1 Kings 19. 9–18 of Elijah's sojourn in a cave on Mount Horeb, to which Milton refers in 353–4 below, and by the description in George Sandys, *Relation of a Journey Begun An. Dom. 1610* (6th ed., London, 1670, pp. 142–3) of the reputed cave of John the Baptist in the wilderness.

309 *hunger'd then at last.* Cf. Matt. 4. 2: 'And when he had fasted forty days and forty nights, he was afterward an hungred.' Cf. 2. 244 below.

310–13 Mark 1. 13, which states that in the wilderness Christ 'was with the wild beasts', is the original of the present scene. In *C.V.* 2. 3–5 Fletcher describes the same scene in greater detail, representing Christ as like another Orpheus whose music interrupted the warfare among the animals. See Claudian 34. 25–8 (2. 316). In *PL* 4. 340–52, a passage which gives most emphatic expression to the view, Milton describes the peace which prevailed among all living creatures before the fall—an inference from Gen. 1. 26–30—which is in sad contrast with the strife after the fall described in *PL* 10. 706–14. Cf. *DocCh*

---

[10] numquam...minus solum, quam cum solus esset.

1. 13 (*Works* 15. 217), and see also Jean Passerat, *Hymne de la paix* 83–5, 103–5; Spenser, *F.Q.* 4. 8. 30–1; Joseph Beaumont, *Psyche* 9. 122–9. In Sylvester's Du Bartas, *D.W.W.*, through the more than eight hundred lines of *The Furies*, the discord brought about among all things by sin is described in great and horrifying detail.

The belief that the wild animals will lose their savage natures, and that the primal peace will be restored by the Messiah, derives from a literal reading of the prophecies in Isa. 11. 6–9 and Ezek. 34. 25, which, however, before Milton's time were being allegorically interpreted, as notably in *The Commentary of David Kimchi on Isaiah*, ed. Finkelstein (*Columbia University Oriental Studies* 9), by Calvin in *Comment. in Isa.* 11 (*Opera Omnia* 36. 241–6), and in the Geneva Bible. The belief may also owe something to the accounts of the Golden Age in Hesiod, *W.D.* 109–20 and Virgil, *E.* 4. 4–45 and *A.* 8. 319–27, in which, though the evidence is slight, it has been thought that amity among the animals is implied. In the present passage Milton is cautious. He says that in Christ's presence the wild beasts are harmless; he does not, however, say that their savage natures have been changed, and that they will henceforth live peaceably together.

In 'Satan's Disguises: *PL* and *PR*', *MLN* 73 (1958), 9–11, J. I. Cope suggests that in mentioning the serpent, the lion, and the tiger Milton intended a subtle link with *PL* 4. 386–408 where Satan, spying upon Adam and Eve, assumed the forms of various animals, among them those of the lion and the tiger; and that the mention here of these animals means that before disguising himself as an old man, he again took the forms of the lion and the tiger, but then decided that 'if God has become man, so must the tempter.' This interpretation appears most improbable to me. How could Satan in the guise of a lion or a tiger with the slightest plausibility have presented the temptations to Christ? He was too shrewd a strategist to think of making such a mistake.

312 *fiery Serpent*. In Num. 21. 6–7; Deut. 8. 15; Isa. 14. 29; 30. 6 serpents are called 'fiery' probably because of the burning sensation caused by their venom (Diodati, *Pious Annotations*, Num. 21. 6), or because of their gleaming eyes. Svendsen (*Science*, p. 144), however, believes that 'fiery Serpent' means the cockatrice or basilisk, whose breath burned leaves off trees, scorched grass, and killed everything near it. Milton uses cockatrice and basilisk, Svendsen suggests, 'not as articles of scientific faith but as fixed images'.

Worm. Possibly here used in a general and archaic sense: 'Applied (like *vermin*) to four-footed animals considered as noxious or objectionable. *Obs.*' (*OED*).

313 Cf. *PL* 4. 343–4, 402–3.

314 *an aged man in Rural weeds.* Cf. Fletcher, *C.V.* 2. 15. 1–2; 16. 1:

> At length an aged Syre farre off he sawe
> Come slowely footing...
> A good old Hermit he might seeme to be.

In many of the incidents of the second book of *The Faerie Queene*, e.g. 2. 3. 11 ff., Archimago, who stands for Satan, appears as an old man.

The Scriptural accounts of the temptation tell nothing about the form in which Satan appeared, but since he had come in the guise of a serpent to tempt Eve, and since Paul in 2 Cor. 11. 14 had declared that 'Satan himself is transformed into an angel of light', there was from antiquity a tradition that, in keeping with his lying nature, he assumed whatever disguise suited his purpose (Louis Ginzberg, *The Legends of the Jews*, Philadelphia, 1946–7, 1. 276, 287; 2. 234). Many commentators agreed that the Gospels *imply* some disguise; but since they could not agree upon what it was, Satan was so variously represented that finally the tradition became uncertain and confusing. The disguises most common are that of a benevolent old hermit, of an old man of mean appearance, and of a handsome young man. Some represent him as assuming a different disguise for each of the three temptations. See the plates at the end of Miss Pope's volume. In his own way so does Milton, who has him first appear as an old man, a dweller in the wilderness, a plausible disguise, which, as Miss Pope observes (*PR, Tradition and Poem*, p. 47), answers his 'purposes much better than the more familiar and widely accepted one of the friendly hermit.'

At the beginning of the second day, however, Satan appears as

> a man...
> Not rustic as before, but seemlier clad,
> As one in City, or Court, or Palace bred (2. 299–300).

The term 'man', Miss Pope believes (p. 49), 'is rather ambiguous', because it does not make clear whether Satan has returned as an entirely different person, or is still the grey old man now in courtly dress, in keeping with the splendours of the banquet and the glories of the world which he is about to offer Christ. But 'As one in City, or Court, or Palace bred' I take to mean a change of person as well as of dress; for it is most improbable that, after Christ has at once seen through the first disguise, Satan on his second appearance would be so stupid as to change only his clothing, which would be no disguise.

Finally on the third day, when he emerges from the wood, Satan comes 'in wonted shape' (4. 449). Cf. *PL* 4. 819: 'So started up in his own shape the Fiend.' Miss Pope (pp. 49–50) here finds another, even greater ambiguity. Does 'wonted shape' mean '"the shape he usually wears"...his own shape, with no attempt at disguise'? Or does it mean 'no more than "the shape in which he usually appeared in the wilderness"'? In that case, the "courtier" of the second day must be the "aged man" of the first, for there would be no point in referring to the devil's *accustomed* shape, if he had actually assumed more than one...On the whole, however, I think "wonted shape" makes better sense if it is interpreted as "usual disguise" rather than "ordinary form." But either interpretation is possible; and both have the support of the tradition. The question thus becomes one which every reader must decide for himself.' Miss Pope is going out of her way to create difficulties.

If my interpretation be correct that on the first and second appearances Satan assumed completely different disguises—and according to the tradition he assumed several—'usual disguise' becomes meaningless. 'Wonted shape' I take to mean no disguise at all, but the ugly monster with horns, wings, claws, and tail as he is represented in Plates VIII and XI in Miss Pope's volume.

That Satan assumes a second disguise, after Christ has detected who he is (see note on 348 below) indicates how desperately he hopes that if one disguise has failed, another may succeed. When he finally appears in 'wonted shape', he knows the futility of all disguises, but he will not accept the fact that he is defeated.

315 Possibly an ironic allusion to the shepherd who leaves his flock to search for one lost sheep (Matt. 18. 12–13; Luke 15. 4), and to the good shepherd who gives his life for the sheep (John 10. 11).

319 *curious*. 'Careful, attentive' (Lockwood, *Lexicon*), as in Shakespeare, *Romeo* 1. 4. 31.

320 *Perus'd*. Scrutinized (Lockwood, *Lexicon*), as in *PL* 8. 267; Shakespeare, *Troi.* 4. 5. 231; *Romeo* 5. 3. 74; *Ham.* 2. 1. 90.

323 *Caravan*. In Sandys, *Relation* (p. 108), a caravan such as Milton may have had in mind is described in some detail.

325 *pin'd*. 'Exhausted or wasted by suffering or hunger' (*OED*). Cf. *PL* 10. 597; 12. 77; Spenser, *F.Q.* 1. 10. 48. 9.

326 *admire*. See note on 214 above.

327 *For that.* Because, as in 2. 458 below; Gen. 41. 32; 1 Tim 1. 12.

328 *new baptizing Prophet.* Satan is scornful. See notes on 18–32 above.

333–4 *ought…* / *What.* Anything that. Cf. 'all what' in *PL* 5. 107.

334 *Fame.* Report, rumour, Lat. *fama*, as in *PL* 1. 651; 2. 346; Spenser, *F.Q.* 1. 7. 46. 2. There seems to be a slight echo of Dido's speech in *A.* 1. 562–78, especially of 565–6: 'Who would fail to know of the race of Aeneas, who of the city of Troy, her brave deeds and brave men, and the fires of so great a war?'; and of Aeneas' words (461) earlier in the same scene: 'Here, too, virtue has its rewards.'[11]

335 On the omission of the antecedent, see note on 262–3 above.

339 *stubs.* The stumps left after trees, less commonly shrubs, have been cut down (*OED*), as in Spenser, *F.Q.* 1. 9. 34. 1. To show the futility of searching for food Satan mentions the most inedible things.

339–40 At least from the time of Pliny (*N.H.* 8. 26. 68) the camel's ability to go for days without water has been so often commented upon that it has become a conventional image (Svendsen, *Science*, p. 165).

342–3 Cf. Matt. 4. 3: 'And when the tempter came to him, he said, If thou be the Son of God, command that these stones be made bread.' Cf. also Luke 4. 3. Satan's method, as in the following temptations, is sophistically to conceal his real purpose, and it is diabolically clever, for as Warner Rice observes ('PR', *PMASAL* 22, 1936, 497), his proposal is casual and abrupt, as if it were of no great importance, and it seems charitable. But it involves great things, for if Christ performs the miracle, he will not only have arrogated to himself extraordinary power, but also have called in question God's intentions toward him. In short, Satan will have achieved his object of leading Christ to distrust divine providence, instead of humbly submitting to it, which is his prime duty. Moreover, as Lancelot Andrewes points out (*Ninety-Six Sermons* 5. 482), Satan is defaming God to Christ, as if God were careless in providing for him.

342 *if thou be the Son of God.* Satan is not, as has often been supposed, attempting to discover who, as the Son of God, Christ is. Of his identity he is not really in doubt, as is evident from Christ's statement in 356 below; he is

---

[11] quis genus Aeneadum, quis Troiae nesciat urbem
virtutesque virosque aut tanti incendia belli?
…sunt hic etiam sua praemia laudi.

attempting to arouse distrust. See note on 91 above. Andrewes (*Ninety-Six Sermons* 5. 499), commenting on Satan's words, writes: 'The heathens have observed, that in rhetoric it is a point of chiefest cunning, when you would outface a man or importune him to do a thing, to press and urge him with that which he will not or cannot for shame deny to be in himself'.

346 To the question asked by many, Why did Christ give Satan any answer? Andrewes (*Ninety-Six Sermons* 5. 503) replies: 'Christ answered...to teach us to answer; willing us thereby...to do as he had done before. So Christ is our example'.

348 It is a sign of Christ's divine nature that he at once detects who Satan is, for in *PL* 3. 683–4 we are told that 'neither Man nor Angel can discern / Hypocrisie', which is 'Invisible, except to God alone'. Satan's present artful humility is in striking contrast with his belligerence when in *PL* Ithuriel and Zephon haled him before Gabriel.

349–51 Christ's answer, which closely follows the words of Matt. 4. 4 and Luke 4. 4, ultimately comes from Deut. 8. 3: 'man doth not live by bread only, but by every word that proceedeth out of the mouth of the Lord.' In *Pious Annotations* (Deut. 8. 3) Diodati has the following comment on this verse: '*By every word*] Namely by any thing, to which God shall bee pleased to grant the power of nourishing. Or by the onely issuing forth of his power, called in the Scripture, word: without using of any externall meanes.'

352 When Moses was summoned to Mount Sinai, he 'was in the mount forty days and forty nights' (Exod. 24. 18), and 'did neither eat bread, nor drink water' (34. 28). Cf. Deut. 9. 9.

353 When Elijah was threatened by Jezebel, 'he arose, and did eat and drink, and went in the strength of that meat forty days and forty nights' (1 Kings 19. 8).

The spelling 'Eliah', which occurs also in 2. 19 below, and which seems to be Milton's own invention, more nearly approximates Heb. 'Eliahu' than does Elijah. He uses it presumably for the sake of euphony.

Nearly twenty references to Elijah scattered through Milton's works usually bespeak his admiration for the great prophet who bravely resisted wicked, tyrannical kings and worshippers of heathen gods. In his Outlines for Tragedies (*Works* 18. 238) one of the subjects (39) is 'Elias in the Mount. 2 Reg. 1. 'Ορειβάτης. or better Elias Polemistes.'

354 *this barren waste.* According to 1 Kings 19. 8 it was not to the Desert of Quarentana, supposedly the scene of the present action (see note on 119 above), but to Mount Horeb that Elijah withdrew for forty days.

355 *distrust.* Although the first temptation may appear to be merely an appeal to bodily appetite, and by some has been so interpreted, appetite is only a means to an end. The more reasonable and generally accepted view is that the temptation is far more fundamental; that, as Christ is quick to see, Satan, as in trying Job, is attacking his faith that, whatever his need may be, God in his own time and in his own way, will provide for him. In *Harm. Evang.*, Matt. 4. 3 (*Opera Omnia* 45. 131) Calvin is contemptuous of any other interpretation. See also Geneva Bible on Luke 4. 3; Andrewes, *Ninety-Six Sermons* 5. 497; Diodati, *Pious Annotations*, Matt. 4. 3; Poole, *Annotations upon the Holy Bible*, Matt. 4. 3.

356 Cf. Fletcher, *C.V.* 2. 30. 1–2:

> Well knewe our Saviour this the Serpent was,
> And the old Serpent knewe our Saviour well.

See note on 91 above.

358–405 See note on 348 above. In *PL* 4. 32–113 Satan makes the most damning admissions, but he does so in a soliloquy, not before an audience. It is an indication of his progressive moral deterioration that now with daring hypocrisy he admits to Christ his wrongdoing, and even attempts yet to claim some remnants of virtue. His speech is a sophistical mixture of truth, half truth, and untruth, intended by deceiving Christ to disarm his further resistance. But all his efforts fail, because Christ lays bare his insincerity and his sophistry.

358 *that Spirit unfortunate.* In his lecture on *PR* (*Milton Memorial Lectures, 1908*, London, 1909, pp. 199–200), Edward Dowden writes: 'In that word "unfortunate" the sophist is apparent.... It was not fortune but insensate pride that cost Satan his happy station.'

359 *rash revolt.* See *PL* 5–6.

360–1 In Jude 6 it is said that 'the angels which kept not their first estate, but left their own habitation, he hath reserved in everlasting chains under darkness.' See note on 46–7 above.

362 *that hideous place.* See note on 46–7 above.

363 *unconniving.* 'Not giving aid or encouraging a wrong by silence or forbearance' (Lockwood, *Lexicon*). Satan is admitting the common doctrine, stated in Origen, *Princip.* 3. 2 (Migne, *Pat. Gr.* 11. 312); Cyprian, *Ad Quirin.* 3. 80 (Migne, *Pat. Lat.* 4. 772); Augustine, *Ioan. Evang.* 7. 7 (Migne, *Pat. Lat.* 35. 1440–1); Calvin, *Inst.* 1. 14. 17 that he can do nothing without the will and consent of God. But there is another part of the doctrine, stated in Origen, *Cels.* 6. 44 (Migne, *Pat. Gr.* 11. 1366–7); Augustine, *Enarrat. in Ps.* 77. 30 (Migne, *Pat. Lat.* 36. 1003–4); and in Milton, *DocCh* 1. 9 (*Works* 15. 109), which Satan does not mention, and which makes his admission ironic, namely that he is permitted to act, as in trying Job and seducing Ahab, whom he is about to mention, only because the powers of evil exist to carry out God's purpose.

365   *to round.* In speaking of the sun in *PL* 10. 684 Milton uses the same expression. In F. Quarles, *Job Militant* (1624) 2. 31–2, Satan, replying to God, says: 'Hell's my Home, / I round the World, and so from thence I come.'

366   *range in th' Air.* See note on 39 above.

366–7   The 'Heav'n of Heav'ns', as Milton explains in *DocCh* 1. 7 (*Works* 15. 29), is the highest heaven, 'which is the throne and habitation of God, and the heavenly powers, or angels.' In the same work (15. 109) he further states that the evil angels are sometimes 'permitted to wander throughout the whole earth, the air, and heaven itself, to execute the judgments of God.' For this view Scriptural authority is found in 1 Kings 22. 19–22; Job 1. 6; 2. 1; Rev. 12. 7–9. That these angels may appear in the presence of God is explained in Augustine, *Civ. D.* 12. 1, and Gregory the Great, *Moral.* 2. 4 (Migne, *Pat. Lat.* 75. 557), on the ground that, although they have lost beatitude, they have not lost their nature.

The astronomical theory here implied, as in the *Divine Comedy* and generally in Milton, apart from Raphael's discourse in *PL* 8. 66 ff., is that of the Ptolemaic, geocentric universe consisting of a system of concentric spheres or heavens; a hard outer shell, a Primum Mobile, a crystalline sphere, spheres of the fixed stars, of the seven planets, of fire, and of air, and at the centre the earth (Svendsen, *Science*, p. 48). As a typical example of the diagrams of such a universe, which were numerous in the Renaissance, Svendsen (p. 49) reproduces the frontispiece from Robert Fage's *Description of the Whole World* (1658).

368–70   These three lines summarize Job 1. 6–12 (substantially repeated in 2. 1–6), where it is said that 'the sons of God came to present themselves before the Lord, and Satan came also among them.' To test Job's faith and righteousness God permitted Satan to afflict him, saying, 'Behold, all that he hath is in thy power.' Note that Satan says nothing of *his* purpose to ruin Job as he ruined Adam and Eve. See Christ's reply in 424–6 below.

369 Biblical references to the land of Uz, where Job is said to have dwelt (Job 1. 1; Jer. 25. 20; Lam. 4. 21), which in 3. 94 below Milton calls 'a land obscure', tell nothing about its location. According to *Encyc. Bibl.* 4. 5238 it is still 'a land of uncertain situation'.

370 On the idea of temptation 'for good', see note on 155–6 above.
    illustrate. 'To render illustrious...or famous' (*OED*), as in *PL* 5. 739; 6. 773.

371–6 The story of the seduction of wicked King Ahab by prophets inspired by a lying spirit with God's permission, and of Ahab's consequent defeat and death is told in 1 Kings 22. 19–35. The similarity between the situation presented in verses 19–21 and that in Job 1. 6 and 2. 1 may explain the identification of the lying spirit and Satan. 'In *RES*, n.s. V (1954), 249–55, Audrey I. Carlisle shows that Ludwig Lavater's Commentary *In Libros Paralipomenon sive Chronicorum* bracketed Satan's roles with Job and Ahab to illustrate the readiness of the "liar from the beginning" to do evil to men, of which God cannot rightly be held guilty. Milton's summary of Lavater's passage is in the Trinity *MS.*, p. 36' (Hughes, p. 491).

372 *fraud.* 'By Milton used in passive sense (as L. *fraus*): State of being defrauded or deluded' (*OED*). See *PL* 9. 643.

373 *they demurring.* Cf. 1 Kings 22. 20: 'And the Lord said, Who shall persuade Ahab, that he may go up and fall at Ramoth-gilead? And one said on this manner, and another said on that manner.'

375 *glibb'd.* Rendered 'glib or fluent' (*OED*). The word, which is fairly uncommon, does not occur elsewhere in Milton's poetry.

377–8 In *PL* 1. 97 Satan first admitted that he had 'chang'd in outward lustre'. The loss of brightness and glitter, which outwardly symbolizes his moral deterioration, is mentioned in *PL* 1. 591–2; 4. 835–7; 10. 450–2.

378–9 According to *PL* 2. 482–3 'Spirits damn'd' do not 'loose all thir virtue', and in 4. 847 even Satan is still capable of feeling 'how awful goodness is'.

383–4 *What can be then less in me then desire | To see thee and approach thee...*

In *TLS* (9 Sept. 1960, p. 577) I. A. Richards asks if 'we should for "less" read "more"'. The three writers replying in the same periodical do not accept the suggested emendation. A. D. Fitton Brown (16 Sept. 1960, p. 593) explains that 'the text can be understood along the lines of the modern idiom: "I can do no less than desire"', and cites somewhat similar expressions in *PL* 1. 591 and *Lear* 2. 4. 135. Philip H. Mankin (7 Oct. 1960, p. 645) asks if Satan does not mean that, 'since he claims not to have "lost To love, at least contemplat [*sic*] and admire, What I see excellent in good, or fair, Or vertuous", nothing could be less in him—nothing could be less surprising or remarkable—than to desire to see and approach Him who has been "Declar'd the Son of God".' In the same issue of *TLS*, D. H. Woodward explains the meaning thus: 'How can I have anything less than the desire to see and approach thee...? If I had less than this desire, I would not be what I am, a creature of sense (1, 382). To substitute *more* for *less* would be to change Satan's argument unfairly: to say that one wishes at least to pay one's debts is not to say that one wishes nothing more than to pay one's debts. Satan is too smooth a hypocrite to try that kind of argument, especially before his present audience.'

385 *attent*. 'Attentive, full of attention' (*OED*), as in 2 Chron. 6. 40; Spenser, *F.Q.* 3. 9. 52. 3; 6. 9. 26. 2; Shakespeare, *Ham.* 1. 2. 193. Milton does not use the word elsewhere in his poetry.

386–7 Satan—the 'adversary', be it remembered—in now denying hostility to man is denying what he emphatically avowed in *PL* 2. 368–70 when he proposed to 'seduce' men 'to our Party' so that God would destroy them; and in 10. 402 when he said to Sin and Death, 'Him first make sure your thrall, and lastly kill.'

390–3 When Satan is returning to hell after the fall of man, Sin assures him (*PL* 10. 372) that 'Thine now is all this World.' Satan replies (392) that hell and this world have been made 'one Realm, one Continent', and bids Sin and Death proceed to Paradise and

> There dwell and Reign in bliss, thence on the Earth
> Dominion exercise and in the Aire,
> Chiefly on Man... (399–401).

393–6 See note on 24–37 above. Satan is expressing the pagan view of presages, oracles, and the various forms of divination as valuable aids in the direction of human life which Cicero states in the following passage in *N.D.* 2. 65. 163: 'Diviners at sacrifices make many observations; augurs foresee many events; oracles, prophecies, dreams, and portents reveal events, knowledge of which often has led to acquiring many things that gratify men's wishes and supply their needs, and to avoiding dangers.'[12] In *N.D.* 2. 65. 163, however, Cicero limits the validity of divination to signifying events; it can tell a man nothing about his duty.

But because divination in all its forms was believed to be the work of the devil and demons, it was condemned by the Mosaic law, as in Lev. 19. 26, 31 and Deut. 18. 10–11, and by the earliest Christians, as appears from Acts 16. 16–18 and 1 Cor. 10. 19–20. Patristic writers have much to say against divination, as for example Augustine, who in his unregenerate days believed in it, as he admits in *Conf.* 4. 3, but who later in *Doc. Ch.* 2. 23 (Migne, *Pat. Lat.* 34. 53) condemned it as either futile or harmful superstition arising from evil association of men and devils. Clement of Alexandria in *Cohort ad Gr.* 2 (Migne, *Pat. Gr.* 8. 67–75, 87–90) and Tertullian in *De Idol.* 9 (Migne, *Pat. Lat.* 1. 671–3) condemned it as absurd, impious, and idolatrous. See also 430–3, 455–9 below and notes, and the well-known passage, *Nat* 173–96, on the cessation of the oracles.

397–402 Satan himself has admitted in *PL* 9. 175–6 that envy was one of his chief motives in ruining man; and in 9. 124–8 that it was his intent to make men his companions in misery. In 6. 900 Raphael warned Adam that Satan 'envies now thy state'.

399 *it may be.* Not exactly signifying, Jerram (p. 88) believes, '"it may *have been* so," but "it may be *the fact* that it was so." Lat. "fieri potest ut sic fuerit."'

400 *Nearer.* The first edition reads 'Never', which is corrected in the Errata. *by proof.* See note on 11 above.

401 Carey (p. 1093) quotes 'the Latin tag *solamen miseris socios habuisse doloris*' and Shakespeare, *Lucr.* 790: 'And fellowship in woe doth woe assuage.' The same thought occurs in *Romeo* 1. 2. 47 and in Seneca, *Cons. Polyb.* 12. 2.

405 Editors note the artfulness of Satan's words. In mentioning the restoration of man, he subtly endeavours to lead Christ to reveal the manner of that restoration, which it is important that he should know so that, if possible, he may avert it. But Christ shrewdly ignores his remark. Stein (*Heroic Knowledge*, p. 44)

[12] Multa cernunt haruspices, multa augures provident, multa oraclis declarantur multa vaticinationibus multa somniis multa portentis; quibus cognitis multae saepe res ex hominum sententia atque utilitate partae, multa etiam pericula depulsa sunt.

notes the 'virtuoso skill' with which Satan in this speech uses 'sincerity as he traditionally uses flattery, to soften up an opponent.'

406 To Satan's hypocritical justification of himself and appeal for pity Christ 'sternly' replies. The hardness which he consistently shows to Satan throughout the poem has led many readers and commentators to see him as a cold, un-emotional, even priggish superman; but as Blondel (pp. 62–4) with greater discernment points out, he is not addressing a creature who can have any part in salvation, but an enemy who must be confounded. If he presents only an inhuman face, he does so because he is addressing Satan, who is as impenitent as ever in the evil which he has irrevocably chosen (*PL* 4. 110–13), who has deliberately forfeited the possibility of God's grace and therefore all claim to consideration (*PL* 3. 198–201). In the particular situation in which Christ is, his usual gentle kindness would manifestly be out of place. Cf. 1 Cor. 2. 14–15; *Apol* (*Works* 3. 288, 313).

407–8 In John 8. 44 Christ says of the devil: 'there is no truth in him. When he speaketh a lie, he speaketh of his own: for he is a liar, and the father of it.' In *PL* 1. 121 and 645–7 Satan declared his intention to use force or guile to gain his ends.

409–10 See 363 above and note.

410 See notes on 122 and 366–7 above.

411 *captive thrall*. These stinging words may be reminiscent of Spenser, *F.Q.* 1. 7. 19. 3: 'And valiant knight become a caytive thrall'; and 4. 4. 34. 5: 'Like captive thral two other Knights atween.'

413 In *PL* 1. 86–7 Beelzebub said that Satan 'Cloth'd with transcendent brightness didst out-shine / Myriads though bright.'
  Among the Prime. Equivalent to Lat. *inter primos*, among 'the choicest, principal, or chief…members of a company' (*OED*).

414 *emptyed*. This may be an echo of ἑαυτὸν ἐκένωσε, 'emptied himself' in Phil. 2. 7, which the A.V. translates 'made himself of no reputation'.
  gaz'd. Looked at intently (Lockwood, *Lexicon*), become a gazing stock, as in *PL* 5. 272. Blakeney (p. 106) remarks upon the slow effect of the collocation of participles in this line. It expresses the accumulation of scorn.

416–20 The peculiar force of these lines is that they are a bitter reminder to Satan of his own admission in *PL* 4. 75 that 'Which way I flie is Hell; myself am Hell.' See also *PL* 1. 255; 4. 18–23; 9. 467–72.

423 *pleasure to do ill.* In *PL* 1. 159–60 Satan declared

> To do ought good never will be our task,
> But ever to do ill our sole delight.

425 *righteous Job.* In Job 1. 1 Job is characterized as 'perfect and upright, and one that feared God, and eschewed evil'; and in the eighth verse of the same chapter, God, addressing Satan, says of Job: 'there is none like him in the earth, a perfect and an upright man.'

426 *patience.* Although Job is hardly an example of what we should call patience, except in his first submission to misfortune; and although there is a Jewish legend that the Lord remonstrated with him because of his *lack* of patience (Ginzberg, *Legends* 2. 225; 5. 382), the statement in Jas. 5. 11, 'Ye have heard of the patience of Job', which apparently implies a matter of common knowledge (cf. Vulgate, Tobit 2. 12), has given rise to the general acceptance of patience as one of Job's chief attributes.

427–8 *thy chosen task.* The spirit mentioned in 1 Kings 22. 21 *volunteered* to put lies in the mouths of the prophets who would lead Ahab astray. See note on 371–6 above.

four hundred mouths. According to 1 Kings 22. 6 the false prophets were 'about four hundred men'.

430 *Oracles.* Oracles, notably those of Zeus at Dodona and Apollo at Delphi, since through them the gods were believed to give messages to men, occupied an extremely important place in Greek popular religion, as is evident from the great frequency with which they are mentioned, for example in Pausanias, and from the authority obviously attached to their utterances. See A. Bouché-Leclerq, *Histoire de la divination dans l'antiquité* (Paris, 1879–82), 1. 41 ff. But there is evidence of scepticism concerning their reliability, as in Herodotus 1. 47–8; Thucydides 5. 103; Lucian, *J. Trag.* 6; *J. Conf.* 12. 14; Pausanias 8. 11. 10–11; Claudian 26. 552 (2. 166). In *Div.* 2. 56. 115 Cicero declares that many oracles of Apollo in the no longer extant collection of Chrysippus are utterly false, some accidentally true, others ambiguous; and in *Ann.* 2. 54 Tacitus mentions an oracle which spoke *per ambages ut mos oraculis*.

Patristic writers almost universally condemned oracles, not only because they were false or ambiguous, but also because they were the work of demons hostile to man. Characteristic expressions of this condemnation are found in Eusebius, *P.E.* 4–6 (Migne, *Pat. Gr.* 21. 229–506); Minucius Felix, *Oct.* 26–8 (Migne, *Pat. Lat.* 3. 320–31); Tertullian, *Apol.* 22; *De Idol.* 9 (*Pat. Lat.* 1.

404-10, 671-3); Clement of Alexandria, *Cohort ad Gr.* 2 (*Pat. Gr.* 8. 67-90); Augustine, *Civ. D.* 4. 30; *Doc. Ch.* 2. 23-34; *Div. Daem.* 5-6 (*Pat. Lat.* 34. 52-4; 40. 586-7).

But despite patristic and subsequent condemnation, e.g. Hooker, *Eccles. Pol.* 1. 4. 3, oracles had for men of the 17th century far more than merely historical interest, as we may gather from the bibliography of Renaissance works on oracles in G. G. Wolff, *Porphyrii de Philosophia ex Oraculis Haurienda* (Berlin, 1856, pp. 229-31), and from L.-F. A. Maury's discussion of the subject in *La Magie et l'astrologie dans l'antiquité et au moyen âge* (3rd ed., Paris, 1864). Nor is the interest surprising at a time when there was much excitement over portents, prodigies, signs, and revelations. See note on 24-37 above. Oracles were still thought worthy of consideration by Anthony van Dale, whose *De Oraculis Ethnicorum* appeared at Amsterdam in 1683 (2nd ed., 1700), and by Bernard Fontenelle, whose *Histoire des oracles* appeared at Paris as late as 1687, both of which explained oracles as the tricks of priests to maintain superstition. Other evidence of the rational, sceptical attitude to oracles appears in Francis Bacon, *De Aug.* 4. 3; Hugo Grotius, *De Ver. Rel.* 4. 9; Sir Thomas Browne, *Pseud.* 1. 10; John Selden, *Table-Talk*, ed. Singer (London, 1890), p. 203; Thomas Hobbes, *Lev.* 1. 12. These writers regard oracles, in so far as they are not explicable on naturalistic grounds, as false and superstitious. Milton has little to say about oracles and divination, but that little indicates agreement with the writers just mentioned. See note on 456 below.

The term 'oracle' had been appropriated by Christian writers at least as early as Augustine, who uses it in *Civ. D.* 10. 23 and in *Ep. ad Cath.* 3. 6 (Migne, *Pat. Lat.* 43. 395) to mean the Lord speaking through the divine canon of Scripture, the sense in which Hooker uses it in *Eccles. Pol.* 1. 14. 1. In 460 below Milton applies it to Christ; in *PE* (*Works* 3. 101) to the Gospel; and in *DDD* (3. 444) to divine law, as each of these is a medium whereby God communicates his will to men.

433 Editors quote a passage said to come from Augustine, *Div. Daem.* 12, but not in any edition of that work which I have seen, to the effect that in divination demons mix truth with falsehood, and, because they cannot know the truth, are not so much teachers as deceivers.[13] However, the whole sixth chapter of Augustine's treatise (Migne, *Pat. Lat.* 40. 586-7) deals with the deceptiveness of divination.

---

[13] Miscent tamen isti fallacias; et verum quod nosse potuerunt non docendi magis quam decipiendi fine praenuntiant.

434-41 In *Div.* 2. 56. 115-16 Cicero gives the following examples of ambiguous and hence deluding oracles: the oracle of Fortune concerning Croesus: 'When Croesus has the Halys crossed, / He will a mighty kingdom overthrow', which he believed to be an assurance of victory; but the kingdom that was overthrown was his own. Equally ambiguous was the oracle of Apollo given to Pyrrhus: 'I tell you, son of Aeacus, / That you the Romans will subdue', which Pyrrhus might have seen evaded his question. There is also the irrelevant and evasive answer given to Oedipus when he asked who his parents were (Apollodorus 3. 5. 7). Blakeney (p. 107) quotes Lucian, *D. Deor.* 16: 'Apollo...takes good care to give ambiguous answers that nobody can understand, though there are plenty of fools to be imposed upon.'

442-4 Cf. 2 Thes. 2. 11: 'And for this cause God shall send them strong delusion, that they should believe a lie.' Cf. also 1 Kings 22. 22; Matt. 24. 5, 11; Rom. 1. 24-5, 32; 1 Tim. 4. 1.

446 The common belief of patristic writers that the fallen angels retained their original spiritual nature is stated in Augustine, *Civ. D.* 12. 1, and Gregory the Great, *Moral.* 2. 4 (Migne, *Pat. Lat.* 75. 557). By virtue of their nature, Tertullian explains in *Apol.* 22 (*Pat. Lat.* 1. 409), they are able to learn the processes of nature, and thus they can predict the weather. He also declares that they have taken many of their prophecies from God's true prophets. In *Sum. Th.* 2. 2. 172. 6 Aquinas says: 'The prophets of demons do not always speak from the demons' revelation, but sometimes by divine revelation...because God makes use of the wicked for the benefit of the good.'[14]

447-8 According to Jewish angelology, the angels are spirits of clouds, winds, rain, of earth, sun, moon, and stars; there is nothing on earth, not a blade of grass, which has not an angel to watch over it (*Enoch* 39. 12; 61. 12; *Book of Jubilees* 2. 2; Heywood, *Hierarchie*, pp. 194-5; Ginzberg, *Legends* 5. 110). 'Angels President / In every Province', Hughes (p. 492) notes, refers to the belief that the points of the compass were angelic provinces. In *Three Books of Occult Philosophy* 3. 24 (tr. J. F., London, 1651, p. 416), Cornelius Agrippa says: 'There are also four Princes of the Angels, which are set over the four winds, and over the four parts of the world, whereof *Michael* is set over the Eastern wind; *Raphael* over the Western; *Gabriel* over the Northern; *Nariel*, who by some is called *Uriel*, is over the Southern.'

[14] Prophetae daemonum non semper loquuntur ex daemonum revelatione, sed interdum ex inspiratione divina.... Quia Deus utitur etiam malis ad utilitatem bonorum.

454 *retrench'd.* 'To cut short, check, repress. *Obs.*' (*OED*).

455–9 See 24–37, 393–6, 430–3 above and notes.

456 *Oracles are ceast.* When in *Nat* 173 Milton says 'The Oracles are dum', he is following, as he does here, a tradition traceable, if not further, at least to Cicero, who, in *Div.* 1. 19 and 2. 57, mentions, as does Juvenal (6. 555), the declining reputation of the Delphian oracle. Strabo (7. 7. 9) remarks that the oracle of Dodona, 'like the rest', is virtually silent; and Lucan (5. 111–14) laments the silence of the Delphian oracle, and suggests that because of the increasing evil of the age Apollo has ceased to speak to men. Even more important than these witnesses is Plutarch, who, in *The Obsolescence of the Oracles*, discusses at length the failure of the oracles and the reasons therefor.

The Church Fathers, in order to discredit the pagan gods, maintained that at the birth of Christ the oracles became dumb. Eusebius, notably, expresses this view in *P.E.* 5. 1, 16–17 (Migne, *Pat. Gr.* 21, 309–14, 349–58); and Porphyry, whom Eusebius quotes, is clearly speaking of a widely accepted belief.

That this belief had become traditional is evident from Du Plessis-Mornay, *A Woorke Concerning the Trewnesse of the Christian Religion*, tr. Sidney and Golding (3rd ed., London, 1604, p. 552); William Drummond, *Miserable Estate of the World* 13–41; Spenser, *S.C.*, May, Gloss; Fletcher, *C.V.* 1. 82. 2; Browne, *Pseud.* 7. 12; *Rel. Med.* 1. 29.

458 *Delphos.* This spelling from the accusative Δελφούς rather than Delphi from the nominative Δελφοί Richard Bentley defended, but Alexander Dyce in his edition of Bentley's *Dissertation upon the Epistles of Phalaris* (*Works*, London, 1836, 1. lviii–lix) calls it a 'common error' which ought to be 'sent back to Barbary, its native country'. Milton uses also 'Delphos' in *Nat* 178.

460–4 On the term 'oracle' as it is here used, see note on 430 above. Christ's function as the revealer of truth is repeatedly stated in the N.T., as in John 1. 16–17; 4. 25; 18. 37; Heb. 1. 1–2; and from the earliest times, as in Origen, *Cels.* 5. 5 (Migne, *Pat. Gr.* 11. 1185–8) and Augustine, *Civ. D.* 9. 15; 11. 2, has been accepted as orthodox Christian theology. In *DocCh* 1. 15 (*Works* 15. 287–9), in discussing Christ's office as mediator, Milton writes: 'His function as a prophet is to instruct his church in heavenly truth, and to declare the whole will of his Father.'

462 In John 16. 13 Christ, comforting his disciples, promised them that 'when he, the Spirit of truth, is come, he will guide you into all truth.'

465 *subtle. OED*, which quotes this line, gives the meaning: 'Crafty, cunning; treacherously or wickedly cunning, insidiously sly, wily.' Cf. 2. 323 below and *PL* 7. 495.

Fiend. Satan is so called also in 2. 323; 3. 345; 4. 576 below; *PL* 1. 283; 2. 815. 'Fiend' is related to Ger. *Feind*, and at least until the early 18th century was a common name for the devil (*OED*), and the equivalent of 'adversary'. See note on 33 above.

466 *inly*. See note on 228 above.

469–74 Satan admits Christ's charge in 430–64 that he is untruthful, but defends himself on the ground that misery has often forced him to depart from truth. In *PL* 4. 389–92 he uses a like argument, on which in 393–4 Milton comments:

> So spake the Fiend, and with necessitie,
> The Tyrants plea, excus'd his devilish deeds.

In 3. 96–8 Milton cites the example of Socrates, who, for truth's sake, suffered death.

474 Several earlier editors suggest that Milton may here be alluding to the Englishmen who in 1660 abjured their republican principles and supported the restored monarchy.

476 *submiss*. 'Not quite the same', Jerram (p. 92) explains, 'as "submissive," which implies more of *voluntary* obedience. "Submiss" (= "placed under") is the literal opposite of "placed above" in the former line. Cf. *PL* 8. 316.'

477 *quit*. Freed, cleared from a charge (*OED*), as in *PL* 11. 548 and often in Spenser, as in *F.Q.* 2. 1. 20. 2; 2. 12. 27. 1.

478 The difficulty of attaining truth or any other form of goodness has often been represented by the figure of a narrow or steep and hazardous road, as in Matt. 7. 14; Hesiod, *W.D.* 289–91; Silius Italicus 15. 101–6; Simonides, frag. 37 (*Anthologia Lyrica Graeca*, ed. Diels, Leipzig, 1925, 2. 78); Tasso, *Jerusalem* 17. 61. 3–4; Spenser, *F.Q.* 1. 10. 46–7; Donne, *Sat.* 3. 79–84. In *Sonn* 9. 1–4 Milton writes:

> Lady that in the prime of earliest youth,
>   Wisely hast shun'd the broad way and the green,
>   And with those few art eminently seen,
>   That labour up the Hill of heav'nly Truth.

And in *Educ* (*Works* 4. 280), shortly before recommending the *Tabula* of Cebes, in which the road of learning is difficult and has precipices on either side, Milton goes on to say: 'I will point ye out the right path of a virtuous and noble Education; laborious indeed at the first ascent, but else so smooth, so green, so full of goodly prospect, and melodious sounds on every side, that the Harp of *Orpheus* was not more charming.'

479–80 Cf. *Comus* 475–9:

How charming is divine Philosophy!
Not harsh, and crabbed as dull fools suppose,
But musical as is *Apollo's* lute,
And a perpetual feast of nectar'd sweets,
Where no crude surfet raigns.

480 *tuneable*. Tuneful, harmonious (*OED*), as are the prayers of Adam and Eve in *PL* 5. 151.

482–3 Reminiscent of Rom. 7. 19: 'For the good that I would I do not: but the evil which I would not, that I do'; and Ovid, *M*. 7. 20–1: *video meliora proboque, | deteriora sequor.*

484 *since no man comes.* Cf. 321–5 above. The meaning, Jerram (p. 93) explains, is that 'since in this desert no *man* comes to hear thee, may I be allowed to do so, in the absence of better auditors?'

486–90 Cf. *PL* 1. 494–6:

the Priest
Turns Atheist, as did *Ely's* Sons, who fill'd
With lust and violence the house of God.

See 1 Sam. 2. 12–17 and cf. *Ref* (*Works* 3. 19); *Animad* 13 (3. 160). Jerram (p. 93) suggests that Milton may be alluding to the immorality in the Church of England after the Restoration, and quotes Bishop Burnet's condemnation thereof. But it is more significant that Satan is virtually maintaining the Roman Catholic doctrine, stated in Aquinas, *Sum. Th.* 3. 64. 5, and officially reiterated in the canons of the Council of Trent, Sess. 7, can. 12 (*Canons and Decrees of the...Council of Trent*, tr. Waterworth, London, 1848, p. 55), that the efficacy of the sacraments does not depend upon the worthiness of the minister, but only upon the will of God, which is also an Anglican doctrine (Article XXVI).

The real purpose of Satan's speech, as Rice ('PR', *PMASAL* 22, 1936, 498) observes, has been half apparent from the beginning, but now clearly emerges.

And as Dunster (p. 52) remarks, 'An argument more plausible and more fallacious could not have been put into the mouth of the Tempter.'

487 *Hypocrite.* Cf. *PL* 3. 682–4:

> For neither Man nor Angel can discern
> Hypocrisie, the onely evil that walks
> Invisible, except to God alone.

Atheous. From ἄθεος, as in Cicero, *N.D.* 1. 23. 63: *Diagoras*, ἄθεος *qui dictus est. OED* notes only two other occurrences of the word.

490 *Praying or vowing.* Besides the sacrifices of prayer and thanksgiving, the Jews had vow-sacrifices (Lev. 7. 16), oblations of vows (22. 18), and sacrifices in performing their vows (Num. 15. 3, 8).

491–2 Balaam, whose complicated story is told in Num. 22–4, knew and prophesied the will of God; but he also desired the rewards of unrighteousness. From antiquity he has been infamous. See Num. 31. 16; 2 Pet. 2. 15; Rev. 2. 14; Josephus *A.J.* 4. 6. 2–6. In *Ref* 2 (*Works* 3. 53) Milton calls him 'the Reprobate hireling Preist' who sought 'to subdue the Israelites to *Moab*, if not by force, then by this divellish *Pollicy*'.

491 *Reprobate.* 'Depraved, degraded, morally corrupt. *Obs.*' (*OED*). In A.V. Jer. 6. 30, Blakeney (pp. 109–10) notes, the prophet calls the men of Judah 'reprobate', i.e. spurious metal to be rejected. Cf. also 1 Cor. 9. 27 in the Vulgate where *reprobus* translates Greek ἀδόκιμος, which means 'rejected', 'worthless'.

494 *scope.* 'Purpose, aim', from σκοπός, a mark to shoot at, as in *PL* 2. 127; a meaning now rare but common in the 17th century (*OED*).

495–6 In *PL* 4. 1006–9 Gabriel says:

> *Satan*, I know thy strength, and thou knowst mine,
> Neither our own but giv'n; what follie then
> To boast what Arms can doe, since thine no more
> Then Heav'n permits, nor mine.

498 *gray dissimulation.* Equivalent to 'his gray head with which he disguised himself'. The expression occurs in Ford, *The Broken Heart* 4. 2 (Blondel, p. 249). On the use of abstract instead of concrete terms, see note on 146 above.

499 *Into thin Air diffus'd.* So the phantoms sent to Penelope by Athene in

Homer, *Od.* 4. 838–9, Mercury in Virgil, *A.* 4. 278, and Canens in Ovid, *M.* 14. 432 vanish into the air. Cf. Shakespeare, *Tem.* 4. 1. 150: 'Are melted into air, into thin air'.

500 *Night with her sullen wing.* Possibly reminiscent of Virgil, *A.* 8. 369: 'Night rushes down and enfolds earth with her swarthy wings', in which 'swarthy' (*fuscus*)[15] is equivalent to 'sullen', i.e. of a dull colour; hence of gloomy and dismal aspect (*OED*), as in *Sonn* 20. 4. But, as editors note, the figure, the wing or wings of night, is conventional, and is found in *L'All* 6; Tasso, *Jerusalem* 8. 57. 1; Spenser, *F.Q.* 6. 8. 44. 5; Shakespeare, *Troi.* 5. 8. 17.

double-shade. To double the natural gloom of the desert. The present line and *Comus* 334, 'In double night of darkness and of shades', may be echoes of Ovid, *M.* 11. 550: 'The image of night is doubled' (*duplicataque noctis imago est*).

501–2 Cf. Ps. 104. 20: 'Thou makest darkness, and it is night: wherein all the beasts of the forest do creep forth.' The unadorned style, like that of the A.V., the monosyllables with long vowels bring the first book to an appropriately dignified and solemn conclusion.

[15] nox ruit et fuscis tellurem amplectitur alis.

Book II

1–57 Commentators generally have had little to say about the significance of these lines in which the disciples of Christ, troubled by his disappearance, begin to doubt that he is the Messiah, the earthly deliverer for whom they have been looking. Theirs, however, 'is not the uncertainty of ignorance', like that 'attributed to Satan, but rather a sacred unknowingness, an eager expectancy' made strong by the certainty of promise (Allen, *Vision*, pp. 115–16). Though they do not understand Christ's mission, are even perplexed about his Messiahship, much more important is their faith, which bespeaks their love, and which in the end overcomes perplexity and doubt, and enables them to lay all their fears on 'his Providence'. Never can Satan be thus delivered from doubt and fear. The disciples, ordinary fishermen, provide *dramatically*, and so effectively, an example of the love and faith that are possible for any devoutly disposed man.

1–2 See I. 18–32 above.

2 *At Jordan.* See note on I. 184 above.

3–4 *expresly call'd | Jesus Messiah.* In the Scriptural accounts of the baptism of Jesus, while the voice from heaven pronounced him to be the Son of God, it did not expressly call him the Messiah. See note on I. 24–37. But that his disciples believed him to be the Messiah is clear from Matt. 16. 16, where Peter, speaking for the Twelve, makes the great confession, 'Thou art the Christ, the Son of the living God.' Cf. Mark 8. 27–30; Luke 9. 18–20; John 1. 29, 41. But it is equally clear that Jesus was not generally regarded as the Messiah, for to the question in Matt. 16. 13–14 (cf. Mark 8. 28; Luke 9. 19), 'Whom do men say that I the Son of man am?' the disciples replied: 'Some say that thou art John the Baptist: some, Elias; and others, Jeremias, or one of the prophets.'

5–7 See John 1. 35–41.

6 *I mean.* Editors find excuse for this prosaic expression in that it is common in Harington's translation of *Orlando Furioso*. Jerram (p. 95) suggests that

Milton is 'probably imitating the λέγω of Greek tragedy, as Φιλοκτήτην λέγω (Soph. *Philoct.* [1261])'.

9–10 For similar uses of repetition, see 287–8 below; *Comus* 221–4; *Lyc* 8–9, 37–8; *PL* 2. 585–6; 4. 641–56; 7. 25–6.

14–15 See note on 1. 352 above.

16–19 For the account of Elijah's ascent to heaven in a fiery chariot and the search for him by fifty men, see 2 Kings 2. 11, 16–17. Cf. 266–8 below and notes, and 1. 353 above; *Eli* 49–50; *ProdBom* 1. 8; *PL* 3. 522.

16 *Thisbite.* In A.V. 1 Kings 17. 1 (cf. 21. 17) Elijah is called the 'Tishbite', but Milton uses 'Thisbite', which is closer to the Θεσβίτης of the LXX, presumably because he disliked the *sh* sound, and when possible avoided it, as in Basan for Bashan, Sittim for Shittim (*PL* 1. 398, 413), and Silo for Shiloh (*SA* 1674).

17 *once again to come.* Belief in the second coming of Elijah rests upon Mal. 4. 5: 'Behold, I will send you Elijah the prophet before the coming of the great and dreadful day of the Lord.' The belief is implicit in Matt. 16. 14; Mark 8. 28; Luke 9. 19. But in Matt. 11. 14 Jesus tells the Jews that John the Baptist was 'Elias, which was for to come'. The purpose of his coming, Augustine (*Civ. D.* 20. 29) explains, was to teach the Jews the true meaning of the law, and to convert them to faith in the true Messiah, who is our Christ.[1]

18 *those young Prophets.* According to 2 Kings 2. 15–17, after the translation of Elijah, the 'sons of the prophets' said to Elisha: 'There be with thy servants fifty strong men; let them go, we pray thee, and seek thy master...and they sought three days, but found him not.'

20–5 For other instances of proper names used possibly for the sake of verisimilitude, and certainly for their harmonious sound, see *PL* 1. 396–413, 580–7; 11. 388–411. The same device is used in Virgil, *G.* 4. 334–46; *A.* 7. 706–44; Ovid, *M.* 2. 217–27; Ariosto, *O.F.* 14. 11–24; Spenser, *F.Q.* 4. 11. 13–16; Drayton, *Poly.* 1. 18–30, 320–39, and often by later poets.

All the places here mentioned are on or near the Jordan, not far from Bethabara, the place of baptism, and appear in the maps of Adrichomius, *Theatrum*, pp. 24, 30, 126.

[1] Per hunc Heliam magnum mirabilemque prophetam exposita sibi lege ultimo tempore ante iudicium Iudaeos in Christum verum, id est Christum nostrum.

20 *Bethabara.* See note on 1. 184 above.

Jerico. Called 'the city of palm trees' in Deut. 34. 3. The site is about five miles north-west of the Dead Sea in the plain of Jordan.

21 *Ænon.* According to John 3. 23, 'John also was baptizing in Ænon near Salim.' In Thomas Fuller, *Pisgah Sight of Palestine* (London, 1869, p. 159 map) Ænon is near the western bank of the Jordan, a short distance from Salim.

Salem old. The usual spelling is Salim, but Gilbert (*G.D.*, p. 251) believes that Milton's spelling may be explained by his identifying the place with the Salem of Gen. 14. 18. Or he may have adopted it from Adrichomius, *Theatrum*, p. 74. If 'old' has any special significance, it also may lie in the identification with a place mentioned in earliest O.T. history.

22 *Machærus.* A fortress in Peraea, north-east of the Dead Sea, described in Josephus, *B.J.* 7. 6. 1–2 and Adrichomius, *Theatrum*, p. 128.

23 *On this side.* This side as opposed to Peraea, which was on the other side of the Jordan.

Genezaret. The Sea of Galilee, called Gennesaret in Luke 5. 1 from a district of that name on the west side toward the north, mentioned in Matt. 14. 34 and Mark 6. 53.

24 *Perea.* A rugged district north-east of the Dead Sea, extending in length, according to Josephus, *B.J.* 3. 3. 3, from Machaerus to Pella, and in width from Philadelphia to Jordan.

26 *Reeds and Osiers.* 'The reeds', Gilbert (*G.D.*, p. 163) explains, 'may be accounted for by the words of Jerome on Zechariah 11. 3 where he speaks of "arundineta" (thickets of reeds) and "carecta" (places covered with sedge) by the Jordan. Cf. also "the marish of Jordan" (1 Maccabees 9. 42, 45.) The question of Jesus about John the Baptist, who taught by the Jordan, is also suggestive: "What went ye out into the wilderness to see? A reed shaken with the wind?" (Matt. 11. 7.)'

whisp'ring play. Cf. *El* 5. 89–90; *Lyc* 136–7; *PL* 8. 515–16; Fletcher, *C.V.* 3. 2. 4: 'Or whistling reeds, that rutty Jordan laves'.

27 Cf. Spenser, *S.C.*, Jan. 1: 'A Shepeheards boye (no better doe him call)'.

30–1 Almost a translation of the well-known line in Terence, *Heaut.* 250: *vae misero mi, quanta de spe decidi.*

31–6 See notes on 1. 24–37, 245, 261, 262–3 above. The Messianic hope of the

Jews for 'the advent of an ideal king was only one feature of that larger hope of the salvation of Israel from all evils, the realisation of perfect reconciliation with Yahwè, and the felicity of the righteous in him, in a new order of things free from the assaults of hostile nations and the troubling of the wicked within the Hebrew community, which was constantly held forth by all the prophets' (*Encyc. Bibl.* 3. 3058). The disciples of Jesus, when they asked (Acts 1. 6): 'Lord, wilt thou at this time restore again the kingdom to Israel?' were expressing the burning desire of the Jews to be delivered from their Roman conquerors.

34 *full of grace and truth*. Cf. John 1. 14: 'And the Word was made flesh, and dwelt among us...full of grace and truth.'

36 *Kingdom*. As in 3. 171; 4. 363 below; *PL* 6. 815, equivalent to Lat. *regnum*, kingship, sovereignty.

38 *amaze*. 'Bewilderment, mental confusion. *Obs.*' (*OED*).

40 *rapt*. Taken by force, probably from Lat. *raptus* (*OED*). Cf. *PL* 3. 522; 7. 23.

42–8 The sudden interruption of the speech by these earnest words of prayer is happily calculated to heighten one's sense of the emotion of the speakers and their fervent hope for deliverance by the Messiah foretold by the prophets. Cf. 1. 55–65, 286–9 above.

44–5 Cf. Ps. 2. 2: 'The kings of the earth set themselves, and the rulers take counsel together, against the Lord, and against his anointed.' Some editors believe that in these lines there is an allusion to the position of Milton and his political sympathizers after the Restoration.

46–7 Cf. Neh. 9. 26: 'Nevertheless they were disobedient, and rebelled against thee, and cast thy law behind their backs.'

50 *his Anointed*. The Messiah. See notes on 1. 24–37 and 245 above.

51 *his great Prophet*. John the Baptist. See 1. 25 ff. above.
pointed at and shown. Cf. Horace, *C.* 4. 3. 22: 'I am pointed out by the fingers of passersby';[2] and Persius 1. 28: 'But it is a fine thing to be pointed out and to have it said, "There he is".'[3]

53–4 Cf. Ps. 55. 22: 'Cast thy burden upon the Lord, and he shall sustain thee'; 1 Pet. 5. 7: 'Casting all your care upon him; for he careth for you.'

[2] monstror digito praetereuntium.
[3] at pulchrum est digito monstrari et dicier hic est.

54-5 Cf. Joshua 1. 5: 'I will be with thee: I will not fail thee, nor forsake thee.'

56 Cf. Virgil, *A.* 1. 407-8: 'Why do you too so often cruelly mock your son with false phantoms?'[4] and 6. 869-70: 'The fates will but show him to earth, nor longer suffer him to stay.'[5]

60-4 Although the clauses intervening between 'Mary' and 'got head' make the sentence involved, the meaning is clear. Jerram (p. 98), to make it more clear, thus renders it in Latin: *At matri Mariae, videnti...quum neque filius rediisset, &c., imo pectore...curae maternae oriebantur.*

60 *To his Mother Mary.* Equivalent to a Latin dative of reference.

61-2 Milton evidently liked the effect of 'none' in the emphatic position which it here occupies. See 4. 315 below; *PL* 3. 132, 289, 443, 669, etc. Desire for emphasis may also explain the double negative in line 62, which editors regard as a Latinism.

63 *calm...pure.* Both Scripture and tradition ascribe to Mary great personal sanctity. She showed in daily life and in the most trying circumstances the greatest humility and patience. See Luke 1. 38, 48; 2. 7, 35, 48; John 19. 25-7; Ambrose, *Expos. Luc.* 2. 16-22; *Inst. Virg.* 5-7 (Migne, *Pat. Lat.* 15. 1558-60; 16. 315-19); Augustine, *Nat. et Grat.* 36 (*Pat. Lat.* 44. 267); Aquinas, *Sum. Th.* 3. 28. 4; Council of Trent, Sess. 6, can. 23 (*Canons and Decrees of the...Council of Trent,* tr. Waterworth, p. 47); Jeremy Taylor, *Life of Christ* 1. 1 (*Works,* ed. Heber, London, 1822, 2. 53-5).

65 *clad.* In a figurative sense, 'invested, arrayed, decked' (*OED*). Editors note the similar metaphorical use of *vestire* in Cicero, *Brutus* 79. 274; *De Orat.* 1. 31. 142; Horace, *Ep.* 1. 18. 22; Quintilian 8, praef. 20.

66-104 Mary, whose experience, related in the first part of her soliloquy, gives her, even more than the disciples, reason for doubts and fears, ends, like them, with an assertion of faith that enables her to 'wait with patience' the fulfilling of the promise of God. See note on 1-57 above. The soliloquy mainly consists of summary paraphrases of various passages of Scripture skilfully wrought into a single whole. Dunster (p. 69) notes the likeness to Mary's lament beneath the cross in Vida, *Christ.* 5. 865-80: 'But assuredly the swift

[4] quid natum totiens, crudelis tu quoque, falsis
  ludis imaginibus?
[5] ostendent terris hunc tantum fata, nec ultra
  esse sinent.

messenger from heaven gave not this promise to the trembling maid. Thus I alone am blessed before all others; thus do I appear as a queen of heaven? This is my great glory, this my high honour? Why after your birth did kings bring me rich gifts? Why did celestial choirs sing hymns of joy, if such a lot remained for me, and I was to live to behold this great misfortune? Happy were those whose innocent children the frenzy of an impious king devoured on the threshold of life, when in vain fear he sought to bring about their bitter death. O would that you had fallen in that devastation! These, these are the sorrows for which the dread elder in his fearful prophecy bade my trembling heart to hope. And he foretold that it would come to pass that a sword would pierce my heart. Now has its point been driven deep, now deep is the wound.'[6]

In 'The Second Eve in *PR*' (*PMASAL* 44, 1959, 365-9), H. H. Petit explains Milton's purpose in introducing Mary in *PR*. She serves as a contrasting link with *PL*. As Christ is the second Adam, so is Mary, artistically if not theologically, the second Eve, as she is called in *PL* 10. 183, one of several passages in the poem which prepare for her part in *PR* (5. 385-7; 11. 382-3; 12. 149-50, 233-4, 327, 379-82). Mary, like Eve, is puzzled by God's ways; she cannot understand why Christ has not returned from his baptism; she questions the meaning of Gabriel's salutation (see note following). But whereas the first Eve was impatient and gave way to rash pride, doubt, and disobedience, the second Eve is patient, faithful, and obedient. And as appears from Christ's soliloquy (1. 196-293), thirty lines of which are quoted from Mary, whereas Eve induced Adam to sin, Mary nurtured Christ in his office. He learned from the law and the prophets, but first he learned from his mother. See note on 4. 636-9.

[6] At non certe olim praepes demissus Olympo,
nuntius, haec pavidae dederat promissa puellae.
sic una ante alias felix ego, sic ego caeli
incedo regina? mea est haec gloria magna?
hic meus altus honos? quo reges munera opima
obtulerunt mihi post partus? quo carmina laeta
caelestes cecinere chori, si me ista manebat
sors tamen, et vitam, cladem hanc visura trahebam?
felices illae, natos quibus impius hausit
insontes regis furor ipso in limine vitae,
dum tibi vana timens funus molitur acerbum;
ut cuperem te diluvio cecidisse sub illo!
hos, hos horribili monitu trepidantia corda
terrificans senior luctus sperare iubebat,
et cecinit, fore quum pectus mihi figeret ensis,
nunc alte mucro, nunc alte vulnus adactum.

67–8 Cf. Luke 1. 28: 'Hail, thou that art highly favoured, the Lord is with thee: blessed art thou among women.'

69–71 The tradition that Mary was a woman of sorrows rests upon John 19. 25: 'Now there stood by the cross of Jesus his mother'; and upon Luke 2. 35, the prophecy of Simeon, paraphrased in lines 90–1 below: 'Yea, a sword shall pierce through thy own soul also'. Her sorrow is the subject of one of the most famous and pathetic of medieval Latin hymns, the *Stabat mater dolorosa*, ascribed to Innocent III and to Jacobus de Benedictis.

72–4 Although there is no historical evidence that Christ was born during the winter, the Roman Church, about the middle of the fourth century, accepted the date, 25 Dec., which ever since has been agreed upon throughout western Christendom (*Encyc. Bibl.* 3. 3346).

74–5 Cf. Luke 2. 7: 'And she...laid him in a manger; because there was no room for them in the inn.' Cf. *Nat* 29–31.

75–8 These lines summarize Matt. 2. 13–16, which tell of the flight of Joseph, Mary, and Jesus into Egypt, and of the slaughter by Herod of the children in and about Bethlehem.

79–80 Milton here gives a greatly condensed summary of the account in Matt. 2. 19–23 of the return of Joseph, Mary, and Jesus to Israel and their settlement in Nazareth.

80–1 Some editors here see an allusion to Milton's own way of life after the Restoration, or, as Blakeney (p. 113) suggests, to his years at Horton. But such personal allusions are dubious, and in any case there is a tradition that Christ spent his early years in contemplation and prayer. See J. de Q. Donehoo, *Apocryphal and Legendary Life of Christ* (New York, 1903), p. 166 n.

83–92 See 1. 24–37 above and note.

86–9 Cf. Luke 2. 34: 'And Simeon blessed them, and said...Behold, this child is set for the fall and rising again of many in Israel, and for a sign which shall be spoken against'. Cf. also Isa. 53. 5–8 and 1. 255 above.

90–1 See note on 69–71 above.

92 *Exaltation.* Carey (p. 1100) quotes Donne, who points out that 'in pure, and Originall Hebrew, the word [Mary] signifies *Exaltation*, and whatsoever is best in the kinde thereof' (*Sermons*, ed. Potter and Simpson, Berkeley, Cal., 9, 1958, 193).

93–5 The thoughts which Mary expresses are consistent with her character as Milton represents it in lines 63–5. Her sudden question, 'But where delays he now?' arises from the natural but only momentary impatience caused by anxiety, not by doubt.

94 *argue*. Reason in opposition, contend, dispute (*OED*), like Lat. '*arguere*... "to find fault with;" properly "to refute an opponent by proving him to be in the wrong"' (Jerram, p. 99).

96–9 These lines are a greatly condensed summary of the account in Luke 2. 42–51 of Christ's tarrying in Jerusalem and being found in the temple talking with the doctors.

97–8 Some editors question Milton's taste in admitting a play upon words, which, however appropriate when Belial and Satan are the speakers, as in *PL* 6. 560–7, 609–19, they feel is not in keeping with the otherwise dignified style of Mary's soliloquy. But see note on 269 below.

103–4 Cf. Luke 2. 19: 'But Mary kept all these things, and pondered them in her heart.'

107 *Salutation*. See 67–8 above and note, and cf. *PL* 12. 595–7.

111 *Into himself descended*. Editors note the reminiscence of Persius 4. 23: 'How nobody attempts to descend into himself.'[7] The meaning is that Christ spent his time attempting to make clear to his own mind the nature of his mission as Messiah. See note on 1. 196–293 above.

115–235 Satan, tortured by fear, in the earlier council (1. 40–118) gloomily warned his followers of danger, but tried to encourage them to hope that the 'fatal wound' might be averted. Now, after a first encounter with Christ in which he has signally failed, terrified he appears before another council, ostensibly to seek advice and to secure a second confirmation of his dictatorial powers (see note on 1. 113 above), but actually to prepare his followers for ruin. This time he does not even attempt to encourage them. See Allen, *Vision*, p. 113.

115 *slye preface*. The reference is to Satan's words in 1. 483–5 which are a 'preface', something said before to prepare for his return.

117 *middle Region*. See 1. 39 above and note.

119–20 See note on 1. 37–42 above. Note the contrast with Satan's proud

---

[7] ut nemo in sese temptat descendere.

boasting in *PL* 10. 460–503 when he reported to his followers his success in corrupting man.

120 *Sollicitous.* 'Full of care or concern' (*OED*).
blank. 'Of persons...utterly disconcerted' (*OED*).

121 Cf. 1. 44 above; *PL* 1. 315–16; 2. 11, 310–13, 430; 10. 460.

122–4 Blakeney (p. 114) explains 'Demonian Spirits' as the 'demons of the elements', στοιχεῖα, the imaginary beings believed to control the various phenomena of nature, and refers to *Enoch* 60. 11–21 and *Encyc. Bibl.* (s.v. 'elements'). It is such phenomena of nature as hoar-frost, snow, fog, dew, and rain which, according to *Enoch*, the spirits control; it was not, however, to elements in this sense that the Greeks applied the term στοιχεῖα, but to the component parts of matter which Empedocles and others after him believed to be fire, air, water, and earth, and with which he and the Homeric allegorists identified the gods. See John Burnet, *Early Greek Philosophy*, 4th ed. (London, 1930), pp. 12n., 228 ff. Since it is these elements which Milton mentions, he is here indebted to Greek rather than to Jewish conceptions. See note on 1. 447–8 above. Cf. Diogenes Laertius 1. 27; Epictetus, *Diss.* 3. 13. 15. That each element had living creatures proper to it became a common belief, as appears from Philo, *Gigant.* 2. 7; Augustine, *Civ. D.* 8. 16; Apuleius, *De Deo Socratis* 8; Hooker, *Eccles. Pol.* 1. 4. 3; Heywood, *Hierarchie*, pp. 502 ff.; A. Dieterich, *Abraxas: Studien zur Religionsgeschichte des spätern Altertums* (Leipzig, 1891), pp. 57, 61; Svendsen, *Science*, pp. 51–2, 259.

125–6 Satan, fearing that the new enemy may confine him and his followers to hell, hopes that they may be able to maintain their comfortable position as elemental spirits. He had more grandiose notions when, in *PL* 10. 391–3, he praised Sin and Death for having made

> one Realm
> Hell and this World, one Realm, one Continent
> Of easie thorough-fare.

and when in 466–8 he confidently bade the fallen angels to possess

> As Lords, a spacious World, to our native Heaven
> Little inferiour.

129–30 See 1. 94–105 above.

130 See 1. 128 above and note.

131   *tasted.* Had experience or knowledge of (*OED*), as in *PL* 9. 867; *SA* 1091; Spenser, *F.Q.* 6. 2. 32. 8; Chapman, *Od.* 21. 211.

135   *Man.* See note on 1. 4 above.

136   The first edition places a comma after 'at least', but some editors place it after 'side', believing that 'at least' more logically goes with the following phrase. Satan, for obvious reasons, is suggesting to his followers the doubt that Christ is human *even* on his mother's side.

139   Satan, as he would, thinks of Christ as actuated by ambition to achieve greatest deeds in a worldly sense, which he conceives as magnanimity. But of magnanimity in either the Aristotelian (see *Nic. Eth.* 4. 7) or the Miltonic sense (see introduction, pp. 41–3) he has no true conception. And shut up as he is within his own pride, he utterly fails to understand that Christ, possessing magnanimity, must reject the riches, power, and glory which he is about to offer him, because they are disproportionate to his virtue, and as they are offered by an evil person are incompatible with his dignity.

140–7   See note on 1. 37–43 above.

143–6   When he set out to ruin man (*PL* 2. 450–66), and when he undertook to tempt Christ (1. 100–5 above), although even then he was frightened, Satan asked his followers for no aid either of hand or counsel. Nor, although he admitted danger, did he even suggest that he might be 'over-match'd'. But now in 'the cold damp of fright' after an encounter with Christ, he is preparing his followers for the ruin which he foresees (Allen, *Vision*, p. 113).

147   *the old Serpent.* Cf. Rev. 12. 9: 'And the great dragon was cast out, that old serpent, called the Devil, and Satan.'

150–3   *dissolutest...sensuallest...fleshliest.* Cf. 'exquisitest' (346 below), 'famousest' (*SA* 982), 'virtuousest' (*PL* 8. 550). This use of *-est*, common in Elizabethan English, is a remnant of the indiscriminate application of the inflection found in early English (Abbott, *Shakes. Gram.* 9).

150   *Belial.* In *PL* 1. 490–505 and 2. 109–17 Belial appears to outward seeming 'graceful and humane'—'a fairer person lost not Heav'n'; but of all the fallen angels none was 'more lewd' or 'more gross to love / Vice for it self'. He is the arch hedonist to whose brood, as Milton declares in the preface to *DDD* (*Works* 3. 370), 'no liberty is pleasing, but unbridl'd and vagabond lust.' He is the horrifying result to be expected when pleasure becomes man's chief end.

Although Belial, or Beliar, frequently occurs in the O.T., it is there a common noun, the etymology and exact meaning of which are uncertain, but it probably means 'worthlessness' (*Encyc. Bibl.* 1. 525–7). It is only in pseudepigraphical literature that Belial attains personality, and the personality is always that of a lawless, Satanic spirit. Finally the myth of Belial became fused with that of Antichrist and that of *Nero redivivus* (*Asc. of Isa.*, ed. Charles, London, 1900, pp. lv ff.).

151 *Asmodai.* Milton uses the forms 'Asmodeus' and 'Asmedai' in *PL* 4. 168 and 6. 365. Asmodeus, Ἀσμοδαῖος, or Asmedai, the counterpart of Lilith, is first mentioned in the apocryphal Tobit 3. 8, in the Hebrew and Chaldaic versions of which he is called the 'king of demons'. He killed seven men on the nights of their marriages to Sarah, but was finally exorcized by Tobias. Since the scene of the story of Tobit is Persia, it is likely that Asmodeus is of Persian origin, and came into Jewish demonology in the period of the exile, and thereafter in popular imagination and rabbinical writings underwent many changes, as in the *Testament of Solomon* (*Jewish Encyc.* 2. 217–20; P. I. Hershon, *The Pentateuch According to the Talmud*, tr. Wolkenberg, London, 1883, pp. 188–91). From Tobit to Burton's *Anatomy* (1. 2. 1. 2) the characteristics for which Asmodeus has been notorious are lust and malice toward the newly wed (J. G. Frazer, *Folk-Lore in the Old Testament*, London, 1918, 1. 499 ff.).

152 *Incubus.* The word is post-classical, but it occurs in Servius *ad A.* 6. 776. An incubus, perhaps originally a personification of the nightmare, was a demon which had sexual intercourse with women in their sleep, the male counterpart of the succubus (Augustine, *Civ. D.* 15. 23; Aquinas, *Sum. Th.* 1. 51. 3. 6; Isidore, *Etym.* 8. 11. 103). How common in the Middle Ages and even much later was the belief in incubi may be gathered from the *Malleus Maleficarum* 1. 1. 3–4; 2. 1. 4; 2. 21. King James devoted a chapter (3. 3) of his *Demonologie* to incubi and succubi; Heywood in *Hierarchie*, pp. 501–3, tells 'a history of an incubus' followed by that of a succubus; Jean Bodin in his *Daemonomania* (Frankfort, 1603) 2. 7 records many accounts of witches and demons having intercourse; and in *An Antidote Against Atheism* (London, 1655) 3. 12. 3 Henry More declares that it is a 'shrewd presumption' that the devil lies with witches, and 'that it is not a meer *Dream*, as their friend *Wierus* would have it.'

Concerning this passage Woodhouse ('Theme', *UTQ* 25, 1955–6, 175) makes the point that Milton, departing from a long tradition of patristic, scholastic, and Protestant commentary, is content with the simple contrast between Christ's obedience and Eve's disobedience, and endeavours to parallel the two temptations step by step. The parallels which Milton draws between Christ's temptations and those of our first parents 'are all with his own account of the earlier temptation in *Paradise Lost*', and these parallels on occasion lead him outside the tradition altogether. For example, finding nothing in the tradition corresponding to the predicament of his Adam 'fondly overcome with Femal charm', he has Belial propose 'Set women in his eye and in his walk', and Belial is rebuked by Satan for his stupidity.

In his account of the Satanic council in *Jerusalem* 4, which contributed some details to the council in Pandemonium, Tasso gives a description of the charms of women, like the present one but more elaborate, when Satan suggests to the wizard Idraote that he use Armida, the fair young witch, to seduce the Christian lords (stanzas 25–33). Cf. *El* 1. 52–3; 7. 63–74; *SA* 710–24.

155 Cf. *El* 1. 63–70; Ovid, *A.A.* 1. 53–6.

156 Cf. *El* 7. 53, 63–4.

157–9 Cf. Tasso, *Jerusalem* (tr. Edward Fairfax, London, 1600) 4. 89. 5–6:

> Yet tempred so her deignfull looks alway,
> That outward scorne shew'd store of grace within...

and 4. 83. 7–8:

> Her lips cast forth a chaine of sugred words,
> That captiue led most of the Christian Lords.

159–60 *mild...sweet.* See note on 1. 26–8 above.

160 *terrible to approach.* Cf. *PL* 9. 490–1; Song of Sol. 6. 4: 'Thou art beautiful, O my love...terrible as an army with banners'; Claudian 1. 91–2 (1. 8): 'Her goodness is mingled with beauty, and her lovely modesty armed with awe';[8] Tasso, *Jerusalem* 4. 93. 1–2:

> While thus she them torments twixt frost and fier,
> Twixt ioy and griefe, twixt hope and restlesse feare.

161 *Skill'd to retire.* So do the damsels of Acrasia first show and then conceal their charms in Spenser, *F.Q.* 2. 12. 66–7. The same effect is vividly described in *El* 7. 75–88. Cf. *PL* 8. 504–5.

162 *Amorous Nets.* Cf. *El* 1. 60; *PL* 10. 897; 11. 586–7; *SA* 409, 532; Tasso,

[8] miscetur decori virtus pulcherque severo
    armatur terrore pudor.

Jerusalem 4. 23. 2: 'What dart to cast, what net, what toile to pitch'; 4. 26. 2: 'Frame snares, of lookes; traines, of alluring speach'; Spenser, *F.Q.* 5. 5. 52. 1: 'There all her subtill nets she did unfold.' On 'amorous nets' as 'a favorite conception of Milton's', see E. S. Le Comte, *Yet Once More* (New York, 1953), pp. 6–7.

163–8 On a woman's power to 'soft'n and tame' consider the examples of Samson (Judges 16. 4–17; *SA* 381–406), of the Christian lords whose story Tasso tells in *Jerusalem* 4, and of those whom Satan mentions in lines 186–91.

164 *rugged'st brow.* The brow wrinkled with care, as in Spenser, *F.Q.* 4. Pr. 1. 1–2. Cf. *IlPen* 58.

165 *Enerve.* Enervate. Now obsolete but fairly common in the 17th century (*OED*).

166 *Draw out.* 'A metaphor', as Jerram (p. 104) notes, 'for enticing an animal from his lurking-place by a bait. Cf. Terence, [*And.* 648]: *nisi me...falsa spe produceres?'*
    credulous desire. Cf. Horace, *C.* 1. 5. 9: 'Who now enjoys thee credulously thinking thee all golden?'[9]

168 In the 17th century 'magnetic' was used as a noun meaning 'magnet' (*OED*). That woman's beauty attracts the lover as the magnet, or adamant, attracts iron is a common figure found in Lucian, *Im.* 2; Claudian, *S.P.* 29. 22–39 (2. 236–7); Shakespeare, *Dream* 2. 1. 195–6; Donne, *H.S.* 1. 14; *First Ann.* 221; Burton, *Anat.* 2. 3. 2; William Browne, *Brit. Past.* 1. 1. 639–41. Blondel (p. 250) notes that in *Anat.* 3. 2. 2 Burton gives a list of the victories of Venus over heroes, and remarks: 'No king so strong, but a fair woman is stronger than he is.'

169–71 Even Solomon, reputedly the wisest of men, led in old age by his heathen wives, 'turned away his heart after other gods', and 'went after Ashtoreth the goddess of the Zidonians, and after Milcom the abomination of the Ammonites' (1 Kings 11. 4–5). Cf. *PL* 1. 399–505; 9. 442–3; and especially 1. 442–6.

172–234 Satan, in this matter at least on the 'right' side, condemns Belial as guilty of damaging the reputation of the pagan gods. He and his followers have indulged in all manner of amorous escapades, and then to cover up the

[9] qui nunc te fruitur credulus aurea?

facts have invented fine fables attributing their own misdeeds to the gods. 'It is a delightful piece of mythological debunking by a puritanical Satan' (Stein, *Heroic Knowledge*, pp. 50–1). It is ironic that by both the first part of the speech in which he condemns Belial and the second in which he recognizes Christ's nobility, he is self-condemned.

173–4 It is also ironic that Satan, shut up as he is within himself, cannot avoid judging Christ by himself. As Northrop Frye explains in 'Typology', *MP* 53 (1956), 231, by heroic action Satan understands 'his own type of aggressive and destructive parody-heroism' which attempts to rival God. 'His assumption that the Messiah's heroism will be in some way of this type is genuine', and so he is willing to credit Christ with contempt for 'effeminate slackness'.

178–81 Commentators have generally believed that in *PL* 11. 574–92 Milton represents the Sons of God as the posterity of Seth, but that in the present passage he inconsistently makes them the fallen angels. About the meaning of the former passage there is no disagreement; but R. H. West in 'Milton's Sons of God', *MLN* 65 (1950), 187–91, and in *Milton and the Angels* (Athens, Ga., 1955), pp. 129–31, has convincingly shown that there is no conflict between the two passages, as Milton's deliberate qualification, 'False titl'd' ought to have warned commentators. Belial and his associates have cloaked their amorous activities under the name of Sons of God, to which they have no right; but actually they are pagan gods, as the names Apollo, Neptune, Jupiter, and Pan in line 190 make plain. West also notes that of the story of angels mixing with women and begetting devils, and of Justin Martyr who told it, Milton speaks with scorn in *Ref* 1 (*Works* 3. 21). On the identification of the fallen angels and the pagan gods, see note 1. 117 above.

180–2 See note on 152 above.

184–5 Cf. Shakespeare, *Dream* 2. 1. 28–9:

> And now they never meet in grove, or green,
> By fountain clear or spangled starlight sheen.

185–8 The nymphs named here, and frequently mentioned in classical literature, are personifications of nature in all its fundamental aspects, the goddesses which give life, βιόδωροι (*Schol. Aristoph., Ran.* 1344). Milton's references to nymphs are numerous, as in *Comus* 54, 120, 229, 421, 823; *PL* 4. 707; 5. 381, etc. See also 297 below.

186–91 The 'arraignment of the gods' in these lines, Osgood (*Mythology*, p.

10) observes, 'is not unlike that in the *Protrepticus* of Clement of Alexandria, 27 P ff., where among others Poseidon, Apollo, and Zeus are named with Amymone, Daphne, Semele, and others.' Milton must have known Ovid's recital in *M*. 6. 107 ff. of the loves of Jupiter, Neptune, Apollo, and Bacchus, and Spenser's description in *F.Q.* 3. 11. 29–46 of the arras in the house of Busyrane on which were depicted the loves of Jupiter, Phoebus, Neptune, and Saturn.

186–8 *Calisto*. Jupiter became enamoured of the Arcadian nymph Calisto, and, disguised as Diana, ravished her (Apollodorus 3. 8. 2; Ovid, *M*. 2. 409–40).

Clymene. Clymene, wife of Merops, was loved by Apollo and by him became the mother of Phaeton (Ovid, *M*. 1. 765–75; 4. 204; *Tr*. 3. 4. 30).

Daphne. The first love of Apollo was Daphne, who as she fled from him was transformed into a laurel tree (Ovid, *M*. 1. 452–567). Cf. *El* 5. 13; 7. 31–6; *Comus* 660–1; *PL* 4. 273.

Semele. By union with Jupiter, Semele, daughter of Cadmus, became the mother of Dionysus (Hesiod, *Theog*. 940–2; Ovid, *M*. 3. 520; *Am*. 3. 3. 37). Cf. *El* 5. 91.

Antiopa. By her great beauty Antiopa, daughter of Nykteus, attracted Jupiter and by him became the mother of twin sons, Amphion and Zethus (Pausanias 2. 6. 1; Ovid, *M*. 6. 110–11).

Amymone. Poseidon, after rescuing the beautiful Amymone from a satyr who was about to ravish her, carried her off into the sea (Statius, *The*. 6. 288; Apollodorus 2. 1. 4–5; Lucian, *D. Mar*. 6; Hyginus, *Fab*. 169).

Syrinx. The pure and beautiful Syrinx, an Arcadian wood-nymph, who had eluded pursuing satyrs, was at last pursued by Pan, but before he could overtake her, she was transformed into marsh reeds (Ovid, *M*. 1. 698–706). Cf. *Arc* 106.

189 *scapes*. Breaches of moral restraint, outrageous sins; 'often applied to a breach of chastity' (*OED*). Cf. Donne, *Womans Constancy* 14. The word does not occur elsewhere in Milton's poetry.

190–1 Cf. Ovid, *M*. 1. 192–3: 'I have demigods and rustic deities, nymphs, fauns, and satyrs, and sylvan gods upon the mountain sides.'[10]

Pan. Pan was the Greek god of all things concerned with pastoral life, whose home was the hills of Arcadia where, with the nymphs, he indulged his love of noise and dancing. He is represented as a theomorphic being having the

---

[10] sunt mihi semidei, sunt rustica numina, nymphae
faunique satyrique et monticolae silvani.

horns, shaggy hair, and feet of a goat (*Homeric Hy. to Pan*; Silius Italicus 13. 326–42; Lucian, *D. Deor.* 2). Cf. *Nat* 89; *Comus* 175; *PL* 4. 707.

Satyr. The satyrs, attendants of Dionysus (Apollodorus 3. 5. 1; Ovid, *F.* 3. 737; *A.A.* 1. 542) were creatures with shaggy hair, pointed ears, horns, and tails, like those of goats (Silius Italicus 3. 103–5). They were generally regarded as sensual and voluptuous (Apollodorus 2. 1. 4; Ovid, *F.* 1. 397), and much given to dancing (Ovid. *M.* 14. 637; Horace, *C.* 1. 1. 31; Virgil, *E.* 5. 73), as in *Lyc* 34. They were often represented in art, as notably in the satyr of Praxiteles (Pausanias 1. 20. 1).

Fawn. This spelling occurs in the 16th and 17th centuries (*OED*). A faun, not to be identified with the Roman god Faunus mentioned in *El* 5. 127; *Sals* 27; *EpDam* 32, was one of the *fauni*, the silvan deities of indefinite number, the *agrestum numina* of Virgil, *G.* 1. 10, who became identified with the Greek satyrs (Ovid, *M.* 6. 329; Osgood, *Mythology*, p. 87). Cf. *Lyc* 34.

Silvan. Silvan, i.e. Silvanus (*OED*), who greatly resembles Pan and Faunus, was a Roman god of forests and husbandmen (Virgil, *E.* 10. 24; *G.* 1. 20; *A.* 8. 600–1; Horace, *Ep.* 2. 1. 143; Lucan 3. 402), who protected cattle and increased their fertility (Tibullus 1. 5. 27; Cato, *R.R.* 83). Cf. *Comus* 267; *IlPen* 134.

haunts. Habits or possibly companionships, though the latter meaning is rare (*OED*).

196–8 The '*Pellean* Conquerour' is Alexander the Great, born at Pella in Macedonia. Milton probably refers to the treatment of the mother, wife, and daughters of Darius, whom he captured after the battle of Issus (Arrian, *Anab.* 2. 11–12; Diodorus Siculus 17. 36–8; Plutarch, *Alex.* 21; Athenaeus 13. 603). But as Blakeney (p. 119) points out, 'he was moved by compassion rather than by *contempt*', as Milton seems to imply by the word 'slightly'.

199–200 *hee sirnam'd of Africa.* The name Africanus was conferred upon P. Cornelius Scipio because he defeated the Carthaginians (Livy 30. 45. 6). Earlier in his career, after the capture of New Carthage in Spain, he restored to her lover a beautiful young woman who was among the prisoners (Livy 26. 50; Silius Italicus 15. 268–82; Polybius 10. 18–19).

201–3 The honour shown to Solomon, his wealth, even his rich food, are frequently mentioned in 1 Kings 3 ff. and 2 Chron. 1 ff. That he had no 'Higher design then to enjoy his State' may be a conclusion drawn from these accounts and from Ecclesiastes, of which he was believed to be the author, and in which the doctrine of *carpe diem* is prominent. Moreover it is a conclusion to be expected from Satan.

205–6 *wiser far | Then Solomon.* Cf. Matt. 12. 42: 'Behold, a greater than Solomon is here.'

207–8 See note on 139 above.

208–23 In these lines W. B. C. Watkins, in *Anatomy of Milton's Verse* (Baton Rouge, La., 1955, p. 118), believes that Satan steps out of character and antagonizes us with his sweeping and indiscriminate contempt for beauty and women. In the whole 'savage and inept' denial of beauty, an embarrassment to the poem, Watkins sees Milton betraying his own character in that of Satan. But this is a very dubious interpretation, for if Milton were to deny beauty and women, it would be he, not Satan, who was stepping out of character. Hughes (p. 478) is unquestionably right in maintaining that what Milton intended was 'only one of several confessions by Satan that in Christ he saw the perfect, Platonic "shape" or ideal of the "good, wise," and "just" (III, 11).'

210–11 Editors note the same figure in Aeschylus, *Supp.* 1003–5: 'So all men, as they pass, mastered by desire, shoot an alluring arrow of the eye at the delicate beauty of maidens';[11] and *Prom.* 654: 'The eye of Zeus may find respite from its longings.'[12]

212–13 By means of a magic girdle, which on false pretences she had obtained from Aphrodite, Hera beguiled Zeus (Homer, *Il.* 14. 197 ff.). Cf. Spenser, *F.Q.* 4. 5. 3–4; Burton, *Anat.* 3. 2. 2. 5.

215 *so Fables tell.* In *Mythology and the Renaissance Tradition in English Poetry* (Minneapolis, Minn., 1932, p. 278), Bush notes that all the relatively few allusions to myth in *PR* are accompanied by disparaging phrases, unless it is Satan who makes the allusion, and even he can express Miltonic scepticism.

216–17 The meaning is 'one look from the majestic brow of him who is seated'; but as the sentence reads there is no word which 'seated' can logically modify. Cf. *PL* 2. 59; 5. 502–3.

219 *deject.* 'To cast down from high estate or dignity...to abase, humble' (*OED*).

---

[11] καὶ παρθένων χλιδαῖσιν εὐμόρφοις ἔπι
πᾶς τις παρελθὼν ὄμματος θελκτήριον
τόξευμ' ἔπεμψεν, ἱμέρου νικώμενος.
[12] ὡς ἂν τὸ Δῖον ὄμμα λωφήσῃ πόθου.

220–2 In *El* 7. 61 ff. Milton describes his own state when he was captivated by a woman's beauty. Cf. *SA* 1003–7:

> Yet beauty, though injurious, hath strange power,
> After offence returning, to regain
> Love once possest, nor can be easily
> Repuls't, without much inward passion felt
> And secret sting of amorous remorse;

and Spenser, *Colin Clout* 871–4:

> For beautie is the bayt which with delight
> Doth man allure, for to enlarge his kynd,
> Beautie the burning lamp of heauens light,
> Darting her beames into each feeble mynd.

222–4 Editors note the reminiscence of Ovid's remark about the peacock in *A.A.* 1. 627–8: 'The bird of Juno displays its feathers if you praise them; but if you look at them in silence, it hides its treasures.'[13]

226 Constancy, Milton explains in *DocCh* 2. 2 (*Works* 17. 47) is 'that virtue whereby we persevere in a determination to do right, from which nothing can divert us.' It is exemplified in the Lady in *Comus* and in Abdiel in *PL*. Christ is about to prove himself the supreme example of constancy.

227 In rejecting the subsequent temptations, Christ exposes the speciousness of such honours, glory, and praise as Satan offers, and hence the folly of seeking them. See note on 3. 21–30 below.

228 *greatest men.* For example Alexander the Great, Scipio, Pompey, and Julius Caesar, whom Satan will mention in 3. 31–42 below. But ironically enough Satan 'Insatiable of glory had lost all.'

230–1 Cf. 368–77 below.

232 I see no reason to believe, as Blakeney (p. 120) does, that 'wide' is probably a slip for 'wild' as in *PL* 12. 234.

235 In their applause they granted him the commission to act for them.

236–7 Editors note the resemblance to Matt. 12. 45: 'Then goeth he, and taketh with himself seven other spirits more wicked than himself.' Cf. Luke 11.26.

---

[13] laudatas ostendit avis Iunonia pinnas;
   si tacitus spectes, illa recondit opes.

239-40 The use of players in 'some active Scene', since it is a device of Satan, might appear to be an oblique expression of Puritan hostility to the theatre as evidenced notably in the *Histrio-Mastix* (London, 1633) of William Prynne, who called theatres 'the Divels Chappels' (sig. * 3ᵛ), and actors 'the Arch-agents, Instruments, Apparitors, of their originall Founder and *Father, the Devill*...' (p. 134). But that Milton was not hostile to the theatre is clear from *El* 1. 27-46; *L'All* 131-4; *IlPen* 97-102; *ComBk* (*Works* 18. 207) in which, after discussing the unfavourable opinions of Tertullian, Cyprian, and Lactantius, he adds: 'He [Lactantius] does not even once seem to have reflected that, while the corrupting influences of the theater ought to be eliminated, it does not follow that it is necessary to abolish altogether the performance of plays... for what in the whole of philosophy is more...uplifting than a noble tragedy, what more helpful to a survey at a single glance of the hazards and changes of human life?'

242 *from shade to shade.* 'passing from one shelter to another' (Jerram, p. 109).

244 See note on 1. 309 above.

245-59 In this soliloquy, only at the close of which is there any echo of Scripture, Christ is seeking the meaning of the experience through which he is passing. What does it mean to have fasted forty days without hunger? It means, as Jerram (p. 109) paraphrases the argument, that '*either* nature may not feel need at all, *or*, though she may do so, God can satisfy her by other means than food. But my feeling hunger tells me that the former alternative is not true, therefore the second remains.' His experience, then, assures him that he is sustained by God, and confirms him in his humble faith in God. He is also sustained by 'better thoughts', that is such thoughts about his mission as he has already expressed in the soliloquy in 1. 196-293, especially 259 ff., thoughts which intensify his desire to do his Father's will.

These lines are an acknowledgment by Christ that the miracle of his fast was performed *by God*, not by himself, and they cannot be used to prove, as G. W. Whiting has argued in 'Christ's Miraculous Fast', *MLN* 66 (1951), 12-16, that Christ *in his divine nature* is the hero of *PR*.

258 Cf. *PL* 3. 37-8.

259 Cf. John 4. 34: 'My meat is to do the will of him that sent me.'

262-3 Editors note the reminiscence of Virgil, *G*. 4. 24: 'A tree in their way may shelter them with its friendly leaves';[14] and Horace, *C.* 2. 3. 9–11: 'Why do the great pine tree and the white poplar uniting to make a hospitable shade delight with their branches?'[15] Cf. *Comus* 185–6.

264 *appetite.* See note on 1. 146 above. Editors compare Lucretius 4. 1024–5 where it is said that in dreams 'a thirsty man often sits beside a stream or a pleasant fountain and gulps down almost the whole river.'[16]

266 *Him thought.* It seemed to him. Cf. 'methinks', 'meseems'. 'Him' is a dative and 'thought' is from O.E. *þync(e)an*, 'to seem', which was distinct from *þenc(e)an*, 'to think'; but in M.E. the two became confused and finally fell together (*OED*). Cf. *PL* 4. 478; 5. 114; Spenser, *F.Q.* 1. 8. 7. 5; 2. 3. 5. 6.

266–76 Accounts of Elijah's sojourns in the wilderness are found in 1 Kings 17. 3–7 and 19. 3–8.

269 Puns such as that upon 'ravens' and 'ravenous' were approved, Hughes (p. 500) observes, as ornaments of epic poetry by Abraham Fraunce in *Arcadian Rhetoric* 24.

275 *eat.* This may be either the infinitive after 'bid' or the past tense.

277 After 'Sometimes' supply 'him thought' from line 266.

278 The story of Daniel's refusal to eat the rich food of Nebuchadnezzar, and his determination to live upon his usual spare diet of pulse, is told in Dan. 1. 8–19.

279–81 Milton speaks of the lark as the herald of morning also in *L'All* 41–3 and *Comus* 316–17. The conceit, as editors note, was often used before his time, as in Chaucer, *Kn. T.* 1491–4; Lyly, *Campaspe* 5. 1; Spenser, *F.Q.* 1. 11. 51. 8–9; Shakespeare, *Sonn.* 29. 11–12; and in the well-known song, 'Hark, hark the lark' in *Cym.* 2. 3. 20.

In 'Aural Imagery as Miltonic Metaphor', *LSUSHS* 18 (1966), 32–42, C. R. Mackin notes that the song of the lark and the 'chaunt of tuneful Birds' ten lines below signify Christ's harmony with God, since in the 17th century there was an old tradition that the song of birds symbolizes the harmony and order

[14] obviaque hospitiis teneat frondentibus arbos.
[15] quo pinus ingens albaque populus
umbram hospitalem consociare amant
ramis?
[16] flumen item sitiens aut fontem propter amoenum
adsidet et totum prope faucibus occupat amnem.

of the cosmos. Mackin, however, does not make fully clear, as does James Hutton in 'Some English Poems in Praise of Music', *English Miscellany*, ed. Praz, 2 (1951), 43–59, that when Milton mentions music as he does here, he has in mind the theory which began with Pythagoras, which he first treated as early as *De Sphaerarum Concentu*, the second of his *Prolusions* (*Works* 12. 148–57), and to which, as Hutton shows, he often reverted thereafter, the theory, namely, that since, imprisoned as he is in the body, sinful man cannot hear the harmonious music of the spheres, it is the function of earthly music, which in a degree reproduces the heavenly harmony, to compensate for man's loss by reaching his soul, and bringing the motions of his spirits into accord with the motions of the heavenly spheres, uniting him with what is highest. Is it not, then, ironic that at a banquet of Satan's providing there should be 'Harmonious Airs' (362), though it is understandable that he should attempt to use them to deceive Christ? See notes on 402–3; 4. 410–25, 434–8 below.

285–8 Jerram (p. 110) notes that these lines are modelled on Virgil, *A.* 1. 180–3: 'Aeneas meanwhile climbs up a rocky headland and seeks a full view far over the sea, if he may catch any sight of tempest-tossed Antheus and his Phrygian ships, or of Capys, or of Caicus' arms on the high stern.'[17]

287–97 The description of the 'pleasant Grove', one of the few descriptions of natural beauty in *PR*, suggests the greenwood, the scene of Armida's banquet in Tasso, *Jerusalem* 10. 63–4, and the grove of Error in Spenser, *F.Q.* 1. 1. 7. 2–9. Osgood (*Mythology*, p. 64) observes that 'Milton dwells often upon the beauty of places haunted by the nymphs (*P. L.* 4. 705–8...*Pens.* 133–146).' Is the 'pleasant Grove' a natural grove, or is it, like the banquet which follows, another part of Satan's evil artifice; and is Christ rejecting beauty itself as worthless or evil? That the grove is artificial may seem to be implied by line 295, 'Natures own work it seem'd (Nature taught Art)'; but the words 'to a Superstitious eye' in the next line indicate the circumstances in which the scene might be deceptive and evil; and when the banquet disappears, the grove remains. 'The point', as Woodhouse explains ('Theme', *UTQ* 25, 1955–6, 179), 'is that Christ accepts this scene of natural beauty just before he rejects the splendours of the banquet speciously offered as homage from the powers of

---

[17] Aeneas scopulum interea conscendit, et omnem
prospectum late pelago petit, Anthea si quem
iactatum vento videat Phrygiasque biremis,
aut Capyn, aut celsis in puppibus arma Caici.

nature, but really of Satan's procuring and destined to vanish "With sound of harpies' wings and talons heard." As in *Comus*, it is not beauty that is condemned, not natural beauty in its appointed place, but beauty in the service of evil and, specifically, in competition with obedience to God.'

In 'A Fairer Paradise? Some Recent Studies of *PR*', *ELH* 32 (1965), 275–302, Howard Schultz offers a new interpretation of the present scene. What purports to be a grove is actually a church, probably a cathedral, he believes, as ought to be evident if we reverse Satan's false assurance to Christ (328–30) that the banquet is neither idolatrous nor Anti-Christian. By the 'stripling youths' and 'Nymphs of Diana's train' are meant members of the secular and the regular ministry. The Nymphs, the regulars, as they are women, properly do not mingle with the youths but remain apart. The youths, the seculars, appear serving or standing beside a 'stately side-board' (350), in which Schultz sees an allusion to the long dispute over the proper position of the Lord's table. Should it be a stately altar placed against the wall of the chancel or an unstately table standing in the midst of the church? Schultz nowhere expressly states that what is being described is the service of the mass, but that *seems* to be implied. Of the validity of this unusual interpretation of the scene readers may judge for themselves.

293 *brown*. 'Dusky, dark' (*OED*). As an epithet applied to shade 'brown' occurs also in *IlPen* 134; *PL* 9. 1088, and in 3. 326 below.

295 Milton may have remembered Spenser, *F.Q.* 2. 12. 59. 1, 3–7:

> One would haue thought...
> That nature had for wantonesse ensude
> Art, and that Art at nature did repine;
> So striuing each th' other to vndermine,
> Each did the others worke more beautifie;
> So diff'ring both in willes, agreed in fine.

296–7 Editors note the resemblance to Lucretius 4. 580–1: 'These places the neighbours believe are haunted by goat-footed satyrs and nymphs, and they say there are fauns.'[18] On the significance of the words 'to a Superstitious eye' with respect to classic myth, see note on 215 above. In *Def 1* 12 (*Works* 7. 553) Milton declares that tyranny and superstition are 'the two greatest mischiefs of this life, and most pernicious to virtue'; and in *DocCh* 1. 1 (14. 3) that they

---

[18] haec loca capripedes satyros nymphasque tenere
finitimi fingunt et faunos esse locuntur.

are curses from which nothing but the Christian religion 'can so effectually rescue the lives and minds of men'.

297 *Wood-Gods...Wood-Nymphs.* See notes on 190–1 and 186–8 above.

302–16 Satan now begins the second temptation, 'the essence' of which for Milton 'resides in the world *glory*', common to the 'accounts in both Matt. 4 and Luke 4', and in 'the word *power*' found in Luke. Having discovered that essence, 'he is ready to amplify four verses of scripture into over one thousand lines, in the interests of his theme and pattern. So he surrounds the offer of power and its glory with other examples. The glory of wealth and of fame lead up to the glory of power, all presented under the specious colouring of means to establish Christ's Messianic kingdom....He frames these temptations to the active pursuit of glory with two others which are...contemplative in character: the glory of beauty or of the senses, and the glory of knowledge or of the intellect, thus running the whole gamut of worldly glory as conceived by the Renaissance man' (Woodhouse, 'Theme', *UTQ* 25, 1955–6, 175–6).

302 *With granted leave.* See note on 1. 363 above.
   officious. Ready...to serve or please (*OED*), i.e. by doing *officia*, kindnesses; like Lat. *officiosus.* This is Satan's hypocritical meaning, but it is ironic that he uses a word which also means 'unduly forward in proffering services or taking business upon oneself...meddlesome' (*OED*).

307–14 Satan is inaccurate. Hagar's wanderings were not in the Desert of Quarentana, where he and Christ now are (see note on 1. 119 above), but in the wilderness of Beersheba (Gen. 21. 14); the wanderings of the Israelites were in the wilderness of Sin (Exod. 16. 1); and Elijah went from Beersheba 'a day's journey into the wilderness' (1 Kings 19. 4).

308–10 Hagar, the bondwoman, and her son Ishmael, when driven into the desert because of Sarah's jealousy, would have died had not 'the angel of God' shown her 'a well of water' (Gen. 21. 17–19). According to Gen. 25. 13 Nebaioth was the eldest son of Ishmael.

310–12 The children of Israel in the wilderness of Sin 'did eat manna forty years, until they came to a land inhabited' (Exod. 16. 35).

312–14 As Elijah 'slept under a juniper tree' in the wilderness, 'an angel touched him, and said unto him, Arise and eat' (1 Kings 19. 5).

313 *Thebez.* This, Gilbert (*G.D.*, pp. 294–5) explains, 'was a city of the tribe

126

of Ephraim. (Judges 9. 50.) Milton is apparently without authority for making this city, rather than Thisbe across the Jordan, the city of Elijah the Tishbite.' See note on 1. 353 above.

The first edition reads 'Thebes' which in the Errata is changed to 'Thebez', probably because Milton wanted to be sure that the word would be pronounced as two syllables, which are metrically necessary (Fletcher, facsimile ed. 4. 100).

318   *I...none.* See note on 245–59 above.

319–404   About the banquet scene there has been much disagreement among commentators. Some have thought that it inartistically repeats the first temptation in other terms; T. H. Banks, in 'The Banquet Scene in *PR*', *PMLA* 55 (1940), 773–6, argues that it involves the aims of both the first and the second temptations; others, among them Gilbert ('Tempt. in *PR*', *JEGP* 15, 1916, 604), Blondel (p. 53), and Woodhouse ('Theme', *UTQ* 25, 1955–6, 175–6) regard it as the first phase of the second temptation and completely distinct from the first. That it must be the last of these ought to be obvious. Glory and power are the very essence of the second temptation (see note on 302–16 above), and the sumptuousness and beauty, the luxury, of the banquet are the first form in which Satan offers Christ the glory of the world.

321–2   *as I like / The giver.* Cf. 4. 171 below and *Comus* 701–3.

323   *Fiend.* See note on 1. 465 above.

324–6   In like manner Satan appealed to Eve in *PL* 9. 539–40, when he said: 'All things [are] thine / By gift'. But his argument is sophistical, for the matter of first importance to Eve and to Christ is not their *right* to all created things but their *duty* to trust and obey God. Satan's words, which like 4. 166–7 below, suggest the rendering of feudal service (cf. Phil. 2. 10–11), are another indication that he knows who Christ really is. See note on 1. 91 above.

328–9   The unclean meats from which the Jews were to abstain are mentioned in Lev. 11. 2–31 and Deut. 14. 3–20. On the meats offered to idols and Paul's reassurance to certain Christians who scrupled to eat them, see Acts 15. 29 and 1 Cor. 8. 1–10; 10. 20, 25–9. Daniel refused to eat the king's rich food (Dan. 1. 8) no doubt because it included the flesh of animals forbidden in the Mosaic law.

When Satan says 'Nor mention I / Meats by the Law unclean', he contradicts himself, for he has just said that Christ has a right 'to all Created things'; and he is lying, and repeats the lie in lines 368–71; for many of the meats and fish and all the shellfish mentioned in 342–5 are absolutely forbidden in the Mosaic dietary laws. And since the lie is too patent to deceive Christ, Satan's purpose, as Michael Fixler explains in 'The Unclean Meats of the Mosaic Law and the Banquet Scene in *PR*', *MLN* 70 (1955), 573–7, is more elaborate and sophisticated. Unaware that Christ has come to abrogate the Mosaic law, he assumes that these laws are binding upon Christ. If the laws are the criteria, then the food which Satan offers is manifestly unclean; and it would seem that Satan is, in effect, asking Christ to accept the laws and contradict him. Christ, however, has said that only the acceptability of the giver would determine his accepting or rejecting the banquet. If Satan could induce him to deny his own words and shift his ground, he would win at least a minor victory. Or he may have hoped that Christ would accept the laws, but after his fast would prove too weak to reject the proffered food. Were he to do so, and take no exception to the lie, he would implicate himself in it, and thus be condemned in his own eyes for eating, like Eve, food forbidden by the word of God.

331 *scruple*. 'Make scruples about...question the propriety...of...something...' (*OED*).

332 *Nature*. Personified as in *Nat* 32, and as there almost equivalent to Earth, Γαῖα or Γῆ, the all-producing, all-nourishing mother.

333 Cf. Juvenal 11. 14: 'Meanwhile they are searching all the elements for relishes.'[19]

337–67 There are many scenes of feasting in literature, as in Homer, *Od.* 7. 167–85; Virgil, *A.* 1. 695–711; Petronius, *Cena* 31 ff.; Plutarch, *Luc.* 40–1; *Sir Gawain and the Green Knight* 884–94; Spenser, *F.Q.* 1. 12. 38–40. The present banquet, since it is designed to beguile Christ, may have been suggested by others designed for a similar purpose, such as that given by Cleopatra, when she was captivating Caesar, which Lucan (10. 107–68) describes in all its lavish details; at which, as he says (155–8), 'On golden dishes they served a banquet of every delicacy that earth, air, sea, or the Nile provided, all that extravagance, unspurred by hunger and maddened by vain love of display has sought out over the whole earth.'[20] Cf. Macrobius, *Sat.* 3. 16–18. Milton probably remem-

---

[19] Interea gustus elementa per omnia quaerunt.
[20] Infudere epulas auro, quod terra, quod aer,
quod pelagus Nilusque dedit, quod luxus inani
ambitione furens toto quaesivit in orbe
non mandante fame.

bered also the description in Tasso, *Jerusalem* 10. 64, of false Armida's feast intended to ensnare the Christian lords:

> Vnder the curtaine of the greene-wood shade,
> Beside the brooke, vpon the veluet grasse,
> In massie vessell of pure siluer made,
> A banket rich and costly furnisht was,
> All beastes, all birds beguil'd by fowlers trade,
> All fish were there in floods or seas that passe,
> > All dainties made by art, and at the table
> > An hundreth virgins seru'd, for husbands able.

And he may have recalled the description in Fletcher, *C.V.* 2. 39–52, of the garden to which the devil conducted Christ to tempt him with sensuous pleasures.

In *Grace Before Meat* (Works, ed. Lucas, London, 1903–5, 2. 93–4), Charles Lamb objected that, 'The mighty artillery of sauces, which the cook-fiend conjures up, is out of proportion to the simple wants and plain hunger of the guest.' But in his essay *On Milton* (*Collected Writings*, ed. Masson, Edinburgh, 1889–90, 10. 403), De Quincey, perceiving the effect of contrast, suggested that Milton's purpose is to show 'subtle and lurking antagonism' in Satan, and that this explains everything in the passage 'which has been denounced under the idea of pedantry in Milton'. David Daiches points out in *Milton* (London, 1957, pp. 223–4) that the banquet is described in the style of the more ornate passages of *PL*; but the classical mythology is used not to create 'a powerful and moving suggestion of ideal beauty (as it is in the first account of Eden and of Eve)', but 'almost ironically to suggest excess and exhibitionism'. So 'domestic objects and activities' are described in 'high epic language'; the youths at the sideboard and the nymphs under the trees, who after all are only 'waiters and waitresses', are described in such exaggerated terms that the description becomes 'almost...parody'. Milton has deliberately violated decorum 'to achieve irony'; and yet, since the banquet '*is* a temptation', there is also 'splendour and beauty in the description'. It may be remarked further that the very elaborateness of the banquet shows the full extent of Satan's terror. No 'crude apple' can now serve his purpose. Terror impels him to offer what he believes to be the most attractive sensuous pleasure he can conjure up.

340 Editors compare Virgil, *A.* 1. 637–8: 'The interior of the palace is laid out with the splendour of regal magnificence, and in the midst of the halls they are preparing a banquet';[21] and 6. 604–5: 'Before their eyes is laid a banquet in regal splendour';[22] and Silius Italicus 11. 271: 'They give banquets on tables heaped with regal splendour.'[23] See Shakespeare, *Temp.* 3. 3. 17, stage direction.

342 The Mosaic law (Lev. 11. 3) forbade the eating of any animals except those which are cloven-footed and chew the cud. It also forbade the use of many birds (Lev. 11. 13–20).

343 *pastry.* Milton probably refers to the elaborate pastries of the 17th century, such as a 'pasty royal', or to the 'sotyltyes' which as early as the 15th century began to adorn the tables at banquets. These were large, extremely elaborate structures, often allegorical or heraldic, of sugar, flour, wax, tinsel, and other materials. See Charles Cooper, *The English Table in History and Literature* (London, 1929), pp. 48–50; *Two Fifteenth Century Cookery-Books*, ed. Austin, E.E.T.S. (London, 1888), pp. 57 ff. Editors tell of a pie served at an entertainment given by the Duke of Buckingham in which Geoffrey Hudson, later King James's dwarf, was concealed.

344 *Gris-amber.* Ambergris, grey amber, an intestinal secretion of the sperm whale, because of its delicate, sweet odour, was used, Hawkins (3. 91) explains, 'as a main ingredient in every concert for a banquet; viz. to fume the meat with, and that whether boiled, roasted, or baked; laid often on the top of a baked pudding.'
   all Fish from Sea or Shore. The Mosaic law (Lev. 11. 9–10) permitted the eating of only fish which have fins and scales. Hence all shellfish were forbidden. According to Juvenal 5. 92–106, to capture fish wherewith to satisfy their gluttony the Romans ravaged not only all the waters in and around Italy, but also those of the provinces.

345 *Freshet.* 'A small stream of fresh water' (*OED*).

346 *exquisitest name.* See note on 150–3 above. Early editors quote Warburton's comment that Milton 'here alludes to that species of Roman luxury, which gave *exquisite names* to fish of exquisite taste, such as that they called *cerebrum Jovis.*'

[21] at domus interior regali splendida luxu
instruitur, mediisque parant convivia tectis.
[22]   epulaeque ante ora paratae
regifico luxu.
[23] regifice extructis celebrant convivia mensis.

347 *Pontus.* Athenaeus (6. 275) mentions salt fish from Pontus as a rich and costly delicacy. Cf. Juvenal 4. 41–4.

Lucrine Bay. Oysters and other shellfish from Lucrinus, a salt water lagoon near Baiae, were famous in ancient Rome (Horace, *Epod.* 2. 49; Juvenal 4. 141; Martial 6. 11. 5; 13. 82).

Afric Coast. The Romans greatly prized many good kinds of fish from the Nile (Athenaeus 7. 311–12; cf. Juvenal 10. 155–6).

348–9 It is an ironic contrast that in the midst of the beauties of paradise Eve was tempted by a 'crude apple', whereas in the bleakness of the desert Christ will not be tempted by the 'cates', the delicacies of a splendid banquet.

349 *crude.* 'Of fruit: Unripe; sour or harsh to the taste' (*OED*), but here more probably 'coarse, common' (Lockwood, *Lexicon*).

diverted. Led 'astray from duty or right' (Lockwood, *Lexicon*).

352 Many young and beautiful attendants are a common feature of the banquets described in Homer, *Od.* 7. 172; Virgil, *A.* 1. 703–5; Lucan 10. 127–35; Petronius, *Cena* 30–1; Silius Italicus 11. 284; Tasso, *Jerusalem* 10. 64. 7–8; Spenser, *F.Q.* 4. 11. 29. 1–2.

353 Ganymede, the most beautiful of mortals, was caught up to heaven to be cup-bearer to Zeus (Homer, *Il.* 20. 231–5; *Homeric Hy. to Aphrodite* 202–4; Virgil, *A.* 5. 252–5; Ovid, *M.* 10. 155–61; Apollodorus 3. 12. 2. Cf. *El* 7. 21.

Hylas was famed for his beauty, and in the land of the Mysians a nymph who guarded a fountain, becoming enamoured of him, carried him into the depths of the water whence he never returned (Apollonius Rhodius 1. 1207–60; Theocritus 13; Hyginus, *Fab.* 14. 271). Cf. *El* 7. 23–4.

355 *Nymphs of Diana's train.* Nymphs attending Diana are often mentioned, as in Homer, *Od.* 6. 102–5; Callimachus, *Diana* 13–17; Virgil, *A.* 1. 498–500; Ovid, *M.* 2. 441–65.

355–6 *Naiades | …Amalthea's horn.* According to Apollodorus 2. 7. 5 Amalthea possessed a bull's horn that yielded whatever was desired either of food or drink. With it Achelous ransomed the horn which Hercules had torn from him in their struggle for the hand of Deianira. The two horns eventually became identified, as in Ovid, *M.* 9. 87–8, where the Naiads take the horn, fill it with flowers, and hallow it.

357 The Hesperides, daughters of Hesperus, kept the garden in which grew the golden apples which Ge gave to Hera on her marriage to Zeus. In *Comus* 981

Milton mentions '*Hesperus*, and his daughters three'; but their genealogy and number, even their names, vary, as in Hesiod, *Theog.* 215 and Apollonius Rhodius 4. 1399. As editors note, Milton here applies the name Hesperides to the garden itself, as does Shakespeare in *L.L.L.* 4. 3. 338.

358–61 Note that in rebuking Belial in 206–11 above Satan has rejected women as a means of tempting Christ.

360 *Logres.* Loëgria, as the name appears in *HistBr* 1 (*Works* 10. 14–15), was, according to Geoffrey of Monmouth 2. 1; 4. 19, the central part of Britain, east of the Severn and south of the Humber, and was named after Locrin, the eldest son of Brutus. Cf. Spenser, *F.Q.* 2. 10. 14. 5.

Lyones. Lyonesse was the legendary land of Arthur's birth, between Land's End and the Scilly Isles, which was believed to have been submerged by the sea (William Camden, *Britannia*, London, 1600, p. 150).

361 Lancelot, Pelleas, and Pellenore, who frequently appear in Arthurian stories, as in Malory, *Morte d'Arthur* 1. 20, 24; 4. 21–2; 6. 7, 14, 16, because of their amorous adventures, are appropriately mentioned here. Cf. *EpDam* 162–8; *Mansus* 80–4; *Apol* (*Works* 3. 304).

362 As appears from Horace, *Ep.* 2. 2. 9; Seneca, *Vit. Beat.* 11. 4; Petronius, *Cena* 28, 32, 36; Silius Italicus 11. 288–97; Athenaeus 14. 627; Macrobius, *Sat.* 2. 4. 28; Ariosto, *O.F.* 7. 19; Spenser, *F.Q.* 1. 12. 38. 6–9, music has from antiquity been a regular accompaniment of feasting.

363 *chiming.* 'Sounding in harmony' (Lockwood, *Lexicon*).
charming. 'Enchanting, fascinating, delightful' (*ibid.*).

364 *Arabian odors.* Arabia supplied the rest of the ancient world with such common perfumes as frankincense and myrrh (*Encyc. Bibl.* 2. 1563–4). In antiquity perfumes were much used at feasts (Matt. 26. 7; Seneca, *Vit. Beat.* 11. 4; Petronius, *Cena* 28; Athenaeus 2. 46; 9. 409; 12. 517; Q. Curtius 5. 1. 12. Cf. Spenser, *F.Q.* 1. 12. 38. 2–4, and *PL* 4. 162–3.

365 In *F.* 5. 195 ff. Ovid tells the story of Chloris, whose name *corrupta Latino sono* became Flora, and who was stolen away by Zephyrus and became the goddess of flowers. Osgood (*Mythology*, p. 36) believes that the words at the end of Ovid's story (375), *tenues secessit in auras,* / *mansit odor* may have suggested to Milton the expression 'Flora's earliest smells.'

368 *What doubts.* Why hesitates, like Lat. *quid dubitas.*

369   See *PL* 1. 1–3; 5. 51–2.

370   *Defends.* Forbids, prohibits '*Obs.* exc. *dial.*' (*OED*), like Fr. *défendre*, as in *PL* 11. 86; 12. 207.

371–81   Cf. Sir Guyon's reply to Mammon in *F.Q.* 2. 7. 39. 1–4:

> Suffise it then, thou Money God...
> That all thine idle offers I refuse.
> All that I need I haue; what needeth mee
> To couet more, then I haue cause to vse?

371   Satan implies that there is an analogy between the temptation of Christ and that of Adam and Eve; but the analogy is false, since Christ is not bound by the Mosaic dietary laws, whereas Adam and Eve were absolutely bound by God's command.

374   See note on 122–4 above.

378–91   Christ often answered the Pharisees by asking them embarrassing questions, as in Matt. 12. 3–8; 15. 3–9; 22. 18–21; Mark 2. 19; Luke 5. 22–3; so he now answers Satan with questions which expose the fallacy of offering to give him what is already his own. As Rice remarks ('PR', *PMASAL* 22, 1936, 499), Christ does not 'wish to torment and exasperate Satan', though his questions have that effect. In the circumstances, 'assertion would be unfitting; irony must suffice'.

378   *temperately.* Cf. 432: 'patiently'; 3. 43: 'calmly'; 3. 121: 'fervently'. Although in the course of the temptations Christ's temper becomes more and more strained, it is always firmly controlled.

382   *likes me.* '*Impers.*....it likes me = I am pleased...Now only *arch.* and *dial.*' (*OED*); cf. Lat. *placet mihi* and It. *mi piace.* Impersonal verbs were much commoner in the 16th and 17th centuries than they now are. Many examples are given in Abbott, *Shakes. Gram.* 297.

384   Cf. Ps. 78. 19: 'Can God furnish a table in the wilderness?' In *The Paradise Within* (New Haven, 1964), p. 187, Louis Martz believes that there is here an allusion to the communion table; and in *Brief Epic*, p. 218, Mrs Lewalski explains the 'Table in the Wilderness' as a typological allusion to such manifestations of Christ's proper banquet as the 'celestial food' supplied to him by the angels after his victory over Satan, and to the feeding of the five thousand, and to 'the Eucharistic banquet with which his church will be

nourished in the wilderness of this world'. But if Milton had intended such allusions, is it not likely that he would have given his readers some clearer hint of his meaning than is to be found in this line?

385 Cf. Ps. 91. 11: 'For he shall give his angels charge over thee, to keep thee in all thy ways.' Note that this is the passage of Scripture which Satan will later quote (see 4. 556–9) when he tempts Christ to throw himself from the pinnacle of the temple. Cf. *Comus* 454: 'A thousand liveried Angels lacky her.'

391 *gifts no gifts*. Editors note the reminiscence of Sophocles, *Ajax* 665: 'A foe's gifts are no gifts and profit not';[24] and Euripides, *Med.* 618: 'The gift of a bad man profits not';[25] and Virgil, *A.* 2. 43–4: 'Do you think that any gifts of the Greeks are free of guile?'[26] Cf. *Apol* (*Works* 3. 354) where Milton speaks of 'enemies...whose guifts are no guifts, but the instruments of our bane'.

392 See note on 1. 37–43 above.

399 See note on 1. 180 above.

401 *fet*. A synonym of 'fetched', of which *OED* gives many examples from the 16th and 17th centuries.

402–3 Editors note the reminiscence of Virgil, *A.* 3. 225–6: 'But suddenly with a fearful swoop from the mountains the Harpies are upon us, and with loud clapping shake their wings';[27] and the stage direction in Shakespeare, *Temp.* 3. 3. 52: 'Enter Ariel like a Harpy; claps his wings upon the table, and with a quaint device the banquet vanishes.' Cf. *Prol* 4 (*Works* 12. 175); *Comus* 604; *PL* 2. 596. At least as early as Aeschylus, *Eumen.* 50 the Harpies were known as filthy, predatory creatures, and so appear in Apollonius Rhodius 2. 178–93; Apollodorus 1. 9. 21; Ovid, *M.* 7. 4.

Here the 'sound of Harpies wings and Talons', like the hiss which greeted Satan when he reported to his followers his success in seducing Adam and Eve (*PL* 10. 508), is a harsh, discordant sound, the negation of music. See note on 279–81 above.

[24] ἐχθρῶν ἄδωρα δῶρα κοὐκ ὀνήσιμα.
[25] κακοῦ γὰρ ἀνδρὸς δῶρ' ὄνησιν οὐκ ἔχει.
[26]   ulla putatis
dona carere dolis Danaum?
[27] at subitae horrifico lapsu de montibus adsunt
Harpyiae et magnis quatiunt clangoribus alas.

404 *importune.* Persistent, 'irksome through persistency' (*OED*), as in Spenser, *D*. 387; *F.Q.* 1. 12. 16. 5; 2. 11. 7. 7; 5. 9. 44. 8.

406–31 Satan, knowing that the very virtues of a noble nature, if misdirected, will, as Plato explains in *Rep*. 6. 491, distract from philosophy, and destroy the soul that possesses them, appeals to Christ's noble nature by offering him riches as a means of achieving the power whereby he may accomplish the 'high designs, / High actions' on which all his heart is set. But in his reply Christ exposes the fallacies of Satan's argument.

406–7 See 245–59 above and note.

410 See 1. 196–293 above and note.

414 Cf. Matt. 13. 55: 'Is not this the carpenter's son?'

416 *hunger-bit.* The expression apparently is not common. *OED* gives only three examples of its use, including the present one.

420–1 As parallels to these lines editors cite Horace, *Ep*. 1. 19. 37–8: 'I do not hunt for the votes of the fickle crowd at the cost of dinners and worn-out clothes';[28] and Shakespeare, *Tim*. 2. 2. 178–80:

> Ah! when the means are gone that buy this praise,
> The breath is gone whereof this praise is made:
> Feast-won, fast-lost.

See also 3. 49–50 below where Christ calls the people 'a herd confus'd'.

422 Editors note the reminiscence of Spenser, *F.Q.* 2. 7. 11. 1–5, where Mammon tempts Guyon with riches, saying:

> Vaine glorious Elfe...doest not thou weet,
> That money can thy wantes at will supply?
> Sheilds, steeds, and armes, and all things for thee meet
> It can puruay in twinckling of an eye;
> And crownes and kingdomes to thee multiply;

and Horace, *Ep*. 1. 6. 36–7: 'Of course, a wife and dowry, credit and friends, birth and beauty, are the gift of Queen Cash';[29] and *S*. 2. 3. 94–6: 'For every-

---

[28] non ego ventosae plebis suffragia venor impensis cenarum et tritae munere vestis.

[29] scilicet uxorem cum dote fidemque et amicos et genus et formam regina Pecunia donat.

thing—virtue, reputation, honour, things divine and human—all are slaves to the beauty of wealth';[30] and Ovid, *F.* 1. 217-28: 'Nowadays money is the measure of worth; wealth brings honour and friends; the poor man is everywhere despised.'[31]

423-5 The history of Antipater the Edomite, or Idumean, and of his son, Herod the Great—certainly an unfortunate example to place before Christ—is most fully recorded in Josephus, *A.J.* 14. 1. 3-4, 5. 2, 6. 2, 7. 3; *B.J.* 1. 9. 3-5, 10. 5, 11. 4. The father, as a result of energetic and unscrupulous use of his great wealth, was by Julius Caesar appointed Procurator of Judaea. His notoriously violent son by the same means secured from the Roman Senate appointment as King of the Jews. Of his later acts of cruelty the most infamous was the slaughter of the innocents (Matt. 2. 16).

427-31 In placing wealth above virtue, Satan makes it a final good; but as Aristotle (*Nic. Eth.* 1. 5) maintains, wealth is useful only for something else, and therefore cannot be a final good. Moreover, as he also maintains (4. 1), wealth can be properly used only by a virtuous man. Plato (*Rep.* 9. 580; *Laws* 9. 870) insists that wealth is inferior to virtue because it appeals to the lowest element of the soul, the appetitive. He, then, who gives first place to wealth is selling his divine being to that which is most godless and detestable; he is enslaving the noblest part of himself to the worst part (*Rep.* 8. 550; *Laws* 5. 728; 8. 831). See also notes on 433-86 and 453-7 below.

429-30 Satan's claim to riches contradicts Hag. 2. 8, which reads: 'The silver is mine, and the gold is mine, saith the Lord of hosts.' As the possessor and dispenser of wealth Satan resembles Pluto, who is concerned with wealth (πλοῦτος), and whose name means 'the wealth-giver' (Liddell and Scott; Plato, *Crat.* 403; Lucian, *Tim.* 21; Cicero, *N.D.* 2. 26. 66). Cf. the following words addressed to Sir Guyon by Mammon in *F.Q.* 2. 7. 8. 5-8:

> Riches, renowme, and principality,
> Honour, estate, and all this worldes good,
> For which men swinck and sweat incessantly,
> Fro me do flow into an ample flood.

[30] omnis enim res,
virtus, fama, decus, divina, humanaque pulchris
divitiis parent.

[31] in pretio pretium nunc est; dat census honores,
census amicitias; pauper ubique iacet.

431 Cf. *Def I* (*Works* 7. 543): 'If you desire riches, liberty, peace, and empire, how much more excellent, how much more becoming yourselves would it be, resolutely to seek all these by your own virtue, industry, prudence, and valour, than under a royal despotism to hope for them in vain?'

432 See note on 378 above.

433–86 Christ answers Satan with the Platonic doctrine that the very existence of the state depends upon virtue which controls the conflicting passions and desires of the many (*Protag.* 322, 325–7; *I Alcib.* 134), and which provides the rulers with their power of governing (*Meno* 73). Plato also maintained that the state is not great by reason of wealth, to which it must give last place (*Laws* 3. 697; 5. 742–3). Aristotle (*Pol.* 4. 1) declared that 'it is not the virtues which are gained and guarded by external goods but these external goods by virtues.' Hughes ('Christ of *PR*', *SP* 35, 1938, 271) notes that substantially the same doctrine is expounded in the *Dialoghi d'amore* of Leo the Jew, who 'completes the thought with an allusion to the verse in Proverbs [16. 32] which says that "he that ruleth his spirit [is better] than he that taketh a city."' Cf. 466–72 below.

435 *ancient Empires.* For example Assyria, Babylon, the empire of Alexander, and Carthage.

439 *Gideon.* Although Gideon came of a poor family and was the least in his father's house, he obeyed the command of God and with three hundred men routed the army of the Midianites (Judges 6–7).

Jephtha. Driven from his father's house because he was the son of a harlot, and become a fugitive, Jephtha was recalled by the elders of Gilead to deliver his people from the Ammonites (Judges 11. 1–33). Mrs Lewalski (*Brief Epic*, p. 253), ever finding typology, sees Jephtha as exemplifying not only poverty but also a 'conception of kingship relevant to Christ's situation', since he had attained the judgeship only after being rejected by his own people and sacrificing his own flesh.

the Shepherd lad. When Goliath was challenging the army of Israel, and no man dared to accept the challenge, David, a youth who tended his father's sheep, killed him with a stone from his sling (1 Sam. 17. 14–54; Ps. 78. 70–1).

440-1 The kings of the house of David reigned in Judah for over three hundred years until Nebuchadnezzar extinguished the kingdom (2 Kings 25; *Camb. Anc. Hist.* 3. 400–2).

442 The angel Gabriel at the annunciation said of Christ (Luke 1. 32–3): 'The Lord God shall give unto him the throne of his father David: And he shall reign over the house of Jacob for ever; and of his kingdom there shall be no end.' For earlier prophecies of the perpetual Messianic kingdom, see Isa. 16. 5; Ezek. 34. 23–4; Amos 9. 11. See note on 1. 24–37 above.

443–9 In the rebuke which Christ here delivers to Satan, Hughes (p. 477) finds 'a key to Milton's treatment of the devil. In the typology of *Paradise Regained* Satan is an obvious parody of the epic hero of the poem, just as in *Paradise Lost* he parodies God's heavenly council with his parliament of devils in Pandemonium, Christ's rule over the angels "by merit" with his own dictatorial rule of the demons, and in general parodies the divine goodness by his own resolve to make evil his good.' In 'Christ of *PR*', *SP* 35 (1938), 266–7, Hughes finds the passages intelligible only in the light of Tasso's theory of heroic virtue, that is '" an excess and perfection of the good, something which has nothing to do with moderation, as the moral virtues have"'. Tasso treated the heroic virtue of the Romans as a shadow and figure of the divine love that Christ brought into the world. See Tasso, *Prose diverse*, ed. Guasti (Florence, 1875), 2. 200.

446–9 The four men here commended for their integrity belonged to the period of the Roman republic when the Romans were celebrated for their frugality and austere virtue (Polybius 6. 52–3, 56; 18. 35; Horace, *C.* 2. 15. 10–20; Sallust, *Cat.* 12–13; Juvenal 11. 77–116; Aulus Gellius 2. 24; Tacitus, *Ann.* 3. 54). J. P. Pritchard in *The Influence of the Fathers upon Milton with Especial Reference to Augustine* (unpublished Cornell dissertation, Ithaca, N.Y., 1925, pp. 110–11) notes an 'almost parallel' between the present passage and *Civ. D.* 5. 18, where Augustine praises the virtues of the ancient Romans, and cites as examples Torquatus, Camillus, Mucius, Curtius, the Decii, Pulvillus, Regulus, Valerius, Quintus Cincinnatus, and Fabricius. An even closer parallel is the following in Quintilian 12. 2. 29: 'But have any others ever more effectively taught fortitude, justice, faithfulness, temperance, frugality, contempt of pain and death than the Fabricii, Curii, Reguli, Decii, Mucii, and countless other [Romans]? For as the Greeks are rich in precepts, so the Romans, in what is the greater part, are rich in examples.'

Quintus. L. Quintus Cincinnatus was called from some rustic work on his little farm to deliver the Romans from the Aequians (Livy 3. 26–9; Cicero, *Senec.* 16. 56).

Fabricius. C. Fabricius Luscinus, who was renowned for his virtue, when sent upon an embassy to Pyrrhus, although he was poor, refused to accept all the latter's gifts and inducements to enter his service (Cicero, *Off.* 3. 22. 86; *De Orat.* 2. 66. 268; Claudian 3. 200-1 (1. 40); 8. 414-15 (1. 316). Aulus Gellius gives another notable example of Fabricius' contempt for riches. When envoys of the Samnites, in return for his kindness and generosity to them, offered him a great sum of money, he 'drew his open hands from his ears to his eyes, from them to his nose and mouth and thence to his throat and finally down to the lower part of his belly, and replied to the envoys that while he could restrain and control all those members which he had touched, he would never lack anything, and therefore could not accept money for which he had no use.'

Curius. M. Curius Dentatus, after defeating the Samnites, the Sabines, and Pyrrhus, gave to the Roman Republic all the booty that he had taken and retired to end his days in simple frugality on his farm (Cicero, *Senec.* 16. 55–6; Seneca, *Cons. Helv.* 10. 8; Aurelius Victor, *Vir. Ill.* 33; Claudian 8. 413 (1. 316).

Regulus. M. Atilius Regulus, who was captured by the Carthaginians in the First Punic War, was later, upon his promise to return, allowed to go with an embassy to Rome, where he persuaded the Senate to reject the Carthaginian terms. Despite all persuasions he returned to Carthage to be tortured to death (Cicero, *Off.* 3. 26. 99; Horace, *C.* 3. 5. 13–56; Seneca, *Cons. Helv.* 10. 7; Aurelius Victor, *Vir. Ill.* 40; Claudian 15. 78–9 (1. 104); Silius Italicus 6. 346–573).

453–7 For other contemptuous statements about riches by Milton, see *Patrem* 93–4; *Epistol* 4 (*Works* 12. 15); *PL* 1. 690–2. Cf. Mark 10. 23: 'How hardly shall they that have riches enter into the kingdom of God!'; Plato, *Rep.* 8. 550: 'There is such a gulf between riches and virtue that, when weighed as it were in the two scales of a balance, one of the two always falls as the other rises'; and Bacon, *Of Riches*: 'I cannot call riches better than the baggage of virtue.' Bacon may be echoing Seneca, *Ep.* 87. 11, where rich possessions are called *impedimenta*.

456 *aught may merit praise.* 'Aught, which' occurs in *PL* 8. 636, 'aught that' in 9. 347; here, then, 'which' or 'that' may have been omitted for metrical convenience only.

458 *for that.* See note on 1. 327 above.

460–5 Perhaps an echo of Shakespeare, *2 H. IV* 3. 1. 31: 'Uneasy lies the head that wears a crown'; and *H. V* 4. 1. 235–42:

Upon the King! Let us our lives, our souls,
Our debts, our careful wives,
Our children, and our sins, lay on the King!
We must bear all....What infinite heart's ease
Must kings neglect, that private men enjoy.

462–5 Milton repeatedly denies the divine right of kings, and insists that they derive their authority from the people to whom they are responsible. See *TKM* (*Works* 5. 10–12); *Def 1* 2 (7. 113); *Eikon* (5. 202). This is virtually the theory of kingship expressed in Plato, *States.* 301–2; Aristotle, *Pol.* 5. 6–7; Augustine, *Civ. D.* 4. 4; 19. 4; John of Salisbury, *Pol.* 4. 1; Aquinas, *De Regimine Principum* 1. 1; Hubert Languet (?), *Vindiciae Contra Tyrannos* (Edinburgh [Basel?], 1579), 3.

466–7 Editors note the reminiscence of Pr. 16. 32: 'he that ruleth his spirit [is better] than he that taketh a city'; and Horace, *C.* 2. 2. 9–12: 'You may have wider dominion by mastering a greedy spirit than if you joined Libya with distant Cadiz, and either Carthage served you alone';[32] and *S.* 2. 7. 83–6: 'Who then is free? The wise man who rules himself, whom neither poverty nor death nor bonds terrify, who resists his passions and scorns public honours.'[33] As Blakeney (p. 129) points out, Milton is expressing the Stoic doctrine of ἐγκράτεια, self-control, as it is stated for example in M. Aurelius 8. 41: 'The freehold of the mind no other man can contravene..."Once it is formed, a sphere remains round."'[34]

The bitter significance of Christ's statements for Satan appears if they are read in the light of earlier statements by Satan himself, notably his soliloquy in *PL* 4. 32–113, in which he admitted the anarchy, the hell, within him, ruled as he is not by reason but by lawless passion.

469–72 Abdiel has already told Satan in *PL* 6. 176–81 that

[32] latius regnes avidum domando
spiritum, quam si Libyam remotis
Gadibus iungas et uterque Poenus
serviat uni.

[33] quisnam igitur liber? sapiens, sibi, qui imperiosus,
quem neque pauperies neque mors neque vincula terrent,
responsare cupidinibus, contemnere honores
fortis.

[34] τὰ μέντοι τοῦ νοῦ ἴδια οὐδεὶς ἄλλος εἴωθεν ἐμποδίζειν·..."ὅταν γένηται σφαῖρος, κυκλοτερὴς μένει."

God and Nature bid the same,
When he who rules is worthiest, and excells
Them whom he governs. This is servitude,
To serve th' unwise, or him who hath rebelld
Against his worthier, as thine now serve thee,
Thy self not free, but to thy self enthrall'd.

473–80 See Christ's earlier statements in 1. 215–26 above. In *DocCh* 1. 15 (*Works* 15. 299–301) Milton writes: 'The pre-eminent excellency of Christ's kingdom over all others' is that 'he governs not the bodies of men alone, as the civil magistrate, but their minds and consciences, and that not by force and fleshly weapons, but by what the world esteems the weakest of all instruments.'

479 *force.* See note on 1. 219 above.

481–3 Cf. Seneca, *Thy.* 529: 'Wielding power is the work of chance, bestowing it the work of virtue.'[35] Editors suggest that Milton may here allude to the Roman Emperor Diocletian, who in A.D. 305 abdicated and withdrew to his native Dalmatia (Aurelius Victor, *Caes.* 39), or to the Emperor Charles V, who in 1555 abdicated and retired to a monastery (*Camb. Mod. Hist.* 2. 90), and to Christina of Sweden, who in 1654, when not yet thirty, gave up her kingdom (R. N. Bain, *Scandinavia*, Cambridge, 1905, pp. 226–7). In view of Milton's praise of Christina in *Def 2* (*Works* 8. 103–9, 193), an allusion to her is likely, if he was unaware of the almost incredible follies and extravagances of her later career. See Bain, pp. 218, 220, 225–6.

483 *magnanimous.* See note on 139 above.

[35] habere regnum casus est, virtus dare.

Book III

⁂

2–6 See note on 1. 37–43.

3 *convinc't.* Overcome in argument, proved to be wrong (*OED*), as in Job 32. 12; *Comus* 791.

4 *drift.* 'The conscious direction of action or speech to some end' (*OED*), as in *Animad* 2; *Tetr* (*Works* 3. 128; 4. 65, 143); Spenser, *F.Q.* 2. 1. 3. 4.

7–11 Satan here speaks the truth, but only with the ulterior intention of flattering. He characterizes Christ as an ideal hero of Renaissance Neoplatonism in whom there is an integrity of thought, word, and deed, a harmony of the whole man (Stein, *Heroic Knowledge*, p. 24).

10 *large heart.* Wisdom, as in 1 Kings 4. 29; *PL* 1. 444; 7. 486. Cf. Virgil, *G.* 4. 83: *ingentis animos.*

11 *the perfect shape.* The true form or absolute perfection of the thing, the Platonic 'idea' or pattern (Plato, *Rep.* 5. 476; 10. 596–7; *Parm.* 132). Cf. *Comus* 214–15; *PL* 4. 848; *Areop* (*Works* 4. 337): 'Truth...was a perfect shape most glorious to look on.' The shape (*forma*) of moral goodness, says Cicero (*Off.* 1. 5. 15), if it could be seen with the eye, would awaken a marvellous love of wisdom. In *De Christiana Religione* 23 (*Opuscula*, Venice, 1503, sig. h2), Ficino speaks of Christ as 'the divine idea itself of virtue manifest to human eyes' (*divina ipsa idea virtutum humanis oculis manifesta*).
    perfect. See note on 1. 83 above.

13–16 Urim and Thummim are mentioned in Exod. 28. 30; Lev. 8. 8; Num. 27. 21; Deut. 33. 8; 1 Sam. 28. 6 (cf. Philo, *Vit. Mos.* 2. 23. 112–13, 24. 123); but none of these passages explains the original significance of the words, or what the objects in the breastplate of the high priest were. But from 1 Sam. 14. 41–2 in the fuller Greek text, the most illuminating Biblical passage, it appears that they were two lots in some way used in divination, and closely connected, in a way no longer intelligible, with the equally mysterious ephod. The Geneva Bible (Exod. 23. 30), following Jewish tradition, explains Urim as signifying light and knowledge, and Thummim, perfection and holiness. See Ginzberg, *Legends* 3. 172; Hastings, *Dict.*, p. 955. From Joseph Mede, *Disc.* 36 (*Works*, London, 1677, p. 271) it also appears that they are traditionally regarded as an oracle. As appears from 1. 460 and 463 above, Milton regarded the pagan oracles as infernally inspired, but he can accept as authentic Urim and Thummim, Hebrew methods of divination.

15–16 *Seers... | Infallible.* The belief that seers, prophets (1 Sam. 9. 9) were infallible, men who knew and understood God (Jer. 9. 24), finds support in 2 Pet. 1. 21: 'For the prophecy came not in old time by the will of man: but holy men of God spake as they were moved by the Holy Ghost.' As Philo (*Quis Rerum Divinarum Haeres Sit* 53) expresses the belief, the prophet is but a passive instrument who, 'even when he seems to be speaking, really holds his peace, and his organs of speech...are wholly in the employ of Another, to shew forth what He wills.'

18 *conduct.* The leadership or command of an army, as in *PL* 1. 130; 6. 777; Spenser, *Gn.* 548.

19 *sustain.* 'Bear up against, withstand' (*OED*), like Lat. *sustinere*, as in *PL* 2. 209; 5. 904; 6. 423; 11. 302; *SA* 1258.

21–30 As in Spenser, *F.Q.* 2. 7, Guyon, after leaving the 'delve of Mammon', comes to the place of glory to be tempted by Philotime; and as in Fletcher, *C.V.* 2. 42–62, Christ, after other temptations, finally reaches the palace of Panglory, who presides over pleasures, avarice, and 'ambitious honour'; so is he now to be tempted with fame and glory. In endeavouring to induce Christ to use his 'God-like Vertues' to secure for himself worldly fame and glory, Satan in effect proposes that he make these virtues the slaves of glory. But thus to enslave them, as Augustine maintains in *Civ. D.* 5. 20, is no less shameful than to enslave them to bodily pleasure. Satan's argument is sophistical, nor is he adroit enough to conceal the sophistry. The fallacy lies in his statement that glory is the reward 'That sole excites to high attempts the flame / Of most erected Spirits.' Milton truly states the matter in *Lyc* 70–2:

> *Fame* is the spur that the clear spirit doth raise
> (That last infirmity of Noble mind)
> To scorn delights, and live laborious dayes.

Fame, he admits, is a spur, but not the only one. Moreover it excites the 'Noble mind', not the 'most erected Spirits', that is the noblest; and even of the 'Noble mind' it is an infirmity. Cf. also *Def 2* (*Works* 8. 218–19).

22 *Affecting.* Aiming at, desiring, like Lat. *affectare*, as in *PL* 3. 206; 6. 421; 12. 81.

23 *savage.* 'Uncultivated, wild.' '*Obs.*' (*OED*).

27–8 *most temper'd pure | Ætherial.* Of most pure heavenly temper. Jerram (p. 123) remarks that '"Pure-ethereal" is like "sudden-bold," "deep-contemplative", in Shakespeare, and perhaps "massy-proof" in *IlPen* 158. *Temper* = "constitution," from the idea of mixing in proportion (Greek τέμ-νω; Lat. *tem-pus*, *tem-perare*, &c.).'

27 *erected.* 'High-souled, noble'. '*Obs.*' (*OED*), like Lat. *erectus*, as in Quintilian 11. 1. 16 and Tacitus, *Agr.* 4. The present passage is no doubt intended as an ironic echo of *PL* 1. 679, where Mammon is called 'the least erected Spirit that fell | From heav'n.'

28 See *Lyc* 72, quoted in the note on 21–30 above.

31–4 Alexander the Great, son of Philip of Macedon, in 334 B.C. embarked upon his victorious wars in Asia, and in 330, at the age of twenty-six, had included in his conquests the Persian empire founded by Cyrus (Arrian, *Anab.* 1. 17 ff.; 3. 8 ff.; Q. Curtius 5. 1 ff.).

34–5 Scipio Africanus in 210 B.C., when twenty-four—or according to Polybius 10. 6, twenty-seven—was given command of the Roman armies in the war against the Carthaginians in Spain. Eight years later he defeated them near Zama in Africa, and brought to an end the Second Punic War (Livy 30. 30 ff.; Polybius 14–15). See also 101–2 below and 2. 199–200 above; *Pro se Def* (*Works* 9. 5). Scipio, one of the greatest Romans, excelled perhaps only by Julius Caesar, is for Milton the model of ancient heroism, the exemplar of the balance of action and contemplation, a man who explicitly rejected Satan's idea of glory (Kermode, 'Milton's Hero', *RES* n.s. 4, 1953, 320–3).

35–6 Cn. Pompeius in 65 B.C. defeated Mithridates, King of Pontus, and subjugated his kingdom. Upon his return to Rome he was voted a triumph, although at the time of the Mithridatic War he was forty-seven. See Dio Cassius 36. 48 ff. Seneca (*Ep.* 94. 64) mentions him as an example of 'insane love of false glory'.[1]

---

[1] insanus amor magnitudinis falsae.

39–42 Julius Caesar had declared that he would rather be first in a wretched, barbarian village in the Alps than second at Rome, and when in 68 B.C., aged thirty, he was quaestor in Spain, after reading the history of Alexander, he burst into tears. When asked why he wept, he replied: 'Do you not think it matter for sorrow that while Alexander at my age was king of so many peoples, I have as yet accomplished no brilliant success?' (Plutarch, *Caesar* 11). According to Seneca (*Ep.* 94. 65), it was 'renown, ambition, and admitting no limit to pre-eminence over all other men'[2] that impelled Caesar to ruin himself and the state. Cf. *HistBr* (*Works* 10. 34).

43 *calmly.* See note on 2. 378 above.

44 See 2. 412–31 above.

47–8 Hughes (p. 506) notes that 'Milton translates Seneca's question (*Ep.* cii, 19): "What distinguishes clear renown (*claritas*) from glory? Glory consists in the judgment of the many; renown in that of the good."'

In these lines and in 60–4 and 69–70 below, and in *Lyc* 64–84, the distinction is drawn between worldly fame and glory and true glory, which is the approbation of God. The distinction is an old one. Plato taught that since it is the base, passionate element of the soul that is bent upon ruling and securing fame (*Rep.* 9. 581), the life of ambition is inferior to that of philosophy (*Phaedrus* 256). Cicero (*Tusc.* 3. 2. 3–4), while he believed that good men ought not to scorn the glory which consists in the universal praise of good men, who can truly judge pre-eminent virtue, thought that popular fame, because it is hasty and ill-considered, and most often commends sinful acts, brings honesty itself into discredit by assuming a false semblance of it. Among the ancients as the worth of all things came to be questioned, philosophers, especially the Stoics, taught that it is a duty to despise worldly fame. See Cicero, *Off.* 1. 19. 62; *Som. Scip.* 6–7; Tacitus, *Hist.* 4. 6; Seneca, *Ep.* 43; 79. 18; 94. 64–6; M. Aurelius 4. 3, 19. The pagan tradition was in time reinforced by Christian teaching based on such passages of Scripture as 1 Cor. 3. 21; 10. 31; Gal. 5. 26; and that teaching was expounded, as in Origen, *Cels.* 7. 24 (Migne, *Pat. Gr.* 11. 1455); Augustine, *De Pat.* 3 (Migne, *Pat. Lat.* 40. 612); Thomas à Kempis, *Imitat.* 1. 3. 6. For the Middle Ages and the Renaissance probably the most influential expressions of this unfavourable attitude toward the glory of the world were the *De Contemptu Mundi* of Innocent III—of which nearly five hundred manuscripts are extant—and the *Secretum*, often called the *De Contemptu Mundi*, of Petrarch. How

---

[2] Gloria et ambitio et nullus supra ceteros eminendi modus.

influential may have been Erasmus' early work with the same title I am unable to say. In the 17th century Milton was far from alone in his contempt for popular fame, as is evident from Grotius, *Annot. Evang.* (*Op. Th.* 2. 453); Donne, *Second Ann.*; Fulke Greville, *An Inquisition upon Fame and Honour* (*Certain Learned and Elegant Works*, London, 1633, pp. 68–9); Joseph Hall, *Med.* 3 (*Works* 3. 88). As Miss Mahood (*P. & H.*, p. 235) observes, Christ's present speech is Milton's maturest and most complete statement on the problem of fame. His final feeling is that the desire for fame, 'like other human-ist impulses', is divinely bestowed, but whether it exalts or debases the mind depends upon 'whether it is given a Godward or selfward direction'.

Hughes ('Christ of *PR*', *SP* 35, 1938, 257) is convinced that '*Contemptus mundi* was never carried further by medieval pope or doctor of the Church than it was by Milton in this poem.' Blondel (p. 60), less positive, believes that Milton inclines in favour of an ascetic contempt for the world. But Stein (*Heroic Knowledge*, p. 131), I think, is surely right in maintaining that '*contemptus*, religious decorum tells us, could be carried further by no one than by the protagonist of this poem. But Milton did not interpret the decorum so, and the poem he wrote is consciously organized in another direction. Milton is not trying to declare the business of the world bankrupt. By inveigling, Satan has got control of some of the world's enterprises, but his power is "usurped," and not complete; nor is the world incorrigibly rotten.' If it were so rotten, would there be any point in writing about regaining Paradise, since Paradise, be it remembered, is in *this* world, it is not heaven?

49–56 The view of the people as a thoughtless rabble is much the same as that expressed by Plato, for example in *Protag.* 353, where he asks why we should trouble ourselves about the opinions of the many who say whatever happens to occur to them; and in *Rep.* 6. 493, where he calls the people 'the great brute'. Cf. *Crito* 44, 47–8. Cf. also Christ's denunciation of the scribes and Pharisees as a 'generation of vipers' in Matt. 23, one of the sternest denunciations ever uttered. And on Christ's sternness, see note on 1. 406 above.

56 Carey (p. 1118) notes an echo of Jonson, *Cynthia's Revels* 3. 3. 15–16: 'Of such / To be disprais'd is the most perfect praise'—itself an echo of Seneca, *De Remediis Fortuitorum* 7. 1: *Malis displicere laudari est.* The *De Remediis*, not included in all editions of Seneca, and probably a late abstract of a lost work, may be found in *Senecae Opera*, ed. Fred. Haase (Leipzig, 1886), 3. 446–57, and in *Revue de philologie* 12 (1888), 118–27.

59 Cf. Seneca, *Ep.* 102. 11–12: 'Again does renown need many votes? It can be satisfied with the judgment of one good man; it is one good man who decides that we are good....Glory, I understand, is more widespread, for it demands the judgment of many men.'[3] Seneca further maintains that to be well thought of by one good man amounts to being approved by all, for they will all think alike.

60–4 See note on 47–8 above. Cf. Seneca, *Prov.* 2. 9: 'But behold! there is a spectacle worthy of the regard of God when he contemplates his own work. Behold! here is a contest worthy of God—a brave man matched against ill fortune, and doubly so if his also was the challenge',[4] and Joseph Hall, *Med.* 3. 95 (*Works* 8. 88): 'I will not care whether I be known, or remembered, or forgotten amongst men, if my name and good actions may live with God, in the records of eternity.'

62 *divulges*. Proclaims (a person, etc.) publicly (*OED*), like Lat. *divulgare*, as in *SA* 1248.

64–7 Cf. Job 1. 8: 'Hast thou considered my servant Job, that there is none like him in the earth, a perfect and an upright man, one that feareth God, and escheweth evil?'

69–70 See note on 47–8 above.

71–83 The same thought is expressed in *PL* 11. 689–99, where Michael informs Adam that one of the signs of the progressive deterioration of mankind will be the honour shown to those who conquer by violence, the so-called

> Patrons of Mankind, Gods, and Sons of Gods,
> Destroyers rightlier call'd and Plagues of men.

For Milton's views on the use of violence, see note on 1. 219 above. In *Milton's Literary Milieu* (Chapel Hill, N.C., 1939, p. 168) G. W. Whiting notes that similar views are expressed by Burton and many others whom he quotes in *Democritus to the Reader* (*Anat.*, ed. Shilleto, London, 1893, 1. 60, 64–5) in an extended indictment of war and those who wage war, who, though commonly honoured among men, deserve only the most opprobrious names. If in the present passage a contemporary allusion is intended, it may be to the subjugation of the Netherlands by Louis XIV in 1667. See *Camb. Mod. Hist.* 5. 39.

[3] Deinde claritas desiderat multa suffragia? Potest et unius boni viri iudicio esse contenta; unus nos bonus bonos iudicat...Gloriam...latius fusam intellego, consensum enim multorum exigit.

[4] Ecce spectaculum dignum ad quod respiciat intentus operi suo deus; ecce par deo dignum, vir fortis cum fortuna mala compositus, utique si et provocavit.

74 *Worthies*. Heroes, especially of antiquity (*OED*), but here 'rather in the modern depreciatory sense', as Jerram (p. 125) observes.

81–3 One of the most famous examples of the deification of a king was that of Alexander the Great (Arrian, *Anab.* 7. 23, 26; Aelian, *V.H.* 2. 19; Plutarch, *Alex.* 54; Herodian 4. 8; Dio Cassius 78. 7). But in the ancient world the practice was common (M. L. Strack, *Die Dynastie der Ptolomäer*, Berlin, 1897, pp. 112–13; Hastings, *Encyc. Rel. Eth.* 4. 525–32; *Camb. Anc. Hist.* 7. 13–22). Ptolemy I received the name Σωτήρ, Deliverer, and Demetrius was worshipped at Sicyon (Diodorus Siculus 20. 100, 102–3); Julius Caesar was by law placed among the gods as *Divus Iulus* (Dio Cassius 43. 14, 45; 47. 18; Appian, *B.C.* 1. 4. 44; 2. 20. 148; Suetonius, *Caesar* 88); and *Divus Augustus* marked the beginning of the emperor cult among the Romans (Dio Cassius 56. 46; Suetonius, *Aug.* 97, 100; Virgil, *G.* 1. 25–42; Ovid, *F.* 1. 608). See G. Boissier, *La Religion romaine d'Auguste aux Antonins*, 2nd ed. (Paris, 1878), 1. 109–220; Roscher, *Lexikon* (s.v. Kaiserkultus); Lily R. Taylor, *The Divinity of the Roman Emperors* (Middletown, Conn., 1931), pp. 58–99, 142–80.

84–7 Alexander the Great was reputed to be the son of Zeus (Plutarch, *Alex.* 2; Strabo 17. 1. 43), Romulus, the son of Mars (Livy 1. 4. 2; Plutarch, *Rom.* 2). Alexander by excessive drinking brought on a fever which caused his untimely death (Plutarch, *Alex.* 75; Arrian, *Anab.* 7. 25–6). Among differing accounts of the death of Romulus, one is that in a violent storm he was caught up into the sky and never seen again; another is that he was murdered by the Roman senators (Livy 1. 16; Plutarch, *Rom.* 27).

86 *Rowling in brutish vices*. Cf. *Comus* 77: 'To roule with pleasure in a sensual stie.' Editors note that 'to roll' (*volutare*) in vice is an expression used by Cicero in *Fam.* 9. 3. 1; *Har. Res.* 20. 42; *Her.* 4. 13. 19.

deform'd. 'Morally ugly, base' (Lockwood, *Lexicon*). Cf. Donne, *First Ann.* 336; *Goodfriday* 40.

91–2 Cf. 2 Pet. 1. 6: 'And to knowledge temperance; and to temperance patience.'

94 On the land of Uz, see note on 1. 369 above. Milton apparently knew of the uncertainty among Jewish scholars about Job and the time at which he lived. According to Maimonides (*Guide for the Perplexed*, tr. M. Friedländer, 2nd ed., London, 1904, 3. 22), 'Those who assume that he has existed, and that the book is historical, are unable to determine when and where Job lived.' See also *Jewish Encyc.* 7. 193.

95 *patient Job.* See note on 1. 426.

96-9 See 1. 469–74 above and 4. 274, 293 below. Highly laudatory references to Socrates by ancient writers are numerous, as for example in the works of Epictetus, Seneca, and Marcus Aurelius. The present passage may be reminiscent of the words of the last-named writer, who says (8. 3): 'What are Alexander and Gaius and Pompeius to Diogenes and Heraclitus and Socrates?' Similar references occur in patristic writings, as in Justin Martyr, 2 *Apol.* 10 (Migne, *Pat. Gr.* 6. 460–1); Augustine, *Civ. D.* 8. 3. Erasmus in *Colloquia Familiaria* (*Opera Omnia*, Leyden, 1703–6, 1. 683) could say *Sancte Socrates ora pro nobis*; and Montaigne in *Essays* 3. 2 (tr. E. J. Trechmann, London, 1927, 2. 263) saw in Alexander the Great only a conqueror of the world, but in Socrates a man who could 'lead a human life...a much more general, more important, and more legitimate art'.

In *Rep.* 6. 491–2 Plato represents Socrates as explaining the various inducements which lead to the deterioration of philosophical natures. They are distracted by their own virtues, by the ordinary goods of life, by the opinion of the world, and finally by the compulsion of attainder, or confiscation, or death. In the present state of governments, if the philosophical nature is to be saved at all, it must be 'by the power of God'. In Platonic terms, then, Christ is the philosopher saved by divine power, as were Job and Socrates, for the pursuit of true fame and glory.

101 *young African.* See note on 34–5 above.

103-4 Jerram (p. 126) observes that the thought here expressed 'is not universally true, even when justified by the addition "the *man* at least." A man often gets praised for actions which benefit others, though they be done from unworthy motives. Still there is a *tendency* in mankind to refuse the "verbal reward" to those whom they know [to] have been actuated solely by the desire of praise; hence it is true that in the long run the most self-forgetful are likely to be best remembered. St. Augustine has said, "vis possidere terram? vide ne possidearis a terra."'

104 *his.* Refers to 'deed'. See note on 1. 82 above.

106 Cf. John 8. 50: 'I seek not mine own glory'; and *DocCh* 1. 5 (*Works* 14. 339): 'His glory, even in his divine nature before the foundation of the world, was not self-derived, but given by the love of the Father'.

107 Cf. John 5. 31–2: 'If I bear witness of myself, my witness is not true.

There is another that beareth witness of me; and I know that the witness which he witnesseth of me is true.' Cf. also John 7. 18; 13. 32; 16. 14.

109–20 Satan argues that since Christ is the Son of God, he ought to seek glory as his Father seeks it, as an end in itself. The fallacies of the argument Christ exposes in lines 122–44. It is bitterly ironic that insatiable desire for 'Glory above his Peers' led Satan to rebel against God, and to lose all.

109 *slight.* See note on 1. 203 above, and cf. 4. 155 below.

111 In discussing the creation in *DocCh* 1. 7 (*Works* 15. 5, 15) Milton states that God 'produced every thing that exists... for the manifestation of the glory of his power and goodness', and he cites as his authorities Gen. 1. 31; 1 Tim. 4. 4; Ps. 19. 1; Pr. 16. 4; Acts 14. 15; 17. 24; Rom. 1. 20. Cf. *PL* 3. 162–4.

111–12 *all things | Orders and governs.* Of God's government of the world, Milton writes in *DocCh* 1. 8 (*Works* 15. 55) that he 'regards, preserves, and governs the whole of creation with infinite wisdom and holiness according to the conditions of his decree.' As authority for this view he cites, among other passages of Scripture, Ps. 33. 15; Jer. 32. 19; Deut. 8. 3; Job 7. 20; 14. 5. Cf. 1. 236–7 above, and the seventh answer of the *Westminster Shorter Catechism*: God 'for his own glory... hath foreordained whatsoever comes to pass.'

113 See Job 38. 7; Ps. 148. 2; Neh. 9. 6; Isa. 6. 3; Rev. 4. 8–11. Cf. *PL* 3. 372–82; 7. 182–8; *DocCh* 1. 9 (*Works* 15. 101).

114–15 Of numerous passages of Scripture enjoining man to give glory to God, the following may be cited: 1 Chron. 16. 29; Ps. 29. 1–2; Isa. 42. 12; 1 Cor. 10. 31; Rom. 11. 36; Rev. 14. 7. On such passages as these is based the first answer of the *Westminster Shorter Catechism*: 'Man's chief end is to glorify God and to enjoy him for ever.'

115–19 Satan's words may be reminiscent of Rom. 1. 14, where Paul says, 'I am debtor... both to the wise, and to the unwise.' Satan wishes subtly to insinuate a defence of the pagans essentially the same as that of Themistius, who in *Or.* 12 argues that God is well pleased with the diversity of religions whereby all men may the more revere his majesty. Cf. Sozomen, *Hist. Eccles.* 6. 36 (Migne, *Pat. Gr.* 67. 1401–4).

119 *Barbarous.* Equivalent to βάρβαρος, 'foreign, non-Hellenic' (*OED*). In *States.* 262 Plato divides all men into Greeks and barbarians. In the N.T., however, as in Col. 3. 11, the Jews became a third division.

121 *fervently.* See note on 2. 378 above. Jerram (p. 127) comments: 'lit. "glowing" with the thought of God's goodness, and eager to vindicate his honour.'

122–44 Satan has argued that glory was God's *sole* end in creating all things, and that he requires glory from all his creatures. Christ exposes the sophistical distortion of truth in this argument. God created all things *not* only to achieve glory, but also to express his goodness, and to impart it to all men. The only return, the only expression of gratitude, for his goodness which men can render is to glorify God. But man himself, sinful as he is, has neither right nor claim to glory; nevertheless God, as an act of grace, does glorify those who seek his glory, not their own.

122–6 Cf. *PL* 4. 412–15:

> Needs must the power
> That made us, and for us this ample World
> Be infinitly good, and of his good
> As liberal and free as infinite;

and 7. 170–3:

> Though I uncircumscrib'd my self retire,
> And put not forth my goodness, which is free
> To act or not, Necessitie and Chance
> Approach not mee, and what I will is Fate;

and *DocCh* 1. 7 (*Works* 15. 5): 'Creation is that act whereby God the Father produced every thing that exists by his Word and Spirit, that is, by his Will, for the manifestation of the glory of his power and goodness.'

In opposition to such cosmic determinism as Spinoza propounds in his *Ethics*, Milton tenaciously adheres to the orthodox doctrine that the creative act of God was voluntary. The doctrine begins with Plato, who in *Tim.* 29–30 explains that the supreme soul, god, is all good and completely free of envy; he desires as far as possible to communicate his goodness to all things so that they may be like him; and so his creation of the cosmos is an outpouring of his goodness. Cf. Philo, *De Opificio Mundi* 5; Plotinus, *Enn.* 5. 2. 1–2. See C. Ritter, *Platon* (Munich, 1910–23), 2. 323–4, 746; A. E. Taylor, *A Commentary on Plato's Timaeus* (Oxford, 1928), pp. 75–9.

After it was adopted by Christian theologians, the doctrine was stated again and again through the centuries, as by Aquinas in *Sum. Th.* 1. 44. 4, who writes that God in creating all things 'intends only to communicate his own perfection, which is his goodness. And every creature intends to achieve its own perfection, which is the likeness of the divine perfection and goodness. Therefore divine goodness is the end of all things';[5] and by Boethius, *C.P.* 3. metr. 9. 4–9: 'Who to your work were moved by no external cause, but by a sweet desire, wherein is no envy; your goodness moving you to give each thing its grace, you take the forms of all the creatures from the highest patterns. From your fair mind you fashion the world fair like yourself. Thus perfect yourself, you frame the whole perfect in each part';[6] and by Dante, *Parad.* 7. 64–6: 'The divine goodness, which spurns all envy from itself, burning within itself, shoots forth such sparkles that it unfolds the eternal beauties';[7] and by E. Stillingfleet in *Origines Sacrae* (London, 1663), 3. 2. 7: 'we assert, that it was the *communication* of this *Divine goodness* which gave *being* to the *world*; but withal we acknowledge *God* to bee an *Agent infinitely wise* and *free*, who dispenseth this goodness of his in such a way and manner as is best pleasing to himself, though ever *agreeable* to his *Nature*.' See A. S. P. Woodhouse, 'Notes on Milton's Views of Creation', *PQ* 28 (1949), 213–14. But concerning Plato's and Milton's difficulties in completely avoiding determinism and in reconciling the doctrine of a God of over-flowing goodness with that of a self-sufficient God, see Arthur O. Lovejoy, *The Great Chain of Being* (Cambridge, Mass., 1948), pp. 160–2, 351–3.

122 *his word.* The doctrine that all things were produced by an utterance (ῥῆμα), the 'omnific word' of God, rests upon Gen. 1. 3; Ps. 39. 9; Heb. 1. 3; 11. 2; 2 Pet. 3. 5. Cf. *PL* 7. 163–4, 217; *DocCh* 1. 7 (*Works* 15. 7–13).

126–9 These lines, ironically enough, almost repeat Satan's own admission in *PL* 4. 46–9:

> What could be less then to afford him praise,
> The easiest recompence, and pay him thanks,
> How due!

[5] [Deus] intendit solum communicare suam perfectionem, quae est eius bonitas. Et unaquaeque creatura intendit consequi suam perfectionem, quae est similitudo perfectionis et bonitatis divinae. Sic ergo divina bonitas est finis rerum omnium.

[6] Quem non externae pepulerunt fingere causae
  Materiae fluitantis opus, uerum insita summi
  Forma boni liuore carens, tu cuncta superno
  Ducis ab exemplo, pulchrum pulcherrimus ipse
  Mundum mente gerens similique in imagine formans
  Perfectasque iubens perfectum absoluere partes.

[7] La divina bontà, che da sè sperne
  Ogni livore, ardendo in sè sfavilla
  Si, che dispiega le bellezze eterne.

130-5 Cf. *Comus* 775-8.

134-6 Implied here is the doctrine of original sin, the original depravity of the human mind and its propensity to sin engendered in us by our first parents (Hastings, *Encyc. Rel. Eth.* 9. 558-62), various interpretations of which Milton discusses in *DocCh* 1. 11 (*Works* 15. 193-9). See Maurice Kelley, *Argument*, pp. 143-50.

137-41 These lines imply the terrible condemnation of Satan's own sin against God, a condemnation which he recognizes, and which for the moment gives him pause.

137-9 Adam and Eve in their fall were guilty not only of unbelief, disobedience, and gluttony, but also of ingratitude. Cf. *PL* 3. 96-9; *DocCh* 1. 11 (*Works* 15. 181-3).

138 *recreant.* 'False, apostate', from O.F. *recroire*, Med. Lat. *recredere*, to surrender or give up one's cause. According to *OED* it was 'a term of the greatest opprobrium'. It is so used by Spenser in *F.Q.* 1. 4. 41. 4; 5. 6. 37. 4.

140-1 Cf. *DocCh* 2. 4 (*Works* 17. 117).

142-4 Cf. *PL* 6. 726-9.

146 *had not to answer.* Jerram (p. 128) notes that this expression is 'like "*non habeo dicere*," οὐκ ἔχω λέγειν.'

147-8 Cf. *PL* 1. 38-9; 2. 426-9; 6. 381-4.

150-80 Satan now tempts Christ as a descendant of David (see notes on 1. 24-37 and 240-1 above) to gain control of the earthly kingdom that is his by right, and thus to free his people from servitude to pagan Rome. To this seemingly altruistic proposal in itself there is no objection; moreover in view of the passionate desire of the Jews to be free from Roman rule, it is shrewdly designed to appeal to Christ, a Jew.

152-3 Cf. Luke 1. 32: 'the Lord God shall give unto him the throne of his father David.'

154 *By Mothers side thy Father.* Although the genealogies of Christ in Matt. 1. 1-17 and Luke 3. 23-38 trace his descent from David through Joseph, that in Luke has been supposed to relate to Mary rather than to Joseph; and the words 'of the house of David' in Luke 1. 27 have been interpreted as referring to her. The reason for this view, maintained by Justin Martyr in *Dial. Tryph.*

100 (Migne, *Pat. Gr.* 6. 709), by Augustine in *Faustum* 23 (Migne, *Pat. Lat.* 42. 468–72), is that, if Mary were not of the family of David, her son conceived by the Holy Ghost could not be of the seed of David. In *Sum. Th.* 3. 31. 2 Aquinas argues, first, that Joseph, though not Christ's father by fleshly union with Mary, would be called father even of an adopted son; secondly, that in Scripture it is not customary to trace descent in the female line; and finally that Joseph and Mary were of the same family. With this last explanation Calvin in *Inst.* 2. 13. 3 and Grotius in *Annot. Evang.* (*Op. Th.* 2. 1, 339, 348) agree. In *Nov. Test.*, Erasmus, at the end of a long note on Luke 3. 23, concludes that the differing views of the genealogy arise from a failure to distinguish between descent in a natural and in a legal sense. Diodati in *Pious Annotations*, Luke 3. 23, arrives at virtually the same conclusion.

155–9 The following is a summary of the account in Tacitus, *Hist.* 5. 9, of Roman rule of the Jews in the time of Tiberius: the first Roman who subdued the Jews was Pompey, in 68 B.C. During the Roman civil wars, Pacorus, a Parthian prince, took possession of Judaea, but after he was put to death by Ventidius, the Parthians were driven beyond the Euphrates. The Jews were again subdued by Gnaeus Sosius in 38 B.C. Antony made Herod the Great King of the Jews, and Augustus increased Herod's power. After the death of Herod, Simon, with the authority of Augustus, made himself king, but was punished by Quintilius Varus, Governor of Syria. The Jews were again repressed, their kingdom divided and given to Herod's three sons. As we learn from Josephus, *A.J.* 18. 1. 1 and *B.J.* 2. 8. 1, Judaea in A.D. 6, when added to the province of Syria, lost whatever independence it had possessed, and thereafter was ruled by Roman procurators. See 1. 217 above and note.

159–60 Although in *Hist.* 5. 9 Tacitus reports that in the reign of Tiberius all was quiet in Judaea, the accounts of Josephus in *A.J.* 18. 3 and *B.J.* 2. 9. 2–4, although he may be a hostile witness, indicate that Roman rule was harsh and caused much discontent, as it had in the time of Augustus.

160–2 Josephus records various Roman violations of the temple and of Jewish law: that Pompey entered the holy of holies in the temple, which only the high priest might enter (*A.J.* 14. 4. 4); that Crassus carried away the gold that was in the holy of holies (14. 7. 1); that Herod introduced games every fifth year in honour of Augustus (15. 8. 1); and that Pilate, violating the second commandment of the Decalogue, brought into Jerusalem busts of the Roman emperors (18. 3. 1).

163 *Antiochus.* About 100 B.C. Antiochus Epiphanes, King of Syria, captured and pillaged Jerusalem (1 Macc. 1. 21–4), and, in an effort to suppress Judaism, tried to compel the Jews to offer swine's flesh upon the altar, and to keep their children uncircumcised. Many who disobeyed he put to death (Josephus, *B.J.* 1. 1. 2). See next note.

165–70 The story of Judas, surnamed Maccabaeus, the Hammer (*Encyc. Bibl.* 3. 2850), which Milton summarizes, is told with minor variations in 1 Macc. 2–9 and in Josephus, *B.J.* 1. 1. 3–6 and *A.J.* 12. 6–11. After the death of his father Mattathias, under whom revolt against Antiochus had begun, Judas became the most successful champion of the Jews; and having defeated their enemies, he achieved their virtual independence. Finally he formed a league of friendship with the Romans, but shortly thereafter was killed in a battle with the Syrians.

166 Cf. 1 Macc. 5. 24, 28: 'Judas Maccabaeus also and his brother Jonathan went over Jordan and travelled three days' journey into the wilderness.... Hereupon Judas and his host turned suddenly by the way of the wilderness unto Bosora.'

170 *Modin.* Although the city of Modin is frequently mentioned in the books of the Maccabees, its exact location is unknown (Gilbert, *G.D.*, p. 194).

171 *Kingdom.* See note on 2. 36 above.
 let move. Equivalent to a Latin jussive subjunctive, *moveat.* Cf. 4. 223 below.

173 *Occasions forelock.* Occasion or Opportunity (καιρός) appears very frequently in literature, as in Ausonius, *Epigr.* 33; Phaedrus, *Fab.* 5. 8; *Greek Anth.* 16. 275; Rabelais, *Garg.* 1. 37; Erasmus, *Adagia* (*Tempestive*); Bacon, *Nov. Org.* 1. 121; Spenser, *F.Q.* 2. 4. 3–16; Shakespeare, *Oth.* 3. 1. 50. The epigram in the *Greek Anthology* is especially noteworthy, since many Renaissance writers, among them Giraldi, Politian, Machiavelli, and More, commented on or imitated it (James Hutton, *The Greek Anthology in Italy*, Ithaca, N.Y., 1935, p. 645). The same epigram was probably the inspiration for the many emblems in which Occasion appears, notably that of Andrea Alciati in *Emblematum Libellus* (Paris, 1540, sig. Bii^v). Whether represented as male or female, Occasion's characteristic features are winged feet and a head bald save for a lock of hair hanging over the forehead which can be seized only by those who meet Occasion face to face.

174 As Carey (p. 1123) notes, Satan here changes the meaning of 'occasion' to 'reason, cause', a meaning well established in the 17th century.

175 After Christ had driven the money-changers from the temple, 'his disciples remembered that it was written, The zeal of thine house hath eaten me up' (John 2. 17).

176 See note on 155–9 above.

177 See note on 1. 261 above.

178 *thy endless raign.* See notes on 1. 24–37 and 240–1 above.

182–202 This whole speech, in which Christ rejects the temptation to make himself King of the Jews, the heroic action of which he had already thought (see 1. 215–20 above), is an elaboration upon John 2. 4: 'mine hour is not yet come.' The deliverance of his people is a worthy end; but if he is to accomplish it, he must await God's guidance. Thus he again maintains his humility. See also 396–7, 433 below.

182–3 An allusion to Eccles. 3. 1: 'To every thing there is a season, and a time to every purpose under the heaven.'

183 *Truth.* 'The Scriptures as setting forth the truth' (Lockwood, *Lexicon*), the authority to which Satan has just appealed, and which Christ now turns against him.

184–5 See notes on 178 and 1. 24–37, 240–1 above.

187 Editors quote Christ's words to his disciples in Acts 1. 7: 'It is not for you to know the times or the seasons, which the Father hath put in his own power.'

188–94 These lines are reminiscent of the prophecies interpreted as foretelling the sufferings of the Messiah, notably Isa. 50. 6; 53. 5–11; cf. Acts 3. 18; 1 Pet. 1. 11. The belief that virtue is attained through trial by adversity, to which Milton attached the greatest importance, as is evident from *Areop* (*Works* 4. 311); *PL* 12. 569–71; and *PR* as a whole, is common to both Christian and Stoic teaching, as appears from 1 Thes. 2. 4; 1 Pet. 1. 7; Rev. 2. 10; Seneca, *Prov.* 4; *Cons. Marc.* 1.

195–6 *who first | Well hath obey'd.* From Milton's concept of obedience (see note on 1. 1–7 above) it logically follows that he is best fitted to rule who has first learned to obey, a principle which Christ enunciated in Matt. 20. 26, and which Milton believed that Cromwell exemplified. See *Def 2* (*Works* 8. 215). But the principle was already old, for, as Blakeney (p. 136) notes, it occurs in a saying of Solon: ἄρχε πρῶτον μαθὼν ἄρχεσθαι. It is emphasized also in Plato, *Laws* 4. 715; Aristotle, *Pol.* 4. 14. 6; Cicero, *Leg.* 3. 2. 5; Seneca, *De Ira* 2. 15. 4.

199 See notes on 1. 24–37 and 240–1 above.

201–2 The allusion to the rising and setting of opposite stars continues the figure of Christ as 'our Morning Star then in his rise' in 1. 294 above. Christ's words here, like those in 1. 356, clearly disprove the too common assumption that throughout *PR* Christ is concealing his identity from Satan. See note on 1. 91 above.

203 See note on 1. 37–43 above.
   inly. See note on 1. 228 above.

204–50 Christ's unshaken, patient humility and the horrible doom foretold in the closing words provoke from Satan a 'fervent' reply of exciting dramatic effect, since it suddenly suggests that a real break in the contest may be about to take place. Satan speaks with the reckless weariness born of despair. Since the worst is all that he can expect, whether Christ reigns or not, he would even be glad to reach that end and be done. But then rallying himself with the compulsiveness of his evil nature, he prepares for another temptation. See Stein, *Heroic Knowledge*, pp. 83–8.

204–22 With these lines compare Satan's famous soliloquy in *PL* 4. 32–113.

204–5 Cf. *PL* 3. 131–2: 'Man therefore shall find grace, / The other none.'

206–11 In proud impenitence Satan declared in *PL* 4. 108–10:

> So farwel Hope, and with Hope farwel Fear,
> Farwel Remorse: all Good to me is lost;
> Evil be thou my Good.

Though the pride with which these words were spoken is now hypocritically concealed, and though, after ages of devotion to evil, Satan must more fully understand the meaning of his damning admissions, he is ever impenitent, and declares that there 'is left no fear', only to contradict himself in line 220 below with the admission that he dreads God's ire 'more then the fire of Hell'.

212–14 Satan admits that his crime, whatever it may have been, will be condemned for what it was, and that he will be punished, whether Christ rules or not (Hanford, p. 522). In *PL* 4. 75 he cried, 'Which way I flie is Hell; my self am Hell'.

215–22 Satan with flattery suggests that Christ in mercy shelter him from the wrath of God; but, as we know, he is excluded from grace (*PL* 3. 131–2) and hence from mercy, and condemned to everlasting punishment (Matt. 25. 41; Rev. 20. 10; *PL* 3. 198–202).

219 Cf. *FInf* 69: 'To stand 'twixt us and our deserved smart'.

220 When first expelled from heaven Satan defied God's wrath (*PL* 1. 110–11), but he has since learned to dread it, as his followers did then (*PL* 2. 82–4, 163–8, 291–4).

221–2 Possibly reminiscent of Isa. 25. 4–5: 'For thou hast been a strength to the poor, a strength to the needy in his distress, a refuge from the storm, a shadow from the heat.... Thou shalt bring down the noise of strangers, as the heat in a dry place; even the heat with the shadow of a cloud'.

227–8 See Christ's soliloquy in 1. 196–204 above.

232–3 See 22; 2. 79–81 above.

234–5 See Luke 2. 41 and cf. 1. 209–14 above.

237–9 It is significant that the praise of courts as the 'Best school of best experience' comes from Satan, for Milton's own attitude to courts and their influence was almost invariably hostile, as is evident from *Comus* 321–6; *Eikon* (*Works* 5. 129); and *REW* (6. 120), and as might be expected of a Puritan in the time of the Stuarts.

The wickedness and malign influence of courts had, however, long been a commonplace among Renaissance writers. Antonio Guevara, the Spanish Franciscan, a popular writer of the 16th century, devoted a book, the *Menos-precio de la corte y alabanza de la aldea* (Valladolid, 1539, French tr., Paris, 1544) to the dispraise of courts. In *The Courtier* (Everyman ed., 1928, pp. 260–1) Baldassare Castiglione says that courtly pursuits 'doe many times nothing els but womanish the mindes, corrupt youth, and bring them to a most wanton trade of living'. Roger Ascham in *The Scholemaster* (*English Works*, ed. Wright, pp. 206–7) is equally severe; and Spenser, as in *Hub.* 502–20 and *Colin Clout* 652–730, is stern, even bitter, in denouncing the evil and ingratitude of courts. See also Tasso, *Jerusalem* 7. 12–13. In *A Country Life* 90 Robert Herrick writes, 'Vice rules the Most, or All at Court'; and the *Memoirs* (Cologne, 1713) of the life of the comte de Gramont are a startling picture of frivolity and immorality at the court of Charles II.

242 Saul sought his father's asses but found a kingdom when Samuel anointed him as King of Israel (1 Sam. 9. 3 ff.).

245 *rudiments*. See note on 1. 157–8 above.

247 *inform*. 'To train or discipline in some particular course of action' (*OED*).

249 *Mysteries*. As in *SA* 378, a 'mystery' may be 'a political or diplomatic secret; a secret of state' (*OED*), like μυστήριον in LXX Dan. 2. 18, 19, 22, 27; or it may be a secret office or duty (Med. Lat. *misterium*) as in Chaucer, *Pars. T.* 895; Spenser, *Hub.* 221.

251 See note on 1. 363 above.

252-3 Cf. Matt. 4. 8: 'Again, the devil taketh him up into an exceeding high mountain, and sheweth him all the kingdoms of the world, and the glory of them.' Blakeney (p. 138) mistakenly remarks that Luke 'mentions no mountain, but simply says, "uplifted him" (ἀναγαγών, A.V. "led him up"), descriptive perhaps of an exalted state of mind.' But the reading of A.V. Luke 4. 5 is 'And the devil, taking him up into an high mountain', a rendering of the Greek text as accepted by Biblical scholars in the 16th and 17th centuries, e.g. Stephanus, Beza, Walton. Later scholars, however, have rejected as spurious the words εἰς ὄρος ὑψηλόν (*Nov. Test. Gr.*, ed. Tischendorf, Leipzig, 1872, 1. 454).

The 'specular mount', which Milton does not name, Gilbert (*G.D.*, p. 210) believes to be probably Niphates or some adjoining part of Taurus, the mountains of Armenia north of Mesopotamia.

In *PL* 11. 366–84 the angel Michael, as part of Adam's moral edification, conducts him to 'a Hill / Of Paradise the highest',

> Not higher that Hill nor wider looking round,
> Whereon for different cause the Tempter set
> Our second *Adam* in the Wilderness,
> To shew him all Earths Kingdomes and thir Glory (381–4).

From this hill Adam beholds the panorama of history which, as a result of his fall, is a spectacle of sin and destruction which he can do nothing to repair. Christ, on the other hand, though he refuses to become involved in the kingdoms with which Satan would tempt him, beholds a world which it is his mission ultimately to redeem.

The temptations of the kingdoms of the world, as Frye in 'Typology', *MP* 53 (1956), 232, observes, are all temptations to *false* heroic action. The temptation of Parthia signifies false power, Rome false justice, and Athens false wisdom. The first, though the crudest of the three, is treated at much greater length than the others, because the Jews, passionately desiring armed deliverance from Roman rule, expected that the Messiah would so deliver them, and because Christ had already considered taking that course of heroic action (see 1. 215–17 above). In the temptations of Parthia and Rome, Frye sees Satan dramatizing for Christ the nature of that aspect of law which is to be abrogated by the Gospel—the 'law as a compelling external force in which spiritual authority is subject to and administered by temporal authority.'

255–8 The two rivers, it is generally agreed, are the Euphrates and the Tigris, which, as Milton might learn from several sources, as Strabo 2. 1. 23; 11. 12. 1–3; Pliny, *N.H.* 5. 20. 83–5; and the maps in Ortelius, *Theatrum Orbis Terrarum* (Antwerp, 1592, pp. 4, 104); Mercator, *Atlas* (Amsterdam, 1628, p. 662), rise in the Taurus Mountains in Armenia, flow southward, and after their junction empty into the Persian Gulf.

255 *his.* See note on 1. 82 above.

258 *thir tribute to the Sea.* Todd (5. 171) notes a reminiscence of Tasso, *Jerusalem* 15. 16. 2–3: 'to the sea his tribute Nilus paies / By his seu'n mouthes.'

259–60 The fertility of Mesopotamia is frequently mentioned by ancient writers, as by Strabo 16. 1. 23–4; Pliny, *N.H.* 6. 30. 117; and Q. Curtius 5. 1. 12.

261–2 The many cities of Assyria are mentioned in Herodotus 1. 178; Pliny, *N.H.* 6. 30. 117; Strabo 16. 1. 24; Diodorus Siculus 2. 11; and they are a conspicuous feature of the maps of Ortelius (see note on 255–8 above) and of Ptolemy's map reproduced in G. W. Whiting, *Milieu*, facing p. 124.

261 *high towr'd.* The expression may be reminiscent of Virgil, *A.* 10. 253: *turrigeraeque urbes*, and Hesiod, *Shield* 270: εὔπυργος πόλις. Cf. *El* 1. 74; *L'All* 117.

264 The deserts are probably those of Arabia Deserta and southern Mesopotamia mentioned in Strabo 16. 3. 1 and shown in the maps of Ortelius and Mercator (see note on 255–8 above).

fountainless. This is the only occurrence of the word in Milton's poetry and the earliest recorded by *OED*. It may be Milton's rendering of ἄνυδρος in Strabo 16. 3. 1 and Diodorus Siculus 2. 48.

267–385 The subject of *PR* permits fewer poetical adornments than that of *PL*, but in the present passage, out of the fabric of the poem, Milton creates ornament. Skilfully turning to account his geographical and historical learning, using sonorous proper names, a favourite if not original device, he achieves effects as splendid as those in *PL* 1. 386–521 and 11. 388–411. The occasion here demands a geographical panorama of narrower compass than that in the passages last cited; yet it demands that the poet convey an impression of vast space; and this Milton admirably succeeds in doing. By introducing the episode in lines 298–336 he adds action and variety to the otherwise static description. The musical effect of the proper names is as remarkable as that to be found anywhere in Milton's poetry. T. S. Eliot ('Milton I', *On Poetry and Poets*, New York, 1957, p. 163) objects to such passages as this as 'not serious poetry' but rather 'a solemn game'. He has failed to see that the present roll of names has the justification of Milton's purpose to indicate the utter lack of seriousness, the emptiness of the life that sought expression in the imperial pomp of a parade of names—this 'new train of words' as Milton calls it in line 266—a phrase which Eliot might well have pondered.

269 *shorter many a league.* Because they have gone by a straight course through the air, the journey has been shorter than it would have been by land.

270 The Assyrian empire during the five centuries of its history greatly varied in extent, but between 722 and 626 B.C., the period of its greatest power and expansion, to which Satan probably refers, it had reached the boundaries which he mentions (G. Rawlinson, *History of Herodotus*, 3rd ed., New York, 1875, 1. 502–3).

271 *Araxes.* The *pontem indignatus Araxes* of Virgil, *A.* 8. 728, a turbulent river of Armenia, now called the Aras, flows eastward into the Caspian Sea (Strabo 11. 1. 5, 4. 2, 14. 3).

273 *And oft beyond.* According to Strabo 16. 1. 1–2 Assyria extended westward to Cilicia, Phoenicia, and Judaea, to the Egyptian Sea and the Bay of Issus, and northward to the Euxine Sea.

274 *drouth.* 'Dry or parched land, desert'. '*Obs. rare.*' *OED* records only this and one other occurrence of the word in this sense and none later than the present one. See note on 1. 146 above. Editors note an echo of Silius Italicus 14. 74: *Libyamque sitim*, the reading accepted in the 17th century but later emended to read *situm*.

275–6 Nineveh, the capital of Assyria on the banks of the Tigris, was larger even than Babylon (Herodotus 1. 193; Arrian, *Ind.* 42; Strabo 16. 1. 3). According to Jonah 3. 3 it was 'an exceeding great city of three days' journey', and to Diodorus Siculus 2. 3. 2, where it is mistakenly located on the Euphrates, the circuit of the city was four thousand and eighty furlongs. Its destruction in 608–607 B.C. is referred to in Nahum 3 and Zeph. 2. 13–15.

276 *Ninus old*. According to Gen. 10. 11 Asshur 'builded Nineveh', but according to pagan tradition the legendary and eponymous founder of the city was Ninus, King of Assyria (Diodorus Siculus 2. 3. 2–4; Ammianus Marcellinus 23. 6. 22; Strabo 16. 1. 2). Jerome, whose interpretation of the *Chronicles* (1) of Eusebius (Migne, *Pat. Lat.* 27. 111), as Irene Samuel shows in 'Semiramis in the Middle Ages' (*M & H* 2, 1944, 35–7), was influential for centuries in spreading the legend of Semiramis and Ninus, her husband—a legend in which there is much confusion—disregarding Scripture, follows the pagan tradition, as does Milton. Ninus is called 'old' because he is believed to have lived about 2200 B.C., or even earlier (Justin 1. 1–3; Sir Walter Ralegh, *Historie* 1. 10. 2). Augustine (*Civ. D.* 18. 2) and others say that Abraham was born in his reign.

277 *golden Monarchy*. Editors believe that these words are an allusion to the golden head of the image in Nebuchadnezzar's dream of the four empires recounted in Dan. 2. 31–45. But it is likely that Milton intended an allusion to oriental splendour, like the *Persicos apparatus* of Horace, *C.* 1. 38. 1, and the Βαβυλὼν δ' / ἡ πολύχρυσος of Aeschylus, *Pers.* 52–3. Athenaeus (12. 9) describes in detail the luxuries of the Persian kings. See note on 281–4 below.

278–9 Salmanassar is the Shalmaneser of 2 Kings 17. 3; 18. 9. Milton, presumably for the sake of euphony (see note on 2. 16–17 above) uses the form of the name found in A.V. 2 Esdras 13. 40—there spelled Salmanasar. He was King of Assyria from 727 to 722 B.C. According to 2 Kings 17. 3–6, he made Hoshea, King of Israel, his vassal; but when the latter conspired against him, he besieged and captured Samaria, and carried the Israelites into captivity in Assyria. See *Encyc. Bibl.* 2. 2242–3; Hastings, *Dict.*, pp. 402–3.

280–1 Babylon, the great and very ancient city on the Euphrates, was one of the wonders of the ancient world, as appears from such descriptions of its splendours, notably the temple of Bel and the famous hanging gardens, as are given in Herodotus 1. 178–81; Diodorus Siculus 2. 7–12; Strabo 16. 1. 5. According to Diodorus Siculus 2. 7. 2, the city was founded by Semiramis; but Milton, all of whose references to Babylon Gilbert (*G.D.*, p. 42) finds to be dependent on the Bible, following Gen. 10. 10, in *PL* 12. 38–47, makes Nimrod the builder of Babel, which he identifies with Babylon, as does Augustine in

Book III

Civ. D. 16. 4. By the time of Christ Babylon had long been uninhabited ruins.

the wonder of all tongues. In these words J. E. Parish ('An Unrecorded Pun in *PR*', *N & Q* n.s. 11, 1964, 337) detects a pun, since in *PL* 12. 38–78 Milton, who has identified Babylon with Babel, gives a grimly humorous account of the building of Babel and the wonderful confusion of tongues that occurred there.

281–4 Nebuchadnezzar, more correctly Nebuchadrezzar, King of Babylon from 604 to 561 B.C., excelled all who had reigned before him in Babylon and greatly added to its splendours (Josephus, *A.J.* 10. 11). In 597 B.C. he captured Jerusalem, and carried as captives to Babylon all but the poorest of the Jews (2 Kings 24. 10–17; Dan. 1. 1–2; Josephus, *A.J.* 10. 6. 1–3). In 587 B.C. he again captured Jerusalem, burned the city, and led the remnant of the people into captivity (2 Kings 25. 1–22; Jer. 39. 1–9; Josephus, *A.J.* 10. 8. 5). The Jews remained captive for seventy years, until Cyrus, King of Persia, in 538 B.C., captured Babylon and returned them to their own land (Ezra 1–2).

282 See note on 1. 240–1 above.

284 *Persepolis.* The ancient capital of Persia, a city of great wealth and magnificence, which Alexander the Great destroyed in 339 B.C. (Diodorus Siculus 17. 70–1; Pliny, *N.H.* 6. 29. 115; Ralegh, *Historie* 4. 2. 12).

285 *Bactra.* Also called Zariaspa, a city of Bactria, a mountainous but fertile region between the Hindu Kush Mountains and the Oxus River (Ammianus Marcellinus 25. 6. 14; Q. Curtius 7. 4. 26–31; Strabo 11. 8. 9; 11. 11. 2).

286 *Ecbatana.* The principal city of Media, now Hamadan (Herodotus 1. 98; Q. Curtius 5. 8. 1; Pliny, *N.H.* 6. 17. 43). According to Xenophon, *Cyr.* 8. 6. 22, it was the summer residence of the kings of Persia. The words 'her structure vast' agree with Herodotus' description of the palace and extensive fortifications of Ecbatana.

287 *Hecatompylos.* The city of the 'hundred gates' was the capital of Parthia (Pliny, *N.H.* 6. 17. 44). Q. Curtius (6. 2. 15) calls it *urbs clara.. condita a Graecis.* Its location is hard to determine, since Strabo (11. 8. 9) places it 224 miles east of the Caspian Gates, but Pliny only 133 miles.

288–9 Susa, the Scriptural Shushan (Esther 1. 2; Dan. 8. 2) and modern Shush, was the chief city of ancient Susiana and the winter residence of the kings of Persia (Q. Curtius 5. 1. 7). According to Strabo 15. 3. 2, it was founded by Tithonus, father of Memnon, 'for whom the citadel is called Memnonian'; in Herodotus 5. 54 it is referred to as the palace of Memnon.

Choaspes. A river of Susiana (Strabo 16. 3. 4: Q. Curtius 4. 5. 4).

288 *amber stream.* Jerram (p. 133) takes 'amber' to mean 'clear' (cf. the 'lucid streams' of *PL* 1. 469) and quotes Virgil, *G.* 3. 521–2: 'No stream purer than amber seeks the plain'.[8] Cf. *L'All* 60–1; *Comus* 332; *PL* 3. 358–9. Gilbert (*G.D.*, pp. 85–6), who discusses Milton's several uses of the term 'amber', concludes that it here means 'shining like amber'. *OED*, which cites this line, gives the meaning 'of the colour and clearness of amber'.

289 *The drink of none but Kings.* These words have evoked much comment. The tradition that the water of Choaspes was the drink of kings, the *regia lympha Choaspes* of Tibullus 3. 7. 140, begins with Herodotus (1. 188), who writes that the King of Persia, when he goes to war, takes with him water from Choaspes, 'as that is the only water that kings of Persia taste'. This statement is echoed by Plutarch (*On Exile* 6), Athenaeus (2. 45), Pliny (*N.H.* 31. 6. 35), and others. By the time the tradition reached Solinus (38. 4), it had undergone a significant change, and it was *only* the kings who drank the water of Choaspes. The explanation of the change may well be that on military expeditions it was only the kings who drank the water, which, with much trouble, they carried with them. Jortin, whose laboriously learned note is quoted by Todd (5. 177–9) and Hawkins (3. 138–9), suggests that Solinus was Milton's authority. Editors suggest as another possible authority Peter Heylyn (*Cosmographie*, London, 1667, bk. 3, p. 142), who, however, does *not* say that only kings drank the water.

289–93 Having pointed out the very ancient cities of Assyria, Babylon, and Persia, Satan goes on to cities of later origin built by the Emathians, that is the Macedonian successors of Alexander, and by the Parthians.

291 *Seleucia.* Out of the struggle for power between Alexander's successors, Seleucus Nicator by 301 B.C. emerged as ruler of the vast Greek conquests in Asia, and thus became the founder of the Syrian monarchy of the Seleucidae (Appian, *Syr.* 55–62; Ralegh, *Historie* 4. 5. 7). He built many cities, nine of which he named Seleucia; of these Milton probably refers to the one on the Tigris, about ninety miles from Babylon, called 'the Great' to distinguish it from the other cities of the same name. After it was built, Babylon fell into decay (Strabo 16. 1. 16; Pliny, *N.H.* 6. 30. 122).

Nisibis. Also called Antioch in Mygdonia, the modern Nisibin, a city in western Mesopotamia (Strabo 16. 1. 23; Pliny, *N.H.* 6. 16. 42; Ammianus Marcellinus 20. 7. 1).

---

[8]   non...
purior electro campum petit amnis.

292 *Artaxata.* A city of Armenia on the Araxes River, which, according to Plutarch, *Luc.* 31, and Strabo 11. 14. 6, Hannibal built for King Artaxias.

Teredon. A town near the mouth of the river formed by the junction of the Tigris and the Euphrates (Strabo 16. 3. 2; Pliny, *N.H.* 6. 32. 145). There is a tradition, says Gilbert (*G.D.*, p. 290), that it was built by Nebuchadnezzar; however, it first became known in the time of Alexander.

Tesiphon. The more correct spelling is Ctesiphon, from Κτεσιφῶν, which Milton uses only eight lines below. It was a city on the Tigris near Seleucia, and was the winter residence of the kings of Parthia (Strabo 16. 1. 16). According to Pliny, *N.H.* 6. 30. 122, the Parthians built Ctesiphon with the deliberate intention of ruining Seleucia, as it had been the means of ruining Babylon.

294-7 Since Satan wishes to tempt Christ to win temporal power with which to free the Jews from the hated Roman rule, he now shrewdly shows him the great Parthian empire, of which Artabanus III was ruler from about A.D. 10 to 40 (Tacitus, *Ann.* 2. 3), and which at that time, as Justin (42. 5) points out, was the only power which had been able to offer effectual resistance to the eastward march of Roman conquest (Dio Cassius 40. 12-27; 59. 27. 2-3; Plutarch, *Crassus* 17-33). Ancient historians give varying accounts of the origin of the Parthian empire (G. Rawlinson, *The Sixth Great Oriental Monarchy*, New York, n.d., pp. 42-51); but it appears that Arsaces, a Bactrian or Scythian, about 250 B.C., made himself King of Parthia, which had thrown off the supremacy of the Seleucid kings (Justin 41. 4). Thereafter by successive conquests the Parthians achieved an empire which until A.D. 227 embraced most of western Asia (Strabo 11. 9. 2).

295 *Arsaces.* There is much uncertainty about the events of Arsaces' career. His successors, who bore the same name, were known as the Arsacidae (Tacitus, *Hist.* 1. 40; Justin 41. 4-5; Strabo 11. 9. 3; Photius, *Bibl.* 58, Migne, *Pat. Gr.* 103. 103-6).

Blakeney (p. 140) notes that though in Lucan 1. 108; 8. 218; 10. 51 the second syllable of Arsaces is short, Milton makes it long.

297 Antioch was a city on the Orontes River, about twenty miles from the Mediterranean, built by Seleucus, who named it after his father, Antiochus (Justin 15. 4). It became an early centre of Christianity (Acts 11). In size and wealth it was little inferior to Seleucia (see note on 291 above) (Strabo 16. 2. 5). Milton's mention of the 'luxurious Kings' may be a reminiscence of the account in Livy 41. 20 of Antiochus Epiphanes, who built at Antioch a splendid temple and introduced gladiatorial combats and other elaborate entertainments.

298–336 In the episode here introduced (see note on 267–385 above), Milton apparently had in mind no particular war between Parthians and Scythians, but invented a typical action, such a conflict as often occurred between the Parthians and their barbarian neighbours (Justin 42).

The present passage as a whole, but especially lines 309–12 and 322–6, is one of several in Milton's works which attest his interest in military matters. See *Educ* (*Works* 4. 289); *ComBk* (18. 208–17); *PL* 6 *passim*; J. H. Hanford, 'Milton on the Art of War', *John Milton, Poet and Humanist* (Cleveland, Ohio, 1966), pp. 216–18.

300 *Ctesiphon.* See note on 292 above.

301 *Scythian.* A name commonly applied by both Greeks and Romans to all the peoples of northern Europe and Asia in what is now Russia and Siberia (Aeschylus, *Prom.* 2; Herodotus 4. 1; Strabo 11. 6. 2; Ovid, *M.* 1. 64; Cicero, *N.D.* 2. 34. 88; Pliny, *N.H.* 4. 12. 80). In Elizabethan times it was used in much the same sense (Marlowe, *1 Tam.* 1. 1. 36, 54; Spenser, *Ro.* 4. 3), and so also by Milton in 4. 78 below; *El* 4. 11; *HistBr* (*Works* 10. 114).

302 *Sogdiana.* Ancient writers do not exactly agree upon the boundaries of Sogdiana, but according to Strabo 11. 11. 2, it was a region 'above Bactria to the East, between the River Oxus...and the Jaxartes, which separates the Sogdii from the nomads.' Cf. Q. Curtius 7. 10. It corresponds to modern Turkestan and Bokhara.

303–9 The Parthians, who fought on horseback, would advance, then feign flight, shooting their arrows behind them; hence the expression 'a Parthian shot'. When they had deceived the enemy into thinking that they were retreating, they would again quickly advance, 'so that when you feel most sure that you have conquered them, you have yet to meet the greatest danger from them' (Justin 41. 2).[9] Cf. Dio Cassius 40. 15; Virgil, *G.* 3. 31; Horace, *C.* 2. 13. 17–18; Lucan 1. 230; Claudian 8. 531 (1. 326); *S.P.* 9. 21–2, 47 (2. 182, 184).

309 The battle formations mentioned here are all drawn from ancient military tactics. The 'rhomb' (ῥόμβος) was a battalion in the shape of a lozenge, the 'wedge' (ἔμβολον) was a half rhomb (Aelian, *Tact.* 18. 1–3, 5–9; 36. 7). The 'half moon' (*lunata acies*) was formed by curving back the wings in order to present to the enemy the main body of an army (Frontinus, *Strat.* 2. 3. 4). The 'wings' (κέρατα, *alae*, *cornua*) were the divisions of an army to the extreme right and left (Aelian, *Tact.* 22. 2; Vegetius, *R.M.* 2. 1).

[9] Cum maxime vicisse te putes, tunc tibi discrimen subeundum sit.

310 *numbers numberless.* Cf. *PL* 3. 346: 'numbers without number'; Lucretius 3. 779: *innumero numero*; Tasso, *G.L.* 19. 121. 2: *L'innumerabil numero*. From the several occurrences of 'numbers numberless' which Todd (5. 184–5) found in both prose and verse of the 17th century, it appears that the expression was fairly common.

311 Editors note in this line two echoes from Virgil: *A.* 12. 121–2: 'The troops pour from the crowded gates'; and *G.* 4. 314: 'when the light-armed Parthians enter upon the opening battle'.[10]

312–13 Justin (41. 2) describes the armour of the Parthians and of their horses as formed of metal plates overlapping like the feathers of a bird which completely covered both man and horse. Plutarch (*Crassus* 24) speaks of the consternation of the Romans when they beheld the Parthians thus armed. See also Ammianus Marcellinus 25. 1. 11–19; Claudian 5. 357–65 (1. 82–5).

315–21 The 'Provinces' mentioned in these lines—in a great circuit of the Parthian empire—were either provinces or merely districts of that empire at its greatest extent.

316 *Arachosia.* The most easterly district of the Parthian empire, part of the territory of Asia extending to the Indus River (Strabo 11. 10. 1). It is now part of Baluchistan.

Candaor. This spelling for 'Candahar' may be Milton's invention. Candahar was a province and city of the same name in what is now Afghanistan. In *Purchas his Pilgrimes* (Glasgow, 1905), 4. 430, it is mentioned as 'a Citie of importance...frequented with Merchants of Turkie, Persia, and all parts of India.'

317 *Margiana.* An extensive region east of the Caspian Sea, between Bactria and Parthia (Strabo 11. 10. 2; Q. Curtius 7. 10. 15).

Hyrcania was a fertile region south-east of the Caspian, which was also called the Hyrcanian Sea (Strabo 11. 7. 1–3). 'The *Hyrcanian* cliffs / Of Caucasus', Gilbert (*G.D.*, p. 150) suggests, may refer to the proximity of the Sea to the Caucasus Mountains, since Hyrcania is not near them. Cf. Virgil, *A.* 4. 366–7: 'Rugged Caucasus on its hard rocks begat you';[11] Marlowe, *2 Tam.* 5. 3. 242: 'Through rocks more steepe and sharp than Caspian cliftes.'

---

[10] plenis
agmina se fundunt portis.

[11] prima leves ineunt si quando proelia Parthi.
duris genuit te cautibus horrens / Caucasus.

318 Iberia, corresponding to modern Georgia, lay between the Black and the Caspian Seas, partly surrounded by the Caucasus Mountains (Strabo 11. 3. 1–2). Gilbert (*G.D.*, p. 151) quotes as suggesting Milton's 'dark Iberian dales' the following passage from *Purchas his Pilgrimes* 3. 110: 'In those parts [Georgia] there is a Prouince or Countrey called *Hamsem*...whose whole extent is all couered ouer with such thicke and palpable darknesse, that none can see any thing therein, neither doe any dare to goe into that Land, because they know not the way out againe.'

319 Atropatia, or Atropane, was the northern portion of Media, between the Caspian Sea and Armenia (Strabo 11. 13. 1).

320 *Adiabene.* One of the plains about Nineveh (Strabo 16. 1. 1, 18–19).

Media. Media, now northern Persia, consisted of two parts, Media Magna and Media Atropatia. It was an extensive region between the Caspian Sea on the north-east and Adiabene, Assyria, and Susiana on the west and south (Strabo 11. 13; Pliny, *N.H.* 6. 29. 114).

321 *Susiana.* A province in the south-eastern part of Persia. According to Strabo 15. 3. 2 ff., it is 'part of Persia, between it and Babylon....It stretches to the sea' and 'to the mouth of the Tigris'.

Balsara. Modern Bassora on the Chatt-el-Arab, the river formed by the union of the Euphrates and the Tigris. It did not exist at the time of the action of *PR*, having been founded only in A.D. 626. But Ortelius (*Theatrum*, p. 103, map) identifies it with ancient Teredon. See note on 292 above.

322–36 See note on 298–336 above.

324 *Sharp sleet of arrowie showers.* The first edition reads 'shower', corrected in the Errata to 'showers'. The line is onomatopoeic. Editors cite the following passages which Milton may be echoing: Pindar, *Isth.* 5. 50: 'Slaughter thick as hail fell on unnumbered warriors';[12] Virgil, *A.* 11. 610–11: 'At once they shower from all sides darts as thick as snowflakes';[13] 12. 283–4: 'A thickening storm of javelins flies through all the sky, and fast falls the iron rain';[14] Statius, *Th.* 8. 412–13: 'Their darts shut out the day, a steely cloud hangs across the sky';[15] Spenser, *F.Q.* 5. 4. 38. 3–4, 9:

[12] ἀναρίθμων ἀνδρῶν χαλαζάεντι φόνῳ.
[13]   fundunt simul undique tela
crebra nivis ritu.
[14]   it toto turbida caelo
tempestas telorum ac ferreus ingruit imber.
[15] exclusere diem telis, stant ferrea caelo
nubila.

Book III

But in the middle way they were ymet
With a sharp showre of arrowes, which them staid...
And arrowes haild so thicke, that they could not abide.

326 Editors note that this line may be reminiscent of Euripides, *Phoen.* 110–11: 'The glare of brass there flashes over all the plain';[16] Virgil, *A.* 11. 601–2: 'Far and wide the steely field bristles with spears, and the plains blaze with uplifted arms';[17] Tasso, *Jerusalem* 1. 64. 4: 'Embattailed in wals of iron browne'.

327 *clouds of foot*. Editors suggest that this expression echoes Homer, *Il.* 4. 274: νέφος πεζῶν, and Virgil, *A.* 7. 793: *nimbus peditum*. Cf. Claudian 21. 353 (1. 390): *equitum nimbos*. Some have found this line inconsistent with line 307, which seems to say that the whole army consisted of horsemen. Dunster (p. 164) would remove the difficulty by interpreting 'all horsemen' as meaning 'skilled in the management of a horse, as every Parthian was'. But Jerram (p. 136) maintains that 'Milton's words imply merely that all those who *first* issued forth were "horsemen," and that these were the chief part, though not the whole, of their strength.'

   horn. 'Each of the two wings of an army' (*OED*), Lat. *cornu*, as in Livy 9. 40. 3; Caesar, *B.G.* 1. 52; 2. 23, 25.

328 *Cuirassiers*. Horse soldiers wearing cuirasses (*OED*). See note on 312–13 above.

329 Aelian (*Tact.* 2. 11. 13) speaks of chariots and elephants as regular parts of a mounted military force. The chariots of the Egyptians, Syrians, and Assyrians are often mentioned in the Bible, as in Exod. 14. 7, 9; 1 Kings 20. 21; 2 Kings 19. 23; Isa. 21. 9; 31. 1. By these peoples they were used much earlier than by the Greeks and Romans. See Daremberg and Saglio, *Dictionnaire des antiquités grecques et romaines* (Paris, 1877–1919), 1. 2. 1633–43.

   Ancient writers often speak of the military use of elephants as a practice which the Greeks and Romans learned from oriental and African peoples. Alexander was the first European who acquired elephants (Pausanias 1. 12. 4; Diodorus Siculus 17. 89. 2; Arrian, *Anab.* 5. 18. 2; Q. Curtius 5. 2. 10). The first elephants used by the Romans were those surrendered to them by the

[16]   κατάχαλκον ἅπαν
πεδίον ἀστράπτει.

[17]   tum late ferreus hastis
horret ager campique armis sublimibus ardent.

169

Carthaginians in the Second Punic War between 219 and 201 B.C. (Livy 30. 37. 3; Silius Italicus 3. 459–65; 4. 598–621; Daremberg and Saglio, *Dict.* 2. 1. 536–44).

The 'Towers' with which the elephants are 'endorst' are the howdahs, the *impositae turres* of Livy 37. 40. 4. Cf. Silius Italicus 9. 239–41, 570–643. In 1 Macc. 6. 37 they are called 'strong towers of wood' and are said to accommodate thirty-two men, an absurd exaggeration. Livy (37. 40. 4) says four men.

endorst. Put upon the back, like Med. Lat. *endorsare.* *OED* records no earlier use of the word in this sense.

330 *Archers.* All Parthian soldiers, both cavalrymen and infantrymen, were archers (Dio Cassius 40. 15. 2).

Pioners. This spelling was common in the 16th and 17th centuries (*OED*). Pioneers were foot-soldiers sent ahead of the main body of an army to build or repair roads, dig trenches, and in any way to prepare for the advance of an army—to do such works as those mentioned in the lines immediately following. Cf. *PL* 1. 675–8.

333–4 Editors suggest that Milton may be alluding to Aeschylus' description of Xerxes' bridge across the Hellespont in *Pers.* 71–2: 'casting a stout-clamped roadway as a yoke upon the neck of the deep.'[18] Cf. Virgil, *A.* 8. 728: 'Araxes chafing at the bridge' (*pontem indignatus Araxes*).

335 Mules, camels, and dromedaries were used in antiquity when speed was necessary, as with the messengers of King Ahasuerus mentioned in Esther 8. 10.

336 *Utensils.* Accented on the first syllable as in Shakespeare, *Temp.* 3. 2. 104. As often in the 16th and 17th centuries, 'utensils' here means articles, implements useful for any purpose.

337–42 To convey an impression of the vastness of the Parthian army, Milton compares it to the host of two million two hundred thousand men with which, as Boiardo, with romantic exaggeration, tells the story in *Orlando innamorato* 1. 10 ff., Agrican the Tartar king besieged Albracca, when he sought to win Galfrone's daughter Angelica, the fair but faithless beguiler of Orlando, or Roland, one of the most famous peers of Charlemagne (*Chanson de Roland*, ed. Gautier, Tours, 1897, p. 30 n.; Gaston Paris, *Histoire poétique de Charlemagne*, Paris, 1865, p. 417). On Milton's reading of romances, see *Apol* (*Works* 3. 304).

As Christ will reply in lines 387–98 and 400–2, all the 'ostentation vain' of

[18] πολύγομφον ὅδισμα
ζυγὸν ἀμφιβαλὼν αὐχένι πόντου.

military might, the 'cumbersome / Luggage of war', is an 'argument / Of human weakness rather then of strength.'

The allusions in this passage to Renaissance epics and romances, as J. M. Steadman (*Milton and the Renaissance Hero*, p. 26) points out, are not fortuitous. In them Milton is condemning the epic tradition which glorified military prowess.

342 *Prowest.* 'Prow', meaning 'good', is a doublet of the earlier 'prut', 'prud', 'proud' (*OED*). Spenser uses the word several times, as in *F.Q.* 1. 4. 41. 7; 2. 3. 15. 6; 3. 3. 24. 7. It occurs nowhere else in Milton's poetry.

343 *Paynim.* 'Pagan, heathen; non-Christian; chiefly = Mohammedan or Saracen' (*OED*). In Milton's poetry the word occurs again only in *PL* 1. 765—there spelled 'panim'—but both as noun and adjective Spenser uses it thirty-one times.

344 *Chivalrie.* 'As at one time the "chivalry" constituted the main strength of a mediaeval army (the archers, slingers, etc. being mere subordinate adjuncts), the word had sometimes the value of "army", "host"' (*OED*), the part being named for the whole.

345 *Fiend.* See note on 1. 465 above.

347–85 Satan, choosing to assume that Christ's kingdom is earthly and temporal, and anticipating the objection that what he is offering is dangerous, assures Christ that he will make every provision for his safety. Not only is such an assurance from him ironic, but it reveals his refusal to understand the kind of character with which he is dealing. He then attempts to persuade Christ that if Christ is ever to become king and deliver his people, thus fulfil his mission, he must himself use means to achieve that end, and that the necessary means is by conquest or league, to gain control of the Parthian empire. Again, as in *PL* 4. 389–92, his argument is the necessity of 'public reason just'; he does not consider the morality of the act. The argument, however, is specious and intended to conceal Satan's real motive, which, as Christ perceives (412–13), is to induce Christ to satisfy worldly ambition, and so to become guilty of pride.

348 *Vertue.* Milton often uses 'vertue' to mean 'strength', 'courage', like Lat. *virtus*, as in *PL* 1. 320; 7. 236; *SA* 1690, but more often to mean 'moral excellence', as in 1. 68 above; *PL* 2. 483. Here there may be a blending of the two meanings (Lockwood, *Lexicon*).

351–85 See 1. 240–1, 261–3; 3. 150–80 above and notes.

353 *Endeavour*. A stronger word in the 17th century than it now is, meaning a strenuous, earnest attempt. Jerram (p. 138) cites Eph. 4. 3, where σπουδάζοντες, doing anything earnestly, zealously, in the A.V. is rendered 'endeavouring'. Cf. *PL* 12. 355.

thy Father David. See note on 154 above. The reference is to the long war which David had to wage against the house of Saul before he could make himself king of all Israel (2 Sam. 3. 1; 5. 1–3).

354–6 In asserting that the fulfilment of divine predictions is dependent upon voluntary human agency, Satan wishes to insinuate a doubt concerning God's power, and to appeal to pride in Christ which will lead him to use his power. See Christ's answers in 394–402 and 4. 152–3 below.

357 *David's Throne*. See note on 1. 240–1 above.

358 *opposite*. 'Hostile, antagonistic' (*OED*), as in *PL* 2. 298 and Shakespeare, *Twel*. 2. 5. 162.

359 Immediately after the Jews returned from the captivity, enmity arose between them and their neighbours the Samaritans because the latter tried to prevent the rebuilding of Jerusalem (Ezra 4. 1–7; Neh. 4. 7–8). Thereafter disputes between them were frequent, and on one occasion the Jews appealed to Darius, King of Persia, for redress of grievances against the Samaritans (Josephus, *A.J.* 11. 4. 9). The continued hostility between them is still conspicuous in the Gospels (Matt. 10. 5; John 4. 9). But Satan argues that even these long-standing enemies would unite in the great undertaking which he now proposes.

362–4 See 4. 84–5 below.

362 *Roman*. See notes on 155–9 and 1. 217 above.

364–8 The events referred to in these lines occurred not 'of late' but about 40 B.C., and shortly thereafter, nearly seventy years before the time of the present action. The Parthians then invaded Syria (Tacitus, *Hist*. 5. 9), and when Hyrcanus II, high priest and King of Judaea, went to them as ambassador, they sent him as a prisoner to Parthia (Josephus, *B.J.* 1. 13. 3–4, 11). On his return to Judaea ten years later, he was put to death (*B.J.* 1. 22. 1). Far from taking his nephew Antigonus prisoner, the Parthians made him King of Judaea (*B.J.* 1. 13. 11; Dio Cassius 37. 15–16). It suits Satan's purpose, however, to represent this exhibition of Parthian power as a recent occurrence, and hence his historical inaccuracies.

368 *Maugre.* 'In spite of' (*OED*), O.F. *maugre*. Elsewhere in Milton's poetry the word occurs only in *PL* 3. 255 and 9. 56. Spenser uses it more often, as in *F.Q.* 2. 5. 12. 9; 3. 10. 2. 2; 4. 10. 58. 2.

374–82 Satan's hypocritical argument in these lines, which Christ in lines 407–13 most aptly turns against him, is an example of the stupidity of which the cunning are at times capable. For another argument similarly turned against Satan, see 4. 100–5 and 125–9 below.

374–5 In the revolt following the death of Solomon, only the tribes of Judah and Benjamin accepted his son Rehoboam as king and constituted the kingdom of Judah. The remaining ten tribes chose Jeroboam as their king and formed the kingdom of Israel (1 Kings 12. 15–21). It was these tribes of Israel which Shalmaneser led into captivity from which they never returned (see note on 278–9 above); thus they became known as the lost ten tribes (*Encyc. Bibl.* 4. 5200–13).

376 *Habor.* According to 2 Kings 17. 6, which Milton follows, Habor was a country or district in which the Israelites carried captive to Assyria were placed; but according to Strabo 16. 1. 27 Habor was a river, a tributary of the Euphrates.
   Medes. See note on 320 above.

377 Dunster (p. 168) would emend this line to read 'Eight sons of *Jacob*', since only eight of the lost tribes were descended from the sons of Jacob, the other two, Ephraim and Manasseh, being descended from the sons of Joseph. But the emendation is unnecessary if we understand that Ephraim and Manasseh are included in the ten, the phrase 'two of Joseph' being an elliptical expression meaning 'two of these being sons of Joseph'. Since there was no tribe of Levi, the tribes of Ephraim and Manasseh with those of Reuben, Simeon, Zebulun, Issachar, Dan, Gad, Asher, and Naphtali bring the number to ten.

379 See Exod. 1–12.

382–4 In the covenant with Abraham, God said (Gen. 15. 18): 'Unto thy seed have I given this land, from the river of Egypt unto the great river, the river Euphrates.' The kingdom of Israel finally reached this, its greatest, extent in the reign of Solomon (1 Kings 4. 21).

383 *Throne of David.* See note on 1. 240–1 above.

385 *not need fear.* If we supply an auxiliary 'shalt' or 'do' before 'not'

(Abbott, *Shakes. Gram.*, 305), it is unnecessary to assume with Keightley (2. 276) that Milton probably dictated 'need not' or 'need naught'.

387-440 To all that Satan has just proposed, Christ in masterly fashion opposes three principal, unanswerable objections: first, that for the fulfilment of his mission, military might and shrewd statesmanship are worthless; second, that Satan in urging him to deliver his people is hypocritical, since they are in bondage because of sins into which Satan himself has led them; and third, still maintaining his humility, that he awaits God's 'time and providence', to do whatever he must do.

387 *fleshly arm.* The expression, which Spenser also uses in *F.Q.* 1. 11. 36. 6; 3. 4. 27. 6, is probably an echo of 2 Chron. 32. 8: 'With him is an arm of flesh; but with us is the Lord our God'; and Jer. 17. 5: 'Cursed be the man that trusteth in man, and maketh flesh his arm.'

388 *instruments of war.* Editors compare Cicero, *Acad.* 2. 1. 3: *totius belli instrumento et adparatu.*

394-402 See 354-6 above and note, and 4. 152-3 below.

395 *unpredict.* See note on 429 below. 'Unpredict' does not appear in *OED*.

396-7 *My time...is not yet come.* Repeated from John 7. 6.

401-2 Why the resort to war is an indication of human weakness Christ has already explained in his soliloquy in 1. 215-26. See note on 1. 219.

409-13 According to 1 Chron. 21. 1 'Satan stood up against Israel, and provoked David to number Israel'; because of this act David was punished by a plague from which seventy thousand of his people perished. Cf. 2 Sam. 24. 1-25. In 'The Sin of the Census' (*Folk-Lore in the Old Testament*, 2. 555-63), J. G. Frazer explains David's sin as a violation of the very old and common belief, not yet extinct, that to count people, cattle, any of one's possessions— Catullus (5, 7) includes even kisses—places the powers of evil in possession of knowledge which they can use to the injury of man. But according to Josephus (*A.J.* 7. 13. 1) and the rabbinic tradition, David in ordering the census forgot the Mosaic injunction (Exod. 30. 12) that, when the people were numbered, every man should give half a shekel as 'a ransom for his soul unto the Lord'. See Ginzberg, *Legends* 4. 111-13; 6. 270. But in interpreting the census as an act of pride Milton may have remembered that Du Bartas so interprets it (Sylvester's Du Bartas, *D.W.W.*, *The Trophies* 1245); and he may also have remembered the following comment on 1 Chron. 21. 1 in the Geneva Bible: 'It was a thing indifferent and usual to number people, but because he did it of an ambitious mind, as though his strength stood in his people, God punished him.'

414-19 Because of their many heathenish practices the ten tribes of Israel were carried into captivity in Assyria (2 Kings 17. 7-18).

416-18 Jeroboam made two calves of gold, one of which he placed in Bethel and the other in Dan; these, he told the Israelites, were the gods which had brought them out of Egypt, and these they worshipped (1 Kings 12. 28; 2 Kings 17. 16). Cf. *PL* 1. 482-6. In calling them 'Deities of Egypt' Milton may be following John Selden, who, in *De Diis Syris* 1. 4 (*Opera Omnia*, London, 1726, 2. 293), says that the Israelites in worshipping a golden calf were adopting an Egyptian superstition.[19] It is now known, however, that this worship was far more extensive than Selden supposed. See Robertson Smith, *Religion of the Semites*, new ed. (London, 1901), pp. 297-304.

Baal. The Hebrew word 'ba'al', pl. 'ba'alim', means primarily 'owner', 'possessor', but not in the sense of 'lord' or 'master'. When a god is called 'ba'al', the term signifies that he is the proprietor or inhabitant of a place, and hence is worshipped at the 'high places' often mentioned in the O.T. Since there were multitudes of local 'ba'alim' (Jer. 2. 28; 11. 13), 'ba'al' is a general name, as Milton evidently knew (*PL* 1. 421-2). They were worshipped as producers of fertility both of soil and of cattle (*Encyc. Bibl.* 1. 401). The many references to Baal in the O.T. make clear that Baal-worship, which the Israelites learned from the Canaanites, was one of their besetting sins (Selden, *op. cit.* 2. 1, *Opera Omnia* 2. 324 ff.; *Encyc. Bibl.* 1. 402-3).

Ashtaroth. The singular form of the name is Ashtoreth, Gr. ᾿Αστάρτη, the name of a Semitic goddess of love, identified with Cyprian Aphrodite (Robertson Smith, *op. cit.* pp. 470-1). She was the consort of Baal, and like him a producer of fertility. According to Pseudo-Lucian, *De Syria Dea* 4, she was also a moon-goddess. Although mentioned in the O.T. less often than Baal, she was one of the chief Semitic deities. In Judges 10. 6 the name in the plural is coupled with Baalim, evidently in the general sense of heathen gods and goddesses (*Encyc. Bibl.* 1. 337; Roscher, *Lexikon* 1. 1. 645-55). Milton here, as in *Nat* 200 and *SA* 1242, uses the plural form. Since he uses the singular Baal, did he intend to use the singular Ashtoreth?

419 The 'other worse then heathenish crimes', Blakeney (p. 146) believes,

---

[19] Aegyptia superstitione iniquitatos Israelitas vitulum aureum coluisse certum est.

citing Jer. 19. 5, no doubt refer to the practice of human sacrifice. Such sacrifices, part of the worship of Moloch, are what is meant by the words 'to pass through the fire' in 2 Kings 17. 17, 31; 21. 6; 23. 10 and elsewhere (*Encyc. Bibl.* 3. 3184). They were explicitly forbidden in Lev. 18. 21; Deut. 12. 30–1. But, as Milton says, the Israelites were guilty of *worse* than heathenish crimes; he probably means their lack of faith in Yahwè which permitted them to adopt heathenish practices.

425 *Circumcision vain.* An allusion to Rom. 2. 25 where Paul maintains that 'if thou be a breaker of the law, thy circumcision is made uncircumcision.' 'The outward circumcision, if it be separated from the inward, doeth not only not justify but also condemn them that are indeed circumcised, of whom it requireth that which it signifieth, that is to say cleannesse of heart, & the whole life according to the commandment of the Law' (Geneva Bible, Rom. 2. 25).

427 Blondel (p. 257) compares *TKM* (*Works* 5. 1): 'For indeed none can love freedom heartilie, but good men; the rest love not freedom, but licence.'

429 For further evidence of Milton's fondness for words beginning with *un*-, see any Milton concordance. Cf. Tasso, *Jerusalem* 2. 16. 8: 'Unseen, unmarked, unpitied, unrewarded'; and Spenser, *F.Q.* 7. 7. 46. 5: 'Unbodied, unsoul'd, unheard, unseen'. Blakeney (p. 147) believes that Milton may have been influenced by lines in Greek tragedies in which alpha privative is equivalent to *un*-: e.g. Sophocles, *Ant.* 1071: ἄμοιρον, ἀκτέριστον, ἀνόσιον νέκυν; Euripides, *Iph. T.* 220: ἄγαμος, ἄτεκνος, ἄπολις, ἄφιλος. Like collocations may be found in Greek prose writers: e.g. Plato, *Phaedrus* 240: ἄγαμον, ἄπαιδα, ἄοικον; Demosthenes, *1 Phil.* 36: ἄτακτα, ἀδιόρθωτα, ἀόρισθ' ἅπαντα.

430–1 Editors have paraphrased and emended this passage to make it more clear. The expression is compressed, it is true, but the meaning, I think, clearly enough is: 'Headlong would follow their forefathers, and return to their gods.' See note on 416–18 above.

431–2 Editors note a possible reminiscence of Jer. 5. 19: 'Like as ye have forsaken me, and served strange gods in your land, so shall ye serve strangers in a land that is not yours.'

433 See 182–203 and note, and 396–7 above.

434 *Remembring Abraham.* Remembering the covenant made with Abraham. See note on 382–4 above.

436 *Assyrian flood.* The Euphrates River. Editors note an allusion to the prophecy in Isa. 11. 15–16 that the Israelites returning from Assyria to their own land shall pass through the Euphrates as they passed through the Red Sea. Cf. Rev. 16. 12.

438–9 An allusion to Exod. 14. 21–2 and Joshua 3. 14–17 which tell of the passage of the Israelites through the Red Sea and the Jordan.

441–2 Dunster (p. 173) sees a resemblance to the passage in Vida, *Christ.* 1. 198–202, in which Satan reports to the fallen angels his failure to tempt Christ: 'In how many shapes, and with how many voices have I not approached him, but to no avail? He has ever repelled me without weapons or the use of force. But by repeating the songs of ancient prophets he has baffled my temptations and my wiles and escaped all my power.'[20]

441 *Fiend.* See note on 1. 465 above.

443 Throughout the second encounter between Christ and Satan, truth and falsehood have been contending. The rejection of the banquet contrasts the true needs of nature with what Satan declares to be her needs. When he offers riches and a way to buy David's throne, Christ meets the offer with a discourse on true 'rule'. When he offers glory and fame, Christ answers rejecting the false and defining the true. In the vision from the specular mount the contest is between outer vision or illusion and inner clarity of moral vision (A. H. Sackton, 'Architectonic Structure', *UTSE* 33, 1954, 40–1).

[20] Quas non in facies, quae non mutatus in ora
accessi incassum? Semper me reppulit ipse,
non armis ullis fretus, non viribus usus;
sed tantum veterum repetito carmine vatum,
irrita tentamenta, dolos, et vim exiit omnem.

Book IV

❧

1–6 See note on 1. 37–43.

1 *Perplex'd.* As Jerram (p. 141) observes, this is 'a word which has now lost much of its force....It meant sore distress, not merely embarrassment, as in Luke 21. 25, "distress of nations with perplexity;" Chapman, *Il.* 5. 347, "perplexed with her late harm," i.e. "sorely pained."'

success. 'Issue', 'result', not merely in a good sense, a meaning common in the 16th and 17th centuries (*OED*). Cf. *PL* 2. 9. 123; 6. 161.

3 *thrown from his hope.* Cf. 2. 30 above. The expression is the equivalent of *spe deiectus*, as in Livy 44. 28 and Caesar, *B.G.* 1. 8.

4–5 Cf. Fletcher, *C.V.* 2. 18. 3–5:

> For well that aged Syre could tip his tongue
> With golden foyle of eloquence, and lime,
> And licke his rugged speech with phrases prime.

For the 'perswasive Rhetoric' by which Satan 'won so much on Eve', see *PL* 9. 532–732; but as in Sylvester's Du Bartas, *D.W.W.*, *The Imposture* 224, it was 'glozing rhetoric'; it persuaded by specious, deceitful arguments. Cf. *Prol* 3 (*Works* 12. 163). Todd (5. 209) believes that Milton here probably had in mind the *Eva* of Fed. Malipiero (Venice, 1540) in which (p. 98) Satan is called 'the master of tempting rhetoric' (*il maestro della rettorica tentativa*).

From Milton's contemptuous references to rhetoric, as in *Def 1* (*Works* 7. 41, 43, 225, 343); *TKM* (5. 5); *Comus* 789, it is not to be assumed that he, a skilful rhetorician himself, is condemning rhetoric as such. Whether rhetoric, the art of finding the means of persuasion, is good or bad depends upon the ethical purpose of him who uses it. See Aristotle, *Rhet.* 1. 2, 4; 2. 1, 5; Cicero, *De Orat.* 2. 20; 3. 14. 55; 3. 20. 76; Quintilian 12. 1. What Milton does condemn is rhetoric which would persuade to a bad end, as would that of Comus, Salmasius, and Satan. For rhetoric in the good sense we need only turn to the speeches of Abdiel and Christ. See J. M. Major, 'Milton's View of Rhetoric',

SP 64 (1967), 685–711; W. S. Howell, *Logic and Rhetoric in England, 1500–1700* (New York, 1961), pp. 213–19.

5 *sleek't.* 'Sleek' used as a verb may denote 'the assumption of friendly or flattering looks or speech' (*OED*).

7 *This.* This man. Cf. 2. 131–2 above.
over-match. See 2. 146 above.

8 *rash.* See note on 1. 359 above.

11–14 As pride was the cause of Satan's revolt against God, so is it now, however foolishly, the cause of his temptation of Christ. See notes on 1. 358 and 2. 139 above.

12 *spight.* Cf. 446 below; *PL* 2. 384–6; Sylvester's Du Bartas, *D.W.W.*, *The Imposture* 54–5:

> Hate, *Pride*, and *Envious* spight,
> His hellish life do torture day and night;

and Beaumont, *Psyche* 9. 227. In *PL* 9. 178 Satan declared that 'spite then with spite is best repaid', but he did not see—grim irony—that he would not only make but receive payment.

15–17 The figure in these lines, well calculated to convey the impression of a persistent if futile enemy, as editors note, is probably reminiscent of Homer, *Il.* 2. 469–71: 'Even as thick swarms of flies hover about a herdsman's farm-yard in spring when milk drenches the pails'[1] and 17. 570–1, where Homer speaks of the annoying persistency of the fly. Milton may also have recalled Ariosto's comparison in *O.F.* 14. 109 of the Moors attacking the Christians to flies attacking ripe grapes, and Spenser's in *F.Q.* 2. 9. 51 of deluding temptations to buzzing flies.

18–20 The present figure emphasizes Christ's steadfastness and Satan's persistent futility, and like the one in the preceding lines, as editors observe, is probably reminiscent of Homer, *Il.* 15. 618–21: 'They stood steadfast and embattled, like a great, steep rock beside the gray sea that abides the swift paths of the shrill winds and the swelling waves that dash against it';[2] and

---

[1] ἠύτε μυιάων ἁδινάων ἔθνεα πολλά,
αἵ τε κατὰ σταθμὸν ποιμνήιον ἠλάσκουσιν
ὤρῃ ἐν εἰαρινῇ ὅτε τε γλάγος ἄγγεα δεύει.

[2] ἴσχον γὰρ πυργηδὸν ἀρηρότες, ἠύτε πέτρη
ἠλίβατος μεγάλη, πολιῆς ἁλὸς ἐγγὺς ἐοῦσα,

Virgil, *A.* 7. 586–9: 'He, like an immovable ocean-cliff resists; like an ocean-cliff which, when a great crash comes, stands unshaken in its bulk in the midst of many roaring waves';[3] and Vida, *Christ.* 4. 634–6—written, be it noted, of Satan's tempting Christ: 'As when the south-east winds raise the restless sea into waves, raging it beats again and again with threatening roar upon the steep land, but the waves dashed upon the rocks are hurled back';[4] and Fletcher, *C.V.* 3. 23:

> So have I seene a rocks heroique brest,
> Against proud Neptune, that his ruin threats,
> When all his waves he hath to battle prest,
> And with a thousand swelling billows beats
> The stubborne stone, and foams, and chafes, and frets
>   To heave him from his root, unmooved stand;
>   And more in heapes the barking surges band,
> The more in pieces beat, flie weeping to the strand.

In 'The Iconography of Renunciation: the Miltonic Simile', *Critical Essays on Milton from ELH* (Baltimore, 1969), p. 79, Kingsley Widmer comments that in the comparison of Satan to a 'swarm of flies' and Christ to a 'wine press', Christ is paradoxically tempting Satan. In the immediately following simile the swarming flies become a 'vain battery', like the breaking of waves upon a rock. How, Widmer asks, can the two similes form 'a coherent image of the action'; how can the flies be waves, the wine press a rock, the buzzing of the flies a battery; and how can Satan be compared both to the flies and the waves? His answer is that in these similes Milton has not attempted to elaborate 'the visual logic of a scene or character', but rather requires 'the application of a dialectical rather than a visual principle'. As Widmer paraphrases the similes, they mean: that Satan's temptations, at once parasitic and futile—in reality tempting himself to commit other evil acts—are aptly likened to a swarm of flies; but the assaults of evil upon goodness, as in Christ, persist throughout

---

ἥτε μένει λιγέων ἀνέμων λαιψηρὰ κέλευθα
κύματά τε τροφόεντα, τά τε προσερεύγεται αὐτήν.

[3] Ille velut pelagi rupes immota resistit,
ut pelagi rupes magno veniente fragore,
quae sese, multis circum latrantibus undis,
mole tenet.

[4] Ut cum sollicitum tollunt mare fluctibus Euri,
crebra ferit, saevitque minaci verbere in alta
littora, sed saxis allisa revertitur unda.

time and must be more threateningly compared to waves beating upon a rock. The action of evil, then, is at once trivial and immense, and its significant duality is revealed in the linkage of the disparate similes. And likewise 'the apparently rich and seasonable energy of Christ (the wine press) is really the principle of immutability (a rock).'

Finally these similes bear out James Whaler's observation in his most penetrating article, 'The Miltonic Simile', *PMLA* 46 (1931), 1036–7, that 'Milton employs simile to explain or to emotionalize or to ennoble or to relieve or to anticipate, or to fulfil two or even several of these functions at once.... It is never purely decorative.'

20 *froth or bubbles.* Satan's foolish, fallacious arguments have as little firmness and strength as froth or bubbles.

25–6 Satan has shown Christ the kingdoms of the world to the east and the south-east of the 'specular mount' (see note on 3. 252–3). Now in another supernatural vision he will show him those to the west. The temptation is the same as that at the close of the third book, but it is presented in what Satan assumes to be a more attractive form, namely that Christ make himself master of the Roman empire, the greatest of all earthly powers.

In making this offer Satan is expressing the classical conception of Rome as the *urbs æterna* current in Latin literature from the late republican period, and for political and religious reasons effective throughout the Middle Ages. Cf. Virgil, *A.* 1. 278–9; 3. 97–8, 157–9; 4. 229–31; 6. 852–4; 7. 98–101; Horace, *Carm. Saec.* 61–8; Ovid, *F.* 1. 85–8; Ammianus Marcellinus 14. 6. This Roman conception of the *urbs æterna*, S. Kliger maintains in 'The "Urbs Æterna" in *PR*' (*PMLA* 61, 1946, 474–91) provides Milton's literary milieu. 'Christ's rejection of the Roman imperial throne in the specific terms [of *PR* 4. 146–51]', he writes, 'is explicable in terms of the effort, successful or otherwise, of Saint Augustine, Lactantius, Tertullian, Prudentius, Dante, and many others, to reconcile Christian eschatology with their fervent hope, paradoxically, for the continuation in prosperity of the pagan "urbs æterna" and all that the imperial idea stood for.

'The effort at reconciliation may be described simply as an attempt to convert the "urbs æterna" into an "urbs sacra" (pp. 483–4). Rome was seen as "providing the earthly order on the basis of which it was the Church's mission to create a spiritual order" (p. 485). Christ's stern rebuke of Satan [in *PR* 4. 149–51]...obviates the entire problem faced by the Christian panegyrists of Rome as they attempted to reconcile the "urbs sacra" with the "urbs æterna."

Christ's rebuke is in reality a call to repentance not of the pagans but of the believers, those who themselves eagerly awaited the Messiah's advent' (p. 490).

27–33 The plain is the long, narrow coastal plain of Italy, comprising Etruria, Latium, and Campania, washed by the Tyrrhenian, or Southern, Sea, and bounded on the east by the Apennines. The river dividing the plain is the Tiber, and the 'Imperial City' is Rome. Milton is now describing a country with which he became familiar during his sojourn in Italy in 1638–9.

31 *Septentrion blasts.* North winds (*OED*), the *venti septentriones* of Cicero, *Att.* 9. 6. 3; Columella, *R.R.* 11. 2. 21. The *septentriones*, or 'seven plough-oxen', are the seven stars forming the northern constellation, the Wain or the Bear; hence *septentrionalis*, northern. See Aulus Gellius 2. 21. 4; 22. 3.

thence. That is, rising in the Apennines. Cf. Ovid, *M.* 15. 432: *Appenninigenae ...Thybrides.*

32 *of whose banks.* Masson (3. 590) has 'little doubt' that Milton dictated 'off' and so emends the line. The emendation, Jerram (p. 142) admits, gives the right sense, but is hardly Miltonic. 'On' would be the obvious substitution for 'of' were it not for 'on' in the phrase immediately following. The meaning clearly is 'on each of whose banks', the normal order of the phrase being inverted.

33–60 There is a general resemblance between Milton's description of Rome and that in Claudian 28. 35–52 (2. 76–8) but not sufficient to warrant Dunster's belief (p. 191) that Milton used Claudian as his model. The details, of which Milton uses the greater number, are the prominent features of ancient Rome mentioned by so many writers that it is impossible in any particular instance to determine whence Milton's information came. He may well have known the description of the marvellous buildings of Rome in Pliny, *N.H.* 36. 24. 101–25, and the discussion of the excessive luxury in buildings of the Romans in George Hakewill's *An Apologie for the Power and Providence of God in the Government of the World* (London, 1630, pp. 392–412). But he must also have drawn upon his own observations of the surviving monuments of ancient Rome when he was in the city in October and November 1638 and in January and February 1638/9.

There are anachronisms in the description of Rome (see notes on 50–4 and 55–60 below), for the Rome which Milton describes is that of the later emperors rather than that of Tiberius. But his purpose in this vision, which, it must be remembered, is supernatural, does not demand historical accuracy. It does demand that the luxurious capital of a powerful people be so described by Satan that it will arouse in Christ a desire to make himself master of it.

34 *Towers.* Such buildings as the tall houses, rising storey upon storey (Seneca, *Ep.* 90. 7), or the tower of Maecenas (Horace, *C.* 3. 29. 10; Suetonius, *Nero* 38), and the tower of the *Domus Augusti* (Suetonius, *Aug.* 72).

Temples. From the period of the kings there had been many temples in Rome, and others were built by the emperors, as the temples of Apollo, Mars, Ceres, Venus (Suetonius, *Aug.* 21, 29; Tacitus, *Ann.* 2. 49), and, most famous of all, the great temple of Jupiter (Pliny, *N.H.* 33. 5. 16, 6. 19; 35. 3. 14; 36. 6. 45).

35 The seven 'small Hills' frequently mentioned by Roman writers are: the Palatine (*Palatium*), the Capitoline (*Capitolinus*), the Quirinal (*Quirinalis*), the Caelian (*Caelimontium*), the Aventine (*Aventinus*), the Esquiline (*Esquilinae*), and the Viminal (*Viminalis*).

Palaces. By the time of Tiberius there were many palaces in Rome, of which may be mentioned the *Domus Augusti* (Suetonius, *Aug.* 72), the palace of Tiberius (Suetonius, *Otho* 6; Tacitus, *Hist.* 1. 27), and later the vast and incredibly luxurious *Domus Aurea* built by Nero (Pliny, *N.H.* 36. 24. 111; Suetonius, *Nero* 31). Seneca (*Ben.* 7. 10. 5) writes of private palaces which cover more ground than great cities. See S. B. Platner and T. Ashby, *A Topographical Dictionary of Rome* (London, 1929), pp. 154 ff.

36 *Porches.* A porch was a covered colonnade (*porticus*, στοά) consisting of a wall and one or more rows of columns forming a long gallery bordering a street or enclosing a rectangular space. Such were the *porticus Liviae* and the *porticus Octaviae* built by Augustus (Dio Cassius, 54. 23. 6; 49. 43. 8; Ovid, *F.* 6. 639–40; Suetonius, *Aug.* 29), and the *porticus Minucia* (Velleius Paterculus 2. 8. 3). In *El* 1. 69 Milton mentions Pompey's porch, the *porticus Pompeii* (Pliny, *N.H.* 35. 37. 114).

Theatres. Often mentioned by Roman writers are the *theatrum Marcelli* (Suetonius, *Caes.* 44; Dio Cassius 43. 49) built by Julius Caesar and Augustus, and the *theatrum Pompei* (Tacitus, *Ann.* 3. 23; 14. 20; Dio Cassius 39. 8). The great *amphitheatrum Flavium*, the Colosseum, was not built until the reign of Vespasian nor dedicated until A.D. 79 (Suetonius, *Vesp.* 9). In *N.H.* 36. 14. 113–20 Pliny describes large theatres built by Scaurus and Curio.

Baths. The earliest of the great Roman baths, the *thermae Agrippae*, were built by Agrippa in 25 B.C. (Dio Cassius 53. 27; Pliny, *N.H.* 34. 19. 62; 35. 9.

26), but the vast structures, 'baths the size of provinces' (Ammianus Marcellinus 16. 10. 13), the *thermae Antoninianae*, the baths of Caracalla (*Script. Hist. Aug.*, *Carac.* 9; Eutropius 8. 20), and the *thermae Diocletianae*, the baths of Diocletian (*C.I.L.* 6. 1130; Aurelius Victor, *Caes.* 39) were not built until A.D. 216 and 302 respectively.

Aqueducts. The first aqueduct to supply water to Rome was the *aqua Appia*, built in 315 B.C. (Livy 9. 29. 6; Frontinus, *Aquaed.* 1. 4–7). Others built before the time of Tiberius were the *aqua Marcia* (Pliny, *N.H.* 36. 24. 121; Frontinus 1. 4, 7, 9), the *aqua Tepula* (Frontinus 1. 4, 8, 9), and the *aqua Alsetiana* (*ibid*. 1. 4, 11, 18).

37   *Statues*. From the frequency with which Roman writers mention statues, it is evident that they were one of the most conspicuous features of Rome. Pliny (*N.H.* 34. 9–18) mentions many statues, so many, indeed, that he asks (34. 17. 37) what man could recount them all.

Trophees. Roman generals regularly brought to Rome the richest spoils of the lands which they conquered. After the capture of Corinth in 146 B.C., the Romans stripped the temples of statues and ornaments of every kind (Pausanias 7. 16. 8; Velleius Paterculus 1. 13. 4). Titus did likewise in A.D. 70 after capturing Jerusalem (Josephus, *B.J.* 7. 1. 3; 7. 5. 7). Lucan (3. 154–68) gives a long list of the rich spoils stored in the Roman treasury. Cf. Livy 10. 46. 1–8; 33. 27. 2–4.

Triumphal Arcs. The two earliest triumphal arches in Rome were built in 196 B.C. (Livy 33. 27. 4). Others built by the time of the present action were the two arches of Augustus, the *arcus Augusti* (Dio Cassius 51. 19; 54. 8) and the arch of Tiberius, the *arcus Tiberii* (Tacitus, *Ann.* 2. 41). By the time of the later empire many others had been built (Claudian 28. 50–1 (2. 78); Platner and Ashby, *Topog. Dict.*, pp. 32–47). When he was in Rome, Milton no doubt saw such arches as still exist, as notably the *arcus Titi* erected in honour of Titus and in commemoration of the siege of Jerusalem.

38   *Gardens*. There were many gardens, both public and private, in Rome long before the time of Tiberius, as appears from numerous references to them in Horace, *S.* 1. 8. 7; Ovid, *P.* 1. 8. 37–8; Tacitus, *Ann.* 2. 41; 11. 1, 32, 37; 13. 47; Plutarch, *Pomp.* 44; Dio Cassius 54. 29; 65. 10; Velleius Paterculus 2. 60. 3.

Groves. By 'groves' presumably are meant the trees in the inner courts of large houses mentioned in Horace, *C.* 3. 10. 5–7; *Ep.* 1. 10. 22; Nepos, *Att.* 13. 2; Tibullus 3. 3. 15. Suetonius (*Nero* 31) mentions woods as part of the gardens of the Golden House. See note on 50–4 below.

40–2 Since in these lines and in line 57 Milton mentions certain optical instruments, he is almost certainly alluding to various scientific or pseudo-scientific explanations of Christ's vision, of which Miss Pope (*PR, Tradition and Poem*, pp. 112–14) finds eight, some of them purely fantastic, as, for example, a series of reflecting mirrors, a great map spread out by Satan, and an actual flight through the air. She concludes that clearly Milton 'did not consider the matter a fit subject for the minute inquiry and ample theorizing some theologians had indulged in; and he deliberately kept his whole discussion of the topic as vague and indeterminate as he could.' But if that were his intention, why did he mention it at all? The words 'were curious to enquire', that is idly inquisitive, I take to be a derisive dismissal of what he considered pedantry. See Blondel, pp. 87–8. In an action including other patent marvels, there ought to be no difficulty in accepting a marvellous vision. See next note.

40 *Parallax.* Not here used in the modern astronomical sense (*OED*) but in the sense of παράλλαξις, a change or apparent change of position, as, to use Masson's (3. 308) illustration, 'the apparent raising of a coin in a basin, so as to make it visible farther off. . .by merely pouring water into the basin.'

'Optic Skill / Of vision multiplyed through air', Jerram (p. 144) suggests, may mean 'the effect of mirrors *successively* reflecting objects over a vast distance through the air.' But this expression and 'Aerie microscope' in line 57, Svendsen ('Milton's "Aerie Microscope"', *MLN* 64, 1949, 525–7) believes may be an allusion to a strange instrument described in Thomas Digges's *A Geometrical Practical Treatize Named Pantometria* (London, 1591, p. 28) consisting of a system of lenses set at adjustable angles, which was supposed to enable the user not only 'to set out the proportion of an whole region', but to see particular objects therein, even the insides of houses, '*so that ye shall discerne any trifle, or reade any letter lying there open*'. This instrument, a 'project' in the terminology of the 17th century, which produced many projects great and small, good and bad, is an example of the sort of crack-brained schemes which Ben Jonson, as Milton may have known, ridiculed in *The Devil is an Ass*. See Alex Keller, 'The Age of the Projectors', *History Today* 16 (1966), 467–74.

45 In Rutilius, *De Reditu Suo* 1. 47 Rome is called *regina pulcherrima mundi*. Hughes (p. 516) notes an 'ironical echo of St. John's description of *Rome*, who "saith in her heart, I sit a queen, and am no widow, and shall see no sorrow" (Rev. xviii, 7).'

46 *spoils.* See note on 37 above.

185

47–50 The Capitol (*Capitolinus mons*) is the smallest of the seven hills of Rome; on it stood the great temple of Jupiter, Juno, and Minerva. On all sides except the south-east it was surrounded by steep cliffs called the Tarpeian rock (*Tarpeium saxum*) (Varro, *L.L.* 5. 41; Livy 6. 20. 12; Tacitus, *Ann.* 6. 19).

50–4 The imperial palace on the Palatine hill which Milton describes cannot be the *Domus Augusti*, the unpretentious palace of Augustus (Suetonius, *Aug.* 72–3), nor the *Domus Tiberiana*, the palace of Tiberius, about which little is known, but rather the vast and incredibly splendid *Domus Aurea*, the Golden House, built by Nero after the fire of A.D. 64 (Suetonius, *Nero* 31). Milton may have visited the ruins of the Golden House, which have been known since the early Renaissance.

54 Terraces there may have been, but ancient Roman buildings had no turrets and spires. Is Milton, as Dunster (p. 191) suggests, blending 'the old English Castle [Windsor] with his Roman view'?

55–60 In his account of the marvellous buildings in Rome, Pliny (*N.H.* 36. 24. 101–25) writes that in 78 B.C. the finest house in the city was that of Lepidus (36. 24. 109). Within thirty-five years its splendours were surpassed by a hundred other houses, and by his own time even these had been surpassed by others without number.

57–8 See notes on 40–2 above.

59 *hand.* 'The performance of an artist, etc.; execution, handiwork' (*OED*), as in *PL* 9. 438.

61–79 See the earlier description of the Parthian power in 3. 298–309. In the present passage there is less emphasis upon military power, possibly because, as is stated in line 80, all nations are already subject to Rome.

63 *Pretors.* The praetors were Roman judicial officers next in rank below the consuls (Livy 43. 14. 3; Cicero, *Att.* 9. 9. 3; *Leg.* 3. 3. 8). In the time of Tiberius there were as many as sixteen praetors (Dio Cassius 58. 20. 5; 59. 20. 5).

Proconsuls. The governors or military commanders of the Roman provinces, who, as the name implies, exercised the delegated authority of the consuls (Livy 8. 23. 12; 23. 30. 19; Caesar, *B.G.* 3. 20; Tacitus, *Ann.* 15. 22).

65 *Lictors.* Officers who attended and executed the orders of the chief Roman magistrates, and symbolized authority and justice (Livy 1. 8. 2; 8. 7. 19 Caesar, *B.G.* 1. 6).

rods. The *fasces*, a bundle of rods and an axe borne by the lictors before superior magistrates as an emblem of their power (Livy 2. 7. 7; Cicero, *Rep.* 2. 17, 31; Tacitus, *Ann.* 3. 2).

66 *Cohorts*. A cohort was a 'body of infantry in the Roman army, of which there were ten in a legion' (*OED*).

turmes. Troops, crowds, from Lat. *turma*. Some editors believe that Milton coined the word, but *OED* gives earlier examples.

68 *Appian road*. The *via Appia*, the oldest and most famous of Roman roads, leading south-east to Brundisium (Livy 9. 29. 5–6; Statius, *S.* 2. 2. 12; Diodorus Siculus 20. 36). It was the road by which travellers would reach Rome from the countries mentioned in lines 69–76.

70–9 The countries and peoples here mentioned, first those to the east and south, then those to the west and north, all at the outermost limits of the Roman empire, are chosen to give an impression of its vast extent; nor does Satan hesitate to make it appear more vast than it is, for he includes among the subject peoples Britons, Scythians, and Sarmatians, who had not been conquered by the Romans.

70 *Syene*. Modern Assuan in Egypt, 'five thousand stadia' south of Alexandria and at the limit of the summer tropic (Pliny, *N.H.* 2. 75. 183; Strabo 2. 2. 2; 2. 5. 7).

where the shadow both way falls. 'It was well known in antiquity that between the tropic of Cancer and the equator the shadow fell in summer to the south and in winter to the north. This is discussed by Sacrobosco [*De Sphaera*, Paris, 1608, p. 46], and the climate ("clima") of Meroe is said to occupy this region' (A. H. Gilbert, 'Milton's Textbook of Astronomy', *PMLA* 38, 1923, 306).

71 *Meroe*. A region partly surrounded by the Nile, the Blue Nile, and the Atbara, and supposed by the ancients to be an island. According to Strabo 1. 2. 25 (cf. 16. 4. 8; 17. 1. 2) it was the seat of empire and the metropolis of the Ethiopians.

72 *Realm of Bocchus*. Mauretania, of which Bocchus, father-in-law of Jugurtha, was king (Sallust, *Jug.* 19. 7; 62. 7).

Black-moor Sea. The Mediterranean off the Barbary coast, the land of the Moors or Blackamoors. Juvenal (10. 148–9) calls it *Mauro oceano*, and Horace (*C.* 2. 6. 3–4) *Maura unda*.

73 *Asian Kings*. The rulers of such kingdoms as Pontus and Cappadocia.

Parthian envoys came to Rome in A.D. 16 and 18 (Tacitus, *Ann.* 2. 2. 58); and a deputation was sent from Ilium to Tiberius (Suetonius, *Tib.* 52). Since Christ was unmoved by Parthian power, Satan now offers him an even greater power.

74-5 Indian envoys came to Augustus to sue for his friendship (Suetonius, *Aug.* 21; Horace, *Carm. Saec.* 55-6); I find no record of Indian envoys coming to Tiberius, nor of envoys from Chersonese and Taprobane ever coming to Rome. Satan may be deliberately inaccurate in order to exaggerate the importance of Rome.

74 *Chersoness.* 'A region east of India, usually identified with the peninsula of Malacca. (Ortelius, *Parergon* [*Theatrum*, Pt. 2], p. 1). Purchas writes "The Kingdome of Siam comprehendeth that Aurea Regio of Ptolemy by Arrianus in his Periplus...called Aurea Continens; nigh to which is placed that Aurea Chersonesus..."' (Gilbert, *G.D.*, p. 82). Gilbert quotes from Purchas the account of a banquet given by the King of Sumatra, who evidently lived in a world of gold. Cf. Ariosto, *O.F.* 15. 17. 1: *l'aurea Chersonesso.* Probably to avoid rhyme with 'these' in the preceding line Milton does not use the form 'Chersonese'.

75 Milton probably 'thought of Taprobane as Ceylon, as do modern geographers. It has also been identified with Sumatra...[*Purchas his Pilgrimes* 1. 92, 151]. It frequently appears on old maps as the last island toward the east (Ortelius, *Parergon*, p. 1).' (Gilbert, *G.D.*, p. 284). Pliny (*N.H.* 6. 24. 81-91), who, among the ancients, gives the fullest account, writes of it as *extra orbem a natura relegata* (89).

76 *Turbants.* '*Tulipant, turbant* were the most usual English forms' of this word in the 17th century (*OED*). See Spenser, *F.Q.* 4. 11. 28. 6, where the spelling is 'turribant'.

77 *Gades.* The Latin name of Cadiz. Its Greek name, Gadier, occurs in *SA* 716, and Cales, a form common in the 17th century, in *Eikon* (*Works* 5. 153). In the time of Augustus, Gades was the chief city of the Iberian peninsula and, among the cities of the empire, was second only to Rome (Strabo 3. 5. 3-10). It is here mentioned as the most western city of the world.

Brittish West. Since in the time of Tiberius there was little communication between Rome and Britain, which the Romans conquered only in the reign of Claudius, after A.D. 43, 'Brittish West' probably means Armorica, modern Brittany, whose people, in *HistBr* 2 (*Works* 10. 101), Milton says 'were call'd the *Britans* of *France*'.

78 *Germans*. Both before and after he became emperor, Tiberius engaged in military campaigns against the Germans (Suetonius, *Tib*. 18–19; Dio Cassius 55. 6–7).

Scythians. See note on 3. 301 above.

Sarmatians. A people who occupied the country between the Vistula and the Don (Mela 1. 3. 5; Pliny, *N.H.* 4. 13. 97), modern Poland and part of Russia. They were never subject to Rome.

79 *Danubius*. The Danube, the north-eastern boundary of the Roman empire (Mela 3. 4; Pliny, *N.H.* 4. 12. 79).

Tauric Pool. The Sea of Azov, the *lacus Maeotis* (Pliny, *N.H.* 4. 12. 75; 6. 1. 3).

83 In *HistBr* 2 (*Works* 10. 51) Milton writes: 'The *Romans*...beate us into some civilitie; likely else to have continu'd longer in a barbarous and savage manner of life.' Of the fall of Rome he says (10. 101): 'With the Empire fell also what before in this Western World was cheifly *Roman*; Learning, Valour, Eloquence, History, Civility, and eev'n Language it self'.

84–5 In 3. 362–4 above Satan advised Christ *first* to make himself master of the Parthian empire. The present inconsistency is not only in keeping with his character, but it also indicates the increasing desperation of his effort to tempt Christ. Moreover, Christ has refused (3. 387–93) to make use of *any* temporal power, but Satan pretends to assume that he has refused only that of Parthia.

84 Satan again introduces fame, although Christ has already rejected it. See 3. 47–8 above and note.

85–7 See note on 3. 294–7 above.

86 Unless Satan uses 'barbarous' in the Greek sense (see note on 3. 119 above), his statement is false.

88–9 Satan has offered all the kingdoms of *this* world; but, as Christ maintains throughout the poem, there is another kingdom *not* of this world. In offering Christ all the learning of the Greeks, as he is about to do, Satan most artfully attempts to seduce him by means of the kind of riches for which he has rejected all other riches. As B. Rajan observes ('Jerusalem and Athens: the Temptation of Learning in "Paradise Regained"', *Th'Upright Heart and Pure*, ed. A. P. Fiore, Pittsburgh, 1967, p. 67), this is a move on Satan's part arising 'strictly out of the logic of combat'. Thus viewed 'the temptation of learning' has little to do with Milton's supposed 'disillusionment', or with a concern to follow precedent, or with a 'passion for innovation'.

90–7 Tiberius Claudius Nero, successor to Augustus and Roman Emperor from A.D. 14 to 37, having been born in 42 B.C., was at the time of the present action over seventy. His adopted son, Germanicus, died in A.D. 19, and his own son, Drusus, four years later (Tacitus, *Ann.* 2. 71–2; 4. 8). In A.D. 26 Tiberius left Rome never to return (*ibid.* 4. 57; Suetonius, *Tib.* 39), and the next year retired to Capri, there freely to indulge his incredibly bestial lusts (Tacitus, *Ann.* 4. 67; 6. 1). The 'Favourite', whom he distrusted and the Roman people hated, was Aelius Sejanus (*ibid.* 1. 69; 4. 1–3; Suetonius, *Tib.* 61; *Calig.* 12; Dio Cassius 58. 2–5; Seneca, *Tranq.* 11. 11). So cruel and tyrannical was Tiberius, and so hated by the Roman people, that at his death there was general rejoicing (Tacitus, *Ann.* 4. 42, 69–70; 6. 19, 30; Suetonius, *Tib.* 59–62, 75). This is the tradition which Milton knew, and which Ben Jonson followed when he wrote *Sejanus*. In *Psyche* 225–6 and 229 Beaumont's indictment of Tiberius is very similar to Milton's, as Mrs Lewalski points out in *Brief Epic*, p. 122. Despite this tradition, modern historians find no serious evidence that Tiberius was the evil monster depicted by Tacitus and Suetonius. See F. B. Marsh, *The Reign of Tiberius* (London, 1931), pp. 218–19, R. S. Rogers, *Studies in the Reign of Tiberius* (Baltimore, 1943), pp. 3–88, and R. Syme, *Tacitus* (Oxford, 1958), 2. 420–34.

100–5 For Christ's retort to this hypocritical argument, see lines 125–9; and for a similar argument and retort, see 3. 374–82 and 407–13 above.

102 *victor people.* Between these words in the first edition of 1671 there is a comma which is removed in the Errata.

103–4 Cf. Luke 4. 6: 'And the devil said unto him, All this power will I give thee, and the glory of them: for that is delivered unto me; and to whomsoever I will I give it.' See note on 1. 363 above.

108 *David's Throne.* See 1. 240–1; 3. 150–80 above and notes.

109–53 In offering Rome Satan has offered Christ the sum of all the wealth, glory, and military might of pre-Christian civilization. But Christ's kingdom is not of this world. Even as the banquet and worldly glory have their heavenly counterparts, so the *civitas terrena* has its counterpart in the *civitas Dei*. Of the nature of the earthly city Christ is not in doubt, and in rejecting it he is making certain of the heavenly, to which he alludes in the reference to the stone and the tree in Daniel's prophecy (2. 34; 4. 11). Since Rome signifies worldly power and glory, and, under Tiberius, brutality and sensuality, the temptation is inclusive; and Christ's 'unmov'd' rejection of it—and note that it is *unmov'd* (cf. 3. 386 above)—is the rejection of all the rewards possible to an un-Christian hero of the active kind (Kermode, 'Milton's Hero', *RES* n.s. 4, 1953, 327).

114-21 Wealthy Romans of the later republic and the empire went to great excesses in feasting (Tacitus, *Ann.* 3. 55). Juvenal (6. 292-5), Martial (3. 22), and Seneca (*Cons. Helv.* 10) write of extravagance in food and drink as a common evil of their time. Cf. Cicero, *Fin.* 2. 8; Pliny, *N.H.* 9. 53. 104; Valerius Maximus 9. 1; Macrobius, *Sat.* 2. 8; Plutarch, *Luc.* 39-41. Perhaps the best picture of this form of Roman luxury is that in the *Cena Trimalchionis* of Petronius. In *A.P.P.G.* (pp. 360-92) George Hakewill, with an imposing array of evidence from Roman writers, discusses the matter at length.

115 Round tables of *citrum*, the wood of the *citrus*, a North African tree, were so greatly prized by the Romans that they often sold for incredibly large sums (Petronius, *Sat.* 119. 28; Martial 2. 43. 9; 9. 22. 5; 9. 59. 7-10; 10. 98. 6; Silius Italicus 13. 354; Cicero, 2 *Ver.* 4. 17. 37; Seneca, *Ben.* 7. 9. 2; Pliny, *N.H.* 13. 29. 91-5).

Atlantic stone. Probably Numidian marble (*marmor Numidicum*) from the Atlas Mountains (Pliny, *N.H.* 5. 2. 22; Seneca, *Ep.* 86. 6). Blakeney (p. 154) suggests that '*Atlantic* stone' may mean the marble *Atlantes* to support the citrus-top tables, since such supports evidently were commonly used. See Daremberg and Saglio, *Dict.* 1. 1. 526; K. J. Marquardt, *Privatleben der Römer* (Leipzig, 1879-82), p. 310; Pauly-Wissowa, s.v. *Atlantes.*

116 See note on 1. 290-3 above.

117-18 The Italian wines of Setia, Caecubum, and Falernum are often mentioned by Roman writers (Horace, *C.* 1. 20. 9-10; 1. 31. 9-12; *S.* 2. 8. 16; Virgil, *G.* 2. 96; Martial 13. 106-25), as also are Greek wines from Chios and Crete (Horace, *C.* 3. 19. 5; *S.* 1. 10. 24; Aelian, *V.H.* 12. 31). In *A.P.P.G.* (pp. 362-72) George Hakewill assembles much evidence that excessive drinking was a serious Roman vice.

118-20 Costly drinking cups, as well as all manner of other gold and silver plate, were a luxury which the Romans carried to excess. Cicero several times mentions cups embossed and set with gems which were ever objects of Verres' rapacity (2 *Ver.* 4. 18. 38-9, 22. 49, 24. 54, 27. 62; Juvenal 1. 76; 5. 37-41; Martial 9. 59. 14; Silius Italicus 13. 356-7; 14. 661-4; Petronius, *Sat.* 52; Plutarch, *Luc.* 40). See also Hakewill, *A.P.P.G.*, pp. 372-3. Whether 'Myrrhine', Lat. *murra* or *murrha*, referred to glass, onyx, or Chinese porcelain is uncertain (Marquardt, *Privatleben der Römer*, pp. 765-8).

121-5 Dunster (p. 202) suggests that in these lines there is possibly an allusion to embassies which came to congratulate Charles II upon his restoration.

125 *Outlandish.* 'Foreign and extravagant' (Lockwood, *Lexicon*). The word occurs nowhere else in Milton's poetry and never in Shakespeare or Spenser.

130-54 The Romans, once a free and victorious people, through the loss of their earlier virtues, have become the vassals of the emperors. See 2. 446-80 above. Milton expresses the same idea of freedom in *Def 1* (*Works* 7. 285, 373). The principle, as Plato (*Protag.* 322, 325-7; *Rep.* 4. 428; 8. 546) maintains, is that the very existence of the state depends upon virtue; and hence as virtue degenerates, the state also degenerates, and freedom is lost. See 143-5 below and note, and cf. *Ref 2* (*Works* 3. 38); *Tetr* (4. 137).

Luxury began to be an evil among the Romans after the return of the armies from Asia in 188 B.C. (Livy 39. 6-7); and by the beginning of the empire and long thereafter Roman writers again and again exemplify variations of the later theme of Goldsmith,

> Ill fares the land, to hastening ills a prey,
> Where wealth accumulates, and men decay.

See Horace, *C.* 3. 5. 5-12; 3. 6. 33-4; Sallust, *Cat.* 9-12; 52. 19-23; Juvenal 11. 77-182; Valerius Maximus 4. 4; Tacitus, *Ann.* 3. 52-5; Seneca, *Ep.* 86. 1-13; 87. 9-11; 90. 10; Lucan 1. 160-82; Martial 3. 47; Petronius, *Sat.* 119; Augustine, *Civ. D.* 1. 29; S. Dill, *Roman Society from Nero to Marcus Aurelius* (London, 1904), pp. 58-99.

130 As Jortin (*Tracts* 1. 332-4) notes, Milton alludes to the account in Tacitus, *Ann.* 6. 6, of Tiberius' confession of the sense of guilt which tormented him. In a letter to the Senate he wrote: 'May all the gods and goddesses destroy me more miserably than I feel myself to be daily perishing, if I know at this moment what to write to you, Senators, how to write it, or what, in short, not to write.' Tacitus then adds: 'Assuredly Tiberius was not saved by his elevation or his solitude from having to confess the anguish of his heart and his self-inflicted punishment.'[5]

135-7 Some Roman provincial governors treated the provinces as sources of

---

[5] Quid scribam vobis, patres conscripti, aut quomodo scribam, aut quid omnino non scribam hoc tempore, di me deaeque peius perdant quam perire me cotidie sentio, si scio.... Quippe Tiberium non fortuna, non solitudines protegebant, quin tormenta pectoris suasque ipse poenas fateretur.

wealth to be extracted by any means, however unscrupulous (Justin 38. 7. 7; Juvenal 8. 87–124). Cicero (*Pis.* 40. 96; cf. *Prov. Cons.* 3–6) gives an appalling list of Piso's plunderings of Macedonia, and in the Verrine orations he draws up a damning indictment of Verres for his exploitation of Sicily.

136 *Peeling.* 'Plundering', pillaging (*OED*), as in *HistBr* 1 (*Works* 10. 27); *ComBk* (18. 211). The word occurs nowhere else in Milton's poetry.

138 Cicero (*Pis.* 25. 60) considered the pomp and spectacle of a Roman triumph as 'the idle amusement of children' (*inania delectamenta puerorum*). Of pomp and ceremonial Milton usually speaks with disapproval, implied or explicit, as in 3. 246 above; *PL* 5. 354; 11. 748; *Ref* 1 (*Works* 3. 24); *HistMosc*, Pref. (10. 327).

139–40 Seneca (*Ep.* 7. 2–5; cf. 95. 33; *Brev. Vit.* 13. 6–7) condemned gladiatorial combats between men and between men and wild beasts not only because of their brutality, but also because of their demoralizing effect upon those who witnessed them. For the same reasons, among others, Tertullian in *De Spec.* 21 (Migne, *Pat. Lat.* 1. 655) condemned such sports, and Lactantius in *D.I.* 6. 20 (*Pat. Lat.* 6. 706–8) said that those who witness these cruelties do so at the cost of their humanity. See also Petronius, *Sat.* 119. 14–18; Tacitus, *Ann.* 1. 76; Calpurnius, *E.* 64–72; Augustine, *Conf.* 6. 8. 13; Dill, *Roman Society from Nero to Marcus Aurelius*, pp. 234–44.

142 *Scene.* Theatre, Lat. *scaena*. This may be an allusion to the theatre of the Restoration, notorious for its 'profaneness and immorality', and it may be reminiscent of Tertullian, *De Spec.* 10 ff. (Migne, *Pat. Lat.* 1. 642), of Augustine, *Conf.* 3. 2. 2–4, and of other patristic writings which condemn the theatre as idolatrous and morally corrupting.

143–5 The idea that 'true Libertie...always with right Reason dwells', and that loss of inward liberty entails the loss of outward liberty, is more fully expressed in *PL* 12. 83–101.

147 *David's Throne.* See note on 1. 240–1 above.

147–8 Christ, as editors note, appropriates Nebuchadnezzar's dream (Dan. 4. 10–12) in which he saw a tree, 'and the height thereof reached unto heaven, and the sight thereof to the end of all the earth'. The dream, as Daniel interpreted it (4. 20–7), signified the degradation of Nebuchadnezzar until he should 'know that the most High ruleth in the kingdom of men'. See also the parable of the mustard seed in Matt. 13. 31–2.

149-50 Editors also note the allusion to another dream of Nebuchadnezzar (Dan. 2. 31–5) in which he saw an image and a stone 'which smote the image upon his feet that were of iron and clay, and brake them to pieces...and the stone that smote the image became a great mountain, and filled the whole earth.' The image, Daniel (2. 37–45) explained, symbolized four empires which were to be overthrown by the everlasting kingdom of the God of heaven represented by the stone. The empires have been identified as the Babylonian, Persian, Macedonian, and Roman (Geneva Bible, Dan. 2. 38–40; cf. Diodati, *Pious Annotations*, Dan. 2. 38–40).

151 See note on 1. 240–1 above.

152-3 See 3. 354–65 and 394–402 above and notes.

154-69 This speech is the angry, impudent retort of one who, fearful and intensely irritated by a failure which deeply wounds his pride, is reduced, for want of argument, to accusing his opponent of perversity and fastidiousness. In this assertion he is attempting to enhance the value of his proffered gifts not only in Christ's eyes but also in his own. At last he brazenly blurts out the 'abominable terms', that all his gifts are offered on condition that Christ acknowledge him as his superior lord.

155 *slight.* An adverb. See note on 1. 203 above.

157 *difficult.* 'Hard to induce or persuade...obstinate' (*OED*), like Lat. *difficilis*, as in Cicero, *Senec.* 18. 65; Horace, *S.* 2. 5. 90; Terence, *Heaut.* 535, 933.
    nice. As 'nice' was used in the 16th and 17th centuries, it is often 'difficult to say in what particular sense the writer intended it to be taken' (*OED*); but here it almost certainly means 'fastidious', hard to please, as in *PL* 5. 433.
    For 'the difficult' some commentators would read 'thee difficult', but the meaning demands no emendation.

158 *still.* Perpetually, continually, as in *PL* 1. 68, 165; 10. 120.

163-7 A paraphrase of Matt. 4. 9 and Luke 4. 5–7, where Satan asks Christ to 'fall down and worship' him. Here, like a feudal lord, he is asking Christ to render the fealty due from a vassal. See also 2. 325–6 above and 198–200 below. On Satan's claim to the kingdoms of this world there is the following comment in the Geneva Bible (Luke 4. 6): 'That is sure true, for he is prince of the world, yet not absolutely, and as the souvreign of it, but by sufferance, and way of intreatie, and therefore he saith not true, that he can give to whom he will.'

171–94 Christ now delivers the most stinging rebuke which Satan has thus far had to meet, and which leaves him 'with fear abasht'. It has this effect not only because of the explicit statement, terrifying as that is, that his present impious act has made him more than ever accursed, nor because of the challenge, which he cannot meet, to show any right to the kingdoms of the world beyond what God allows him, but also because in the presence of Christ's goodness he feels 'how awful goodness is', and how impotent he is to overcome that goodness. As Augustine says in *De Trin.* 13. 17 (Migne, *Pat. Lat.* 42. 1026–7), the devil is overcome not by might but by righteousness.

176–7 Cf. Matt. 4. 10: 'Thou shalt worship the Lord thy God, and him only shalt thou serve.' See also Luke 4. 9; Exod. 20. 3–5; Deut. 6. 13.

181 *blasphemous.* By blasphemy Milton means 'any slander, any malitious or evil speaking, whether against God or man or any thing to good belonging' (*CivP, Works* 6. 11).

183 *permitted.* See note on 1. 363 above.

184 *donation.* In Roman law a donation (*donatio*) is 'a transaction whereby one person, from motives of liberality, i.e. with a view to enriching another person, makes over to that other person some property or benefit' (Sohm, *Institutes of Private Law*, tr. Ledlie, 3rd ed., Oxford, 1907, pp. 211–12).

185–6 Cf. 1 Tim. 6. 15: 'the blessed and only Potentate, the King of kings, and Lord of lords'; Rev. 17. 14: 'for he is Lord of lords, and King of kings'.

188 *gratitude in thee is lost.* These words must bitterly remind Satan of his admission in *PL* 4. 50–7 that in attempting to 'quit / The debt immense of endless gratitude' to God, he had failed to understand

> that a grateful mind
> By owing owes not, but still pays, at once
> Indebted and dischargd.

193 *Get thee behind me.* Quoted from Luke 4. 8; cf. Matt. 4. 10.

195 See note on 1. 37–43 above.

196–284 Christ's rebuke, ending with the horrifying words, 'thou now appear'st / That Evil one, Satan for ever damn'd', leaves Satan more discomfited than he has been before. He must, however, answer Christ, and he begins his long speech with a feeble and preposterous defence of himself. He has proposed to Christ only what he receives from both men and angels. Since it has been foretold that Christ's coming would be fatal to him, it most concerns him to discover who Christ is. See note on 1. 91 above. This last statement, however, is false, for he already knows who Christ is. The temptations which he has offered, he continues, have in no way injured Christ, but have left him with more honour and esteem. Thus in effect he admits the dishonourable course that he is pursuing. Furthermore he, Satan, has gained no advantage from the temptations. He will say no more about the kingdoms of the world, but will leave Christ to win them or not as he pleases. Finally, ever persistent in evil-doing, seizing upon what he believes to be Christ's fondness for intellectual pursuits, he offers *another* temptation higher in the ascending scale of values, human learning; he calls it wisdom. See notes on 88–9 above and 286–384 below. But as Gilbert ('Tempt. in *PR*', *JEGP* 15, 1916, 600) points out, the learning of the Greeks, which Satan is now about to offer, is not a 'kingdom' which it is within his power to bestow upon Christ. Wealth, glory, and the might of empire are within his power, but Milton is careful not to imply that Greek learning, severely as he criticizes it, is controlled by the devil.

199–200 That men and angels submit to Satan, that is to evil, is no argument that they *ought* to submit.

201 In 2. 122–4 above (see note) Satan addressed his followers as

> Demonian Spirits now, from the Element
> Each of his reign allotted, rightlier call'd,
> Powers of Fire, Air, Water, and Earth beneath.

Here, expressing the same idea, he uses the term 'tetrarch' (τετράρχης) which originally meant a governor of a division, strictly a fourth, of a Roman province or protectorate, as Palestine under Augustus (Matt. 14. 1; Josephus, *B.J.* 1. 12. 5); hence the word came to mean 'a ruler of a fourth part, or of one of four parts, divisions, elements, etc.; also a subordinate ruler generally' (*OED*).

203 See note on 1. 117 above. In 2 Cor. 4. 4 Satan is called 'the god of this world' who 'hath blinded the minds of them which believe not'. On his permitted power in the world, see note on 1. 363 above. He is here taking the position of the Manichaeans, who held that there are two first principles, virtually two gods, one good and the other evil (Hastings, *Encyc. Rel. Eth.* 8. 397).

  world beneath. In *PL* 10. 390–2 Satan congratulates Sin and Death—who are but extensions of himself—on the building of the bridge from hell to this world, telling them that they 'Triumphal with triumphal act have met'—have matched his corruption of Adam and Eve with 'this glorious Work' and thus

> made one Realm
> Hell and this World, one Realm, one Continent
> Of easie thorough-fare.

Traditionally, however, his realm was the air (see note on 1. 39 above), but even of that he was a usurper (*PL* 10. 189).

206–8 Cf. *Comus* 588–98; *PL* 5. 117–19.

207 If by rejecting Satan's temptations Christ has won more honour and esteem, Satan then stands self-condemned.

215–20 See 1. 209–14 above and note.

216 Jerram (p. 151) observes: 'An artful version of the statement in Luke 2. 43, "the child Jesus *tarried behind*" in Jerusalem.'

219 *Moses Chair*. An allusion to the account in Exod. 18. 13–16 of Moses sitting to judge the people and to make known to them the law of God; and to Matt. 23. 2: 'The scribes and the Pharisees sit in Moses' seat.' 'Questions fitting *Moses* Chair' are, then, questions concerning the law.

221–2 *Be famous then | By wisdom*. Satan has offered Christ the kingdoms of the world in all their material forms. Of their glory there remains only human learning, which he now proceeds to offer. But it is learning only for the sake of fame and earthly power, which Christ has already rejected.

223 *let extend*. See note on 3. 171 above.

225–8 The Pentateuch and the Prophets are two parts of the Torah, the third part being the Hagiographa. But Torah is also a name commonly applied to the Pentateuch, and connotes doctrine rather than law; however, since Hellenistic Jews translated it as νόμος, it came to be generally understood to mean law (Ginzberg, *Legends* 3. 79; *Jewish Encyc.* 12. 196). In saying that all knowledge is not contained in the law of Moses, the Pentateuch, and the Prophets, Satan is attempting to arouse in the mind of Christ, a Jew, a doubt concerning the most sacred Jewish Scriptures and the divine truth there made known by revelation. He is controverting the belief in the authority of Scripture, the Word of God, the belief which is summarily stated in the second answer of the *Westminster Shorter Catechism*: 'The Scriptures of the Old and New Testament are the only rule to direct' man in fulfilling his chief end, the glorification and enjoyment of God. In *Milton and This Pendant World* (Austin, Texas, 1958, pp. 35–58), G. W. Whiting has assembled many statements of this belief; in the works of Milton it is repeated again and again. The Gentiles, Satan argues, have by 'Natures light', that is by unaided reason, also attained wisdom. His argument is valid as far as it goes, but it suppresses the more important consideration of the sufficiency of the wisdom thus attained, the consideration which Christ promptly raises in his reply (286–90). '*God*, infinite in goodnesse', says Alexander Gil in *A Treatise Concerning the Trinitie* (London, 1635, p. 215), 'hath together with this understanding and light of Nature, given us withall His Word.' The *Book of Homilies* opens with the following statements: 'Unto a Christian there can be nothing either more necessary or profitable, than the knowledge of holy Scripture; forasmuch as in it is contained Gods true word, setting forth his glory and also mans duty. And there is no truth nor doctrine necessary for our justification and everlasting salvation, but that it is (or may be) drawn out of that fountain and Well of truth. Therefore as many as be desirous to enter into the right and perfect way unto God must apply their minds to know holy Scripture; without the which they can neither sufficiently know God and his will, neither their office and duty.' See also note on 356–64 below.

According to B. Rajan ('Jerusalem and Athens', *Th'Upright Heart and Pure*, ed. Fiore, pp. 67–8), lines 225–8 are 'among the most crucial passages' in *PR*, because, in order 'to know what is happening in the poem', readers must fully grasp their implication. To complete 'the world of understanding', Satan offers 'natural knowledge' as a supplement to Moses' law, the Pentateuch, and the Prophets. 'Christ can agree with the first two lines of the statement, but he cannot agree with the consequence, since he himself is to bring Old Testament wisdom to a far more decisive and transforming fulfillment.' With his limited knowledge 'Satan offers all that he can'; but now, in the process of his 'becoming', Christ both knows and is something that Satan cannot comprehend. If at this point the reader understands what is going on, he will perceive the deep irony of the situation. 'Christ *must* refuse' to accept Greek learning in order to declare his own nature, not so much 'as perfect man' but rather 'as the historic Christ' whose mission it is to introduce 'into history a power of grace' which the light of nature can never give. And when in lines 288–9 below he refers to 'the inner light' which comes to him 'from the fountain of light', he is not withdrawing from the world into an 'interior kingdom', but stating the new dimension which will be added to 'the kingdoms of the world'.

229–35 Satan uses 'two arguments for philosophy as *ancilla theologiae*' which 'had been the stock pleas of every prelate and presbyter jealous for medieval prerogatives.... First, to be socially acceptable ("hold conversation meet")... second, to refute heresy, Christ must wound the pagans with their own feathers. At any rate, the ministry of Christ must do so. Actually, Jesus himself is to meet few pagans. We have read the answers in *Likeliest Means*: scripture best refutes heresy. Scripture, too, can supply all the culture that a minister will need for his calling.... But as always, Milton distinguished carefully between learning itself and the dogma of learning's necessity.... The difference between Satan's position and Christ's is the difference between must and may. Christ himself is not unwilling to be thought learned. "Think not but that I know these things," he begins, thereby exculpating the arts; yet he can preach without them and found a Kingdom on scripture alone—"or think I know them not; not therefore am I short Of knowing what I ought".... If he neglects the last point, he opens the door to Antichrist.... The spiritual minister will be no enemy of good learning, then, if he simply counts it a thing indifferent in the sight of God' (Schultz, *Forbidden Knowledge*, pp. 226–7).

230 Satan seems to refer to Christ's statement about himself in 1. 221–3 above, where, however, he was speaking of moral rather than of intellectual persuasion.

234 *Idolisms*. Blakeney (p. 158) interprets this word as 'idolatrous practices' and believes it to be a Miltonic coinage; but *OED* gives two examples of its use in Sylvester's Du Bartas, *D.W.W., Decay* 502, 518, where it means false notions, fallacies. 'Idolisms' then, are 'idols' in the Baconian sense. See *Nov. Org.* 1. 38; *De Aug.* 5. 4.

Traditions. Probably, as Dunster (p. 211) suggests, 'opinions collected from those philosophers who instructed publickly, without committing any of their precepts to writing; which was the case with Pythagoras, Numa, and Lycurgus.'

Paradoxes. Probably, as Dunster (p. 211) also suggests, the so-called paradoxes (παράδοξα) or admirable moral maxims of the Stoics, as for example the six which Cicero discusses in *Paradoxa Stoicorum*.

235 'The offer of universal knowledge and with it the power of universal persuasion is ever the mark of the Sophist in Plato; and if we need another sign [that Satan is a Sophist], Satan gives it in his next maxim: "Error by his own arms is best evinc't." Socrates did not think so in spite of Anytus, Polus, and the rest, and Jesus is not more likely to admit that anything but truth can conquer falsehood' (Miss Samuel, *P. and M.*, p. 124).

evinc't. Confuted, convicted of error (*OED*).

236–84 'Now follows the most splendid episode in the poem. The stately rhythm, the vivid yet concise description, the whole style of these lines are without rival, even in Milton; and with all this is united perfect fitness of thought and phrase. Milton had never seen Athens, but his whole mind was so permeated with the mind of Greece that he could lay bare the panorama of its past, for he beheld it with "that inward eye which is the bliss of solitude." Yet (says Bailey, *Milton*, p. 206) "it is difficult not to regret that it is the Devil who is made to pay Milton's great debt to Athens and Christ who is made to repudiate it"' (Blakeney, p. 158). In reply to Bailey it may be said that the noble description is part of the 'perswasive Rhetoric / That sleek't' the tongue of Satan, who is characteristically and with subtle skill using something good for an evil purpose. As Stein (*Heroic Knowledge*, p. 96) points out, the real object of the temptation, though deftly concealed—and never more successfully than in the remarks about Socrates—is still power. Stein regards it as Satan's chief temptation, to be followed by Christ's chief answer.

236 *specular Mount*. Mount of observation which affords an 'extensive view' (*OED*). Cf. Lat. *specula*, look-out, watch tower. In *PL* 12. 588–9 the mountain from which Adam viewed the world is called 'this top / Of Speculation'.

237 *Westward, much nearer by Southwest*. The expression probably means 'westward or, more exactly, westward by southwest'.

239 *Built nobly*. Homer, whom Milton virtually translates, speaks in *Il.* 2. 546 of Athens as well built, ἐϋκτίμενον πτολίεθρον.

pure the air. Euripides (*Med.* 829–30) mentions the clear air of Athens, and Cicero (*Fat.* 4. 7) speaks of the rarefied climate which is thought to cause the sharp wit of the Athenians.

light the soil. Plato (*Critias* 111) describes Attica as a once fertile land from which all the richer, softer soil had been lost through erosion until only a skeleton, as it were, is left. Thucydides (1. 2. 3) also mentions its thin, poor soil.

240–1 *Mother of Arts | And Eloquence*. Thucydides (2. 41) calls Athens the 'school of Greece'; Cicero (*Flac.* 26. 62), the source whence humanity, learning, religion, rights, and laws have spread through all the earth; and Augustine (*Civ. D.* 18. 9), 'the mother or nurse of liberal doctrines'.

240 *the eye of Greece*. *OED* quotes the present expression to illustrate the figurative use of 'eye' as 'applied to a city, country, province, etc.: The seat of intelligence or light'.

Justin (5. 8. 4) writes that the Spartans, when urged to destroy Athens, said that they would not put out 'the other of the two eyes of Greece' (*ex duobus Graeciae oculis alterum*). Aristotle (*Rhet.* 3. 10. 7) quotes Leptines as saying, in allusion to Sparta, that he would not let the Spartans stand by and see Greece 'lose one of her eyes' (ἑτερόφθαλμον γενομένην).

241 *native to famous wits.* Wits are 'learned, clever, or intellectual' persons (*OED*), the opposite of dunces (*OED*). In *Areop* (*Works* 4. 299) Athens is the city 'where Books and Wits were ever busier then in any other part of *Greece*'. Among the 'wits' who were natives of Athens or of Attica were Aeschylus, Sophocles, Euripides, Demosthenes, Pericles, Thucydides, Socrates, and Plato.

242 *hospitable.* Pericles in his famous funeral oration (Thucydides 2. 39) mentions among the superior qualities of the Athenians their readiness to receive strangers. Cf. Diodorus Siculus 13. 27. Among the men, not natives, who contributed to the glory of Athens were Herodotus, Lysias, Aristotle, and Theophrastus.

recess. Place of retirement, like Lat. *recessus*.

243 *studious.* Conducive to study, contemplation, as in *IlPen* 156.

244 The Academy (᾽Ακαδήμεια) was a gymnasium in the suburbs of Athens, the exact location of which is not known, named for the hero Academus (Plato, *Lysis* 203; Pausanias 1. 29. 2; Cicero, *Fin.* 5. 1. 1). See W. Judeich, *Topographie von Athen* (Munich, 1931), p. 412. Aristophanes (*Nubes* 1005) mentions the olive trees of the Academy, and Plutarch (*Sulla* 12. 3; cf. *Cimon* 13. 8) describes it as the most thickly wooded suburb of Athens.

245-6 Editors note that Martial (1. 53. 9) calls the nightingale *Atthis*, that is the Athenian bird; and that Sophocles (*O.C.* 670–3) speaks of Colonus, near the Academy, 'where the nightingale, a constant guest, trills her clear note beneath the green shades.'[6]

thick-warbl'd. 'Is Milton half-consciously thinking', Blakeney (p. 161) asks, 'of the Greek word πυκνότης in its technical sense? or, more likely, of the word

---

[6]   ἔνθ'
    ἁ λίγεια μινύρεται
    θαμίζουσα μάλιστ' ἀηδών
    χλωραῖς ὑπὸ βάσσαις.

πυκνώματα, which occurs in Plato, *Rep.* 531 and means "frequently recurring notes" (Lat. *frequentamenta*)?'

247–9 Hymettus is the mountain rising from the plain of Attica about four miles south-east of Athens. Pausanias (1. 32. 1) describes it as producing the best food for bees except the land of the Alzones. In calling it 'flowrie' Milton may have remembered *florens Hymettus* in Ovid, *M.* 7. 702; *A.A.* 3. 687.

249–50 The Ilissus, a small river, rises on Mount Hymettus and flows through the plain of Attica to the sea (Pausanias, ed. Frazer, London, 1898, 1. 19. 5 and note). A quiet spot on its banks was the scene of the discussion between Socrates and Phaedrus (Plato, *Phaedrus* 229).

250–3 Aristotle, the tutor of Alexander (Diogenes Laertius 5. 1. 6), taught at the Lyceum, one of the most famous gymnasia of Athens (Lucian, *Anach.* 1. 7; Suidas, s.v. Λύκειον), which derived its name from the neighbouring temple of Λύκειος. According to tradition it was Aristotle's habit to pace (περιπατεῖν) the walks of the Lyceum while he taught, and hence his school of philosophy came to be known as the Peripatetic school (Diogenes Laertius 5. 1. 2; Cicero, *Acad.* 1. 4. 17; Aulus Gellius 20. 5). Milton is mistaken in placing the Lyceum within the walls of Athens, for it is clear from Plato, *Lysis* 203, and Strabo 9. 1. 19 that it was without the walls, perhaps between Mount Lycabettus and the Ilissus (Judeich, *Topographie von Athen*, p. 415).

253 The 'painted *Stoa*' (ἡ στοὰ ἡ ποικίλη), a colonnade on the market place, was one of the most famous buildings of ancient Athens. Pausanias (1. 15) describes the paintings by Polygnotus which adorned its walls. There philosophers were in the habit of congregating to teach or argue among themselves (Lucian, *J. Trag.* 16; *Icar.* 33; *D. Meretr.* 10. 1; Alciphron 3. 53, 64). The Stoa is most famous, however, because Zeno there discussed philosophy with his disciples, who became known as Stoics (Diogenes Laertius 7. 1. 5–7).

254–6 Here 'Harmony', embracing vocal and instrumental music and poetry, is almost equivalent to 'music' in the Greek sense, in which it signified reading, writing, poetry, mathematics, and music as we understand it (Plato, *Rep.* 2. 376, 398; *Tim.* 88; *Protag.* 326). In education it was distinguished from 'gymnastic' as mental is distinguished from physical training (Plato, *Rep.* 3. 403; *Crito* 50). As Horace (*A.P.* 333–4) believed the function of poetry to be instruction and delight, so does Milton think of the function of 'harmony'.

257 The two main branches of Greek lyric poetry are the Æolian, represented by Alcaeus and Sappho—to whose monodic poems the term 'charm', that is *carmen*, song, is appropriate (cf. Horace, *C.* 3. 30. 13; 4. 3. 12: *Aeolium carmen*)—and the Dorian, of which Pindar, Alcman, and Stesichorus were representatives: poets who composed choric odes in noble style upon lofty subjects (cf. 1. 182 above and note; Pindar, *Ol.* 1. 25; *Pyth.* 8. 29; Croiset, *Hist. Litt. Grec.*, Paris, 1896–1928, 2. 200 ff.).

In explanation of the term 'Æolian' as it is applied to vocal and instrumental music, Fletcher (*Intellectual Development* 1. 352) quotes the following from Charles Butler's *The Principles of Musik, in Singing and Setting* (London, 1636, p. 2): 'The Aeolik [mode] is that, which, with its soft pleasing sounds, pacifies the passions of the mind, and with instruments or dittiles *fa-las*, in continued discant, delighting the sense, and not intending the mind of the hearer, like Mercury's *Caduceus*, charmeth affections and cares, and so lulleth him sweetly to sleep.'

From *OED* it appears that 'charm' in the sense of 'song', and with little suggestion of magical power, occurs but rarely; it is, however, so used in *PL* 4. 642; Spenser, *T.M.* 244; *As.* 46; Phineas Fletcher, *P.I.* 1. 18. 2.

258 Pseudo-Plutarch (*De Vita Homeri*, 2. 1, 213–15) who considered Homer superior to other ancient poets, believed that in his poems tragedy, comedy, and epigram had their origin; and Aristotle (*Poet.* 8, 23, 24) regarded him as the best of all the epic poets whose works he knew. Cf. *Prol* 6 (*Works* 12. 219).

259 According to the *De Vita Homeri* (3, 13) attributed to Herodotus, and the *De Vita Homeri* (1. 2) of Pseudo-Plutarch, Homer's mother, Critheis, named him Melesigenes, because he was born on the banks of the river Meles in Ionia; but after he became blind, the Cumaeans called him Ὅμηρος, their word for blind.

260 Editors note the reminiscence of the epigram in the *Greek Anthology* (9. 455) in which Phoebus says: 'The song is mine, but divine Homer wrote it down.'[7] The epigram was imitated by Politian (*Nut.* 345) and Marino (*Ad.* 20. 515) and several other poets of the Renaissance (Hutton, *The Greek Anthology in Italy*, p. 557).

261–6 In the preface to *SA* Milton writes: 'Tragedy, as it was antiently compos'd, hath been ever held the gravest, moralest, and most profitable of all other Poems: therefore said by *Aristotle* to be of power by raising pity and fear, or terror, to purge the mind of those and such like passions, that is to temper

---

[7] Ἥειδον μὲν ἐγών, ἐχάρασσε δὲ θεῖος Ὅμηρος.

and reduce them to just measure with a kind of delight, stirr'd up by reading or seeing those passions well imitated.' For Aristotle's definition of tragedy and his explanation of its function, with which Milton agrees and of which he is a discerning interpreter, see *Poet.* 6 ff., and consult Miss Langdon, *Milton's Theory of Poetry and Fine Art*, pp. 88–9, 94–6, 243–4.

262 Iambic trimeter, the simplest of all Greek metres, is almost invariably used in the dramatic scenes in Greek tragedies (see Aristotle, *Poet.* 4); but the lyric metres of the choruses are extremely varied and elaborate. See Milton's statement about the verse in the preface to *SA*. The dramatic scenes perform their function by presenting examples; the choruses are more interpretive and directly instructive. As Horace (*A.P.* 196–201) says, the chorus 'should side with the good and give friendly counsel; it should sway the angry and cherish the righteous. It should praise the fare of a frugal board, wholesome justice and law, and peace with her open gates. It should keep secrets, and should pray and beg the gods that good fortune may return to the unhappy and depart from the proud.'[8]

263 Prudence, as Milton defines it in *DocCh* 2. 2 (*Works* 17. 37), 'is that virtue by which we discern what is proper to be done under the various circumstances of time and place.' 'What is that virtue called prudence?' Augustine asks (*Civ. D.* 19. 4). 'Is it not most keenly to distinguish good from evil, so that in things chosen and things avoided no error may be incurred?'[9] Need it be said that Satan's recommendation of prudence, though ludicrous, is wholly in keeping with his hypocrisy and sophistry?

264 Editors note that Quintilian (10. 1. 68) says of Euripides: 'He is full of striking reflections, in which indeed, in their special sphere, he rivals the philosophers themselves';[10] and of Aulus Gellius (11. 4. 1) that he observes: 'In the *Hecuba* of Euripides there are some verses remarkable and brilliant in their diction, their thought, and their terseness.'[11] In *Rhet.* 2. 21 Aristotle in dis-

---

[8] Ille bonis faveatque et consilietur amice,
    et regat iratos et amet peccare timentis;
    ille dapes laudet mensae brevis, ille salubrem
    iustitiam legesque et apertis otia portis;
    ille tegat commissa, deosque precetur et oret,
    ut redeat miseris, abeat fortuna superbis.

[9] Quid illa virtus, quae prudentia dicitur? Nonne tota vigilantia sua bona discernit a malis, ut in illis appetendis istisque vitandis nullus error obrepat?

[10] Sententiis densus et in iis, quae a sapientibus tradita sunt, paene ipsis par.

[11] Euripidis versus sunt in Hecuba verbis, sententia brevitate insignes inlustresque.

cussing maxims draws four of his examples from Euripides. He might have drawn others from Sophocles, as *Ant.* 67–8, 326, 730.

265 Satan, who in *PL* 1. 116, 133; 2. 396; 10. 480 has shown himself to be a kind of fatalist, here, like many in our time, is making tragedy as the Greeks understood it turn upon fate or chance; but the 'change in human life', the reversal of fortune (Aristotle, *Poet.* 11, 13) that we find, for example, in *Agamemnon, Oedipus Rex, Antigone*, and *Medea*, does not turn upon fate, or even upon chance, but upon the *ethos* and *dianoia* of the agents. The fall, the reversal of fortune, as Aristotle (13) explains, comes about 'through a serious defect in judgment, or shortcoming in conduct'. To 'the sins of a darkened soul', to 'the wretched blindness of my counsels', to his own folly Creon attributes the misfortunes which have overtaken him and his house (Sophocles, *Ant.* 1261–9). As W. C. Greene, in *Moira* (Cambridge, Mass., 1944, pp. 91–2), explains: 'the finest and most profound tragic effect comes when the poet is not content merely to set forth external events, nor even the fact of guilt, but exhibits also the moral attitude of his protagonist toward events and toward his own action. He answers the call of honor, come what may; he endures what fate or the gods send. His act may have caused his downfall, but his will remains noble; he learns by suffering; and there may be a final vindication of the sufferer, though of an unexpected kind.... The greatest Greek drama, in other words, rests on the interplay between fate and character, between what man can not change and what remains within his power.'

266 *High actions.* The serious actions of noble agents such as Oedipus, Antigone, and Agamemnon are the materials of tragedy. See Aristotle, *Poet.* 6, 13.

high passions. The passions, for example, of Clytemnestra, Oedipus, and Medea.

267–71 Lysias, Demosthenes, Aeschines, and Isocrates show the highest achievements of Greek oratory; after their time, beginning with Demetrius Phalereus, came the decline of eloquence. See Quintilian 10. 1. 76–80; R. C. Jebb, *Attic Orators* (London, 1876), 2. 369 ff.; Eduard Norden, *Die antike Kunstprosa* (Leipzig, 1898), 1. 126 ff.

268 *resistless eloquence.* Editors believe this to be an allusion to the eloquence of Pericles, of whom Aristophanes (*Ach.* 530–1) says: 'In wrath Olympian Pericles thundered and lightened and confounded Greece.'[12] Cf. Thucydides 1.

---

[12] ἐντεῦθεν ὀργῇ Περικλέης Οὐλύμπιος
ἤστραπτ᾽, ἐβρόντα, ξυνεκύκα τὴν Ἑλλάδα.

140–4; Quintilian 2. 16. 19; 12. 10. 24. There may also be an allusion to the *Philippics*, the famous speeches in which Demosthenes sought to convince the Athenians of the evils arising from jealousies within the state, and to warn them of the common danger of Philip of Macedon. Cicero (*Att.* 15. 1a) speaks of Δημοσθένους *fulmina*.

269 *Wielded*. 'Ruled', a meaning common in the 17th century (*OED*). 'The Demos of Athens', Blakeney (pp. 163–4) comments, 'was not fierce only, but frivolous, with rapid alternations of severity and sentimentality; it was, like all democracies, too much inclined to be a government of words. Hence its levity, its recklessness, and its easy susceptibility to the flatteries of the demagogue.... The real greatness of Athens owed little or nothing to its ochlocracy; [it] was due to men of outstanding qualities.'

270 *Shook the Arsenal*. These words, long a puzzle to editors, are explained by E. C. Baldwin in '"Shook the Arsenal": A Note on Paradise Regained', *PQ* 18 (1939), 218–22. The Arsenal, a naval storehouse at the Piraeus, of which there is a detailed description in the so-called 'Arsenal Inscription' (T. W. Ludlow, 'The Athenian Naval Arsenal', *AJP* 3, 1882, 317–28), was one of the most famous buildings of Greek antiquity. Work on the Arsenal began in 346 B.C.; it was interrupted in 339 because of the war with Philip of Macedon, was resumed in 338, and completed in 329.

Milton's use of the word 'shook', Baldwin believes, may have been suggested by the Greek word ξυνεκύκα in Aristophanes, *Ach.* 531 (see note on 268 above), since κυκάω, like Lat. *turbo*, means disturb, shake, or weaken. The English word 'shake' was frequently used in the 17th century, as in the A.V. of the Bible— e.g. Isa. 14. 16; 23. 11; Ezek. 31. 16; Hag. 2. 7—meaning 'to weaken or disturb something regarded as normally fixed'. Since work on the Arsenal was interrupted at the instigation of Demosthenes so that public funds could be diverted to the war-chest, it may in a real, though not literal, sense be said that he 'Shook the Arsenal'. See Philochorus, *Frag.* 126–35; Dionysius of Halicarnassus, *Epistula ad Ammaeum* 11.

fulmin'd. Literally 'sent forth thunder and lightning', Lat. *fulminare*; metaphorically, 'spoke out fiercely and energetically'. The word is aptly chosen to translate ἤστραπτ' ἐβρόντα (see note on 268 above). When the word now occurs, it is 'chiefly in echoes of Milton's use' (*OED*).

272–4 Editors note the reminiscence of Cicero's statement in *Tusc.* 5. 4. 10 that 'Socrates was the first to call philosophy down from heaven, and place it in cities, and bring it even into the dwellings of men, and compel it to inquire about life and morals and things good and evil.'[13]

273-4 The tradition that Socrates was a poor man rests upon the testimony of Aristophanes (*Nubes* 92), who mentions his small house (οἰκίδιον); of Xenophon (*Oec.* 2. 3), who quotes him as saying that all his goods and chattels, including his house, would sell for the paltry sum of five minae; and of Plato (*Apol.* 23), who says that he lives in utter poverty.

The survey of the philosophers begins with Socrates, with whom the great age of Greek philosophy began. Milton rarely shows much interest in any of the pre-Socratic philosophers except Pythagoras. Satan is shrewd in using Socrates in his argument, since Christ has spoken of him with approval in 3. 96-9 above.

275-6 In Plato, *Apol.* 21, Socrates relates that 'Chaerephon...asked the oracle to tell him whether...any man was wiser than I was, and the Pythian priestess answered there was no man wiser.' What Satan, however, suppresses, and Christ, to correct him, is careful to point out (293-4), is that Socrates' search for a wiser man than himself ended with his finding only men who knew nothing but thought that they knew something. The oracle, he concluded, spoke truly, for he knew nothing, and knew that he knew nothing. Cf. *El* 4. 23; *Prol* 6 (*Works* 12. 219); *Def* 2 (8. 193); *Pro se Def* (9. 53).

276-80 Socrates was the intellectual father of the Platonic or Academic school of philosophy, since he was Plato's great teacher, as Plato in turn was Aristotle's and thus transmitted the Socratic impulse to the Peripatetics. Milton follows the distinction made by Cicero (*Acad.* 1. 4. 13-14; *Tusc.* 5. 26. 75; *Fin.* 2. 11. 34; 5. 3. 7) and based upon the change which, in the course of time, the philosophy of the Academy underwent. The Old Academy, Plato's immediate successors and their followers, until Arcesilas became scholarch, about 270 B.C., sought faithfully to continue the teachings of the master. Arcesilas and those who came after him, the New Academy, introduced a large element of scepticism into their philosophy (Cicero, *Acad.* 1. 12. 45; *N.D.* 1. 5. 11, 25. 70; Augustine, *Civ. D.* 19. 1.

The philosophical systems of the Epicureans and the Stoics, however they may differ from that of Socrates and from each other, are related to his teachings, since his pupil Aristippus founded the Cyrenaic system from which

---

[13] Socrates autem primus philosophiam devocavit e caelo et in urbibus collocavit, et in domus etiam introduxit, et coegit de vita et moribus rebusque bonis et malis quaerere.

developed Epicureanism (Diogenes Laertius 2. 8. 85–93; 10. 3, 9, 12, 18, 85). In much the same way Antisthenes, another pupil, founded the Cynic school (*ibid.* 6. 1. 2–5), from the teachings of which Zeno, the founder of the Stoic philosophy, derived many of his doctrines (*ibid.* 7. 1. 32; Eduard Zeller, *Stoics, Epicureans, and Sceptics*, tr. Reichel, London, 1880, pp. 400–2, 505–10).

276–7 Milton's figure, editors suggest, is derived from Cicero (*Acad.* 1. 4. 18), who says that the Peripatetic and the Academic schools 'both had the same source' (*idem fons erat utriusque*); and from Quintilian (1. 10. 13), who calls Socrates the master (*fons*) of the philosophers.

283–4 When Satan speaks of 'these rules', he is speaking loosely, for he implies that the schools which he has mentioned form one system or set of rules—as if philosophy were nothing more than so many rules; whereas there was obviously much disagreement among them, as for example between Stoics and Epicureans. He then proposes that Christ seek to attain the Stoic ideal of self-sufficiency (αὐτάρκεια) of the wise man. But with characteristic sophistry he confuses self-sufficiency, a form of pride (see 303 below and note), with self-control, which Christ has recommended (see 2. 466–7 above and note). In *PL* 1. 253–5 he boasted of

> A mind not to be chang'd by Place or Time.
> The mind is its own place, and in it self
> Can make a Heav'n of Hell, a Hell of Heav'n.

In his later soliloquy in *PL* 4. 32–113, however, he admitted the bitter futility of self-sufficiency.

The Stoics maintained, as Horace (*Ep.* 1. 1. 106–8) says, that 'The wise man is less only than Jove. He is rich, free, honoured, beautiful; in short he is a king of kings. And above all he is sound—save when he has a cold.'[14]

Cf. *S.* 1. 3. 125–6. In *Fin.* 3. 22. 75 Cicero expresses much the same thought but more elaborately, in effect maintaining the truth of the sixth Stoic Paradox that *solum sapientem esse divitem*. For Seneca (*Ep.* 53. 11; cf. 92. 31–5) the only difference between a wise man and the gods is that the gods live longer.

286–384 Christ's speech and the speeches of Raphael and Michael in *PL* 8. 66–178 and 12. 575–87, which seem a sweeping repudiation of studies of all

---

[14] sapiens uno minor est Iove, dives,
liber, honoratus, pulcher, rex denique regum,
praecipue sanus, nisi cum pituita molesta est.

kinds, have been variously explained; but the most persistent view is that Milton, though himself one of the most learned poets, sometime in his later years came to a complete distrust of intellectual effort. Part of the reason for this view is that his statements have been read out of their cultural context. Schultz (*Forbidden Knowledge*, p. 91), with much evidence to support his conclusion, is correct in saying that 'For any one of Milton's comments on heathen culture in *Paradise Regained* we may establish a tradition among his enlightened contemporaries, or what is equivalent, in the Fathers, whom every educated man knew.' And as Bush (*Our Time*, p. 51) explains, 'Milton is not attacking science as such' in the passage in *PL* 8. 'His words here...are not a fundamentalist and obscurantist attack on science any more than Christ's disparagement of Greek culture in *Paradise Regained* represents a barbarous hostility to the classics. In both cases Milton is simply asserting, with an earnestness born of ripened insight, his lifelong hierarchy of values.' In that hierarchy the ethical and the religious were always supreme, as he makes clear, when in *RCG* (*Works* 3. 229) he distinguishes between 'that knowledge that rests in the contemplation of naturall causes and dimensions, which must needs be a lower wisdom, as the object is low', and 'the only high valuable wisdom' which is knowledge of God and the ultimate ends of life. See also Blondel, pp. 85–6, 91; Douglas Bush, *The Renaissance and English Humanism* (Toronto, 1939), pp. 124–6.

Irene Samuel, in her invaluable article 'Milton on Learning and Wisdom' (*PMLA* 64, 1949, 708–23), agrees with Bush but greatly extends and amplifies the explanation of Milton's position. After considering the three speeches in context and in the light of Milton's many relevant statements elsewhere, she concludes that 'The view of learning in *Paradise Lost* and *Paradise Regained* expands rather than retracts what Milton had said from the first on the place of studies in life, and that the three passages embody convictions central to his whole theory of learning' (p. 709)....From 'youth to age Milton loved all learning, including astronomy, and especially the Greek classics—but always without idolatry. He did not think the Greek classics the most important branch of learning or the best of all literature. Ethics was the one, the Bible the other. He did not think any learning indispensable. He recognized that any learning is useful only as used rightly, and thought the right use knowable to any one who cared to know it. If Jesus in *Paradise Regained* states only the more negative aspects of these doctrines, we must remember that he speaks to a wily opponent. Yet he speaks learnedly throughout, and once at least in highest praise of a person whom he could know only from a Greek classic, the Socrates of the Platonic dialogues...' (pp. 722–3).

Through the earlier dialogues with Satan, Christ has shown a command of whatever knowledge the immediate problem required, and the wisdom necessary to pass authoritative judgment on the problem. But never before has this been so fully evident as in the present speech, in which he proves that he knows what the Greeks knew, and, more important, knows what they did not know. He is now 'declaring his own wisdom'. His speech 'is both general, relevant to Everyman, and particular, the dramatic acting out of illumination by the prophet whose role it is to provide illumination for the human understanding. He is not only saying it in speech, he is doing it in a drama of knowledge. The expression is action, it is happening now' (Stein, *Heroic Knowledge*, p. 106).

Milton's attitude to learning and to ethical and religious wisdom by which we may be saved may be compared to Donne's (*Sermons*, ed. Potter and Simpson, Berkeley, Cal., 8, 1956, 54), who says: 'when *Abraham* went up to the great sacrifice of his son, he left his servants, and his Asse below: Though our naturall reason, and humane Arts, serve to carry us to the hill, to the entrance of the mysteries of Religion, yet to possesse us of the hill it selfe, and to come to such a knowledge of the mysteries of Religion, as must save us, we must leave our naturall reason, and humane Arts at the bottome of the hill, and climb up only by the light, and strength of faith.' In *A Treatise of Human Learning*, 144–7, Fulke Greville (*Certain Learned and Elegant Works*, London, 1633, pp. 50–1) substantially agrees with Milton and Donne.

286–90 Commenting on these lines Irene Samuel (*P. and M.*, p. 125) writes: 'we may well turn to Augustine for help with the doctrine here advanced; for Augustine, next to the Bible itself, guided Milton in theology; and Augustine had dealt with this problem alien to Biblical thought. In the *Confessions*, he says of the time he spent in pagan studies: "I had my back to the light, and my face to the things enlightened" (4. 16). And asking what it profited him to have known these things, he answers: "Nothing." Yet Augustine continued to make use of pagan thought long after his conversion, never attempting to rid his mind of all but Biblical and patristic lore. Apparently he distinguished not so much between a Christian and a pagan learning, as between a Christian and a non-Christian use of learning. His maxim was "*nisi credideritis, non intelligetis*": only he who has faith can understand the truth in any thought, and he who has faith needs no other measure of truth.' Nor, as Miss Samuel (p. 126) adds, was this notion 'peculiar to Milton in the seventeenth century'. Ralph Cudworth, another Christian Platonist, whom she quotes, explains at length. The inadequacy of the Greeks in both philosophy and poetry was their ignorance of the basic matters to be found in Scripture, and their false, or at best diluted, inspiration derived more from man than from God. See Stein, *Heroic Knowledge*, pp. 107–8. Jean Louis Balzac in *Socrate Chrestien* (Paris, 1661, p. 6) declares that 'Toute la Raison, toute l'Eloquence d'Athenes luy [Christ] a cedé. C'est luy qui a humilié l'orgueil du Portique; qui a décrédité le Lycée, & les autres Escoles de Grece. Il a fait voir qu'il y auoit de l'Imposture par tout, qu'il y auoit des Fables dans la Philosophie, & que les Philosophes n'estoient pas moins extrauagans que les Poëtes, mais que leur extrauagance estoit plus graue & plus composée. Il a fait auouër aux Speculatifs, qu'ils auoient resvé, lors qu'ils auoient voulu méditer.'

291–2 Wherein Christ finds the sage philosophy false and ill-founded, he explains in lines 309–21 below.

295 'The next' is Plato, the *fabulator maximus* of *Idea* 38, and 'the wisest of the heathen' of *RCG* (*Works* 3. 182), with whose doctrines Milton so nearly agreed (Miss Samuel, *P. and M.*, pp. 3 ff.), who, unlike the other philosophers, is not criticized in terms of his philosophy, and comes off more easily than the rest. Milton's is not a very serious accusation for a poet to bring against a philosopher; for if Plato 'to fabling fell and smooth conceits', that is, to telling plausible and ingeniously devised myths, he fell from philosophy to poetry, if that be a fall, since the effect produced by the Platonic myths is essentially that of poetry, which in its highest development is indistinguishable from philosophy. If Milton read the *Defence of Poesie*, he would be likely to remember that Sidney, after praising several early Greek philosophers who were poets, added: 'And truly, even *Plato* who so ever well considereth, shall finde that in the body of his worke, though the inside & strength were Philosophie, the skine as it were and beautie depended most of Poetrie. For all stands upon Dialogues, wherein hee fains many honest Burgesses of *Athens* speak of such matters, that, if they had bene set on the Racke, they would never have confessed them: besides his Poetical describing the circumstances of their meetings, as the well ordering of a banquet, the delicacie of a walke, with enterlacing meere tales, as *Gyges Ring* and others, which, who knows not to be flowers of Poetrie, did never walk into *Appollos* Garden' (*Works*, ed. Feuillerat, 3. 5). See also Eduard Norden, *Die antike Kunstprosa* 1. 111–13, and J. A. Stewart, *The Myths of Plato* (London, 1905), p. 22.

 conceits. A conceit (It. *concetto*) is a fanciful, ingenious, it may be a far-fetched notion. Spenser in his *Letter of the Authors* to Sir Walter Ralegh, calls *The Faerie Queene* 'a continued Allegory, or darke conceit'.

296 The Sceptics, chief of whom were Pyrrho, Arcesilas, and Carneades, taught that neither by reason nor by the senses can any certain knowledge be attained. The senses show us only appearances; and reason, even in morals, where it is most certain, is based only on habit and tradition (Diogenes Laertius 9. 9. 69–76). So, of the true nature of things, we can know nothing; and of every statement concerning it the opposite is equally true (*ibid.* 9. 106; Cicero, *Acad.* 2. 23. 73–4).

297–8 Aristotle and the Peripatetics 'in vertue plac'd felicity'. The principle is stated in *Nic. Eth.* I. 11: 'He is happy who is active in accordance with complete virtue and is sufficiently equipped with external goods, not for some chance period, but throughout a complete life.'

299 Epicurus maintained that because all living things seek pleasure and avoid pain, pleasure is the only unconditional good and pain the only unconditional evil, and hence that pleasure is the end of life (Diogenes Laertius 10. 128, 141; Cicero, *Fin.* 1. 6. 23; 1. 9. 29–30). It is not, however, the pleasure of a mere voluptuary, as the expressions 'corporeal pleasure' and 'careless ease' might imply; for Epicurus believed that pleasures of the mind are more intense and more enduring than those of the body, and that only by a life of virtue can a man find happiness (Cicero, *Fin.* 1. 17. 56–7). However, aware that neither pleasure nor pain is a simple thing, he taught that pleasures won at the cost of greater corresponding pain are to be avoided, and pains that promise greater pleasures are to be endured (Diogenes Laertius 10. 128–30; Cicero, *Fin.* 1. 14. 48; *Tusc.* 5. 33. 95).

300 The Stoics divided all men into two mutually exclusive classes: the wise and virtuous and the foolish and vicious; and they implied that only they themselves were wise and virtuous (Cicero, *Fin.* 3. 22. 75; Plutarch, *How a Young Man Should Study Poetry* 7; *On Common Ideas Opposed to the Stoics* 10; Eduard Zeller, *Stoics, Epicureans, and Sceptics,* tr. Reichel, p. 272).

300–9 While Milton represents Christ as summarily disposing of the other systems of philosophy, he has him treat Stoicism in greater detail, no doubt because he knew that, from the early centuries of the Christian era, Stoicism had strongly appealed to Christians, as Jerome observes in *Comment. in Isa.* 4. 159 (Migne, *Pat. Lat.* 24. 147): 'In many things the Stoics agree with our doctrines.'[15] Cf. Justin Martyr, *2 Apol.* 8 (Migne, *Pat. Gr.* 6. 457). In their views of the world and its governance and in their ethical theory Epictetus and

---

[15] Stoici qui nostro dogmati in plerisque concordant.

Seneca come remarkably close to St Paul's conceptions. See W. L. Davidson, *The Stoic Creed* (Edinburgh, 1907), pp. 242–3, and L. Edelstein, *The Meaning of Stoicism* (Cambridge, Mass., 1966), pp. 72, 90–1.

Through the Middle Ages there must have been some more or less constant Stoic influence from Boethius upon the Christian world; and in the Renaissance, as the philosophical works of Cicero and the great Stoic writers became more widely known, both in the original and in translations, there was such a quickening of interest in Stoicism that Mlle Zanta has entitled her book on the subject *La renaissance du stoïcisme au XVIIᵉ siècle* (Paris, 1914). Whether the revival of interest was sufficient to be properly called a renaissance need not be debated here. At least there was considerable interest, as is attested by the translations just referred to and by such works as the *De Constantia* (Antwerp, 1585) of Justus Lipsius, and *La saincte philosophie, la philosophie des Stoïques* (Lyon, 1600), of Guillaume Du Vair.

302 *perfect*. See note on 1. 83 above.

303 See note on 283–4 above and Seneca, *Prov*. 1. 5; *Ep*. 53. 11; Cicero, *Fin*. 3. 22. 75. Jean François Senault, in *De l'Usage des passions* (2nd ed., Paris, [1643?]), pp. 4–5), a work which appeared in twenty editions between 1641, when it first appeared, and 1669, declares: 'Ces raisons qui sont exprimées auec tant de belles paroles dans les escrits des Stoïciens, n'ont pû faire encore vn Sage qu'en idée: Leurs admirateurs n'en ont remporté que de la confusion; apres auoir fait la cour à vne vertu si glorieuse & si austere ils sont deuenus la moquerie de tous les siecles'.

shames not to prefer. That is, to prefer himself to God.

304–5 According to the Stoics, since moral worth (*honestas*), the whole, of which the virtues, wisdom, justice, courage, temperance, are the parts, is the only absolute good (Seneca, *Ben*. 7. 2. 1; Cicero, *Fin*. 2. 15. 48; 4. 16. 45; *Tusc*. 2. 25. 61; *Acad*. 1. 10. 35–6; Diogenes Laertius 7. 101–2), it follows that health, riches, honour, all external goods, even life itself, are not goods; and their opposites, poverty, disease, disgrace, and death, are not evils. The wise man, therefore, treats them as indifferent, and incapable in themselves of increasing or diminishing his happiness (Seneca, *Vit. Beat*. 4. 3; Plutarch, *On the Contradictions of the Stoics* 18; Sextus Empiricus, *Adv. Eth*. 61; Diogenes Laertius 7. 102). This indifference, which he calls 'stoical apathy', Milton in *DocCh* 2. 10 (*Works* 17. 253) considers one of the opposites of true patience, for 'sensibility to pain, and even lamentations, are not inconsistent with true patience; as may be seen in Job and the other saints, when under the pressure of affliction.'

306 On the ground of indifference to external things, the Stoics not only permitted, but under certain circumstances recommended, suicide (ἐξαγωγή). A wise man, they argued, might reasonably take his own life in the interest of his country or of his friends, or if he suffered acute pain or incurable disease (Cicero, *Off.* 1. 31. 112; Seneca, *Ep.* 70. 5, 11–15; Epictetus, *Diss.* 3. 13. 14). Seneca (*Ep.* 12. 10) believed that a wise man's independence of external things depends, at least in part, on his being able to leave life when he will. Cf. Cicero, *Off.* 1. 19. 62; M. Aurelius 5. 29; 8. 47; Epictetus, *Diss.* 1. 24. 20; 3. 24. 91–102.

307 Early editors agree that 'vain boast' is probably an allusion to the so-called 'paradoxes' of the Stoics. See note on 234 above.

308 In this line editors detect an echo of Cicero, *Fin.* 3. 1. 3: 'But you are not unaware that the Stoics use an extremely subtle or, rather, crabbed style of argument.'[16]

309–12 As Blondel (pp. 83–5) notes, the present criticism of the philosophers has many points in common with that of Tertullian in *Apol.* 46–7 (Migne, *Pat. Lat.* 1. 500–20); but, as Schultz (*Forbidden Knowledge*, pp. 6–10) gives much evidence to prove, Milton is here doing no more than preaching traditional Catholic orthodoxy in which Calvinist, Arminian, and Quaker could agree. 'The specific bill' of the philosophers' ignorance, as Stein (*Heroic Knowledge*, p. 100) explains it, 'includes these essential items: the creation and the fall', and their ignorance of these means that they have no knowledge of the true ethical nature of the self; that their concept of God is dangerously misleading; and that they fail to comprehend the relation of man to God. They do not know that man is a being created in the image of God, and that through evil curiosity and pride man has defaced that image.

313 The ancient philosophers did talk 'much of the Soul', offering many and varied explanations of its nature and functions (Cicero, *Tusc.* 1. 10. 19 ff.; Gregory of Nyssa, *De Anima*, Migne, *Pat. Gr.* 45. 188). Among those who appeared to Milton, and to Christians generally, to have talked 'awrie' were the Stoics and Epicureans. In the views of Plato (*Phileb.* 30; *Rep.* 4. 439; 10. 611; *Phaedo* 78; *Tim.* 30; *Phaedrus* 245–6) and Aristotle (*De An.* 412–13) they would find less with which to disagree. The Stoics maintained that the soul

---

[16] Stoicorum autem non ignoras quam sit subtile vel spinosum potius disserendi genus.

is corporeal, a breath or spirit diffused through the body; but it is rational and may live for a time after the body dies (Cicero, *N.D.* 3. 14. 36; *Tusc.* 1. 31. 77–8; Epictetus, *Diss.* 1. 14. 6; 3. 7. 1–9; M. Aurelius 4. 21; 7. 32; 8. 25; Seneca, *Ep.* 24. 18; 41. 2; 57. 8–9; *Cons. Marc.* 25). See G. Verbeke, *L'Évolution de la doctrine du pneuma du stoïcisme à S. Augustin* (Louvain, 1945), pp. 16–17. The Epicureans also believed the soul to be corporeal, a body of the finest, lightest, and most rapidly moving atoms. Upon the death of the body these atoms are immediately dispersed, and the soul dies (Epicurus, *Ep. ad Hdt.* 65–6; Lucretius 3. 425–8; Diogenes Laertius 10. 63–8). See also E. Rohde, *Psyche*, tr. Hillis (New York, 1925), pp. 363–89, 463–76, 490–507.

314–15 Editors note that in *N.D.* 3. 36. 86–7 Cicero expressed the view here condemned when he wrote: 'No one ever imputed virtue to the bounty of a god. And no doubt rightly so; for our virtue is a just ground of others' praise and a right reason for pride on our part, and this would not be so if we had virtue as a gift from a god and not from ourselves.'[17] Christ's own teaching, in John 7. 18, however, is that 'He that speaketh of himself seeketh his own glory: but he that seeketh his glory that sent him, the same is true, and no unrighteousness is in him.' Cf. 1 Cor. 1. 31; 2 Cor. 3. 5; James 1. 17. See also 3. 134–5 above.

316–18 For the ancients themselves, as is abundantly clear from *De Fato* and *De Divinatione* of Cicero, and *On Fate* and *On Fortune* of Plutarch, and the many other discussions of fate which Grotius assembled in his *Philosophorum Sententiae de Fato et de eo quod in Nostra est Potestate* (Paris, 1648), the concepts of fortune and fate, involved as they are with the apparently irreconcilable concept of free will, presented a host of difficulties, which, Philosophia admits to Boethius (*C.P.* 4. 6), seem all but insoluble. 'Fortune' is chance, luck, hazard, a term applied to an event which might or might not have happened, or might have happened in any other way. Obviously it is difficult to reconcile it with regularity, reason, and divine foreknowledge (Cicero, *Div.* 2. 6. 15; 2. 7. 18–19). 'Fate' (μοῖρα) was the supreme power which determined all things, even the acts of the gods (Cicero, *N.D.* 1. 15. 39; *Fat.* 17. 39; Seneca, *Ben.* 4. 7–8; *Prov.* 5. 8; Plutarch, *On Fate* 1).

That the identification of god and 'Fortune', as far as I have discovered, is much less common than that of god and 'Fate'—it does occur in Cicero, *Acad.*

---

[17] Virtutem autem nemo umquam acceptam deo rettulit. Nimirum recte; propter virtutem enim iure laudamur et in virtute recte gloriamur, quod non contingeret, si id donum a deo non a nobis haberemus.

1. 7. 29—may be explained by the fact that 'Fortune' is pure accident or chance in which nothing rational is discernible (Cicero, *Div.* 2. 6. 15; 2. 7. 18); whereas 'Fate', or the world process, is the expression of a law to which reason submits, although it may not understand it, and hence it is compatible with the concept of a rational god (W. C. Greene, *Moira*, pp. 3–9, 331–98). 'Fate', Milton declares in *DocCh* 1. 2 (*Works* 14. 27), 'can be nothing but a divine decree emanating from some almighty power'; and in *PL* 7. 173 God says 'What I will is Fate'.

When Milton says that the philosophers who call God 'Fortune' or 'Fate' 'accuse him...as one regardless quite / Of mortal things', he means that if all men's acts are determined by 'Fortune' or 'Fate', men are charging their own wickedness to God's decrees; and, as he explains in *DocCh* 1. 4 (*Works* 14. 175), they 'do in effect impugn the justice of God...and might justly be reproved in the words of the heathen Homer, *Od.* 1. 7: "they perish'd self-destroy'd / By their own fault."'

Whether God is 'regardless quite / Of mortal things' was a question on which the ancients were not agreed. Plato (*Rep.* 10. 613; *Laws* 10. 899–905), approaching the Christian position, regarded as a grave heresy the belief that the gods take no heed of human affairs. See F. Solmsen, *Plato's Theology* (Ithaca, N.Y., 1942), pp. 68–9, 92, 111–12, 149–59. Aristotle, however, maintained that the nature of god, who is pure being, or thought, consists only in perpetual self-contemplation; between him and man there is too wide a separation to permit of mutual φιλία (*Cael.* 2. 12; *Nic. Eth.* 8. 9; 10. 8; *Eud. Eth.* 7. 3, 12; *De An.* 3. 10; *Meta.* 8. 4; 12. 7, 9, 10). See W. D. Ross, *Aristotle*, p. 184; W. K. C. Guthrie, *The Greeks and their Gods* (London, 1950), pp. 364–5. The Stoics repeatedly asserted that god in his providence cares for men (Cicero, *N.D.* 1. 44. 122; 2. 65. 164; Seneca, *Prov.* 1. 1. 6; *Ep.* 73. 16). The Epicureans denied divine providence, beneficence, and benevolence; and hence it follows, as Cicero observes (*N.D.* 1. 43. 121), that the gods care neither for men nor for each other.

319 *True wisdom.* In *DocCh* 2. 2 (*Works* 17. 27) Milton defines wisdom, one of the virtues of the understanding, as 'that whereby we earnestly search after the will of God, learn it with all diligence, and govern all our actions according to its rule.'

320–1 Editors see in these lines a probable allusion to the story of Ixion, who, believing that he was embracing Hera, embraced only a cloud which Zeus, to deceive him, had formed in her likeness (Apollodorus, *Epit.* 1. 20; Diodorus

Siculus 4. 69. 5; Hyginus, *Fab.* 33, 62; Fulgentius, *Myth.* 2. 14). In the present context the allusion is ironic.

321–30 In the famous discussion of the use of books in *Areop* (*Works* 4. 306–15), Milton insists, as he does here, upon the importance of the reader's judgment. See also *Epistol* (*Works* 12. 91); *Def 1* (7. 67). 'Milton was always aware that the scholar must bring to his book "a spirit and judgment equal or superior," lest he fall into the vices of the pedant or, worse still, the Sophist; but would he also grant, what readers of *Paradise Regained* are loath to admit, that what the scholar brings he need not seek in his book? Perhaps Milton is here letting Jesus pay Satan with his own coin; perhaps he plays with the words "spirit" and "judgment," and means that these alone the scholar cannot find in his book, while *food* for the spirit and judgment he may find...' (Irene Samuel, *P. and M.*, p. 128). Christ is not talking about learning, but about wisdom, which men can learn from books only if to the books they bring 'a judgment and spirit capable of receiving wisdom; and if they are capable of receiving wisdom, then they already possess within themselves the chief endowment for wisdom. And if wisdom is common and available, then the inner potential may be realized by other means: by study of the self, by inspiration; by study of other books, especially the book of books, which speaks directly to the spirit and may make it equal. Christ is not proposing an educational program....He is defining wisdom and declaring his own' (Stein, *Heroic Knowledge*, pp. 101–2).

321–2 An echo of Eccles. 12. 12: 'of making many books there is no end; and much study is a weariness of the flesh.' Who the wise men are to whom Milton refers it is impossible to say; but among those who in some measure agree with him are M. Aurelius (2. 3), Epictetus (*Diss.* 1. 4. 22–3), Pliny (*Ep.* 7. 9), Seneca (*Ep.* 2. 2–3; *Tranq.* 9. 4), and Bacon (*Of Studies*).

328 *crude.* OED, which quotes this line, gives the meaning 'lacking power to digest [*Obs.*]', a transferred sense of the word.

329 *spunge.* 'As a type of something of small value' (*OED*).

330 Dunster (pp. 234–5) suggests an allusion to the account in Cicero, *De Orat.* 2. 6. 22, of Laelius and Scipio, when they had escaped to Caieta and Laurentum, amusing themselves by collecting mussel and cockle shells.

334–5 Scattered through the historical books of the Bible, the books of the law, and the prophets are such poems or fragments of poems as the song of Lamech (Gen. 4. 23–4), the blessing of Jacob (Gen. 49. 1–27), the song of Moses (Deut. 32), the song of Deborah and Barak (Judges 5), the songs of David (2 Sam. 22; 1 Chron. 16. 7–36), and the prayer of Hezekiah (Isa. 38. 10–20). In *RCG* (*Works* 3. 238) Milton says: 'But those frequent songs throughout the law and prophets beyond all these [i.e. the odes and hymns of Pindar and Callimachus], not in their divine argument alone, but in the very critical art of composition may be easily made appear over all the kinds of Lyrick poesy, to be incomparable.' Thus Milton, agreeing with Hooker (*Eccles. Pol.* 5. 37. 2), has declared his preference for Hebrew lyric poetry not only on moral and religious, but also on aesthetic grounds.

335 Editors generally agree that by 'artful terms', that is technical terms, Milton means the headings of the Psalms, as for example, 'To the chief Musician of Seminith', 'To the chief Musician of Neginith, a Psalm of David', and the like—the meaning of which is still unknown—and that he understood them as in some way directions for the liturgical performance in the service of the temple, as do more recent Hebrew scholars. See Robertson Smith, *The Old Testament in the Jewish Church*, 2nd ed. (London, 1895), p. 96.

336–7 Cf. Ps. 137. 1–3: 'By the rivers of Babylon, there we sat down....We hanged our harps upon the willows in the midst thereof. For there they that carried us away captive required of us...mirth, saying, Sing us one of the songs of Zion.'

338 As part of their defence of Christianity against the surrounding paganism, some of the early Church Fathers maintained that the Greeks had derived their law, philosophy, and poetry from the Jews, who had enjoyed the advantage of greater antiquity and divine inspiration. Clement of Alexandria in *Strom.* 1. 5 (Migne, *Pat. Gr.* 8. 717 ff.), by citing parallel passages, proves to his own satisfaction that Plato and the other Greek philosophers must have made use of sacred Scripture. Tertullian in *Apol.* 47 (Migne, *Pat. Lat.* 1. 515–20) and Eusebius in *P.E.* 13. 12–13 (Migne, *Pat. Gr.* 21. 1097–140) argue to much the same effect; and in *Civ. D.* 8. 11 Augustine reasons that since Plato's conception of God is very nearly that of the Jews, he may have learned it from Jeremiah and the other prophets with whose works he probably became acquainted in Egypt.

Although, as Blakeney (p. 170) remarks, Milton was too good a scholar to accept this theory *ex animo*, it was only what many patristic writers had maintained, and what more than a few of Milton's contemporaries were still vigorously maintaining. See Schultz, *Forbidden Knowledge*, pp. 89–95, 260–2.

Book IV

Zachary Bogan in *Homerus* Ἑβραΐζων *sive Comparatio Homeri cum Scriptoribus Sacris* (Oxford, 1658) laboriously and without regard for chronology compared hundreds of passages in Homer with what he was pleased to think were their originals in the Bible. Edmund Dickinson in his *Delphi Phoenicizantes* (Oxford, 1655) set out to prove that the Greeks borrowed the story of Pythian Apollo from Jewish Scripture. And Daniel Huet in *Demonstratio Evangelica* (Paris, 1679), a work at least demonstrating the author's pedantic erudition, found that all the ancient sages were mythical, most of them fancifully copied from Moses. In his *Conjectura Cabbalistica* (Cambridge, 1662, pp. 3, 100) Henry More asks, 'What is *Plato* but *Moses Atticus?*' More also believed that Pythagoras must have been indebted to Moses for his theory of numbers. See also Ralph Cudworth, *The True Intellectual System of the Universe* (London, 1678), 1. 10. The supposed authority for these notions, which in his *Discourse of the Light of Nature* (London, 1652, p. 94) Nathaniel Culverwell rejected, is a passage in Strabo 16. 2. 24, which tells of a Sidonian named Moschus or Mochus, who lived before the Trojan War, and was reputedly the originator of the atomic philosophy. He, as Cudworth and More conjectured, was none other than Moses; and from his successors at Sidon, they believed, Pythagoras had learned his philosophy and transmitted it to Plato.

But to what absurdities this theory could lead has never, it is to be hoped, been more fully revealed than in the voluminous work of Theophilus Gale, *The Court of the Gentiles, or a Discourse Touching the Original of Human Literature both Philologic and Philosophic from the Scriptures of the Jewish Church*, the four parts of which appeared at Oxford between 1669 and 1677. Gale, with vast learning and no critical judgment, demonstrates, as he believes, the 'traduction' not only of all language from Hebrew, but also of all 'human literature', 'theogonie, physic, and politic, pagan poesie, history, laws, and oratory' from sacred Scripture.

Arts. Not merely the fine arts, but branches of learning as in 368 below, for example those comprising the *trivium* and the *quadrivium*.

339–42 In representing the gods as vicious the Greek poets have 'ill imitated' '*Sion's* songs' in which God is ever the God of righteousness. So in *Rep.* 2. 377–80, Plato indicts Homer and Hesiod for telling stories about the quarrels and intrigues of the gods, and thus making them the authors of evil; whereas they ought to be so represented as to furnish a moral standard for mankind, since Plato conceived the ethical end to be 'assimilation to god', as he explains in *Theaet.* 176. Cf. Augustine, *Civ. D.* 2. 8, 14. That the poets can conceive of

219

the gods as evil-doers and can tell stories discreditable to them, Milton believes, is but a reflection of their own depravity and shamelessness.

341 *Fable.* As in 2. 215 above; *PL* 1. 197; 2. 627, a fictitious story about extraordinary or supernatural persons and events, but possibly more specifically a drama based upon such a story, after Lat. *fabula*, as in Quintilian 5. 10. 9: *fabulae ad actum scenarum compositae.*

Hymn. As in 335; 1. 169 above; *PL* 2. 242, a song of praise to a god, such as the Homeric Hymns to Apollo and Hermes, and the Hymns of Callimachus to Zeus and Artemis.

Song. A lyric poem such as those of Anacreon, Simonides, Pindar, and Bacchylides, for which 'song' is the exact term.

personating. Representing, bearing the character of, like Lat. *personare*; 'cf. It. *personare* "...to act or play the part of any person"' (*OED*). The gods often appear among the *dramatis personae* of Greek plays, as, for example, Phoebus and Athene in Aeschylus' *Eumen.*, Hermes in *Prom.*, Athene in Sophocles' *Ajax*, and Poseidon in Euripides' *Tro.* In *Histrio-Mastix* 79–80 William Prynne censures 'the recitall, acting, and personating of...[the] Names, [the] Histories, and notorious Villanies' of the pagan gods, which 'must needes bee euill'.

343–50 That Holy Scripture is superior to all the writings of the pagans is a common Christian conviction which necessarily follows from the antecedent conviction that Scripture is divinely inspired, and that it alone contains the doctrine necessary for man's salvation. See *DocCh* 1. 30 (*Works* 16. 249–85); Calvin, *Inst.* 1. 6, 7, 10. 'Whatever a man may have learned elsewhere,' says Augustine in *Doc. Ch.* 2. 42 (Migne, *Pat. Lat.* 34. 65), 'if it is harmful, it is condemned [in Scripture]; if it is useful, it is contained therein.'[18]

343 *swelling Epithetes.* Does Milton mean that such compound epithets as 'aegis-bearing' (αἰγίοχος), 'bright-eyed' (γλαυκῶπις), 'wise-counselling' (ὀρθόβουλος) are 'swelling' in the sense of 'inflated, bombastic...pretentiously pompous' (*OED*)—expressions which, however common in Greek poetry, prevent the achievement of sublimity? Compound epithets are a well-known feature of his own style—'deep-skill'd', 'new-baptiz'd', 'high-rais'd', 'vermeil-tinctur'd'; but in his three longer poems he uses them more sparingly than in *Comus*. In *PR* they are comparatively rare.

344 Editors note an echo of Shakespeare, *Ham.* 3. 1. 51: 'The Harlots cheek beautied with plast'ring Art'.

---

[18] Nam quidquid homo extra didicerit, si noxium est ibi damnatur; si utile est, ibi invenitur.

345 Dunster (p. 236) compares Horace, *A.P.* 333: 'Poets aim either to benefit or to amuse',[19] and Plato's dictum in *Rep.* 10. 607 that poetry is justifiable only when it unites the power of pleasing with civil and moral instruction.[20]

346-52 Dunster (p. 237) would rearrange the lines and place 351-2 after 345, and Blakeney (p. 171) agrees that this may be the right order. The rearrangement, however, is unnecessary, if we read 'unworthy to compare / With *Sion's* songs... / Unless where moral vertue is express't', and treat the words here omitted as parenthetical.

346-8 See note on 334-5 above. Hughes (p. 523) quotes Sidney, who in *The Defence of Poesie* (*Works*, ed. Feuillerat, 3. 9), maintains that 'the chiefe [poets], both in antiquitie and excellencie, were they that did imitate the unconceiveable excellencies of God. Such were *David* in his Psalmes, *Salomon* in his song of songs, in his *Ecclesiastes*, and *Proverbes*. *Moses* and *Debora* in their Hymnes, and the wryter of *Jobe*'. J. B. Leishman, in *RES*, n.s. 6 (1955), 425, notes the following parallel in Donne, *Sermons*, ed. Potter and Simpson, 6 (1953), 56: 'now, that a perfect knowledge of those languages hath brought us to see the beauty and the glory of those Books, we are able to reply... that there are not in all the world so eloquent Books as the Scriptures; and that nothing is more demonstrable, then that if we would take all those Figures, and Tropes, which are collected out of secular Poets, and Orators, we may give higher, and livelier examples, of every one of those Figures, out of the Scriptures, then out of all the Greek and Latine Poets, and Orators'. Other tributes to the literary excellence of the Bible Leishman (*RES*, n.s. 8, 1957, 436) notes in *Sermons* 2 (1955), 119, 128, 130, 136, 353.

346 *far be found unworthy*. The transposition of the adverb is an Elizabethan usage of which many examples are given in Abbott, *Shakes. Gram.* 420.

347 *tasts*. *OED* quotes the present line to illustrate the earliest use of 'taste' meaning 'the sense of what is appropriate, harmonious, or beautiful...*spec.* the faculty of perceiving and enjoying what is excellent in art, literature, and the like'.

351-2 Although the Greek poets commended by Satan (262-3) as 'teachers best / Of moral prudence' are censured, they are not absolutely condemned. Their 'swelling Epithetes' are harshly dealt with in the image of cosmetics on a

---

[19] aut prodesse volunt aut delectare poetae.

[20] ὡς οὐ μόνον ἡδεῖα, ἀλλὰ καὶ ὠφελίμη πρὸς τὰς πολιτείας καὶ τὸν βίον τὸν ἀνθρώπινόν ἐστιν.

harlot's cheek; but when these are removed something is left, 'Thin sown with aught of profit or delight' it is true, but still 'sown'. Milton is making an exception of those poets who, though lacking divine inspiration, by reason, 'the light of Nature' (see note on 225–8 above), which not all have entirely lost, express 'moral vertue'—Satan said 'moral prudence'. A somewhat similar exception is made in *DocCh* 1. 12 (*Works* 15. 209) where Milton writes 'that some remnants of the divine image still exist in us, not wholly extinguished by this spiritual death. This is evident…from the wisdom and holiness of many of the heathen, manifested both in words and deeds'. Judging from Milton's tone and from the frequency with which he mentions them, I believe that the poets excepted probably are Homer, Aeschylus, Sophocles, Euripides, and Pindar. See Preface to *SA*; *Prol* 6 (*Works* 12. 219); *DocCh* 2. 9 (17. 221); J. D. Adam, *Religious Teachers of Greece* (Edinburgh, 1908), pp. 10–11, 125, 145–6, 165–6, 296–8.

353–7 See note on 267–71 above. The Greek orators, like the poets, were not worthless. Indeed they had the great merit of being statesmen and of loving their country; but, again like the poets, as they were without divine inspiration, they fell short of the excellences of the Hebrew prophets.

The tone of the present passage is like Jean Balzac's in *Socrate Chrestien* (p. 14) when he writes: 'Que vostre voisin le Delicat allegue tant qu'il voudra son Nestor, son Menelas, son Vlisse; & les propose comme les trois Fondateurs des trois stiles differens. Qu'il conte merueilles à ceux qui l'écoutent, de l'Eloquence Attique, de l'Asiatique, de la Rhodiene. Sur ma parole méprisez en cecy tout ce qu'il admire, & reseruez toute vostre admiration pour le Laconisme de Iesus-Christ.'

354 *top*. The 'most perfect example or type of something' (*OED*), like Lat. *summa*.

Statists. The word, probably of Italian origin, was in the 17th century a very common term for 'statesmen' (*OED*). It occurs several times in Milton's prose works.

356–64 The Hebrew Prophets, as Milton must have known, never attempted to teach the rules of civil government, at least as the term is generally understood, nor to deal with political problems as did Demosthenes and Cicero and the other Greek and Roman orators. What they did attempt, and what Milton probably means, since it was clearly one of their chief functions, was to teach both kings and people to apply to social and political problems the highest religious and moral principles, upon which national prosperity and happiness depend. See Isa. 15–19; Jer. 31. 31–4; Hos. 4–10; Amos 3–6; Mic. 4–5.

In ascribing supreme authority to Scripture, here as throughout *DocCh*, Milton wholly agrees with the orthodox Protestantism of the 16th and 17th centuries, as witness Calvin, *Inst.* 1. 6, 7, 8, 10; Hooker, *Eccles. Pol.* 1. 14; 5. 22; Zanchius, *De Perfect. Script.* and *De Sacr. Script.* 2 (*Op. Theol.*, Geneva, 1613, 7. 2. 12–13; 8. 326); *Westminster Confession of Faith* 1. 6. Until the Council of Trent gave tradition a place beside Holy Scripture, the whole Church had looked to Scripture as the only source of its teaching. See also note on 225–8 above.

357 *divinely taught.* See note on 3. 15–16 above.

359 In *Ref* 1 (*Works* 3. 34) Milton speaks of the 'sober, plain, and unaffected stile of the Scriptures'.

362 Editors note the reminiscence of Horace, *Ep.* 1. 6. 2: 'the one and only thing that can make a man happy and keep him so.'[21] Cf. Prov. 14. 34: 'Righteousness exalteth a nation: but sin is a reproach to any people.'

364 Readers in Milton's time may have understood this line as an implied criticism of Renaissance books of advice to princes, such as the *De Regimine Principum* of Egidio Colonna and *Il Principe* of Machiavelli. If such criticism was Milton's intention, it may specially be aimed at Machiavelli; for, although earlier writers had taught that the ruler ought to surpass his subjects in moral excellence, Machiavelli maintained that not moral considerations but his own security and well-being are the ruler's concern. See A. H. Gilbert, *Machiavelli's Prince and its Forerunners* (Durham, N.C., 1938), pp. 3–16, 38–45.

366 Possibly an echo of Ps. 64. 3 and Eph. 6. 16.

368–540 Commentators have generally agreed that Christ's rejection of learning concludes the second temptation; that the coming of night marks the close of the offer of the kingdoms of the world; and that the following episode of the storm either is an interlude between the second and the third temptations, or is connected as a link with the third temptation on the pinnacle of the temple. Invariably they interpret this episode as the attempt of an enraged and despairing Satan to terrorize Christ by the use of violence, to make him doubt divine protection (Blondel, p. 56). But Dick Taylor in his article 'Storm Scene' (*UTQ*

---

[21] solaque quae possit facere et servare beatum.

24, 1954-5, 360) maintains that these interpretations simply do not fit what happens in the speech and action of the scene. As he explains it, 'The storm scene is neither an interlude, nor a link, nor a prologue...it is not a move by a desperate and enraged Satan to terrorize Christ but...it constitutes in itself a forceful temptation, shrewdly devised and skilfully carried out by a calculating Satan in pursuance of an objective of temptation already set.

'There are three main points concerned in the establishment of this interpretation. (1) The theme of the storm scene is specifically that of the second temptation, further developed in a new phase; thus the storm scene is actually a part of the second temptation, and it, not the offer of learning, is the concluding phase; hence, night does not mark off the end of this series of trials but, as the vehicle of the storm, is rather an implementing agent in Satan's further strategy in pressing his offer of kingship, or power. (2) The method of the trial in the storm does not involve violence and terror by Satan so much as the temptation for Christ to follow false portents—to be deceived into reading false signs as evidence of God's will that he should assume power under Satan's auspices....[22] (3) Concerning the conflicting passages in the text, which have been the basis of the long-held interpretations, I shall offer two suggestions: first, the passages which describe Satan as in despairing rage and without further scheme are less conflicting than appears, since Milton throughout the poem has consistently described Satan in similar terms;[23] second, that Milton, either during the course of composition or afterward, possibly altered his original treatment of the storm episode, giving Satan a strategy of false portents instead of the original strategy of terror, but that in his reworking he did not completely eradicate elements of the original.'

These suggestions appear very dubious to me; and I think it unwise to interpret the storm and the evil spectres of the night—any more than the dream of food in 2. 260-78—as a temptation, though Satan is ready to turn them to his advantage. Persistent as he is, and unwilling to face facts, he, even he, after Christ's repeated and steadfast refusals to accept the kingdoms of the world, now can have no remotest reason to believe that further temptation to accept them will be anything but utterly futile. He therefore resorts to violence, the only method now left to him, and clearly a sign of his desperation. He hopes to make Christ feel alone, deserted, and helpless in a hostile, natural world. He hopes so to terrify him at the prospect of 'many a hard assay / Of dangers, and adversities and pains', which the storm and the spectres are meant to

[22] On the significance of portents in Milton's time, see the note on 1. 24-37 above.
[23] See note on 1. 37-43 above.

portend, that his rational control of himself and his faith in God's providence will be overcome by terror, so overcome that when suddenly put to the final test on the pinnacle of the temple, he will be taken unawares, and his resistance will break down. Satan is attempting to use terror as a means of psychological attrition, as—and let this be well noted—Christ clearly understands, if Taylor does not, for in lines 496–7 he rebukes Satan for 'thinking to terrifie / Mee to thy will'. Finally, that Milton 'possibly altered his original treatment of the storm episode', but failed completely to 'eradicate elements of the original' treatment, is a conjecture which nothing in the scene supports, and it is highly unlikely, Milton being the artist that he was.

369   *Kingdom.* Kingship, sovereignty, as in 2. 36 above.

370–1   Satan makes the Aristotelian distinction between the active and the contemplative life (*Nic. Eth.* 1. 6; 10. 7). Augustine (*Civ. D.* 8. 4), whom Hughes (1st ed., p. 524) quotes, accepts the distinction but gives it an added religious significance when he writes: 'So the study of wisdom concerns either action or contemplation, and hence one part of it may be called active and the other contemplative, of which the active consists in the practice, that is the establishment of morality; whence the contemplative consists in the comprehending the causes of nature and the purest truth.'[24] For mystics such as St Bernard and the *contemplanti spiriti* whom Dante found in the Heaven of Saturn (*Parad.* 21–2), contemplation is the highest form of spiritual activity. In the House of Holiness (*F.Q.* 1. 10. 42–57), after the active virtues comes the higher, contemplation, in the order of Calvin, *Inst.* 3. 7–9. See F. M. Padelford, 'Spenser and the Theology of Calvin', *MP* 12 (1914–15), 13–15. See also *Prol* 7 (*Works* 12. 254). Obviously contemplation in this sense is much more than Satan means—or understands—and it is ironical, to say the least, that he should use a term having this significance.

377   *Nicely.* See note on 157 above.

379   *David's Throne.* See note on 1. 240–1.

380   Cf. Gal. 4. 4: 'But when the fulness of the time was come, God sent forth his Son'; cf. also 3. 182–3, 396–9, 433 above.

381   *Prophesies of thee.* See note on 1. 261 above.

---

[24] Itaque cum studium sapientiae in actione et contemplatione versetur, unde una pars eius activa, altera contemplativa dici potest; quarum activa ad agendam vitam, id est ad mores instituendos pertinet, contemplativa autem ad conspiciendas naturae causas et sincerissimam veritatem.

382–93 William Warburton (*Works of Shakespeare*, London, 1747, 6. 21) suggests that Milton, wishing 'to discredit *judicial Astrology*', not only has it 'patronised by the Devil', but deliberately makes 'him blunder in the expression, of *portending a kingdom which was without beginning*. This destroys all he would insinuate.' But Dunster (p. 240) remarks that 'the language is here intended to be highly sarcastic on the eternity of Christ's kingdom, respecting which the Tempter says he believes it will have one of the properties of eternity, *that of never beginning*.'

Since Milton lived at a time when belief in astrology was widespread but often under attack, especially in its judicial form, the present passage may well be satirical. See D. C. Allen, *The Star-Crossed Renaissance* (Durham, N.C., 1941), pp. viii, 147–80. Svendsen (*Science*, p. 83), after considering many passages in Milton's works which contain astrological lore—with which, not surprisingly, he was well acquainted—concludes that, whatever may have been his own private opinion, Milton found in astrology 'the perfectly logical corollary to the order and symmetry of the world' made for man by God. But as Allen (pp. 155–6) observes, although in the English Renaissance astrology for most authors was a storehouse of rhetorical ornament, their use of astrological tropes does not prove that they believed in astrology. Has Svendsen determined in how far Milton uses astrology as rhetorical ornament, and in how far he is expressing a belief? See note on 1. 24–37 above and Schultz, *Forbidden Knowledge*, pp. 52–7.

382–5 Satan 'casts a nativity' or horoscope to discover Christ's fortune. To do so the important matter was to determine which of the seven planets, each of which has its sign or 'character', was in the 'ascendant', and in which 'house' or sign of the zodiac it was at the exact moment of a person's birth. There may also be a 'conjunction' of planets (see note on 385 below) 'and this is either good or bad, as the Planets are either Friends or Enemies one to the other' (J. Middleton, *Practical Astrology*, London, 1679, p. 3). The foregoing is probably close to the meaning of 'Stars / Voluminous, or single characters, / In their conjunction met.' Milton's expression might well be clearer.

382 *contrary.* An adverb, 'on the contrary'. '*arch.*' (*OED*).

383 *Fate.* See note on 316–18 above.

384 *Voluminous.* 'In volumes or books collectively', used figuratively (Lockwood, *Lexicon*); but here probably 'large in numbers; numerous', a rare meaning (*OED*).

385 *conjunction*. In the astrological and astronomical sense, 'an apparent proximity of two planets or other heavenly bodies; the position of these when they are in the same, or nearly the same, direction as viewed from the earth' (*OED*).

to spell. 'To make out, understand, decipher, or comprehend, by study' (*OED*). Cf. *IlPen* 170–1:

> Where I may sit and rightly spell
> Of every Star that Heav'n doth shew.

L. H. Kendall Jr. ('Two Notes on the Text of *PR*', *N & Q* n.s. 4, 1957, 523) would place a semicolon after 'spell', which, he says, would 'accord with Milton's own standard practices, to indicate a full stop'. But this punctuation makes a sentence of what is merely an introductory subordinate clause.

386–8 The sufferings predicted for Christ, as Dunster (p. 239) notes, are like those of the just man in Plato, *Rep.* 2. 361, who will be scourged, racked, bound, will have his eyes burned out, and finally will be impaled. The passage may also be reminiscent of Isa. 53. 3–10, commonly considered a Messianic prophecy, which describes the Messiah as 'a man of sorrows...wounded for our transgressions...bruised for our iniquities...brought as a lamb to the slaughter...taken from prison and from judgment...cut off out of the land of the living.'

387 *Attends*. Accompanies or waits upon for 'hostile purposes, so as to defeat an enemy's plans' (*OED*). The subject is plural, but the verb agrees with an immediately preceding singular noun, as often in Spenser and Shakespeare (W. Franz, *Die Sprache Shakespeares*, Halle/Saale, 1939, 673).

injuries. Insults, taunts (*OED*), like Lat. *iniuria*. See Matt. 27. 29, 39; Mark 15. 32.

390 *Allegoric*. Figurative (*OED*, s.v. allegorically) (ἀλληγορικός) and hence unreal.

391–2 See note on 382–93 above.

393 This continues the figure begun in 382. The stars form, as it were, a calendar, since a rubric is the entry of a saint's name in red letters in the Church calendar.

394–5 See note on 1. 363 above.

397–400 Darkness and night are unsubstantial; they are not self-existent entities, because they are merely the absence of light. Cf. *PL* 2. 439: 'unessential Night'. Milton's treatment of 'night', like that of the ancients, presents some difficulties, since the line is not always clearly drawn between personification and mythology. What we have here is mainly mythology, but, as Osgood (*Mythology*, p. 63) points out, it is contrary to classical tradition, according to which the parent of 'Night', if she had one, was Chaos, not Darkness (Hesiod, *Theog.* 123) or Phanes (Proclus on *Tim.* 5. 291).

401–9 In the light of the dream and demon lore which, W. B. Hunter in 'Eve's Demonic Dream' (*ELH* 13, 1946, 255–65; and see K. Svendsen, 'Milton and Medical Lore', *Bulletin of the History of Medicine* 13, 1943, 170–2) shows, was part of conservative religious belief in the 17th century, the 'ugly dreams' which disturb Christ's sleep, even if Satan in lines 481–2 did not plainly say that they were meant to be warnings, would at once be recognized by Milton's contemporaries for what they are, namely, an attempt to persuade Christ that he is receiving a warning of the 'dangers, and adversities and pains' that await him. But Christ's refusal so to interpret the dreams significantly illustrates the orthodox belief concerning the infernal powers, stated by Aquinas in *Sum. Th.* 1. 114. 2. 3, that they can to a certain degree change the inferior powers of a man, by which powers the will, though it may be inclined, cannot be forced.

402 *jaunt.* In the 16th and 17th centuries this word meant 'a fatiguing or troublesome journey' (*OED*), as in *Areop* (*Works* 4. 325); *HistBr* 6 (10. 259).

406 See note on 1. 306 above.

409–19 In the description of the storm, earlier editors, Masson (3. 315) remarks, 'have traced shreds from similar descriptions in the *Æneid* and other poems. Milton wrote, I believe, with no idea of such patchwork.' True, he probably did not intend his description to be a piece of *patchwork*, but it is undeniably *like* descriptions in Homer, *Od.* 5. 291–6; Aeschylus, *Agam.* 644–57; Virgil, *A.* 1. 82–123; Lucan 5. 597–677; Tasso, *Jerusalem* 7. 115–17; Spenser, *F.Q.* 1. 8. 9; and with the descriptions in Homer, Virgil, and Tasso it has this in common: it is intended for the discomfiture of a particular person.

Hughes (p. 525) observes that 'It suits Milton's purpose to disregard Reginald Scot's denial in *The Discoverie of Witchcraft* that Satan has any power over the weather, the lightning or thunder, and to assume with Burton [*Anatomy* 1. 2. 1. 2.] that "Aerial spirits...cause many tempests, thunder, and lightnings, tear oaks, fire steeples, houses."' For much further evidence of this belief, see Svendsen, *Science*, pp. 75, 100. Whether or not Milton actually accepted the belief, it serves the purpose of representing Satan as creating not only moral but also physical disorder.

409–10 The tropics or solstices are the points in the ecliptic at which the sun is farthest from the equator, north or south; hence 'either Tropic' means 'north or south'. I take 'both ends of Heav'n' to mean 'east and west'. The thunder, like the winds in 415, comes from all directions.

410–25 The sounds mentioned in these lines, the roar of thunder, the howling, yelling, and shrieking of the 'Infernal Ghosts and Hellish Furies', are all extremely discordant and may be intended, like the 'dismal universal hiss' which greeted Satan in *PL* 10. 508, to signify the negation of music. See note on 2. 279–81.

410 *'Gan.* As the apostrophe indicates, Milton understood 'gan' to be a shortened form of 'began'; but it is the past tense of 'gin' (O.E. *ginnan*) (*OED*), which is common in Spenser but rare in Shakespeare and Milton. The omission of 'to' after 'gin' is very common, possibly because the word is often used as an auxiliary verb meaning 'did'.

411–13 Cf. Aeschylus, *Agam.* 650–1: 'Fire and sea, once bitterest foes, are leagued in firm alliance';[25] Homer, *Od.* 5. 295–6: 'The East Wind and the South Wind clashed together, and the stormy West and the sky-born North';[26] Tasso, *Jerusalem* 7. 116. 4–8:

> On euerie side the fierie light'nings flie,
> The thunders roare, the streaming raine and haile
> Powre downe and make that sea which earst was drie,
> The tempests rend the Oakes and Cedars brake,
> And make not trees, but rocks and mountaines shake.

Spenser, *F.Q.* 1. 8. 9. 1–7:

> As when almightie *Ioue* in wrathfull mood...
> Hurles forth his thundring dart with deadly food,
> Enrold in flames, and smouldring dreriment,
> Through riuen cloudes and molten firmament;
> The fierce threeforked engin making way,
> Both loftie towres and highest trees hath rent.

---

[25] ξυνώμοσαν γάρ, ὄντες ἔχθιστοι τὸ πρίν,
 πῦρ καὶ θάλασσα.

[26] σὺν δ' Εὖρός τε Νότος τ' ἔπεσε Ζέφυρός τε δυσαὴς
 καὶ Βορέης αἰθρηγενέτης.

The wearisome account, too long to be quoted here, of the storm in Lucan 5. 597–677 also represents the elements as in utter confusion.

411 *abortive.* 'Produced prematurely, *hence*, in a confused mass without order (?)' (Lockwood, *Lexicon*).

413–14 Cf. Virgil, *A.* 1. 52–4: 'Here, in his vast cave, King Aeolus rules the rebellious winds and roaring storms, and curbs them with prison bonds';[27] and Lucan 5. 608–10: 'I cannot believe that the threats of the East Wind had ceased, and that the South Wind, dark with storms, lay idle in the prison of Aeolus' cave.'[28]

413 *ruine.* *OED* gives several examples of 'ruin' meaning 'the act of giving way and falling down, on the part of some fabric or structure', which seems to be the meaning here.

415 *the four hinges of the world.* In a transferred sense 'hinges' means 'the axis of the earth, the two poles about which the earth revolves, and by extension the four cardinal points' (*OED*). Cf. *Nat* 122; Pliny, *N.H.* 4. 12. 89: *cardines mundi*; Vulgate, Job 22. 14: *cardines caeli.*

416 *vext.* 'Disturbed', 'agitated' (*OED*), like Lat. *vexatus*, as in *PL* 10. 314.

416–19 Cf. Virgil, *G.* 2. 290–2: 'Deeper and far within the earth is fixed a tree, most of all the tall oak which stretches its roots as far down toward the infernal regions as it lifts its head to the airs of heaven.'[29] See also Tasso, quoted in note on 411–13.

419–21 So was Christ unshaken by the storm on the Sea of Galilee (Matt. 8. 23–6; Mark 4. 36–9; Luke 8. 22–5).
  terror. That which 'excites terror' (*OED*), as in Ps. 91. 5. In *PL* 2. 704 Death is called the 'grieslie terrour'.

422–5 Editors suggest that Milton may here be indebted to Eusebius, *D.E.*

[27]   hic vasto rex Aeolus antro
   luctantis ventos tempestatesque sonoras
   imperio premit ac vinclis et carcere frenat.
[28] non Euri cessasse minas, non imbribus atrum
   Aeolii iacuisse Notum sub carcere saxi
   crediderim.
[29] altior ac penitus terrae defigitur arbos,
   aesculus in primis, quae quantum vertice ad auras
   aetherias, tantum radice in Tartara tendit.

9. 7 (Migne, *Pat. Gr.* 22. 673–81), where Psalm 90. 5–7 is interpreted as a prediction of Christ's nocturnal trials in the wilderness. Carey (p. 1157) cites Shakespeare, *R. III* 1. 4. 58–9: 'With that, methought, a legion of foul fiends / Environ'd me about, and howled in my ears'. Jortin (*Tracts* 1. 336) believes that the scene may be taken from a picture which Milton had seen of the temptation of St Anthony.

423 Possibly reminiscent of Tasso, *Jerusalem* 9. 15. 1, 5–8:

> Their mantle darke, the grisly shadowes spred...
> The moone and stars for feare of sprites were fled,
> The shriking gobblings each where howling flew,
>   The Furies roare, the ghosts and Fairies yell.
>   The earth was fild with deuils, and emptie hell.

and 16. 67. 7–8:

> You might haue heard how through the pallace wide,
> Some spirits howld, some barkt, some hist, some cride.

424–5 Todd (5. 277) notes that Christ's behaviour is very like that of the Christian champions in Tasso's enchanted forest (*Jerusalem* 13. 28, 33, 35) who calmly view the threats and attacks of fearful monsters.

426–31 Cf. Virgil, *A.* 1. 142–3: 'Thus he speaks, and quicker than his word he calms the swollen seas, puts to flight the gathered clouds, and recalls the sun';[30] and Tasso, *Jerusalem* 8. 1. 1–4:

> Now were the skies of stormes and tempests cleered,
> Lord *Æolus* shut vp his windes in hold,
> The siluer mantled morning fresh appeared,
> With roses crown'd, and buskind high with gold...

426–7 Cf. *Lyc* 187: 'the still morn went out with Sandals gray'.

427 *amice*. 'An oblong piece of white linen...originally enveloping the head and neck, now generally folded so as to lie around the neck and shoulders: often taken to symbolize "the helmet of salvation"' (*OED*).

428 *radiant finger*. Cf. Homer, *Od.* 2. 1; 3. 404, 491: 'rosy-fingered Dawn' (ῥοδοδάκτυλος Ἠώς).

---

[30] Sic ait, et dicto citius tumida aequora placat
collectasque fugat nubes solemque reducit.

430–1 One of the oldest and commonest beliefs concerning ghosts and evil spirits is that at dawn they must instantly disappear. Cf. *Nat* 232–6; Virgil, *A.* 5. 738–40; Statius, *Th.* 2. 120–1; Claudian 15. 348 (1. 124); Prudentius, *Cath.* 1. 37–47; Philostratus, *Vit. Apoll.* 4. 16; Lucian, *Philops.* 14; Shakespeare, *Ham.* 1. 1. 142–9.

430 *grisly.* Horrible, fear-inspiring, as in *PL* 1. 670; 2. 704; 4. 821. Spenser often uses the word, as in *Gn.* 544: 'grisly Fiends of Hell'.
Fiend. See note on 1. 465 above.

432–8 With this description compare that in *PL* 2. 488–95, and see *Prol 2* (*Works* 12. 123). Dunster (p. 248) compares Spenser, *Am.* 40. 6–12, and Tasso, *G.L.* 15. 9, with which, however, the resemblance is not striking.

434–8 On the significance of the song of the birds, see note on 2. 279–81 above.

436 *ruinous.* 'Disastrous, destructive, pernicious' (*OED*), as in *PL* 6. 216.

437 *Clear'd up.* *OED* gives the present use of 'clear up' as an example of the meaning 'to make clear (what has become overcast); to brighten up'. But certainly the correct meaning is 'make to sound distinctly, make ring' (Lockwood, *Lexicon*), of which I have found no other example.

438 *gratulate.* 'Express joy at the coming or appearance of; to welcome' (*OED*). Cf. *Comus* 948; *PL* 8. 514; 9. 472.

442–6 See note on 1. 37–43.

449 *in wonted shape.* See note on 1. 314.

452–83 On the significance of the storm, see note on 368–540 above.

452 *rack.* 'The tumult of a storm bringing ruin' (Lockwood, *Lexicon*, s.v. wrack). According to *OED*, which quotes the present line, 'a crash as of something breaking'.

453 *Earth and Skie would mingle.* Cf. Virgil, *A.* 1. 133–4: *caelum terramque...| miscere.*

453–4 Satan declares that he has been absent during the night, but, as we know from line 397, he has only pretended to withdraw from the scene. *Expecting* to be charged with responsibility for the disturbances of the night—as Christ does charge him in line 491—he denies responsibility. But since he is ever a liar, the very denial indicts him.

454 *flaws.* Sudden bursts or squalls of wind (*OED*), as in *PL* 10. 698.

455 *the pillard frame of Heaven.* Possibly reminiscent of Job 26. 11: 'The pillars of heaven tremble.' Cf. *Comus* 597: 'the pillar'd firmament'. See 1. 253 above and note.

457 *main.* The universe, the macrocosm, as opposed to man, the microcosm, 'mans less universe' mentioned two lines below. The notion that man is a microcosm, 'an epitome of the "great world" or universe' (*OED*), was often expressed, as in Seneca, *Q.N.* 2. 45; Epictetus, *Diss.* 1. 14. 6; 2. 8. 11; M. Aurelius 2. 4; 5. 27; Lydgate, *Pilgrimage of the Life of Man* 12. 370; Paracelsus, *Archidoxies* 1; Montaigne, *Essays* 2. 12; Ralegh, *Historie* 1. 2. 5. Bacon (*Adv.* 2. 10. 2) thought it a commonplace which had been 'fantastically strained by Paracelsus and the alchemists'.

458 As Svendsen (*Science*, pp. 38–9) explains, the physiological concept referred to here, the therapeutic value of sneezing, which is as old as Aristotle, is common in medical lore of the Renaissance, and from the popular encyclopedias of the time it appears that sneezing was seriously considered to be a purging of the brain and thus a benefit to health. See Browne, *Pseud.* 4. 9.

460–83 See note on 1. 24–37.

460–4 In these lines and in 477–83 Satan talks like an almanac maker or prognosticator, one of those who, for centuries, all over Europe, on the basis of the common belief that thunder, lightning, wind, rain, the phenomena of nature generally, are omens, had been predicting events in the lives of men. That almanacs were popular is attested by their great number and their persistence through the centuries. See E. F. Bosanquet, *English Printed Almanacs and Prognostications* (London, 1917); V. Champier, *Les Anciens Almanachs* (Paris, 1886), both *passim*; Allen, *The Star-Crossed Renaissance*, p. 210. But despite their popularity, almanacs were often ridiculed from the time when Rabelais wrote the *Pantagrueline Prognostication* until with *Isaac Bickerstaff's Predictions* (1708) Swift demolished Partridge. In 1660 and 1675 Milton's nephew John Phillips, in *Montelion* and *Mercurius Verax*, satirized the pretensions of William Lilly and other 17th-century prognosticators.

467–83. See 1. 240–1; 3. 150–80 above and notes. Satan refers to what he has said in lines 374–93 and in 3. 351–6. Hanford (2nd ed., p. 540) remarks that Milton here 'loses the thread of the grammar' and in line 477 begins a new sentence, which takes the place of an object clause. But Satan's manner of expression, beginning with a question, then changing to affirmative statements, betrays his agitation. For a passage in similar style, see Eve's speech in *PL* 5. 28–93.

On this passage Browne (new ed., revised, 2. 318) has the following comment: 'There is a copy of this poem in the King's Library, carefully corrected throughout, apparently at the date of publication, in accordance with the printed directions. At this place, in the same handwriting, occurs the following alteration, for which those directions give no authority:

> Did I not tell thee, soon thou shalt have cause
> To wish thou never hadst rejected thus
> The perfect season offered, with my aid
> To win thy destin'd seat, prolonging still
> All to the push of Fate? pursue thy way, &c.'

468 *perfect.* This is the reading of the Columbia ed., but the first edition reads 'perfet'. See note on 1. 83 above.

470 *push.* '*Fig.*...A critical juncture, an extremity' (*OED*). Cf. Shakespeare, *2 H. IV* 2. 2. 38; *Caesar* 5. 2. 5; *Macb.* 5. 3. 20.
Fate. See note on 316–18 above.

471 *David's Throne.* See note on 1. 240–1.

472 Todd (5. 283) compares Dante, *Parad.* 21. 46–8: 'But she whose guidance I await for the manner and time of speech and silence is mute, and so, though unwilling, I do well to withhold my question.'[31]

474 See note on 1. 242–3 above.

475–6 Satan's opportunistic counsel is not only unprincipled, but almost as illogical as his statement 'Evil be thou my Good' in *PL* 4. 110 and his argument with Abdiel in 5. 853–69. 'Must' excludes any possibility of 'may be', and 'rightliest' and 'best' are irrelevant.

477–83 See note on 460–4 above.

478 *many a hard assay.* See 1. 143 and 264 above and notes.

481 *ominous.* 'Of ill omen, foreboding evil' (*OED*). Cf. *Comus* 61: 'this ominous Wood'.

---

[31] Ma quella, ond' io aspetto il come e il quando
Del dire e del tacer, si sta; ond' io
Contra il disio fo ben ch' io non dimando.

486–98 Christ answers Satan 'in brief'; but he says all that need be said, namely that all Satan's efforts to terrify him to his will are vain, that the portents are false, and that his evil purpose is discerned.

488 *noising.* Making a noise (*OED*). The word in this sense does not occur in Spenser or Shakespeare nor elsewhere in Milton's poetry.

489–91 The portents are false because they come from Satan, who, as Christ said in 1. 407–8, is ever 'compos'd of lyes'.

495 *Ambitious spirit.* In *PL* 4. 40 (cf. 1. 41, 262; 4. 92) Satan himself admitted that 'Pride and worse Ambition' caused his ruin.

496 *storm'st.* Be 'in a passion, rage' (Lockwood, *Lexicon*); but the word is possibly used with a double meaning, and may also signify 'raisest a storm' in the physical sense.

499 *Fiend.* See note on 1. 465 above.

500–40 Satan now 'answers in a rage that releases all his comic perplexity.... We are getting a recapitulation of Satan's first approach to his problem. This is where he came in, and after all that has happened he is still there, retelling it all in a kind of comic-opera song, but with the addition of the charming dramatic candor about the baptism, and with an authoritatively final comic statement on the subject of the literal-metaphorical title Son of God. The verbal comedy of this last is now fulfilled, though the idea has a little further service to perform.

'The speech continues in angry sincerity which aims only at the relief of expressing itself, and is, if here only, not baited' (Stein, *Heroic Knowledge*, pp. 124–5).

500 *Son of David.* See note on 3. 154 above.

Virgin-born. Satan is sarcastically disparaging Christ. Although, as Bishop Pearson maintains in *An Exposition of the Creed* (6th ed., London, 1692, pp. 106–7), to be born of a virgin is not of itself sufficient to prove that Christ is the only-begotten Son of God, nevertheless were Satan to admit the virgin birth, he would be admitting so material a part of the Messianic prophecy, as given in Isa. 7. 14 (cf. Matt. 1. 23), that he would at least in part be admitting the point which he professes to question.

500–3 See notes on 1. 24–37, 245, and especially 261 above. That the Messianic hope was common among the Jews is clear from the words addressed to

Jesus by the woman of Samaria in John 4. 25: 'I know that Messias cometh, which is called Christ: when he is come, he will tell us all things.'

501 Concerning Satan's professed doubt about Christ's identity, see note on 1. 91 above.

504 *Gabriel.* See note on 1. 129 above.

505–6 See note on 1. 242–3 above.

510 *Ford of Jordan.* See note on 1. 184 and cf. 1. 328–9 and 2. 20 above.

512 *Though not to be Baptiz'd.* Another sneer like 'Virgin-born' in line 500.

518–19 Although in *PL* 4. 43 Satan admitted that God created him, in 5. 860–1 he declared that he and the other angels were 'self-begot, self-rais'd' by their 'own quick'ning power'. See Lewis, *Preface*, pp. 95–6.

524 *collect.* 'Conclude', 'infer' (*OED*), like Lat. *colligere*. The word in this sense does not occur in Spenser or Shakespeare, nor elsewhere in Milton's poetry.

525 Satan admits that all the 'conjectures' or prognostications seem to indicate that Christ is the 'Seed of Eve' destined to inflict upon his head the 'fatal wound'. But how is this admission reconcilable with what he immediately goes on to say in lines 534–40?
fatal. 'Destined, fated' (*OED*), like Lat. *fatalis*, as in *PL* 2. 104.

529 The terms which Satan here uses suggest negotiations between two opposing armies, as if he were still in a position to reach some agreement with Christ.
parl. 'Conference, discussion, debate' (*OED*).
composition. 'A mutual agreement for cessation of hostilities' (*OED*), as in *PL* 6. 613.

531–40 Here ends the second temptation. Satan has to admit that thus far he has been defeated; he refuses, however, to admit, at least outwardly, that Christ has yet proved himself to be more than a man of great moral integrity. Therefore he must subject him to another trial. See note on 1. 91 above.

533–4 *rock | Of Adamant.* Probably an echo of Zech. 7. 12: 'adamant stone'; cf. *Huon of Bordeaux* 109; Spenser, *F.Q.* 1. 7. 33. 7; 1. 11. 25. 5: 'adamant rock'. The basic meaning of 'adamant' as of ἀδάμας and Lat. *adamas* is 'invincible'; hence 'an alleged rock or mineral' of extreme hardness; hence, applied to character, 'that which is impregnable to any application of force' (*OED*).

534 *Center*. 'The fixed or unmoving centre of rotation or revolution' (*OED*). Cf. Chaucer, *Sq. T.* 22: 'Of his corage as any centre stable'; *Comus* 380–1:

> He that has light within his own cleer brest
> May sit i'th center, and enjoy bright day.

Grierson advisedly places a semicolon after 'firm'.

535–7 Satan means to belittle Christ, but in affirming that Christ has done no more than man can do, has done, and will do again, he unwittingly states the significance for man of the temptation of Christ, the great moral exemplar.

538–9 See notes on 500–40 and 500 above.

540–95 As Dick Taylor shows in his article 'Grace as a Means of Poetry' (*TSE* 4, 1954, 57–90), Milton, as a Christian humanist, believed that to achieve salvation man must through trial prove himself worthy of it; 'he must win it "not without dust and heat" along the road' (p. 58); but ultimately salvation comes to man only through the extension of grace from God.

Christ, as Taylor (pp. 86–8) observes, now far advanced on his journey of trial, has reached the crucial point; he must take the last step to prove himself worthy of God's intervention with the miracle of his grace. In the last climactic episode on the pinnacle of the temple, Satan boldly and primarily attacks Christ's divinity by scornfully daring him to stand if he can on that seemingly impossible spot. Taylor believes that earlier commentators have exaggerated the importance of violence and despair in Satan's actions; that his manner is bold and assured, rather than despairing, and his attack shrewdly planned and powerfully executed; that he confidently hopes to force Christ to make a false move on his, Satan's, terms, to manœuvre the heavenly powers into performing a miracle at his direction and at an unappointed time. Thus he will not only prove Christ's identity, but will also defeat God's plan for Christ's wholly human trial, and for the consequent salvation of mankind. To this end he tempts Christ to make an untimely and presumptuous display of his power. But if he were to accept Satan's challenge and cast himself down, looking to God to save him, needlessly putting God's power to the test, he would be calling for God's aid on Satan's terms. Christ's trust in God, however, is profoundly mature; he leaves the whole outcome of the event to God; he will stand or fall, be saved or dashed to pieces, whichever may be God's will;

but he himself will do nothing. To the last he holds his trial to the human level, and thus proves his complete obedience. His answer to Satan, 'It is written, Tempt not the Lord thy God', is the last step along the road of trial. God then immediately intervenes with his grace on the human level of trial, miraculously holds Christ in safety on the lofty pinnacle, while Satan 'smitten with amazement' falls.

With much of Taylor's interpretation I agree; I am, however, unable to agree that Satan's boldness, if we may call it that, arises from assurance; it is rather the boldness of a cornered and terrified beast making a last violent effort to save itself. Satan's attack, it is true, is powerfully executed, but in it there is little, if any, assurance. It is a too ill-concealed attempt at murder.

540 Cf. Joseph Beaumont, *Psyche* (London, 1648), 9. 200:

> *Satan* at this repulse, deep in his Heart
> Stifled his Griefe, and smothered his shame:
> And now resolv'd to act another Part,
> Leap'd on that Cloud upon whose back he came.
> With which He through the wondering Aire did swim
> Hurrying thy patient *Lord* along with Him.

542 *Hippogrif.* A fabulous animal, half horse, half griffin, somewhat resembling Pegasus, which is the winged steed that carries Ariosto's heroes upon their incredible journeys. See *O.F.* 2. 37; 4. 4; 10. 66; 22. 24; Pio Rajna, *Le fonti dell'Orlando Furioso* (Florence, 1876), pp. 98–100; Svendsen, *Science*, pp. 144–6.

sublime. High (Lat. *sublimis*) (*OED*), as in *PL* 2. 528; 3. 72; 7. 421.

543–4 The marvellous aerial journey is from the Desert of Quarentana to Jerusalem. See note on 1. 119 above. The speed with which, evidently, the journey is accomplished is part of Satan's method; he will hurry Christ into an ill-considered act.

545 *The holy City.* Jerusalem is so called in Isa. 52. 1; Joel 3. 17; Matt. 4. 5; 27. 53; Rev. 11. 2; 21. 2.

Towers. Adrichomius (*Theatrum*, pp. 166–8) and Sandys (*Relation*, pp. 156–7) mention the many towers of Jerusalem; and in Josephus' description of the city (*B.J.* 5. 4) towers are one of the most conspicuous features.

546 Josephus (*B.J.* 5. 5), whom Milton is probably following, describes the temple of Herod, that of the time of Christ, as a building of great magnificence, constructed of white marble and adorned with plates of gold which reflected the light of the sun with dazzling splendour.

547-8 Viewed from a distance, the temple, Josephus (*B.J.* 5. 5. 6) says, appeared like a mountain covered with snow. From its top, he adds, rose golden spires to prevent birds from settling upon and polluting the roof.

549 *Pinacle.* The word πτερύγιον (Matt. 4. 5; Luke 4. 9), translated in the Vulgate *pinnaculum* and in the A.V. 'pinnacle', has puzzled Biblical scholars, because the roof of the temple was understood to be flat; but it probably means one of the spires mentioned in the preceding line.

551-9 Cf. Matt. 4. 6: 'If thou be the Son of God, cast thyself down: for it is written, He shall give his angels charge concerning thee: and in their hands they shall bear thee up, lest at any time thou dash thy foot against a stone.' Cf. also Luke 4. 9-11. Satan quotes Ps. 91. 11-12. He quotes Scripture, says Andrewes (*Ninety-Six Sermons* 5. 521), to 'be the better credited. He speaks not now after the manner of men, so that it is not he now that speaketh but Scripture'. But he is sophistically misapplying what he quotes, which means that God will save the righteous man from falling into danger; it does *not* mean that that man may expect God to protect him if he deliberately and unnecessarily exposes himself to danger, as Christ would be doing if he cast himself down. See note following.

Satan, in panic fear attempting a 'poorly concealed murder' (Allen, *Vision*, p. 115), intends that Christ shall fall, and the result will be his answer. 'His injunction to stand is purely ironical: that it is possible, he never for a moment conceives. But if Satan can be ironical, so can Christ and the event. For the first and only time, he complies with Satan's suggestion; but it is not in surrender to Satan: it is in obedience to God—like Samson's going to the festival of Dagon. This is Christ's supreme act of obedience and trust, and it is also the long-awaited demonstration of divinity. The poem's two themes are finally and securely united; and "Tempt not the Lord thy God" carries a double meaning, for, in addition to its immediate application, it is Christ's first claim to participate in the Godhead. In an instant, and by the same event, Satan receives his answer and Christ achieves full knowledge of himself' (Woodhouse, 'Theme', *UTQ* 25, 1955-6, 181).

To Woodhouse's interpretation Stein (*Heroic Knowledge*, pp. 224-5) has the following objections: 'To see this as Christ's "claim" [his statement 'Tempt not the Lord thy God']...is to abandon much of the force of the disciplined demonstration—as well as to abandon Milton's own passionate religious and moral belief, and his own disciplined unwillingness to pry into God's maintained mysteries. These are points Woodhouse must have thought of, but I do not see how he has taken them into account. And I do not see how or why, in his interpretation, "full knowledge" is achieved now. Is it the result of the assertion, the "claim"? I can hardly believe that Woodhouse means that. Is it the result of complying with Satan's suggestion? Is it the assertion of miracle (the motivation and timing clouded in mystery) which first demonstrates and then claims divinity, or vice versa? What becomes of all the careful demonstration of progress toward knowledge? Why should the method and discipline of the poem suddenly be abandoned, or reversed?'

But Stein's objections are in turn open to the following objections. What does he mean by 'to abandon much of the force of the disciplined demonstration'? Demonstration of what and to whom? If of Christ's divinity, it is not to *abandon* the demonstration, but to *announce its completion*, effective to Christ and upon Satan. What does he mean by 'to abandon Milton's own passionate religious and moral belief'? What belief? That Christ is 'By Merit more then Birthright Son of God'? But this is Christ's final act of trust and obedience—that is his merit—and so the demonstration of his sonship. If Stein objects to Woodhouse's phrase 'to participate in the Godhead', Christ does, in Milton's belief, participate in it by God's gift. And what does Milton's 'own disciplined unwillingness to pry into God's maintained mysteries' mean? Has Stein forgotten that in *DocCh* 1. 5 (*Works* 14. 209 ff.) Milton specifically excludes the trinity from these matters (e.g. the incarnation) declared in Scripture to be a mystery? For the rest, Woodhouse has explained 'why full knowledge is achieved now', and also that Christ does not 'comply with' (in the sense of finding his motive in) Satan's suggestion. What does Stein mean when he asks, 'Is it assertion of a miracle...or vice versa?' Christ performs no miracle; his divine power simply asserts itself, as Satan fully understands, if Stein does not, for he falls, headlong. 'What becomes of all the careful demonstration of progress toward knowledge?' Stein asks. The answer is that it reaches a conclusion, as Stein's own terms 'demonstration' and 'progress' both imply. Moreover how can a conclusion be said to 'abandon' or 'reverse' the process by which it is reached? It is difficult, then, to see that Stein has done anything more than rhetorically deny Woodhouse's interpretation of the third temptation.

554 *Progeny.* Lineage, parentage (*OED*), as in Shakespeare, *1 H. VI* 3. 3. 61.

556–9 These lines are a paraphrase of Ps. 91. 11–12.

560–1 Christ's answer, 'Thou shalt not tempt the Lord thy God' (Matt. 4. 7; Luke 4. 12), is quoted from Deut. 6. 16 where 'tempt', Lat. *tentare*, the word used in the Vulgate, means 'to put to the test'. To tempt God, then, is to commit the sin of presumption. 'He tempts God', says Aquinas (*Sum. Th.* 2. 2. 97. 1), 'who, though he has the means to do what he ought to do, nevertheless without reason exposes himself to danger to see whether God can deliver him.'[32] See also *Sum. Th.* 2. 2. 21; Andrewes, *Ninety-Six Sermons* 5. 521; Poole, *Annotations upon the Holy Bible*, Matt. 4. 6. The first temptation, to turn stones into bread, to distrust God's providence, is balanced by the third, to make needless, unreasonable trial of that providence. The extreme of defect is balanced by the extreme of excess.

561–2 'Fall' and 'stood' are made emphatic by position and by the marked pauses that follow them. The repetition of 'fell' and 'fall' seven times in lines 562–81 gives added emphasis. 'The parallel with Adam is emphatically clear, if only by verbal association' (Sackton, 'Architectonic Structure', *UTSE* 33, 1954, 43). Satan's fall after his final defeat may have been suggested by his fall from heaven, to which the angels refer in lines 604–6; or by the following lines in Beaumont, *Psyche* 9. 242. 1–2:

> Confounded *Satan* backward from this Throne
> Fell down the Mount, and tumbled into Hell

or by Fletcher, *C.V.* 2. 38. 2: Presumption 'tombled headlong to the flore'. In 'A Metaphoric Approach to Reading Milton' (*BSUF* 8, 1967, 17–18) John T. Shawcross observes that 'stand' should be read not only in a physical sense, but also metaphorically in the sense of remaining 'steadfast to resistance', faithfully obedient to God. Similarly when Satan 'with amazement fell', that is with bewilderment and dizziness, he fell literally, but also, through his stubborn adherence to evil, he fell even further condemned than when he fell from heaven.

At this point the poem reaches its climax. Christ's obedience has been 'fully tri'd / Through all temptation, and the Tempter foil'd / In all his wiles'. Satan has been ignominiously defeated, not by power but by humble faith, by Christ's patient submission to the will of God. See note on 581–653 below.

563–8 Among the accounts of Hercules' heroic exploits, that of his struggle with the truculent giant Antaeus, ruler of Libya, has been one of the most popular. According to Apollodorus (2. 5. 11) and Lucan (4. 593–660), to whom Milton is chiefly indebted, Antaeus, son of Poseidon and Earth (cf. Statius, *Th.* 6. 893–6), forced strangers who came to his land to wrestle with him, and always overcame and killed them, because at every fall he gained new strength

---

[32] Deum tentat qui, habens quid faciat, sine ratione, se committit periculo, experiens utrum possit liberari a Deo.

from Earth, his mother. Hercules on his way to the Garden of the Hesperides encountered him, and in a wrestling match lifted him up in his arms so that he could not touch the ground, and so was able to throttle him. See Ovid, *M.* 9. 183–4; Juvenal 3. 89; Diodorus Siculus 4. 17. 4; Hyginus, *Fab.* 31; Silius Italicus 3. 40–1; Dante, *Inf.* 31. 100, 139. In 'Christ of *PR*' (*SP* 35, 1938, 269) Hughes writes: 'It was the Neo-Platonic habit of treating Hercules as a supreme example of "heroic virtue" which led Milton to compare Christ's mysterious final triumph over Satan to one of Hercules' most familiar triumphs....[The simile, following immediately after Satan's fall, interprets] the scene for those who could read the allusion to the familiar, allegorical interpretation of the myth', which symbolizes the defeat of violence by truth.

Although, as Milton tells the story, 'there is no hint of allegory', Bush wonders (*Mythol.*, p. 270 n.) if Milton had read the exposition of the myth in Sandys' *Ovid's Metamorphoses* (Oxford, 1632, p. 322) wherein 'Hercules is the soul, or prudence; Antaeus the body, or sensual pleasure. Reason must raise the body above the contagion of earthly things'—an interpretation which (as Bush says), had he read it, Milton would not have fogotten.

It may also be significant that Antaeus is overcome when raised from the earth, the source of his strength, but Satan is overcome *in* the air, the realm which he has 'long usurpt'.

In 'The Iconography of Renunciation: the Miltonic Simile' (*Critical Essays on Milton from ELH*, Baltimore, 1969, pp. 75–6), Kingsley Widmer observes that it is disparity as much as similitude in the comparison with Antaeus which is important, as Milton's parenthetical comment, 'to compare / Small things with greatest', is meant to indicate. The principle of disparity in the simile must be applied to both Christ and Satan, if the 'full realization of Milton's dialectical poetry' is to be achieved. The comparison of Christ with Hercules is ironically disproportionate. By means of physical strength Hercules overcame Antaeus, but Christ by the very renunciation of such strength overcomes Satan. Milton, then, is again asserting that Christian renunciation is the greatest heroism; and since he compares 'small things with greatest', he means that Satan 'is far superior to a classical giant'. While the pagan image is appropriate, it is not sufficient 'for the dramatization of evil'.

563–4 *to compare | Small things with greatest.* Cf. Virgil, *E.* 1. 23: 'Thus I was wont to compare small things with great';[33] *PL* 2. 921–2: 'to compare / Great things with small.' See note on 2. 215 above.

[33] sic parvis componere magna solebam.

564 *Irassa.* Milton does not, like Pindar (*Pyth.* 9. 105–6), say that it was in the *city* Irassa that Hercules strove with Antaeus. 'The scholiast on Pindar says, however', as Osgood (*Mythology*, p. 8) explains, 'that the Antæus living in the city Irassa was not the one who strove with Heracles, but he adds that, among others, Pherecydes says that the latter Antæus came from Irassa (neut.) on Lake Tritonis in Cyrene. Herodotus mentions Irassa (neut. pl.) as a locality of Libya (4. 159). That Milton says "*in* Irassa" indicates reference rather to a region as the home of Antæus, for which he has the scholiast's authority.'

565 *Joves Alcides.* Hercules is often called Alcides by Latin poets, e.g. Virgil, *E.* 7. 61; *A.* 5. 414; Horace, *C.* 1. 12. 25; Propertius 1. 20. 49; Lucan 4. 611, from his grandfather Alcaeus, father of Amphitryon. But here as in *Sonn* 23. 3, following Homer, *Il.* 14. 324, Milton also calls him Jove's son.

568 *Throttl'd.* The cue to this, Osgood (*Mythology*, p. 8) notes, is ἀράμενος ἄμμασι in Apollodorus 2. 5. 11.

572–5 The '*Theban* Monster' was the sphinx sent by Hera to harass the people of Thebes by propounding to them the following riddle: 'What is it that has one voice, but becomes four-footed, and two-footed, and three-footed, and is weakest when it has most feet?' When the Thebans could not give the answer, the sphinx devoured them. However, when Oedipus answered correctly that it is man, the sphinx threw herself from the citadel, or, according to some, over a cliff, and was killed (Apollodorus 3. 5. 8; Diodorus Siculus 4. 64. 3–4; Athenaeus 10. 456b; Sophocles, *O.T.*, ed. Jebb, p. 6). The comparison of Christ and Satan with Oedipus and the sphinx is apt, for, as Hughes (p. 477) says, 'Christ, the divine Word, destroys the monster whose riddles threaten all human life.'

575 *Ismenian.* Near Thebes was the river Ismenus, whence the adjective *Ismenius*, which Latin poets used in the sense of 'Theban', e.g. Ovid, *M.* 13. 682; Statius, *Th.* 2. 307. The '*Ismenian* steep' may mean either the citadel or a cliff near the city.

576 *Fiend.* See note on 1. 465.

577–80 When Satan returned to hell to report his success in tempting Adam and Eve, he met equally 'joyless triumphals' (*PL* 10. 504–47).

578 *triumphals.* Tokens of success. This is the only example of the word used in this sense given by *OED*.

581–635 Christ has now passed through an heroic agony and emerged victorious, but, unlike the old epic heroes, he, the exemplary Christian hero, has overcome his adversaries, Satan and appetite, not by acting but by suffering; by right reason and faith he has extinguished appetite. He has rejected heroic action in the ordinary sense with all its rewards of fame, wealth, and power. He has rejected Satan's Lucullan banquet, has rejected worldly fame and glory; but he has sought 'first the kingdom of God, and his righteousness' (Matt. 6. 33), and 'Blessed is the man who endureth temptation: for when he is tried, he shall receive the crown of life' (James 1. 12). Christ has won his reward, a *heavenly* banquet and *heavenly* fame, the 'perfet witnes of all-judging *Jove*'. 'The whole poem, then, is concerned to establish the character of Christian heroic virtue as distinct from pagan, and to establish the heavenly nature of the rewards which supersede the earthly recompense of the old heroes' (Kermode, 'Milton's Hero', *RES* n.s. 4, 1953, 329).

581–95 Editors note the similarity between these lines and Apuleius, *Met.* 4. 35, the story of Psyche, who was borne by gentle zephyrs from a hill to a deep valley where she was laid on a bed of fragrant flowers.[34]

581–2 In Fletcher, *C.V.* 2. 38. 1–4, Presumption vainly tried to tempt Christ,

> But when she saw her speech prevailed nought,
> Her selfe she tombled headlong to the flore:
> But him the Angels on their feathers caught,
> And to an ayrie mountaine nimbly bore.

Milton seems also to be echoing *C.V.* 4. 13. 6–8:

> A globe of winged Angels, swift as thought,
> That, on their spotted feathers, lively caught
> The sparkling Earth, and to their azure fields it brought.

Cf. Matt. 4. 11: 'angels came and ministered unto him'; *PL* 2. 511–12: 'him round / A Globe of fierie Seraphim inclos'd'; Beaumont, *Psyche* 9. 245. 4–6:

> When loe triumphant Store
> Of Angells hovering down, with high-straind Lays
> Back to the sphears return'd the Victors praise.

581 *Globe*. A compact body of persons, Lat. *globus* (*OED*).

[34] Psychen autem paventem ac trepidam et in ipso scopuli vertice deflentem mitis aura molliter spirantis Zephyri, vibratis hinc inde laciniis et reflato sinu, sensim levatam suo tranquillo spiritu vehemens paulatim per devexa rupis excelsae, vallis subditae florentis caespitis gremio leniter delapsam reclinat.

583 *Vans.* Wings, as in *PL* 2. 927. The word, from Lat. *vannus*, is etymologically the same as 'fan'.

585 *blithe.* Soft, mild, much like 'bland' in *PL* 5. 5; 9. 1047.

587-95 Cf. Fletcher, *C.V.* 2. 61:

> But to their Lord, now musing in his thought,
> A heavenly volie of light Angels flew,
> And from his Father him a banquet brought,
> Through the fine element, for well they knew,
> After his lenten fast, he hungrie grew,
>   And, as he fed, the holy quires combine
>   To sing a hymne of the celestiall Trine;
> All thought to passe, and each was past all thought divine;

and Beaumont, *Psyche* 9. 247. 1-4:

> Their Gratulation ended; on their Knees
> A sumptuous Banquet They to Him present,
> Wherein was choise of all Varieties
> With which *Heav'ns King* could his dear *Son* content.

589-90 Cf. Fletcher, *C.V.* 2. 29. 6-7: 'But he upon ambrosia daily fed, / That grew in Eden.' 'Ambrosial' means of divine fragrance and flavour, as in *PL* 5. 427; 9. 852. Ἀμβροσία, which originally meant immortality, came to mean the elixir of life, which the gods used for food, as they used νέκταρ for drink (Homer, *Od.* 5. 93). Fragrance is a constant attribute of ambrosia, as in *PL* 2. 245. The adjective here probably combines the meanings 'heavenly' and 'fragrant'.

tree of life. Cf. Rev. 22. 2, 14: 'In the midst of the street of it, and on either side of the river, was there the tree of life, which bare twelve manner of fruits, and yielded her fruit every month: and the leaves of the tree were for the healing of the nations....Blessed are they that do his commandments, that they may have right to the tree of life.' See also Gen. 2. 9; 3. 22, 24, and cf. *PL* 4. 218-20. The significance of 'the tree of life' as Milton here treats it is best explained by J. M. Steadman in 'The "Tree of Life" Symbolism in *PR*', *RES* n.s. 11 (1960), 384-91. Although the tree had been interpreted as signifying a sacrament, Milton interprets it as a symbol of immortality, and hence the 'Celestial Food' which it bears can hardly be regarded as sacramental. The fruits of the tree, Steadman explains, signify: (1) a symbol of eternal life; (2) a reward specifically merited by obedience to God's commands; (3) a detail particularly characteristic of Paradise. In *PR* these fruits are the antithesis of the fruits of the forbidden tree; they are the reward of Christ's obedience which is everlasting life, as the 'fruit' of disobedience, 'the wages of sin', is death; and they are the sign of the divine approbation of his steadfast obedience. They are also an unequivocal sign of 'recover'd Paradise', and so they appropriately and logically conclude a poem whose theme is Paradise regained.

fount of life. Cf. Rev. 21. 6: 'I will give unto him that is athirst of the fountain of the water of life freely.' Cf. also *PL* 9. 69–73. 'Milton remembered the Well of Life from which Spenser's Knight of Holiness drank at the crisis of his conflict with the Satanic dragon (*F.Q.* I, xi, 29)' (Hughes, p. 528).

596–635 As in *PL* 6. 886–8 'all his Saints' in a triumphal song celebrated the Messiah's victory over Satan, so they now celebrate Christ's victory over Satan and temptation. The hymn leaves the reader with a sense of the completeness with which the proposition stated in the first lines of *PR* has been treated; he is convinced that by obedience man may possess 'a paradise within' him 'happier farr' than the earthly Paradise which by disobedience was lost. He is also convinced that Christ has made the decision without which he could never become the redeemer of mankind.

To some readers it has seemed that Milton concludes the poem too quickly, even abruptly. But Dick Taylor, in 'Grace as a Means of Poetry', *TSE* 4 (1954), 89–90, observes that 'the sign of God's grace comes to Christ within a phrase', and the miracle takes place before the sound of the phrase has died away. Christ's triumph is complete and needs no further treatment, either because of the needs of the episode itself, or because of the form of the brief epic. The almost breathless speed of the conclusion, in fact, heightens the decisive artistic and moral effect of Christ's victory.

596 Cf. Heb. 1. 3, 8: 'Who being the brightness of his glory, and the express image of his person...when he had by himself purged our sins, sat down on the right hand of the Majesty on high....But unto the Son he saith, Thy throne, O God, is for ever and ever'.

597 *the bosom of bliss*. Cf. John 1. 18: 'No man hath seen God at any time; the only begotten Son, which is in the bosom of the Father, he hath declared him.' Cf. *PL* 3. 238–40; 10. 225–6.

597–8 *light of light | Conceiving*. Unlike the Nicene Creed, Milton does not say that Christ *is* 'light from light' (φῶς ἐκ φωτός) but that he *conceives*, that is receives (Lat. *concipere*), takes into the mind (*OED*) light and truth from the source of light. Cf. 289 above. The distinction implied, Milton explains in *DocCh* 1. 5 (*Works* 14. 337–9), is that 'the nature of the Son is indeed divine, but distinct from and clearly inferior to the nature of the Father—for to be with God, πρὸς Θεὸν, and to be from God, παρὰ Θεῷ—to be God, and to be in the bosom of God the Father—to be God, and to be from God—to be the one invisible God, and to be the only-begotten and visible, are things so different that they cannot be predicated of one and the same essence.'

599 The idea of the incarnation is in Scripture most clearly stated in John 1. 14: 'And the Word was made flesh, and dwelt among us'. See also Rom. 8. 3; 1 John 4. 2–3. Cf. *Nat* 14; *Passion* 15–17. In *DocCh* 1. 14 (*Works* 15. 263–5) Milton writes: 'This incarnation of Christ, whereby he, being God, took upon him the human nature, and was made flesh, without thereby ceasing to be numerically the same as before, is generally considered by theologians as, next to the Trinity in Unity, the greatest mystery of our religion.... Since then this mystery is so great, we are admonished by that very consideration not to assert anything respecting it rashly or presumptuously...but to be contented with the clearest texts, however few in number.'

600 *whatever place*. In whatever place. In Shakespeare prepositions are often omitted after verbs of motion (Abbott, *Shakes. Gram.* 198).

601 *expressing*. Manifesting, revealing, as in 1. 233 above.

602–3 When God sent Messiah to conquer the Satanic host, his purpose, stated in *PL* 6. 676–8, was

> To honour his Anointed Son...
>   and to declare
> All power on him transferr'd.

Addressing him in lines 703–5 God said:

> Into thee such Vertue and Grace
> Immense I have transfus'd, that all may know
> In Heav'n and Hell thy Power above compare.

In *DocCh* 1. 5 (*Works* 14. 339), after quoting Col. 1. 19; 2. 9; Eph. 3. 19, Milton concludes: 'These passages most clearly evince that Christ has received his fulness from God, in the sense in which we shall receive our fulness from Christ.'

604 *Thief of Paradise.* Cf. *PL* 4. 192: 'So clomb this first grand Thief into Gods Fould'. Both passages probably are echoes of John 10. 1: 'He that entereth not by the door into the sheepfold...the same is a thief and a robber.'

604-6 See *PL* 6. 856-66 for the defeat of Satan and his host and their expulsion from heaven.

605 *debel.* Vanquish, expel by force of arms (*OED*), from Lat. *debellare*. The word does not occur in Spenser or Shakespeare, nor elsewhere in Milton's poetry. He may have remembered *debellare superbos* in Virgil, *A.* 6. 853.

607-9 In *Studies in the Gospels* (London, 1867, p. 4), Archbishop Trench writes: 'We cannot estimate too highly the importance of the victory which was then gained by the second Adam, or the bearing which it had, and still has, on the work of our redemption. Milton showed that he had a true feeling of this, when he wrote a poem which contained nothing more than a history of this victoriously surmounted temptation, and called it *Paradise Regained*'.

609 From the beginning of his infernal career, it was Satan's purpose to work by 'fraud or guile', as he declared in *PL* 1. 646-7; and in 10. 485 he boasted that by fraud he had seduced man; in *PR* 1. 51-2, less boastfully, he admitted that 'deceiv'd by me' Adam and Eve lost Paradise.

610-11 In *PL* 10. 391-401 Satan assures Sin and Death that they together have

> made one Realm
> Hell and this World, one Realm, one Continent
> Of easie thorough-fare.

and he bids them

> right down to Paradise descend;
> There dwell and Reign in bliss, thence on the Earth
> Dominion exercise and in the Aire,
> Chiefly on Man, sole Lord of all declar'd.

611 *his snares are broke.* Cf. Ps. 124. 7: 'Our soul is escaped as a bird out of the snare of the fowlers: the snare is broken, and we are escaped.'

612 Since man has sinned and been expelled from Paradise, as far as he is concerned, Paradise has 'fail'd', has ceased to exist. Milton is adverting to the idea expressed in *PL* 11. 829-34 that in the Deluge the mount of Paradise was carried down the Euphrates to the Persian Gulf and there became an island 'salt and bare', one of the widely varying theories concerning the fate of Paradise propounded by commentators. On the lines in *PL* see A. Fowler's note and consult D. C. Allen, *The Legend of Noah: Renaissance Rationalism in Art, Science, and Letters* (Urbana, Ill., 1949), pp. 153 f., 191.

613-15 In *PL* 12. 585-7 Michael told Adam that having learned to obey, which is the sum of wisdom,

> then wilt thou not be loath
> To leave this Paradise, but shalt possess
> A paradise within thee, happier farr.

616 *when time shall be.* At the appointed time, as in *PL* 3. 284; 10. 74.

618 Cf. Rev. 20. 2: 'And he laid hold on the dragon, that old serpent, which is the Devil, and Satan, and bound him a thousand years.' Cf. also 2. 147 above and *PL* 10. 1034-5.

619 *Rule in the Clouds.* See note on 1. 39 above.
  Autumnal Star. A meteor. In the Middle Ages and the Renaissance it was believed that comets and blazing stars were generated in the upper air of the sublunar vault, whence they were often seen falling to earth. In the chapter 'Of the fyre and the sterres that seme to falle', in his *Mirrour of the World* 30 (E.E.T.S., Extra Series, 100, p. 122), Caxton, as Svendsen (*Science*, p. 88) believes, 'anticipates in "sparkles of fyre" Milton's *Comus* simile "Swift as the Sparkle of a glancing Star" or the autumnal star of *Paradise Regained*, an inescapable simile for Satan.' Cf. *PL* 4. 556-7.

620-1 Cf. Luke 10. 18: 'I beheld Satan as lightning fall from heaven'; and Rom. 16. 20: 'And the God of peace shall bruise Satan under your feet shortly.' Cf. also *PL* 10. 190.

622 Christ's 'glorious work' of saving mankind will be Satan's 'last and deadliest wound'.

624 *Abaddon.* According to Rev. 9. 11 Abaddon is the angel of the bottomless pit, the Greek Ἀπολλύων; but in the O.T., as in Job 26. 6 and 28. 22, where the A.V. renders it as 'destruction', it means 'the *place* of destruction'; hence Milton uses it as a name of hell.

626 *all unarm'd.* There is a great contrast between Christ's present victory and the victory of Messiah in heaven where, with the panoply of war, he hurled

Satan and his host to hell. Editors note the likeness to Vida, *Christ.* 1. 199–200: 'Ever has he repulsed me, relying not upon arms, using no force.'[35]

628 *holds.* Dwellings, lurking-places. As Jerram (p. 172) observes, 'holds' here means 'not only the bodies of men "possessed with devils", but every place in earth and air, in which the demons hold sway.' Milton may have intended to imply not only this sense of the word but also 'temporary abode' (*OED*).

629–32 According to Luke 8. 27–33 Christ met in the country of the Gadarenes a man possessed of many devils, which, when he commanded them to leave the man, 'besought him that he would not command them to go out into the deep.' He then allowed them to enter a herd of swine, which plunged into the lake and were drowned.

633 *both worlds.* Heaven and this world. Cf. Matt. 6. 33: 'But seek ye first the kingdom of God, and his righteousness; and all these things shall be added unto you.' In *Rep.* 10. 613 Plato expresses a somewhat similar idea of the rewards bestowed by the gods upon just men.

634–5 In *Counterpoint and Symbol* (Copenhagen, 1956, p. 23), J. Whaler notes the similarity to the first three lines of Fortunatus's hymn, *In honorem Sanctae Crucis*: 'Declare, my tongue, the victory won in glorious conflict, sing a song of triumph about the trophy of the cross, how the redeemer of the world by sacrificing himself has conquered.'[36] Cf. *PL* 12. 310–14:

> *Jesus*...who shall quell
> The adversarie Serpent, and bring back
> Through the worlds wilderness long wanderd man
> Safe to eternal Paradise of rest.

Cf. also Virgil, *G.* 1. 42 where the poet bids Augustus 'to enter upon thy worship, and learn even now to give ear to my prayers.'[37]

In *DocCh* 1. 15 (*Works* 15. 285, 325) Milton explains that the mediatorial office of Christ 'is that whereby, at the special appointment of God the Father, he voluntarily performed, and continues to perform, on behalf of man, whatever is requisite for obtaining reconciliation with God, and eternal salvation....

[35] semper me reppulit ipse
non armis ullis fretus, non viribus usus.

[36] Pange, lingua, gloriosi proelium certaminis
et super crucis tropaeo, dic triumphum nobilem,
qualiter redemptor orbis immolatus vicerit.

[37] ingredere et votis iam nunc adsuesce vocari.

[God] calls all the world individually to repentance. But this gracious call could have been vouchsafed to none, had not Christ interfered to make such a satisfaction as should be not merely sufficient in itself, but effectual, so far as the divine will was concerned, for the salvation of all mankind'.

Christ's victory restores human reason to its true place in its first integrity, and blots out the disobedience of the first man and woman, and thus Paradise is regained; but as Paradise is not heaven, neither is moral perfection identical with salvation, the 'glorious work' which Christ has yet to accomplish (Blondel, pp. 72–3). It is glorious because it merits fame or glory in the sense in which Milton approves of fame. See 3. 47–8 above and note.

636–9 Messiah's triumphal progress through heaven after his victory over the Satanic host, as described in *PL* 6. 880–92, is appropriate for a divine Messiah, who is like a victorious king. Since Milton, however, is to the end maintaining the action of *PR* upon the human level, Christ's unostentatious return to his mother's house is appropriate for a *man* 'meek and lowly in heart' who has been victorious not by force of arms, but by the power of the spirit, and who by that power must yet save mankind. Moreover from the closing lines of *PL* and *SA* it is clear that Milton's artistic sense told him that a poem depicting a great and serious action, expressing and arousing powerful feeling, ought to end with 'calm of mind all passion spent.' The final calm, Blakeney (p. 182) points out, is in the manner of Sophocles and the Greek orators; 'the tumult subsides before the closing sentences, giving "the serenity of a completed harmony" (Jebb, *Attic Orators*, vol. 1. cii).'

These closing lines of *PR*, if they are to have their full value, must be read as a contrast to the closing lines of *PL*:

> The World was all before them, where to choose
> Thir place of rest, and Providence thir guide:
> They hand in hand with wandring steps and slow,
> Through *Eden* took thir solitarie way.

Adam and Eve in *Paradise* have met their trial, disobeyed, and lost their innocence and happiness. They have the promise of man's salvation, but that lies in the far distant future. Now utterly alone, condemned, and grief-stricken, they must leave their home and all that they have held dear. Christ, however, in the *desert*, has met his trial, obeyed, and triumphed. Now, with heavenly approbation and joy, he returns to his home and all that that connotes. As H. H. Petit observes ('The Second Eve in *PR*', *PMASAL* 44, 1959, 369): 'The whole mood of each poem is neatly caught in its last four lines; the mutual relationship of each Adam with each Eve is accented as is their setting apart from the rest of mankind. With the work of Redemption about to begin in full, Milton in these final lines parallels and contrasts the two Adams and their Eves and fulfills his opening promises to sing of the Greater Man who will restore us through firm obedience fully tried.'

636 *meek*. Cf. Matt. 11. 29: 'I am meek and lowly in heart'.

638–9 The basis of these lines doubtless is Luke 2. 51: 'And he went down with them, and came to Nazareth, and was subject unto them: but his mother kept all these sayings in her heart.' Cf. Fletcher, *C.V.* 2. 62. 7–8:

> But now our Lord to rest doth homewards flie:
> See how the Night comes stealing from the mountains high.

STUDIES OF STYLE AND VERSE FORM
IN *PARADISE REGAINED*

by

EDWARD R. WEISMILLER

I

Such fatal consequence unites *Paradise Regained* with *Paradise Lost* that prosodists have, all but invariably, treated the shorter epic simply as an adjunct of the longer one. And in a way this is not unreasonable, since the basic meter of the two poems is the same. There are general differences between them, however, in versification: in the rhythms sought; in the patterning of sound. Even here it is customary to find the versification of *PR* examined, rather briefly, as part of a broad examination of the poem's style—and characterized, once again, in terms of similarities to and contrasts with the versification of *PL*. But if the verse of *PR* deserves more attention in and for itself than it has thus far received, to fail to compare the verse of the two poems would of course make no sense at all.

Though Milton does not say so, the 'Measure' of *PR* is, like that of *PL*, '*English* Heroic Verse without Rime.' With no other poem in English, with the verse of no other poet, have prosodists concerned themselves so insistently as with *PL*; and still we cannot say that there is agreement about the precise nature of '*English* Heroic Verse.' What is in question is not merely Milton's practice. The laws that have governed the writing of English accentual-syllabic verse in general are not agreed on. However deliberately a poet may adopt a meter, he may not be fully conscious of the formal limits within which he is working; if he does understand, it may not occur to him to do more than illustrate his understanding by writing verse. His readers may then be aware only in part of the specifics of his practice. Let it not be forgotten that for centuries the verse of Chaucer was thought to be—however delightful—

rough; let the continuing uncertainty of the form of many lines in Wyatt remind us that we do not yet understand all the difficulties encountered by the poets who attempted to naturalize the meters of French and Italian syllabic verse in English. It is easy enough, we suppose, to recognize what instincts were at work in Tottel when he 'corrected' Wyatt. But the fullness of what lies behind the formal experimentation of a Wyatt—or a Milton—is scarcely suggested by conservative response to it.

It would not be appropriate to review here in detail the studies that have been made of the verse of Milton's long epic, however clearly we may recognize that prosodic analysis of *PL* is analysis of *PR* as well. What we must do is sketch in the verse history which prosodists have tried to understand, and indicate the problems they have raised.

Chaucer's earliest poems introduced into English, from the French, the octosyllabic couplet (see 'The Book of the Duchess') and the decasyllable, which Chaucer used in somewhat longer rhymed forms (see, e.g., the 'Complaints' and 'An ABC'). The 'Complaints' and the later and much longer *Troilus and Criseyde* were written in what we now know as 'rhyme royal'; George Puttenham was to call this form Chaucer's 'meetre Heroicall...keeping the staffe of seuen and the verse of ten.'[1] But the *Troilus*, a product of Chaucer's so-called middle period, was based in part on Boccaccio's *Il Filostrato*, and with it the influence of the Italian *endecasillabo* was brought to bear on Chaucer's English decasyllable. The exact meaning of 'influence,' its real effects, are not, of course, easy to assess. But Chaucer critics seem in general to feel that Italian materials and forms freed in Chaucer what was finally to be strongest and most English in him.

The French decasyllable and the *endecasillabo* must have differed, to

---

[1] George Puttenham, 'The Arte of English Poesie,' *Elizabethan Critical Essays*, ed. G. Gregory Smith, 2 vols. (London: Oxford University Press, 1904), **2**, 3–193, **64**. Hereafter, as here, full bibliographical information will be given in the first footnote mention of every work cited, even where the result is a partial duplication of material already supplied; the reader will thus be enabled conveniently to use the footnotes to amplify far briefer later references to the same work(s), which will be given in the text only.

Page numbers in bold figures in the footnotes indicate the precise pages of articles or books dealing with the point at issue.

Chaucer's ear, especially in the much sharper patterns of accent audible in the Italian line. Technically, however, the accentual requirement on both lines is, we are told, the same: in both an accent was required on the tenth syllable, and on either the fourth or the sixth syllable. Other accents might occur as the sense determined. The midverse accent was associated with a following 'caesural' pause which divided the line into two uneven, and often only lightly distinguished, half-lines. The metrically required accents on even-numbered syllables tended to dispose the *rhythm* of both lines toward what we call the iambic—in other words, toward rising rhythm—though the somewhat diffuse character of accent in French must have qualified this effect in the earlier line. Syllabic verse in the Romance vernaculars having developed out of medieval Latin verse, and having derived from it a convention in terms of which all syllables were read as being of equal duration, in neither French nor Italian verse did rising rhythm precipitate a division of the line into *metrical* sub-groups or feet.

In his reading of syllabic verse in the Romance vernaculars Chaucer may well have noted the devices employed, especially in Italian, to achieve the desired syllable count in the line: the use of certain words in full or shortened form; the blending together of contiguous vowels, whether within or between words, or the alternative separate enunciation of such vowels as or in separate syllables. That he imitated these devices consciously in writing his own verse we cannot say with certainty; comparison of the 'correct' use of the English of his time with its use in familiar speech, plus the operation of a subtle ear, might have yielded him naturally the alternative readings or forms he needed once he had determined to write in English a line of counted syllables in rising rhythm.[2] Certain it is, at all events, that he found ways of achieving

[2] See also W. J. Courthope, *A History of English Poetry*, 6 vols. (London: Macmillan, 1895–1910), 3, Chapter 14, 'The Versification, Vocabulary, and Syntax of Milton,' 422–51, 426–7. Courthope quotes (426) a number of lines from Chaucer in which 'a syllable has somehow to be got rid of in order to make the metre conform to the normal iambic movement of decasyllabic verse,' and says, 'The natural explanation seems to be that the Saxon habit of slurring syllables made it easy to modify the French practice to that extent.' Ultimately, however, Courthope believes in the principle of equivalence (see below, pp. 265-6) and thus in the occurrence of the trisyllabic foot in the line.

a strict syllable count in English as like the ways in use in French and Italian as the nature of the languages would seem to have permitted. Moreover, the devices he used—or such of them as were not ruled out specifically by changes in the language—seem to recur in the syllable-counting verse of the 16th and 17th centuries in England. Again this may be coincidental. It may, on the other hand, suggest the possibility that the technique of Chaucer's French-English line, as modified by the Italian, was better understood in the 17th century (at least by poets exploring the possibilities of the same meter) than we have supposed. Details of Chaucer's practice obscured by linguistic change were not clarified, of course, until linguistic scholarship had advanced sufficiently to illuminate them; some of them doubtless are still not clear. It may none the less be exactly true, as Robert Bridges has suggested, that Milton's rules for the writing of verse of counted syllables 'would appear to be only a learned systemization of Chaucer's practice.'[3]

Owing in part to the rapidity of change in the language (or so it is supposed), the meter of Chaucer's line was not fully comprehensible to his followers; within a century it was lost. Two traveled and cultivated admirers of Petrarch, however, Sir Thomas Wyatt and Henry Howard, Earl of Surrey, introduced the sonnet into English in the first half of the 16th century, and with it recovered for English a version of accentual-syllabic meter. Surrey also found in Italian *versi sciolti* (*endecasillabi sciolti*), and tried the effect of writing the English decasyllable without rhyme, translating into blank verse Books II and IV of Virgil's *Aeneid*. Wyatt and Surrey too had many followers. In the second half of the 16th century the English language, though not yet perfectly stabilized, was stable enough to permit more or less conscious study of the 'new' line, criticism of it, and experimentation with it; cultural advances made possible the retention of the gains made. Suddenly England had, not one or two great poets, but many—Spenser and Sidney, Marlowe and Shakespeare, Jonson and Donne. The English ten-syllable line was secure.

Secure—and yet (as I have suggested) not wholly understood. A

---

[3] Robert Bridges, *Milton's Prosody* (Oxford: Clarendon Press, 1921), 15.

meter cannot perhaps be transferred from one language to another substantially unlike it without suffering change: conventions that operated in the original language may not be recognized, or may be so ill suited to the character of the language adopting the meter that they cannot be carried over; the uncertainties—and the freedoms—that result may elicit from the adopting language new conventions, or choices of form generally accepted though they may not be necessary to the preservation of the meter. Beyond all this, there is a real question as to how exactly any meter has ever been capable of formulation, by its practitioners or by the most sensitive, intelligent and trained of readers. Anyone who has tried to make sense of the voluminous writings on English prosody will recognize the truth of this. Analysts of verse form in English—many of whom have themselves been poets of some distinction—have been (variously) responsive, acute, learned, and articulate. And still their writings contradict one another hopelessly.

What is there to misunderstand? The nature of meter itself; the degree of control exercised by a particular meter over particular physical elements of language. Meter is essentially a regulation, a structuring, of sound; ordinarily poetic meter works with the syllable as a unit, patterning accents or durations, counting syllables or groups of syllables, making designs of specific sounds and sound combinations. Certain of the sounds of speech are all but inflexible. They may be used or not; if used, they may enter into such patterns as alliteration; otherwise they are scarcely capable of regulation, can scarcely be the materials of artifice. Other sounds—all vowels, and many consonants—are subject to modulation, expressive or formal. Imposition of a fixed pattern on them will deny to them a range of possible expressive modulations, but will make use of them to help achieve the eloquence of meter itself, the expressiveness of a *particular* artifice.

No meter has ever proposed to regulate all of the physical elements of language upon which patterns of various kinds can be imposed, for no language could retain its identity, or—even—remain alive, thus rigorously constrained. Meters have, then, generally ordered a proportion of the sounds open to regulation, and left the rest free for expressive variation. The character of a given meter, and its usefulness, are clearly the result of a complex balance between what is controlled and what is left free, and the relationship of that balance to what might be called the genius of the language involved. Since the syllables of words are not pure abstract sound, the imposition of pattern upon some of the elements in language must result in a degree of conventionalization: thus the quantitative patterns of classical verse were based on the convention that the syllables of Greek and Latin in the pre-Christian era were either 'long' or 'short'—and that two shorts are equal in time to one long. This was not literally 'true'; the natural time patterning of the languages in question must, however, have been such that the convention did not seem a repellent distortion. Even in Greek and Latin, quantitative patterns could not be secured, and repeated, without major and continual disturbance of word order—which failed to destroy meaning, which could be metamorphosed into a stylistic value, only because classical Greek and Latin were fully inflected languages, so that syntactical elements which belonged together might be separated and yet recognized by the listener or the reader for what they were. The extraordinary *artificiality* of classical quantitative meters, the demands they made upon their audiences, must nonetheless be recognized.

Still, meter is of its nature artificial, and this too it is important to recognize. In a strong stress meter, stress is to a degree conventionalized; normal sentence accent is modified by the need to produce a pattern of stresses approximately equal. In syllabic meters, there must be a convention, an agreement, as to what constitutes (or is for metrical purposes to be regarded as) a syllable. What makes, e.g.,

> Di sangue un rio, d'uomini uccisi un monte
> (Tasso, *La Gerusalemme Liberata* 8. 19. 5)

and

> Han più opportuno loco. Io taccio adunque
> (Tasso, *Il Mondo Creato*, Quinto Giorno 244)

endecasillabi? When Milton rhymes 'Quire' with 'higher' in *Sonn* 13. 10–12, is the rhyme masculine or feminine? What is the condition of 'highest' in *PR* 4. 106,

Studies of Style and Verse Form

Aim at the highest, without the highest attain'd,

and in *PR* 4. 553,

> I to thy Fathers house
> Have brought thee, and highest plac't, highest is best...?

Acceptance of one or another convention is necessary if we are all to read these lines in the same way. We may not, in the 20th century, wish to write as Homer, or Virgil, or the *Beowulf* poet, or Tasso, or Milton wrote. But to criticize one more than the others for using language artificially in writing verse is simply to betray a misunderstanding of what meters are.

Now let us return briefly to the century before Milton wrote—the century that shaped the meter in which he was to write. That meter had scarcely taken firm hold in English verse when explication and criticism of it began. In 1575 the poet George Gascoigne published, with his *Posies*, 'Certayne Notes of Instruction Concerning the Making of Verse or Ryme in English.' One of Gascoigne's first specifically prosodic suggestions to the prospective poet is this: 'I say then, remember to holde the same measure wherwith you begin, whether it be in a verse of six syllables, eight, ten, twelue, etc....'[4] So the 'measure' is, in part at least, a measure of counted syllables. Later Gascoigne observes, 'Note you that commonly now a dayes in English rimes...we vse none other order but a foote of two sillables, wherof the first is depressed or made short, and the second is eleuate or made long; and that sound or scanning continueth throughout the verse' (Smith, 1, 50). In the two sentences quoted we may find the materials of almost all the problems that have vexed English prosodic criticism for the past four hundred years. Gascoigne's views themselves are an inextricable mixture of accurate observation and confusion.

The reader is likely to have found especially puzzling the phrases 'depressed *or* made short,' 'eleuate *or* made long' (my italics). Though Gascoigne may have been attempting to adapt to verse in English the

[4] George Gascoigne, 'Certayne Notes of Instruction,' *Elizabethan Critical Essays*, 1, 46–57, 49.

classical concepts of *thesis* and *arsis*, 'depressed' and 'eleuate' must in English refer to accent, of which one element is pitch: increase of stress is ordinarily, though not invariably, accompanied by increased loudness and the raising of pitch. But 'short' and 'long' are quantitative terms. In effect, then, Gascoigne seems to have confused accent with quantity. The two are indeed related; the stress element of accent is the *degree* of effort employed in the pronunciation of a syllable, while quantity is the *duration* of the effort. Increased stress (emphasis) is often accompanied by increased length or quantity; and strong stress and length are often found in the same syllable. But they need not be: thus 'ănăpēst' is quantitatively an anapest, but accentually a dactyl. Nonetheless we would not, in English, speak of an 'accentual dactyl' or the like—that is, call grouped *accents* by names used originally to refer to classical *quantitative* feet—if accent and quantity had not early been confused in English. Gascoigne does not refer to the ten-syllable line as an 'iambic pentameter,' but he seems to mean no less; and once the meaning had appeared and found acceptance, the terminology was not long wanting.

But confusion of accent with quantity is not alone remarkable in the sentences quoted above from Gascoigne. Note in the first place that the line is assumed to be made up of 'feet.' Where did the concept come from? It has already been pointed out that the continental originals of the verses Gascoigne is speaking of were not thought of as composed of feet; it has been noted as well that the syllables of the French and the Italian lines were reckoned, indeed, as of equal duration, not as falling into patterns of short and long. Neither was there a tradition of foot verse in English. The alliterative line of the AS and ME strong stress meters was divided by metrical caesura into hemistichs, and the intervals between stress peak and stress peak may have been (in performance) isochronous or equal-timed, but the line was not divided into feet. Only the quantitative lines of classical Latin and Greek verse had been, in fact, so divided. Were Gascoigne and those who followed him simply mistaken about the division into feet of the English line of counted syllables? or were they right? If they were right, is the foot in 16th- and

17th-century English verse a foot by virtue of a patterning of durations, of times, or by virtue of something else?

Note in the second place that Gascoigne leaves us no room to suppose that *trisyllabic* feet may appear together with feet of two syllables in the English line. When we turn to the *Posies*, then, and find such lines as the following in, e.g., 'Dulce Bellum Inexpertis,' only one explanation is available:

> Have given their gesse this subject to define (8. 2)
>
> These spirituall Pastors, nay these spitefull Popes (28. 1)
>
> A smouldring smoke which flieth with every winde (44. 2)
>
> From lofty towre discovering of his foes (49. 6)
>
> The poorest pesant and the homeliest hinde (66. 2)
>
> The debt which hangman claimde earst many a day (83. 7)

Examples could be multiplied, including the astonishing line 59 of Gascoigne's blank verse satire 'The Steel Glas':

> My sistr' and I, into this world were sent.

Compare line 60:

> My Systers name, was pleasant *Poesys*.

It makes little difference whether we reckon 'sistr'' as monosyllabic in line 59, 'Systers' as dissyllabic in line 60, or whether we take 'sistr' and' to be a dissyllabic word group, as is 'many a' in *DBI* 83. 7 above (and in Chaucer's *Troilus and Criseyde*, lines 163, 165, 166, etc.). In each of the lines quoted, and in hundreds more that could be quoted—as hundreds upon hundreds far more daring could be quoted from Chaucer, who was identified by Puttenham, it will be recalled, as writing 'the verse of ten' in *Troilus and Criseyde*—there must be more than ten syllables, and thus an admixture of trisyllabic feet, unless the count of syllables is reduced to ten by speech contraction or some form of metrical compression. Precisely such reduction is taken for granted, obviously, by Gascoigne and Puttenham; in other words, they accept an elaborate but implicit convention as the basis of a meter of counted syllables.

Note in the third place that Gascoigne describes only one kind of accentual foot: what was later to be called the iamb (×′). Inversion of accent is not common in his verse, but it does occur:

> Pléntĭe brings pryde, pryde plea, plea pine, pine peace (*DBI* 9. 6)

> But that the Greene Kníght wăs amongst the rest (*DBI* 131. 6)

Indeed, some prosodists would scan the first of these lines as containing not a single iamb. Gascoigne's verse is on the whole very regular, but apparent failure of accent, and doubling of accent, occur in it as in most comparable English verse:

> Áske *Júlĭus Caesăr* ĭf thĭs tále be true (*DBI* 46. 1)

> Ŏh *Épĭtăph* of honŏr ănd high háppe (*DBI* 51. 2)

Could Gascoigne have believed the line to be composed of five *theoretical* iambs, as a base against which a somewhat wider range of *actual* stress patterns may be heard? The position is one which many later prosodists were to take. Gascoigne, however, gives 'by' an accent in the line

> I vnderstand your meaning by your eye

(Smith, 1, 51), and he cautions the writer of verse not to wrench accent by writing, e.g.,

> Your meaning I vndĕrstănd by your eye,

so we must suspect him of having been, quite literally, a stress regularist. Would he then, by enforcing a 'metrical' accent on the even-numbered syllables, have made five iambs of *DBI* 46. 1 and 51. 2? And what of 'Plentie' in *DBI* 9. 6?

Toward the end of 'Certayne Notes of Instruction' Gascoigne remarks that 'There are also certayne pauses or restes in a verse, whiche may be called *Ceasures*...and they haue bene first deuised (as should seeme) by the Musicians...' (Smith, 1, 54). He gives it as his opinion that 'in a verse of tenne' syllables, the pause 'will best be placed at the ende of the first foure...' A pause or rest 'deuised...by the Musicians' would not seem to be a grammatical pause; and the reader may have noticed that in the lines quoted above from 'The Steel Glas,' a comma that has nothing to do with syntax appears after the fourth syllable. Apparently Gascoigne felt the metrical caesura to be particularly necessary to secure the metrical form of nondramatic blank verse; the comma unrelated to sense appears after the fourth syllable of most of the 1,179 lines of 'The Steel Glas.' But it does not appear in Gascoigne's rhymed verse (though in many lines of that verse there is a *sense* pause after the fourth syllable); and it does not appear in those portions of the blank verse drama *Jocasta* which Gascoigne wrote. Puttenham's chapter 'Of Cesure' (Smith, 2, 77–80) is not perfectly clear, but it is in part a discussion of punctuation—of the comma, colon and period as indicating degrees of sense pause—and no way of establishing (or recognizing) the caesura except through normal use of punctuation is spoken of or implied. What did English poets of the 16th century understand the nature of the caesura in Romance vernacular verse to be? What did they intend in their own verse? Does Milton's 1668 phrase 'the sense variously drawn out from one Verse into another' say or imply enough of what we need in general to know about midverse and end-of-line pause in *PL* and *PR*, or must we, as some critics tell us, assume the presence in Milton's verse of metrical pauses independent of sense, within lines and (particularly) at the ends of lines, reference to them buried perhaps in the antecedent phrase 'apt Numbers'?

The articulation of these questions concludes our identification of the major prosodic problems posed by the English heroic line. We may turn now to a rapid survey of the positions taken by prosodists vis-à-vis those problems, from the beginnings to the present day. In making the survey we cannot confine ourselves altogether to an assessment of the prosodic criticism of Milton's epic verse; but we shall consider nothing which does not have a possible or certain bearing on the structure of that verse.

That time is somehow a part of the 'Measure' of English accentual-syllabic verse is by no means universally accepted (though obviously the relative heaviness or lightness of syllables is part of verse rhythm); prosodists who believe that nothing can be 'measured' in verse *but* time by no means all agree on the way in which they suppose time to be patterned in '*English* Heroic Verse.' The confusion, or strict association, of quantity with accent produces a concept of the line in which a fixed number and arrangement of syllables results in fixed movement as well as in fixed measure (the occurrence, that is, in lines of equal duration, of an invariant number of feet—paired syllables—of equal duration). The concept, as we shall see, did not die with Gascoigne. In 1602, however, the poet and musician Thomas Campion, in an essay entitled 'Obseruations in the Art of English Poesie,' introduced in dim outline an alternative concept of the relationship of time to the English line. It seemed to him 'that the Latine verses of sixe feete, as the *Heroick* and *Iambick*, or of fiue feete, as the *Trochaick*, are in nature all of the same length of sound with our English verses of fiue feet; for either of them being tim'd with the hand...they fill vp the quantity (as it were) of fiue sem'briefs...'[5] After exemplification, he continues, 'The cause why these verses differing in feete yeeld the same length of sound, is by reason of some rests which either the necessity of the numbers or the heauiness of the sillables do beget. For we find in musick that oftentimes the straines of a song cannot be reduct to true number without some rests prefixt in the beginning and middle, as also at the close if need requires. Besides, our English monasillables enforce many breathings which no doubt greatly lengthen a verse...' (Smith, 2, 334–5). In all this there is perhaps the suggestion of the temporal equality of total line with total line, not of foot with foot—not even, necessarily, the equality of English foot with English foot. The most interesting part of Campion's discussion, however, is the analogy with music.

Whatever Campion intended, the analogy suggests to most prosodists who accept it as defining accurately the relationship of time to the English line a sequence of *abstract* durations, lengths of time waiting to be filled by syllables and/or pause, as, in (e.g.) 3/4 or 4/4 time, the musical bar may be said to have an abstract existence, waiting to be filled by sound and/or silence. And as in musical notation the bar line

[5] Thomas Campion, 'Obseruations in the Art of English Poesie,' *Elizabethan Critical Essays*, 2, 327–55, 334.

immediately precedes the metrically accented note of the measure, so in scansions based on the analogy of verse with music the bar line immediately precedes the syllable felt as carrying metrical accent (often associated with length). The 'measure' is then the interval between one stress peak and the next;[6] and the intervals are isochronous or equal-timed.

Each measure which begins with a stressed (and usually long) syllable is completed by a briefer syllable—or syllables. For many prosodists who believe in the analogy of verse with music are—logically enough in their own terms—suspicious of the whole notion of metrical compression. Just as in music two eighth notes are the equivalent of a quarter note, so 'contractions' and other compressions are, they feel, best explained and represented as separate syllables briefly pronounced. Historically-minded prosodists who ultimately accept the structural comparability of verse and music may also accept the existence in 16th- and 17th-century verse of *speech* contractions and even of some more complex compressions if the existence of these is clearly attested in the spelling of early texts; but where compression cannot be, or is not ordinarily, indicated by spelling—see, e.g., the difficult *PR* 3. 375,

> Whose off-spring in his Territor|y yet serve,

or even the relatively commonplace dissyllabic 'many a' ([ˈmɛn-jə])—they find extra syllables in the line, and no theoretical difficulty in accommodating them or accounting for them. Many 19th- and early 20th-century prosodists who did not, so far as one can tell, adopt fully and rigorously a theory of the English line as consisting of equal-timed intervals (whether explained in terms of syllabic quantity or of music) nonetheless found it convenient to adopt the notion of 'equivalence'—that is, the notion that two particularly short, unstressed syllables might at times substitute in the unstressed places of the English line (or in the 'thesis' of the foot) for one longer or weightier syllable.[7] On the

---

[6] Note the similarity of this to the description of strong stress meter given above, p. 260. The meters would differ presumably in the *length* of the 'measure,' however.

[7] The most vigorous proponent of the idea is perhaps George Saintsbury, in his three-volume

whole, the belief that 16th- and 17th-century heroic verse may contain trisyllabic feet interspersed among feet predominantly dissyllabic rests, or has come to rest, on the notion of 'equivalence,' often rather vagrantly held.[8]

Over the centuries, a number of prosodists of great interest have analyzed English accentual-syllabic verse—usually in studies of Milton's verse—as composed of equal-timed measures.[9] These measures have

History of English Prosody (London: Macmillan, 1908–10). Milton's 'whole work,' Saintsbury says, 'from the *Nativity Ode* to *Samson* itself, from the *Arcades* choruses to the stately tirades' of *PR*, 'proclaims...the three great laws of English prosody: Foot-arrangement, Substitution, and Equivalence' (2, 267).

[8] The belief appears to have had its inception principally in a change of taste. In the last half of the 18th century readers and critics began to dislike the sound of the metrical compressions, ceased to wish to perform them, and found reasons to suppose (against the evidence) that they had never really been required. But evidence there was, and such scholars as Edwin Guest (*A History of English Rhythms*, 2 vols., London, 1838) might have been able to persuade others of its commanding importance if the problem had not been complicated almost at once by another circumstance. The Romantic poets *did* mix trisyllabic with dissyllabic feet—trisyllabic feet that could not be reduced by metrical compression. At the same time, the Romantics, who were steeped in 16th- and 17th-century English verse, made extensive use of its locutions and rhythms. But do (e.g.) 'the intent,' 'to adore,' 'many a,' remain two-syllable phrases in verse which admits genuine trisyllabic feet? If not, one may see easily enough that the traditional metrical compressions, relaxed, produce trisyllabic feet of a lightness that makes them fit in among dissyllabic feet especially smoothly, so that they might well be sought just on that account by poets writing the newly modified line. And how should a later critic, accustomed to reading

We have giv|en our hearts | away, | a sor|did boon
(Wordsworth, 'The World Is Too Much With Us,' 4),

fail to have it suggested to him at last that Milton did not mean 'given' to be read as a monosyllable in *PR* 4. 185,

If given, by whom but by the King of Kings,—

or even in the next line following,

God over all supreme? if giv'n to thee...?

Full and systematic belief that prosodically the heroic line is made up, not of counted syllables, but of measured durations of time, could only support such a suggestion.

[9] Coleridge, for example, having defined his terms as follows: 'Semi-breve; Breve; Plusquam breve; Long; Plusquam long,' says, 'In the Iambic Pentameter of the *Paradise Lost*, I assume fifteen breves as the total quantity of each line—this isochrony being the identity or element of sameness, the varying quality of the isochronous feet constituting the difference...' (*Coleridge on the Seventeenth Century*, ed. Roberta Florence Brinkley, Durham, North Carolina: Duke University Press, 1955, 580). To his discussion of this view, however

266

in some theories been very different from the 'feet' of 'iambic pentameter' quantitatively understood—or translated into the simplest musical terms. The reader may wish to investigate the work of Joshua Steele[10] or that of Coventry Patmore,[11] in which the line itself is not a metrically independent entity, but, as in music, part of an ongoing movement, a larger total structure. Of particular note in both studies is the conclusion that there are measured or measurable pauses or silences in or between most or all English verses. A relatively more orthodox analysis, in which the line remains a line of five feet (or the equivalent) is to be found in the prosodic criticism of T. S. Omond.[12] 'Temporal periods, usually occupied by syllables, and habitually denoted by stress, must be regarded as the true basis of our verse,' Omond says (31). Of more recent prosodists, S. Ernest Sprott, in what is perhaps the most detailed study of Milton's verse form thus far published,[13] subscribes to 'the correctness of the "temporal-spacing" theory of rhythm' (52); his Chapter V, 'The Iambic Pentameter and Its Scansion' (38–53), explains his views, and sets them in the broad context of English prosodic study. As the chapter title suggests, the verse units which Sprott believes to be isochronous or equal-timed are, like Coleridge's, like Omond's, the 'feet' conventionally accepted as making up the line. They are also *dissyllabic* feet, since Sprott's work is based essentially on Bridges'. To Bridges himself, however, 'quantity, though a main factor of rhythm, is not considered in the prosody of syllabic verse' (1)—that is, time in Milton's line is not in Bridges' view regularly patterned, is not subject to verse *law*.[14]

Coleridge adds a postscript: 'Milton must be scanned by the *Pedes Compositae*[*sic*], as the Choriambus, Ionics, Paeons, Epitrites, etc., taking the five meters ∪| ∪∪ | ∪∪∪ | – | ∪– as the ground' (*loc. cit.*).

[10] Joshua Steele, *Prosodia Rationalis* (London, 1779).

[11] Coventry Patmore, 'Essay on English Metrical Law,' printed as an Appendix to Patmore's *Poems*, 3rd collective ed., 2 vols. (London, 1887), 2, 217–67; first printed in 1858, in vol. 27 of the *North British Review*.

[12] T. S. Omond, *A Study of Metre* (London: A. Moring, 1920).

[13] S. Ernest Sprott, *Milton's Art of Prosody* (Oxford: Blackwell, 1953).

[14] In 1918 Ada L. F. Snell published in *PMLA* 33, 396–408, a fascinating 'Objective Study of Syllabic Quantity in English Verse.' Miss Snell had recorded on as accurate a measuring instrument as could be devised for her use three readers' performances of *PL* 2. 604–28;

But if time in the line is variable, is an element of changing rhythm rather than of fixed meter, on what basis is the line to be thought of as divided into feet? Bridges' opening generalization would seem to suggest that he did not intend so to divide it: 'English blank verse may conveniently be regarded as a decasyllabic line on a disyllabic basis and in rising rhythm (i.e. with accents or stresses on the alternate even syllables)'—but he then continues, 'and the disyllabic units may be called *feet*.' '*May* be called'? The phrase reminds us, almost, of Puttenham: 'Quantitie...consisteth...with vs in the number of sillables, which are comprehended in euery verse, not regarding his feete, otherwise then that we allow, in scanning our verse, two sillables to make one short portion (suppose it a foote) in euery verse' (Smith, 2, 70). Puttenham goes on to say that it is in fact improper to speak of feet in the English line. And Bridges would seem to make use of the concept of the foot as a convenience only, a device that enables him to discuss rhythmic detail. He does *not* use the conventional terms 'pyrrhic,' 'trochee,' etc.; he speaks instead of 'weak feet' (38), 'inversions of accent' (40).

F. T. Prince, who has probably done more to illuminate the form of Milton's verse than any other writer since Bridges, takes his illustrious predecessor to task for saying even so much. 'In regarding the decasyllabic line as "on a disyllabic basis and in rising rhythm" and calling "the disyllabic units" feet,' Bridges has, says Prince, conceded 'to the traditional view that English prosody must be interpreted in terms of Classical prosody...It is precisely these conceptions which have weighed most heavily on all theories of English prosody.'[15] Prince goes on to remind us of the 'affinity between the structure of the Italian hendecasyllable, as it appears in Dante, and Milton's "English Heroic

analysis of the readings syllable by syllable, foot by foot, revealed that 'in nearly every line there are usually three and often four feet of which it may be said that the stressed syllable is not only long, but approximately twice as long as the unstressed' (405). The feet themselves, however, 'can scarcely be said to be even approximately equal in length, since one is frequently twice as long as another and may be three and four times as long' (408). Averaging all her figures, for all readers, Miss Snell found (407) the average length of the first foot to be 0·64 seconds, the second, 0·6, the third, 0·6, the fourth, 0·63, and the fifth, 0·73. In terms of actual, unaveraged figures, however, the totals varied a great deal, *PL* 2. 621, for example, having for all readers two to three times the length of, e.g., 2. 611.

[15] F. T. Prince, *The Italian Element in Milton's Verse* (Oxford: Clarendon Press, 1954), 137.

Verse"' (137–8). His conclusion is that the laws of that verse 'are simply an equivalent of the principles underlying the Italian hendecasyllable, and may be summarized as:

I. The line has a theoretic ten syllables (not eleven, as in Italian).
II. The tenth syllable must always have, or be capable of being given, a stress; one other stress must fall, in any one line, on either the fourth or the sixth syllable.'

Prince continues,

The elisions possible in English to increase the number of real, as opposed to theoretic, syllables, Milton found to be fewer than in Italian; and, as a consequence of this (for in Italian it is the incidence of elision which most violently shifts the stresses), the variety of his rhythms is not so great in practice as their theoretic liberty. To place against the relatively more limited capacities of English for this kind of verse, Milton has one enormous advantage: the more consonantal and monosyllabic substance of his language makes the texture of his verse more varied than that of Italian, whether in the direction of simplicity or that of rich compression (143).

As valuable as Prince's study must be acknowledged to be, its prosodic conclusions here have been disputed (justly, in my opinion) by M. Whiteley, in a good brief article which argues that our experience of English verse is after all, and necessarily, an experience of verse with feet.[16] Mrs Whiteley quotes (271) a wayward scansion of the last line of Donne's 'A Nocturnall upon S. Lucies Day' published by H. J. C. Grierson. I give the line with those just preceding:

> Since she enjoys her long night's festival,
> Let me prepare towards her, and let me call
> This hour her Vigil and her Eve, since this
> Both the years | and the days | deep mid|night is.

The concluding line, which Grierson divides and marks as shown,[17]

[16] M. Whiteley, 'Verse and Its Feet,' *RES*, n.s. 9 (1958), 268–78.
[17] The scansion, with the lines preceding, is as given in the Introduction to H. J. C. Grierson, ed., *Metaphysical Lyrics and Poems of the Seventeenth Century* (Oxford: Clarendon Press, 1921), xxiv.

is, like the three lines that lead up to it, of ten syllables; those lines preceding, if they were to be divided into feet at all, would clearly be divided each one into five dissyllabic feet. Mrs Whiteley very properly points out the difficulty of regarding the ten-syllable line 'as having a variable number of "measures"' (271). For Prince, 'the metrical unit is...the line itself—with all its possible variations' (144, n. 1); he could not, in his theory, distinguish metrically between the last line of the 'Nocturnall' and the lines that lead up to it. Mrs Whiteley notes (274) that the first line of 'Twicknam Garden,'

> Blasted with sighs and surrounded with tears,

like the last line of the 'Nocturnall,' might seem to be—but is not—a four-foot line; and she says that in *PL* 6. 866,

> Burnt after them to the bottomless pit,

the fifth and sixth syllables 'need to be slightly dwelt on'—not stressed— to preserve the meter, as the first line of 'Twicknam Garden' must 'be read with a slight dwelling on (not stressing) the syllables *and sur-*' (274). My own writings on Milton's prosody have made, independently, somewhat the same points.[18]

PL 6. 866 and lines like it—compare, e.g., *PR* 1. 361,

> With them from bliss to the bottomless deep,

and with the last line of Donne's 'Nocturnall' compare, e.g., *PR* 4. 597,

> In the bosom of bliss, and light of light—

have drawn uneasy comment from prosodists for the last two hundred years. Generally it has not been noted, however, that lines exactly comparable accentually (lines, that is, in which syllables one to six or five to ten are accented ××′××′) are very common in Italian verse, and cause no difficulty there, presumably because of the convention in terms of which all syllables in Italian verse are read as equal-timed. With the lapsing of that convention in the transference of syllabic meter from the Romance

---

[18] See, e.g., 'The "Dry" and "Rugged" Verse,' in *The Lyric and Dramatic Milton*, ed. Joseph H. Summers (New York: Columbia University Press, 1965), 115-52, 118-19.

vernaculars into English, a situation arose in which—unless a strong pause precedes the first accent in the ××ʹ××ʹ sequence, thus isolating and identifying in the third and fourth syllables the familiar character of the midverse accentual trochee—the six syllables involved appear to break into two accentual anapests, and the ten-syllable line becomes a line of four improperly assorted, inexplicably varying measures, not five like measures. Ordinarily the reader does not and need not read two syllables by two syllables, of course; in the reading of most English decasyllables he need not bring to explicit consciousness the organization of the syllables into five duple measures. That such an organization is basic to the line, however, becomes clear when that organization is threatened.

The fact that classical measures or feet are quantitative—are timed, and in most verse equal-timed—does not in turn mean that English duple measures are of necessity equal-timed; there is no reason why a measure should not be based on a simple count of syllables, or of groups of syllables, rather than on a count of 'times.' Nor, in concluding that the duple measure is an element of the basic meter of '*English* Heroic Verse,' need we assume 'that Milton held in the front of his mind, as he composed, the typus of a tiny unit to be fitted against a preceding and succeeding tiny unit.'[19] The flow of thought and the structure of verse are of course different. But the dissyllabic 'short portion (suppose it a foote)' (Puttenham; Smith, 2, 70) may have as real an existence in the English line as the enjambed line itself has in a larger structure, though thought flow through both in such a way as to make us at times forget, at other times be more or less conscious of, the structures that define and at last contain the flow.

Prince was shown Mrs Whiteley's criticism of his position before it was published, and was disposed by her arguments, not to change his formulation (quoted above, p. 269) of the laws followed by Milton's blank verse line, but to add to that formulation, 'Every line is to be

[19] Robert Beum, 'So Much Gravity and Ease,' *Language and Style in Milton* (New York: Ungar, 1967), 333–68, 335–6. Beum is arguing that 'the concept of the foot was employed without literalism' by 'the early analysts,' as 'a working convenience' only (335).

measured against a notional basic line of ten syllables alternately un-stressed and stressed.'[20] The statement corresponds closely to what Bridges says—except that Prince deliberately does not add, 'and the disyllabic units may be called *feet*.' He insists instead that the 'under-lying rhythmic *structure* of Milton's verse...is better indicated by Bembo's requirement' ('that the accents should be in the fourth or the sixth and in the tenth syllable,' *Italian Element*, 141). 'This implies that the whole line results from the combination (in balance, unbalance, or fusion) of two unequal or asymmetrical "halves". These varying com-binations give the English ten-syllable verse its vitality' (Prince, *RES* 9, 279).

Rhythmic 'structure' and metrical structure are not, however, identical; centrally important though it is, meter is only one element of rhythm. Prince's language is the kind of language one uses to discuss versification, not strict prosody—not basic metrical law. If *metrically* the Italian hendecasyllable is divided into, or composed of, 'two unequal or asymmetrical "halves",' Prince has adduced no evidence to show that the same is true of the English decasyllable. The 'rhythmic structure' of the second 'half' of, e.g., *PL* 6. 866 and *PR* 1. 361 would destroy the meter if we did not prevent it from doing so; we accomplish this by thinking of the six syllables as constituting three groups instead of two (not permitting the syntax to confuse us), and by reading in such a way as to make sufficiently audible *as* three the three duple measures our metrical sense tells us are required. If Prince's '*measured against* a notional basic line' (or '*based on* a notional pattern'; my italics) means this, well and good; but it is difficult not to conclude that greater clarity of phrasing would be possible, and is desirable—not to say indispensable. Even as modified, Prince's 'simpler explanation' (*Italian Element*, 143) does *not* 'cover the facts.' It requires—and urgently, because of the

---

[20] Prince's reply to Mrs Whiteley follows her article, *RES*, n.s. 9 (1958), 278–9, 279. Publica-tion of a second impression of *Italian Element* (1962) did not, apparently, enable Prince to revise the text of his Chapter 8 ('Milton's Blank Verse: the Prosody'); instead he added a brief prefatory note to the volume, stating, 'I now think that Milton's blank verse line is based upon a notional pattern of ten syllables alternately stressed and unstressed, in rising rhythm.'

extraordinary overall value of Prince's work—a more thorough revision than his response to Mrs Whiteley would suggest. Doubtless he is reluctant to encourage a return to 'foot-thinking' (the phrase is Beum's, 342) if such thinking must entail a confusion between the English foot and the classical quantitative foot. But if we phrase our analyses with sufficient care, surely it need not do so.

Mrs Whiteley has additional reservations about Prince's phrasing of the 'laws' which 'will be found to cover all the phenomena of Milton's blank verse' (*Italian Element*, 143); again her objections coincide with objections of mine. Prince tells us that 'Milton very seldom ends a line with such words as "modesty", "amity", "misery"' (135). 'Very seldom'? 'Such words as'? Ants Oras tells us that 120 lines in *PR* alone have what he calls, and I should call, pyrrhic verse endings;[21] that is one line in a little over seventeen. They are less common in *PL*; Mrs Whiteley too, however, feels that lines of the sort Prince mentions are 'familiar enough' (274). And what, she asks, does Prince mean when he says that the tenth syllable of the blank verse line 'must always have, *or be capable of being given*, a stress' (my italics)? In, e.g., *PR* 3. 241,

> Timorous and loath, with novice modesty,

Mrs Whiteley would say that the -*y* carries more stress, if only a little more, than the preceding syllable, and that fact is enough in actuality; but is this what Prince means? (274–5). It would not seem to be.

Perhaps in line 8 of Donne's 'Elegie XVI,'

> By all pains which want and divorcement hath,

we might think of 'hath' as being 'capable of being given' stress. The line is on the other hand one of several Mrs Whiteley quotes (277) to show that there are after all perfectly good English lines—unusual, perhaps, but not unmetrical—which do not follow the 'law' that says there must be a stress on either the fourth or the sixth syllable:

> By all | páins whîch | wánt and | divorce|ment hath.

[21] Ants Oras, 'Milton's Blank Verse and the Chronology of His Major Poems,' *SAMLA Studies in Milton*, ed. J. Max Patrick (Gainesville: University of Florida Press, 1953), 128–97, 181.

I should instance as a line which meets *none* of the conditions Prince lays down for stress, *PR* 1. 156:

To ex|er$\overset{\times}{\text{cise}}$ | him $\overset{\times}{\text{in}}$ | the Wil|der$\overset{\times}{\text{ness}}$.

Here again, syllables four, six and ten carry *slightly* more stress, doubtless, than syllables three, five and nine. But the stress they carry is 'rather less than secondary at the most' (Whiteley, 274). And the line is an unusual one. Nothing in it comes close, all the same, to threatening the meter, as does the accentual situation in, e.g., *PR* 1. 361, a line which meets Prince's conditions fully. 'A theory,' as Mrs Whiteley says, 'should fit the facts' (278).

The conception of 'a notional basic line of ten syllables alternately unstressed and stressed' requires further consideration—returns us, indeed, to a problem first posed by 'Certayne Notes of Instruction.' Let us say flatly for the moment that the English heroic line is, unlike its French and Italian analogues, a pentameter—as Gascoigne thought it to be, and as it would seem necessary to conclude on the basis of our examination of Prince's beliefs. Let us assume for the moment also that the metrical subgroups of which the line is made up are dissyllabic (though to this problem too we shall have to return, if only briefly). Is the English pentameter 'iambic' *notionally*, or *actually* 'iambic,' or is it simply composed of varying combinations of the four dissyllabic 'feet,' $\times'$, $'\times$, $\times\times$ and $''$, so ordered as to produce in general the effect of rising rhythm?

The idea that accentual variety, though limited by the necessity of preserving duple rhythms, is natural to English and is itself basic to the English line has recommended itself to a number of prosodists; such prosodists do not, accordingly, speak or think of $'\times$, $\times\times$ and $''$ as *substitutions* for $\times'$. Their attempt is to describe practice, not theory. If they find 'iambic pentameter' an acceptable name for the line (as some though not all of them do), it is only because, in English accentual-syllabic verse, iambs naturally predominate.

The contrasting idea that the English line, though it is *in actuality* made up as just described, is *notionally* iambic supposes the existence of an abstract $\times\prime \mid \times\prime \mid \times\prime \mid \times\prime \mid \times\prime$, a 'norm' or 'base'[22] in a kind of continuing counterpoint[23] to which we hear each actual successive line. The idea is widely held, and seems harmless; something of the kind must even be true, since inversion of accent, for example, would scarcely attract our attention if when we heard it we were not as sharply aware of what $\prime\times$ is not as of what it is. Note, however, that *being aware* of difference implies no correction of what we hear; most rhythmic differences we welcome, indeed, and correction is not desired, far less required.

That an abstract $\times\prime \mid \times\prime \mid \times\prime \mid \times\prime \mid \times\prime$ is an *actual* part of every line we hear is itself, finally, a position numbers of prosodists have taken; a 'metrical' accent thus *enters* the line, reinforces $\times\prime$, changes $\times\times$ to $\times\prime$, changes $\prime\prime$ to $\prime\prime$ or a strong iamb—but, mysteriously, does not affect $\prime\times$, the accentual trochee. The source of the metrical ictus, and the authority by which it is introduced into the line, are no more clear than is its selective operation.

A conception of the working of accent in the line which has somewhat the same result as belief in the metrical accent, without its major inconsistencies, arises from the—part recognition, part feeling—that genuine level accent in dissyllabic feet in English is in practice nonexistent. The scansions $\times\times$ and $\prime\prime$ suggest only that paired syllables are both below, or both above, what might be called the 'accentual threshold'—that

[22] Bridges (1) quotes *PL* 1. 2, 56 and 547 as 'normal lines,' having 'ten syllables with five stresses all on the even places.' Mrs Whiteley, objecting to Bridges' use of the terms 'norm' and 'normal regular line,' prefers 'the more accurate "base" and "basic pattern"' of Lascelles Abercrombie's *Principles of English Prosody*, Part I (London [Martin Secker], 1923)...' (269). Abercrombie gives a version of $\times\prime \mid \times\prime \mid \times\prime \mid \times\prime \mid \times\prime$ (see below, p. 279) as 'the *base* to which actual speech-rhythm is referred when it is heard not merely as rhythm but as metre—in this case as the metre of blank verse' (96).

[23] See Mrs Whiteley, 273. Gerard Manley Hopkins, discussing Milton's 'later rhythms' in a letter dated 5 October 1878, also uses the term, not quite as it is used here. See *The Correspondence of Gerard Manley Hopkins and Richard Watson Dixon*, ed. C. C. Abbott (London: Oxford University Press, 1935), 13-15. 'This is counterpoint: "*Hóme to* his móther's house *private* retúrned" [*PR* 4. 639]...' (15). Hopkins appears in the examples he gives to be referring only to reversal of accent, to the occurrence in the 'iambic' line of enough trochees so that the reader's sense of 'rising rhythm' begins to be qualified; but a more general use of the term 'counterpoint' would seem useful and legitimate provided it is not confused with Hopkins' own application of the idea.

point on the scale of accent above which we think of syllables as being accented. But if we accept the belief of the structural linguists that four degrees of accent—×, ∧, ‛, and ′, in order of increasing intensity—are phonemic, then ×× may represent ×∧ or ∧×; ′′ may represent ‛′ or ′‛. Some prosodists argue that in a two-valued notation, the feet represented above as ×∧ and ‛′ should be given as ×′, since they are 'rising' feet, whereas ∧× and ′‛ are 'falling' feet and should be represented as ′×. Clearly, the use of any two-valued system to make more than two distinctions must involve confusion. Our alternatives are to adopt the four-valued system of the structural linguists (if we accept their claims for it) —or to choose whatever way of using the two-valued system seems to us most intelligible or meaningful, *making clear the assumptions behind our use of* × *and* ′.

The idea of an abstract line as norm or base to which the actual line in some way relates may be, and by a number of prosodists has been, developed more fully than it is in the schema ×′ | ×′ | ×′ | ×′ | ×′, or may take other forms. A possible schema might be ×′ | ×′ || ×′ | ×′ | ×′ ||—in which || represents a caesural pause not identified with grammatical pause. The actual syntactical pattern of the line with its actual pauses might then, once again, be heard in a kind of counterpoint to the notional or 'ideal' line (though there are other possible relationships between the real and the 'ideal,' as we have seen and shall see further). The ideal line might, as was mentioned earlier, be a structure or succession of isochronous periods, 'time-spaces' which 'exist apart from the syllables embedded in them' (Omond, 53). Finally, the basic line might be thought of as composed notionally of (say) ten syllables, but as in fact admitting additional syllables of a specified nature in specified circumstances. Positions related to this theory too have been mentioned above. None of the theoretical representations of the line seems patently false or dangerous, thus simply stated; all might in fact be combined in a single complex abstraction. The reader might wonder by what authority a given regulation (say, of pause at the line's end) was held to be part of the ideal schema. Not until he had studied with care a great deal of prosodic criticism would he be likely to discover that the real difficulty with abstract theories of the line lies in the relationship the ideal schema is held to have to the actual line.

It will be recalled that Mrs Whiteley salvages *PL* 6. 866 etc. for the meter by a *practical* expedient, designed to make us aware that we are reading lines of five two-syllable groups or feet. But 'The foot is notional,' she has said earlier, 'a pattern in the mind, though none the less present and effective' (272). 'Notional' may seem at first to be contradicted by 'present and effective'; but if we understand the entire statement to mean that the 'pattern in the mind' is, in fact, imposed on the verse brought to it, difficulties may seem at first to recede. In one sense, all patterns are 'in the mind'; and 'effective' would seem to mean 'active,' 'operative.'

Later, however, discussing the first line of 'Twicknam Garden,' Mrs Whiteley says, 'Donne's verse, however daringly modulated, does follow a fixed notional pattern of foot and stress' (274). She then tells us how we must read

Blasted with sighs and surrounded with tears

in order to *fit* the line to the pattern. In other words, the line does *not*—as the first line of the second stanza does—*follow* the notional pattern *of itself*. There is a real contradiction, and it reminds us of our difficulties with Prince's revision of his formula: what could be accomplished by 'measuring,' e.g., *PL* 6. 866 or *PR* 1. 361 'against a notional basic line'? What does 'measuring' mean? Does the notional become in some way actual, selectively, when its help is required—but not otherwise? In what way are *PL* 6. 866, *PR* 1. 361, etc., '*based upon* a notional pattern of ten syllables alternately stressed and unstressed, in rising rhythm' (my italics)?

The word 'notional' has, in fact, more meanings than one, and for prosody the differences among the meanings are crucial. One kind of notion, or idea, we have is a generalization of what is actual; perceiving instances and what they have in common, noting the limits of the area within which the instances seem to follow the same rules, recording frequencies of occurrence, we achieve a kind of composite (not 'ideal') sense of what tends lawfully to happen which may indeed come to have a real existence in our minds, so that, all but instinctively, we compare with the 'notional pattern' it supplies individual instances as they occur. The 'notional' here exists, then, as I have said, in a kind of counterpoint with the actual and the individual. But it does not *change* the actual. It will help us to recognize what falls outside the limits it has noted; but it will not of itself regularize what is irregular. If *we* regularize, it will be because what we understand to be a law of the verse—something real, not notional—requires us to do so. It goes without saying that we had better be right.

'A law of the verse,' I have said: 'something real, not notional.' But of course 'notional' as opposed to 'real' may mean either 'imagined' or 'theoretical.' And a 'law' in the sense in which I have used the term is itself 'notional' in that it is idea, principle, abstraction. It is the generalization, not of what is, but of what should or must be. We have now four meanings of 'notional pattern': a pattern imposing or fulfilling certain requirements; a generalization or composite idea of what tends to happen within the area delimited by rule; a theoretical pattern; an unreal or imaginary pattern. No prosodist is likely to suggest comparison of the actual blank verse line with the last of these. The third remains to be discussed.

Many prosodic theories, instead of being distillations of the actual— generalizations which represent both what the poet intends, if he has said what he intends, and what is found, commonly or less commonly, in his practice—are based on conceptions of abstract form: on an ideal patterning scarcely to be realized in the patterning of the actual syllables of a particular language. The necessary divergence here of the theoretical and the actual has, in the event, the effect at times of cutting the theorist adrift, permitting him to claim the abstract existence of structures which the poet does not, often need not, sometimes could not produce in verse. What *actual* laws then govern the writing of verse in a given meter becomes at last a subject of separate study—or a matter of indifference.

But no theory can explain the structure of a line which was not written to embody, to actualize, that theory. That is, verse laws are (see above) real, not theoretical. Sometimes, again as has been pointed out, they cannot be followed without the conventionalization of some element of language—time, or accent, or 'the syllable.' But if this is so, the conventionalization *must take place* at least in a sufficient degree to give the reader the sense that he is in fact producing the meter in the line. When T. S. Omond claims that the English line is made up of equal-timed periods, but finds that one line is in truth, in its articulation, much briefer than another, and may be effective precisely because of the *contrast* in time between the actual line and the base (55–6), he is simply disproving his own theory. When Lascelles Abercrombie takes the base of the line to be

$$- \; \acute{-} \; - \; \acute{-} \; - \; \acute{-} \; - \; \acute{-} \; - \; \acute{-}$$

(83) but after discussion (84–96) finds '*any conceivable* reference' to the base 'convincing' (96; my italics) 'within the prevailing movement,' he is, in spite of his clear attempt to guard against doing so, severing theory from practice, his word 'reference' loses meaning, and what he says ceases to explain the actual writing of the line. We have seen what is required to *make* 'the prevailing movement' prevail in *PL* 6. 866 (which Abercrombie specifically discusses and accepts, 96–8) and in lines like it. Mrs Whiteley admires Abercrombie, who is indeed in most respects a superb verse analyst; and some of the terms she uses in discussing the line she has taken from him—not altogether warily, I think. I do not know where Prince's terms come from; but they are, as I have suggested, in fairly common (if stubbornly ambiguous) use. Clearing them of ambiguity will not be an easy task. But the fact that dialogue between Prince and Mrs Whiteley was possible is obviously encouraging. A much expanded dialogue on the nature of the 'notional' blank verse line and its relation to the actual line could lead to important clarifications.

The language in which Bridges expresses his view of the 'normal line' (stressed ×′ ×′ ×′ ×′ ×′) and of exceptions, themselves normal, to its conditions, could evidently be discussed much as we have discussed Prince's and Mrs Whiteley's language. But Bridges has fallen into an additional, comparable trap, and the consequences of his doing so, for the developed part of his theory, are more serious still; they must accordingly be spoken of here instead. A considerable proportion of Bridges' discussion of theory in the 1921 edition of *Milton's Prosody* (8–37) is taken up with identification and categorization of what he calls 'common-speech elisions' and 'poetic elisions': that is, synaloepha, synaeresis, aphaeresis, apocope, etc.—what I have been referring to generally as contractions and metrical compressions. The same had been true in the 1901 edition of the work. But in both editions Bridges divorces scansion (i.e. meter) from rhythm: in Appendix B of the 1901 edition, for example, we find him saying, 'That Milton regarded his open vowels as "elided," like open vowels in Latin, can hardly be doubted: that is, he intended that they should not count in the scansion: yet though he printed *Th' Almighty*, etc., it cannot be supposed that he wished it to be so pronounced' (50).[24]

Verse critics of the late 19th century, among them David Masson, one of Milton's principal 19th-century editors,[25] believed firmly that 16th- and 17th-century English verse, including Milton's, contained a great many trisyllabic feet intermingled with the dissyllabic feet that were basic to it. Bridges' formulation of his position would seem now to have differed only in emphasis, in phrasing, from the position generally held; nonetheless Bridges came under strong attack. Saintsbury, in particular, devotes the greater part of his chapter on Milton in *A History of English Prosody* (Vol. 2, Book 6, Chapter 1) to scolding—and deriding —Bridges. Accordingly, in his 1921 edition Bridges amplifies his earlier remarks, treating elision not merely as 'optional'[26] but as, at times, an

---

[24] Mrs Whiteley discusses interestingly (273) 'the notation of scansion' and the way in which that notation represents in part (as it shows foot division) the metrical base, in part (as it indicates accent) an actual patterning of sound. She does not speak of metrical compression and what its indication, in spelling or in scansion, would represent; Bridges obviously takes this as representing 'the notional pattern,' the base, whereas I should take it as representing, with accent, a part of the *actual* sound pattern.

[25] David Masson, ed., *The Poetical Works of John Milton*, 3 vols. (London, 1874). Vol. 1 is prefaced by a 'General Essay on Milton's English' (ix–cxxxii); of this essay, Part 6 (cvii–cxxxii) concerns 'Milton's Versification and His Place in the History of English Verse.' For Masson's discussion of 'the trisyllabic variation,' in *PR* as in Milton's other poems, see especially cxx–cxxv.

[26] See 6, 16, 18, 34, etc. In its simplest sense this would appear to mean only that the poet

outright fiction. 'Milton came to scan his verses in one way, and to read them in another,' he says (35).

We may consider one illustration: 'These two lines beginning

| The image | of God | [*PL* 11. 508] |
| The sa|vour of death |. | [*PL* 10. 269] |

are identical in rhythm, but different in their prosodial explanation. Perhaps this condition of things is expressed by saying that the rhythm overrides the prosody that creates it. The prosody is only the means for the great rhythmical effects, and is not exposed but rather disguised in the reading' (36).

But how can prosody be said to have *created* a rhythm that overrides it? A rhythm is real; a rhythm arrived at by prosodic means, a rhythm created by prosody, could not be the same as a rhythm that overrides or disguises prosody. *PL* 11. 508 reads, in the spelling of 1674,

> Th' Image of God in man created once;

PL 10. 269 reads

> The savour of Death from all things there that live.

'The sav|our of Death' is a sequence of two accentual iambs (the *ou*, which = [ə], is in the reading so far reduced as to be asyllabic); 'Th' Image | of God' is a trochee followed by an iamb. The lines are *not* identical in rhythm, and must not be read as identical. Thus, though Bridges' work has been of inestimable value to succeeding prosodists, on this very important point he is I think wrong.

So reassuring and convenient an error—for some of the metrical compressions Milton gives us seem at first very strange, very difficult—will not easily be corrected, however. E. H. Blakeney,[27] John S. Diek-

---

might 'elide' or not, as he chose; compare, e.g., 'Spirit' as a monosyllable in *PR* 1. 8, 31, etc. with the same word as a dissyllable in *PR* 1. 189. Ultimately, however, the idea that a choice existed for the poet seems to lead Bridges to accept the idea that the reader may if he chooses treat elision as theoretical, not actual; if the reader accepts the option, the usual result is that trisyllabic feet appear in the line. Curiously enough, once elision is thought of as theoretical, it escapes the reader, evidently, and he loses the option to perform it; see Bridges' analysis of *PL* 11. 508 and 10. 269, in the text above.

[27] E. H. Blakeney, ed., *Paradise Regained* (London: Eric Partridge, 1932), 9.

hoff,[28] William B. Hunter, Jr.,[29] Michael F. Moloney,[30] George A. Kellog,[31] and Robert O. Evans[32] follow Bridges in treating 'elision,' where it does not correspond to obvious speech practice, as a fiction. Sprott, on the other hand, does not (see below, pp. 359–60), and his general discussion of metrical compression and the grounds for excluding tri-syllabic feet from Milton's line (63–74) is very much worth reading.

Prince's remark that the English line 'has a theoretic ten syllables' (*Italian Element*, 143), and his comment on 'the elisions possible in English to increase the number of real, as opposed to theoretic, syllables' (*ibid.*), need, of course, owe nothing to Bridges, and Prince considers indeed that 'something is clearly wrong when Bridges has to declare ...that "Milton came to scan his verses in one way, and to read them in another."' Much the same thing, however, may be wrong with speaking of 'real, as opposed to theoretic, syllables.' But since Prince is comparing English with Italian prosody, his phrasing is likely to relate to a conception of metrical compression in the Italian line, and of this one need say only that if an *endecasillabo* must be a line of eleven syllables principally to the receiving intelligence of the reader, that intelligence, occupied largely with understanding the meaning of what is being said, cannot constantly draw aside to recognize the theoretical truth of what the ear denies. To varying degrees, but sufficiently always to serve as a guide to the intelligence, the metrical compressions of the Italian line, like those of the English line, must be realized, produced in the reading.

New theories of English prosody, based on analyses of the structural linguists, are beginning to emerge; certain of these theories, or others yet to be formulated, may in the next decades qualify radically our sense

[28] John S. Diekhoff, 'Milton's Prosody in the Poems of the Trinity Manuscript,' *PMLA* 54 (1939), 153–83, 153.

[29] William Bridges Hunter, Jr., 'The Sources of Milton's Prosody,' *PQ* 28 (1949), 125–44, 125.

[30] Michael F. Moloney, 'Donne's Metrical Practice,' *PMLA* 65 (1950), 232–9, 235.

[31] George A. Kellog, 'Bridges' *Milton's Prosody* and Renaissance Metrical Theory,' *PMLA* 68 (1953), 268–85, 268.

[32] Robert O. Evans, *Milton's Elisions*, University of Florida Monographs, Humanities—No. 21 (Gainesville: University of Florida Press, 1966), 3.

of the importance, or the interest, or the accuracy of the theories which have emerged thus far. Reconsiderations of prosodic theory cannot, however, render superfluous the work of the historical prosodist, whose task is to try to collect and read the evidences that will tell us what formal intentions writers of verse such as Milton had, what beliefs and awarenesses, what linguistic conditions had a share in determining their practice. It will be clear that we cannot, as of this writing, claim full understanding of Milton's prosodic intentions. But the student who reads Bridges, Saintsbury and Sprott, Prince and Beum, in the light of what has been said here,[33] will at least understand the issues at stake, and will have some sense of the history behind the positions taken by the chief prosodists of the 20th century as to the nature of '*English* Heroic Verse.'

Because of the relationship between verse form and style, the second part of this essay will concern the style of *PR* (in the context, necessarily, of the style of *PL*); those elements of style that have no clear implications for verse form will, in view of the nature of the materials under consideration, be treated briefly, or omitted. The third part of the essay will examine specific studies of and commentaries on the versification of *PR*. Not all studies of verse effects or techniques have behind them a deeply considered theory of prosody. But the reader, if he goes for further information to the books and articles that will be mentioned in this essay's final section, will often recognize in them traces or fully elaborated expositions of now one, now another of the prosodic beliefs that have been outlined above, and will be the better prepared to estimate the real significance of the individual writers' corresponding remarks on verse form.

II

'The specific excellence of verbal expression in poetry,' says Aristotle in the *Poetics*, 'is to be clear without being low. The clearest, of course,

---

[33] See also my articles on Milton's 'Prosody and Versification' and 'Blank Verse' in the *Milton Encyclopedia*, and my detailed study of *The Prosody of the English Poems*, Vol. 6 of *A Variorum Commentary on the Poems of John Milton*.

is that which uses the regular words for things; but it is low...Impressiveness and avoidance of familiar language is achieved by the use of alien terms; and by "alien" I mean dialectal words, metaphor, lengthening of words, in short anything other than the standard terminology. But if the whole composition is of that sort, it will be either a riddle or a piece of barbarism: riddle if made up of metaphors, barbarism if made up of foreign words.'[34]

Joseph Addison's fourth *Spectator* paper on *PL* (No. 285; Saturday 26 January 1712) similarly takes under consideration 'the language of an heroick Poem,' which, in Addison's words, 'should be both perspicuous and sublime.'[35] To the latter end 'it ought to deviate from the common Forms and ordinary Phrases of Speech...Aristotle has observed, that the Idiomatick Stile may be avoided, and the Sublime formed, by the following Methods. First, by the Use of Metaphors...' Here Addison illustrates by quoting from *PL* metaphors which he finds 'very bold, but beautiful' (130).

Another Way of raising the Language, and giving it a poetical Turn, is to make Use of the Idioms of other Tongues. *Virgil* is full of the *Greek* Forms of Speech, which the Criticks call *Hellenisms*, as *Horace* in his Odes abounds with them much more than *Virgil*. I need not mention the several Dialects which *Homer* has made Use of for this End. *Milton* in conformity with the Practice of the ancient Poets, and with *Aristotle*'s Rule, has infused a great many *Latinisms*, as well as *Graecisms*, and sometimes *Hebraisms*, into the Language of his Poem...

Under this Head may be reckoned the placing the Adjective after the Substantive, the Transposition of Words, the turning the Adjective into a Substantive, with several other foreign Modes of Speech, which this Poet has naturalized to give his Verse the greater Sound, and throw it out of Prose.

The third Method mentioned by *Aristotle*, is...the length'ning of a Phrase by the Addition of Words, which may either be inserted or omitted, as also by the extending or contracting of particular Words by the Insertion or Omission of certain Syllables...That he might the better deviate from the Language of the Vulgar...[Milton has used] several old Words, which also makes his Poem

---

[34] Aristotle, *Poetics*, tr. with an introduction and notes by Gerald F. Else (Ann Arbor: University of Michigan Press, 1967), 58–9.

[35] G. Gregory Smith, ed., *The Spectator*, 8 vols. in 4, Everyman's Library Nos. 164–7 (London: Dent, 1907), 4 (in 2, No. 165), 128. Often reprinted.

appear the more venerable, and gives it a greater Air of Antiquity...[In addition,] there are in *Milton* several Words of his own Coining...By the abovementioned Helps, and by the Choice of the noblest Words and Phrases which our Tongue would afford, [Milton] has carried our Language to a greater Height than any of the *English* Poets have ever done before or after him, and made the Sublimity of his Stile equal to that of his Sentiments...

This Redundancy of those several Ways of Speech which *Aristotle* calls *foreign Language*, and with which *Milton* has so very much enriched, and in some Places darkned the Language of his Poem, was the more proper for his Use, because his Poem is written in blank Verse; Rhyme, without any other Assistance, throws the Language off from Prose, and very often makes an indifferent Phrase pass unregarded; but where the Verse is not built upon Rhymes, there Pomp of Sound, and Energy of Expression, are indispensably necessary to support the Stile, and keep it from falling into the Flatness of Prose (130–2).

At the end of the essay Addison comments briefly on

Milton's Numbers, in which he has made use of several Elisions, that are not customary among other *English* poets...This, and some other Innovations in the Measure of his Verse, has varied his Numbers in such a Manner, as makes them incapable of satiating the Ear, and cloying the Reader, which the same uniform Measure would certainly have done, and which the perpetual Returns of Rhime never fail to do in long narrative Poems. I shall close...with observing that *Milton* has copied after *Homer*, rather than *Virgil*, in the Length of his Periods, the Copiousness of his Phrases, and the running of his Verses into one another (133).

The reader will wish to review sections 21 and 22 of the *Poetics* in their entirety, and compare them with the entirety of *Spectator* No. 285. He will find especially interesting, perhaps, Aristotle's warnings against excess, taken in conjunction with a paragraph in Addison rather more defensive in tone than is the rest of the essay:

I have been the more particular in these Observations of *Milton*'s Stile, because it is that Part of him in which he appears the most singular. The Remarks I have here made upon the Practice of other Poets, with my Observations out of *Aristotle*, will perhaps alleviate the Prejudice which some have taken to his Poem upon this Account; tho' after all, I must confess, that I think his Stile, tho' admirable in general, is in some Places too much stiffened and obscured by the frequent Use of those Methods, which *Aristotle* has prescribed for the raising of it (132).

Two Saturdays later (in *Spectator* No. 297, 9 February) Addison treats of 'the several Defects' which appear in *PL*, including defects in the language.

We must allow...that it is often too much laboured, and sometimes obscured by old Words, Transpositions, and Foreign Idioms. *Seneca*'s Objection to the Stile of a great Author, *Riget ejus oratio, nihil in ea placidum nihil lene*, is what many Cricks make to *Milton*: As I cannot wholly refute it, so I have already apologized for it in another Paper; to which I may further add, that *Milton*'s Sentiments and Ideas were so wonderfully sublime, that it would have been impossible for him to have represented them in their full Strength and Beauty, without having Recourse to these Foreign Assistances. Our Language sunk under him, and was unequal to that Greatness of Soul, which furnished him with such glorious Conceptions (178).

To this criticism, as is well known, Samuel Johnson adverted in the discussion of the major poems that closes his *Life of Milton*. Read out of their full context his remarks on Milton's style sound by turns ill-humored and fulsome. And it is odd, certainly, that in this part of his discussion Johnson should make no reference to Aristotle. Perhaps he felt that the Aristotelian precepts which concern 'the basic principles of poetic style' would be known by the educated audience, and so could be taken for granted. His phrasing does not suggest this, however. He says of Milton:[36]

Through all his greater works there prevails an uniform peculiarity of *Diction*, a mode and cast of expression which bears little resemblance to that of any former writer, and which is so far removed from common use that an unlearned reader when he first opens his book finds himself surprised by a new language.

This novelty has been, by those who can find nothing wrong in Milton, imputed to his laborious endeavours after words suitable to the grandeur of his ideas...But the truth is, that both in prose and verse, he had formed his style by a perverse and pedantick principle. He was desirous to use English words with a foreign idiom...

[36] Samuel Johnson, 'Milton,' *Lives of the English Poets*, ed. G. Birkbeck Hill, 3 vols. (Oxford: Clarendon Press, 1905), 1, 84–194, 189–91.

Of him, at last, may be said what Jonson says of Spenser, that 'he wrote no language,' but has formed what Butler calls 'a Babylonish Dialect,' in itself harsh and barbarous, but made by exalted genius and extensive learning the vehicle of so much instruction and so much pleasure that, like other lovers, we find grace in its deformity.

It would have been in general consistent with the remainder of Johnson's criticism if there had intervened between the second and the third of these paragraphs, first, an allusion to the Aristotelian precepts, and second, a suggestion that Milton had followed those precepts without exercising the moderation which Aristotle himself had recommended. One finds instead a miscellany of criticisms and comments, ending thus: 'One source of his peculiarity was his familiarity with the Tuscan poets: the disposition of his words is, I think, frequently Italian; perhaps sometimes combined with other tongues' (190). The contrast with Addison seems deliberate; it is certainly striking.

Johnson had noted earlier that 'Milton, being well versed in the Italian poets, appears to have borrowed often from them...' (187). Indeed, Milton's commentators had from the beginning given instances of such borrowings; scattered examples are reported in P. H[ume]'s 1695 notes on *PL*,[37] and Bishop Newton's mid-18th-century annotated editions of Milton's poems[38] adduce many more, some in notes written by Newton himself, others in notes signed by Thyer, Bowle, etc. Charles Dunster[39] and the Rev. H. J. Todd[40] continue and very much expand the documentation in the late 18th and early 19th centuries. And since Todd's notes incorporate what is most helpful in preceding commentary, a study of them will provide impressive evidence of the range of Milton's allusions to Italian as to classical verse, and the devoted care of his early editors in compiling a record of them.

[37] John Milton, *Paradise Lost*, 6th ed. To which is added, Explanatory Notes upon each Book...(London, 1695).

[38] Thomas Newton, ed., *Paradise Lost*, 2 vols. (London, 1749); *Paradise Regain'd... Samson Agonistes* and *Poems upon Several Occasions* (London, 1752). These editions were reprinted a number of times during the remainder of the 18th century.

[39] Charles Dunster, ed., *Paradise Regained...*with Notes of Various Authors (London, 1795).

[40] The Rev. H. J. Todd, ed., *The Poetical Works of John Milton*, with Notes of Various Authors, 6 vols. (London, 1801). Todd's *Milton* also was several times revised and reissued; I have the 5th ed. (London, 1852).

Walter Savage Landor's two-part Imaginary Conversation with Southey on Milton's verse[41] begins to make a different kind of connection between that verse and the Italian. Landor (and Southey) stroll through the poems as among the gardens of a vast estate, admiring a flower here, a whole bed of flowers there; now and again discreetly pulling a weed. Landor was interested rather in the prosody and versification of the poems than in sources or allusions, however; and he recognized a great deal that was Italian in Milton's handling of the line. Thus *PL* 6. 866 (mentioned often in part one of this essay) 'is not a verse; it is turned out of an Italian mould, but in a state too fluid and incohesive to stand in English' (4, 456). *PL* 8. 299 also is 'too slippery, too Italian' (4, 459). Of *PR* 1. 175, a line not unlike *PL* 8. 299, Landor has Southey remark that 'It is difficult so to modulate our English verse as to render this endurable to the ear. The first line in the *Gerusalemme Liberata* begins with a double trochee *Canto l'arme*'; here, however, 'the word "But" is too feeble for the trochee to turn on' (4, 480). And in another essay, criticizing adversely the again similar *PR* 4. 597, Landor quotes the beginnings of a number of Italian verses Milton might have used as models, and concludes, 'There is no verse whatsoever in any of his poems for the metre of which he has not an Italian prototype.'[42]

The 19th century shows increasing awareness of the relationship of Milton's versification with certain practices of the Italian poets. From them, says John Addington Symonds, Milton 'learned some secrets in the distribution of equivalent masses of sound. Milton's elisions, and other so-called irregularities, have affinities with the prosody of Dante; for while the normal Italian hendecasyllable runs thus:

Mo su, mo giù, e mo ricirculando,

the poet of the "Inferno" dares to write:

[41] *The Works and Life of Walter Savage Landor*, 8 vols. (London, 1874–6); vol. 4, *Imaginary Conversations*, Third Series, Conversation 18, part 1, 427–75, part 2, 476–528. The *Imaginary Conversations of Literary Men and Statesmen* were first published, in 5 vols., 1824–9.

[42] Walter Savage Landor, 'The Poems of Catullus,' *Works and Life*, 8, 390. Prince quotes this remark, 138, n.

Bestemmiavano Iddio e i lor parenti;

which is an audacity on a level with many of Milton's.'[43]

Important and detailed contributions to our understanding of Milton's debt to Italian verse and verse theory have been made in the 20th century. See, for example, the Introduction to John S. Smart's *The Sonnets of Milton*;[44] see also George A. Kellog's 'Bridges' *Milton's Prosody* and Renaissance Metrical Theory' (already mentioned), and Ants Oras' 'Milton's Early Rhyme Schemes and the Structure of *Lycidas*.'[45] It is especially interesting to read Kellog as a supplement to F. T. Prince. *The Italian Element in Milton's Verse* remains, however, incomparably the most searching treatment of the subject. Prince's Chapters 3, 7 and 8 ('Tasso and the Epic,' 34–57, 'Milton's Blank Verse: the Diction,' 108–30, and 'Milton's Blank Verse: the Prosody,' 131–44) contain a great deal of material designed to show the relationship between the principles upon which Milton formed his epic style (including 'the sense variously drawn out from one Verse into another') and the practices and principles that emerged from 'Italian endeavours to devise an epic form of blank verse' (111); anyone who reads these chapters will come to understand much, not only about the relationship under discussion, but about the interconnections between style and versification generally.

Says Prince,

The artistic purpose of a poem cannot be apprehended except through the structure of its verse; it is embodied in the arrangement of the words, whether these are considered as sense or as sound, and Tasso's account of the 'magnificent' style rightly took metrical devices in its stride. The *asprezza* [roughness, difficulty] he desired might be obtained, so he thought, not only in a complex diction (*parlar disgiunto*), but in weighty rhythms, and certain conjunctions of vowels and consonants, sometimes in the body of the line, sometimes at the end.

The same interdependence of sense and sound is Milton's aim. Milton's prosody cannot be understood independently of Miltonic diction (131).

[43] John Addington Symonds, *Blank Verse* (New York, 1895), 97.
[44] John S. Smart, ed., *The Sonnets of Milton* (Oxford: Clarendon Press, 1966). First published, 1921.
[45] Ants Oras, 'Milton's Early Rhyme Schemes and the Structure of *Lycidas*,' MP 52 (1954–5), 12–22.

Prince means not only that 'Milton's epic style' is in part a function of his versification; he asserts a 'clear connection between Milton's prosodic system in his epic blank verse and the recommendations made by Tasso in the *Discorsi* [*del Poema Eroico*].

'Tasso's verbal devices which approximate to prosodic features are:

I. The clogging of the verse by means of accumulated consonants.
II. The conjunction of open vowels, which may be...either (*a*) elided, or (*b*) unelided.
III. The use of double consonants in the penultimate syllables of the line' (132).

And in the pages following Prince illustrates the ways in which, and the degree to which, Milton is able to accommodate these devices to English.

'The combination of difficult, complex diction and a slow, suspended rhythm had been made in Italian by only one poet before Tasso,' says Prince, '—by Della Casa' (39). Later illustrating briefly something of 'the relationship between the rich Virgilian texture' of *PL* 'and Italian experiments in epic diction' (112), Prince quotes fairly extensively from Della Casa, to show variations of a device the Italian poet 'employs... frequently as a part of his equipment for suspending the sense and slowing down the movement of his verse': that is, 'the addition of a second adjective, as an interjection or afterthought, to an already qualified substantive' (*loc. cit.*). We may excerpt (from 112) a single example, and (from 113) a parallel in Milton:

> *Or viver orbo i gravi giorni e rei*
> (Now live bereaved my heavy days and cruel, *Sonetto* XIII)

> Before all Temples th' upright heart and pure (*PL* 1. 18)

Of course the device illustrated was used, occasionally, in the verse of English poets before Milton. Taken as a whole, none the less, Prince's demonstration is both illuminating and persuasive.

And yet the reader may begin to feel that a kind of circle is being completed. Much in Milton's epic style that Prince attributes specifically to the influence of Della Casa and of Tasso's theory and practice Addison attributed to Aristotelian theory and to example furnished by Homer and Virgil. It is Virgil who in turn supplies 'the all-sufficient model for the supreme diction required' of the Italian epic poet (Prince, 111). We need say little more. The interruptions and inversions of word order possible to English are without question very much more like those possible to Italian than they are like the more astonishing, though ultimately related, effects which could be achieved in Virgilian Latin. Doubtless Milton learned much in other ways also from Italian practice. But 'that sublime Art which in *Aristotles Poetics*, in *Horace*, and the *Italian* Commentaries of *Castelvetro, Tasso, Mazzoni*, and others, teaches what the laws are of a true Epic Poem' (*Educ*; *Works*, 4, 286), Milton learned, obviously, from many sources; and many of the influences he sustained were, as obviously, overlapping influences.

Not surprisingly, as more and more is shown of Milton's clear debt to Italian verse, it seems important to more and more critics to remind us that Milton was after all widely and deeply read in English poetry, and that the prosodic practice of the poets he most admired who wrote in his own language must have influenced him far more than the practice of the Italians. 'You never can teach John Milton—he never could teach himself, though he may have tried—to be aught but an English poet': it is Saintsbury speaking (2, 265, n. 1). In his mind, specifically, is 'the Italian practice of elision.'[46]

Beum, taking direct account of *Italian Element*, accepts some of Prince's arguments, but would be cautious about the conclusions to be drawn from them. 'If...Milton is not a foot prosodist, neither did he go to Italy to find something he had long been familiar with in Albion. He took his practice of elision and some of his peculiarities of diction from the Quattrocento, as Prince has convincingly demonstrated. But Milton's line, considered as a structure, is no more a decasyllabic adaptation of the Italian *endecasyllabo* [*sic*] than it is a mere accentual (and iambic) version of Virgil's hexameter. Listen to Milton himself: "The measure is English Heroic Verse without rhyme"...' (347). Else-

---

[46] It will be remembered that Courthope attributed to 'the Saxon habit of slurring syllables' the modification of the strict French/English decasyllable by what he calls the 'swift triple rhythm' (3, 427) which prosodists who believe rather in contraction, metrical compression etc. tend to ascribe in large part to Italian influence or example.

where Beum notes, cogently, 'that whereas multiple elision occurs in almost every Tuscan line, Milton's elision is really not very frequent' (359). He notes as well, possibly following Courthope, 'that a tendency to slur light syllables is an indigenous English habit,' and remarks 'that most of the features of Milton's elision are also to be found in his respected forebears Chaucer and Spenser' (*loc. cit.*). The final tendency of these observations, together with Beum's reminder that 'Milton was an admirer of Shakespeare and Jonson, his sensibility steeped in the mighty lines of the days of his father' (343), is surely clear.

R. O. Evans grants that Milton doubtless 'found something to be learned in Italian poetry and criticism' (48). However, 'No matter what his debt to the Italians (and it was large),' he says, also in a direct if brief and somewhat muddled response to Prince, Milton 'drew his basic prosodic techniques from a strong English tradition' (12–13). He footnotes to his 1954 dissertation, 'The Theory and Practice of Poetic Elision from Chaucer to Milton, with special emphasis on Milton.'

Bridges' conclusion that Milton's rules for 'elision' 'would appear to be only a learned systemization of Chaucer's practice' (15) has already been mentioned. The influence of Milton's immediate predecessors on his early verse, especially the influence upon him of Spenser, Shakespeare and the Fletchers, has long been accepted.[47] Michael F. Moloney thinks it 'highly possible' 'that Donne may have been one of Milton's prosodic mentors' (238). William B. Hunter, Jr., devoting an entire article to a study of English influences on Milton's prosodic practice, doubts Bridges' conclusion that Milton's practice goes back to Chaucer's (125), and considers, only to dismiss, the possible alternative influences on Milton of Shakespeare and Jonson, Spenser, Marlowe, Daniel, Drayton and Chapman (128–30). His own view is that Milton's practice is based on Joshua Sylvester's (130–3) and on the prosody of the metrical psalters (133–44). Hunter's exclusions are artificial, his arguments for them unsound; but that Sylvester and the metrical psalters participated in 'the traditional system of metrical elision that had been the heritage

[47] See, for example, my essay 'Studies of Verse Form in the Minor English Poems,' *Variorum Commentary*, 2, 1019–21, 1047–8.

of English poets since Chaucer' (Evans, 47), that Milton employed that system, and that 'to it he added no new *categories*' (*loc. cit.*; my italics), my own researches would incline me to agree. Here I should like only to add, first, that English treatment of the syllable in English accentual-syllabic verse is likely to have been directly affected, not once but again and again, over the centuries, by somewhat comparable Italian practice[48] —and second, that treatment of the syllable is (as Beum, at least, recognizes) only one part of prosody. Milton's blank verse, like his earlier verse, is both profoundly English and profoundly influenced by Italian (and classical) precept and example. To Prince's fine study we owe much of our particular understanding of devices of style and versification to which Milton seems to have looked in Italian poetry and criticism as he attempted to forge an English style suitable for unrhymed epic. Doubtless not every emphasis in *Italian Element*, not every interpretation or conclusion, is just. But it does not become us to undervalue what we should be so much the poorer for wanting.

Samuel Johnson makes no attempt to explain, as Addison had explained, as Prince explains, Milton's reasons for writing as he did. Johnson too must have understood those reasons; but understanding did not change his opinion of the propriety of the endeavour. And his charge that Milton wrote 'a new language' which is, at last, 'no language' would seem to lead directly to the most serious of the charges leveled against the poet by those of his 20th-century critics who have least sympathy with him. 'The mind that invented Milton's Grand Style had renounced the English language,' says F. R. Leavis, 'and with that, inevitably, Milton being an Englishman, a great deal else.'[49] Again, 'Cultivating so complete and systematic a callousness to the intrinsic nature of English, Milton forfeits all possibility of subtle or delicate life in his verse' (53). F. L. Lucas speaks to similar effect of the 'marmoreal stiffness which Milton imposed' upon blank verse. 'For it is,

---

[48] We need only recall, for example, Spenser's wide familiarity with and indebtedness to Ariosto, Tasso, and other Italian poets; and Spenser is by no means the only English writer between Wyatt and Surrey on the one hand and Milton on the other who was directly affected by Italian verse.

[49] F. R. Leavis, *Revaluation* (London: Chatto & Windus, 1959), 52. First published, 1936.

indeed, almost as if the author' of *PL* 'had turned the verse of *Hamlet* into stone; to be carved and built by him and others after him into shapes of monumental nobility, but never again to seem like living flesh and blood, as once in Elizabethan hands.'[50] Examples of such criticism could be multiplied; I am tempted rather to turn to a few sentences in which James Whaler speaks of the deep source of order he finds in Milton's late verse: 'Milton's rhythmic style in PL and PR is distinguishable from that of all other blank verse in that it often leads a double life. It cannot always be grasped at one level, the level of obvious rhetoric and accessible prosody...Underneath the surface may move a persistent mathematics interpretable in terms of symbol. The result is what we have always known: we often feel in this verse an element of sculptured, even granitic, precision...'[51] In an earlier essay in this series I wrote (*Variorum Commentary*, 2, 1049), 'Every critic, apparently, has his own *Comus*.' Even more obviously, every critic has his own *PL*, his own *PR*. We may give C. S. Lewis the last word in the present interchange: 'Dr. Leavis does not differ from me about the properties of Milton's epic verse...He sees and hates the very same that I see and love.'[52]

R. D. Havens, preparing to discuss the influence of Milton's epic style upon English poets of the 18th century, devotes several pages to an analysis of the distinguishing features of that style.[53] Though not all the headings under which his analysis is subsumed are equally clear or objective in wording, it may be useful to list them here, in Havens' own language. The epic style, specifically the style of *PL*,[54] shows, to an unusual degree,

[50] F. L. Lucas, *Studies French and English* (Freeport, New York: Books for Libraries Press, 1969), 232. First published, 1934.

[51] James Whaler, *Counterpoint and Symbol*, *Anglistica* 6 (Copenhagen: Rosenkilde and Bagger, 1956), 159.

[52] C. S. Lewis, *A Preface to Paradise Lost* (London: Oxford University Press, 1942), 130.

[53] Raymond D. Havens, *The Influence of Milton on English Poetry* (Cambridge, Mass.: Harvard University Press, 1922), 80–5.

[54] 'We cannot expect to separate the influence' of *PR* from that of *PL*, Havens tells us (549). From evidence available, 'the assumption seems warranted' that *PR* 'exerted a relatively unimportant influence, and that writers who employ the Miltonic style and diction derive them mainly' from *PL*.

1. Dignity, reserve, and stateliness.
2. The organ tone...
3. Inversion of the natural order of words and phrases, one of Milton's many Latinisms.
4. The omission of words not necessary to the sense...
5. Parenthesis and apposition.
6. The use of one part of speech for another.
7. An unusual vocabulary...the general effect...of which...is to give splendor, as well as a certain strangeness or aloofness, to the poem.
8. The introduction into a comparatively short passage of a considerable number of proper names that are not necessary to the sense but add richness, color, and imaginative suggestiveness.
9. Unusual compound epithets.

Havens is, I take it, paraphrasing neither Aristotle's *Poetics* nor Tasso's *Discorsi*, though he might seem at times to be doing one or the other. He notes in addition Milton's frequent repetitions of words—in effect, the use of such rhetorical figures as *antimetabole* and *asyndeton* (85).

James Holly Hanford summarizes Havens' analysis, and elaborates upon it. He then goes on to say,[55]

Milton really has two styles, corresponding to two different kinds of object or two qualities of poetic inspiration. The one is abundant, highly colored, pictorial, figurative; the other direct, closely woven, and relatively plain. The first is the language of Milton's impassioned visual imagination, the second, of his ethical and intellectual intensity. Many passages, to be sure, show the two modes in combination, and both have the fundamental Miltonic qualities already analyzed [above]. The contrast between them in their purity is, nevertheless, strongly marked. It may already be discerned in *Comus*, but it is clearest in the later poems. In the sonnets, *Paradise Regained* and *Samson Agonistes*, the barer style predominates—though there are patches of the other, as in the description of the banquet spread for Christ, or the nightly storm followed by a serene dawn...

Are there then two Grand Styles—both with 'the fundamental Miltonic qualities' Havens defines? Or is 'the barer style' not 'Grand'

[55] James Holly Hanford and James G. Taaffe, *A Milton Handbook*, 5th ed. (New York: Appleton, 1970), 256–7.

after all? There seems no implication, in Hanford's remarks, that of the 'two qualities of poetic inspiration' one is inferior to the other. But answers to the questions raised here are not obvious, all the same. Critics who do not admire the complex style of *PL* do not necessarily approve the style of *PR* for being 'barer.' On the other hand, there have certainly been critics who admired the 'abundance' of *PL* so much that Milton's 'relatively plain' style—and thus the style of the greater part of *PR*—could only seem to them to betray a lessening of the poet's powers. Equally, there have been critics who thought so much in terms of a developing authorial style, an Elizabethan early style (typified, usually, by *L'All*, *IlPen* and *Comus*) and an individual, majestic late style, that *PR* could seem to them successful only where they found in it excellences that recalled to them the excellences of *PL*. There are variants, naturally, of all these positions.

To confound the forms and aims of *PL* and *PR* is of course to invite invidious comparison between them. This is not to say that the sharpest discrimination between the two poems will always result in the most sensitive characterization of their styles. The distinction Milton himself makes in *RCG* (1642) between the diffuse and the brief models of the epic (*Works*, 3, 237) is one that many critics have applied to the two later poems, not necessarily with full appropriateness; if in 1642 Milton foresaw writing diffuse and brief epics we cannot know what subjects he had then in mind for them, and the fact that, substantially later, he wrote longer and shorter epics (both to varying degrees complex in style) is only a very general confirmation of his earlier thoughts and interests.

The reader may recall a second question about epic upon which, Milton tells us in the same passage in *RCG*, he had found himself musing: 'Whether the rules of Aristotle herein are strictly to be kept, or nature to be follow'd, which in them that know art, and use judgement is no transgression, but an inriching of art.' It is interesting that in 1740, Francis Peck, contemplating the entire passage in *RCG*, associated the diffuse and the brief models of the epic with unwritten Miltonic works having Arthur and Alfred, respectively, as their protagonists; he suggested *PL* as an epic written strictly in accordance with the rules of Aristotle (was Peck here thinking of Addison's criticisms?), *PR* as following nature.[56] I have found no earlier critical use of the passage in *RCG* to illuminate Milton's own subsequent practice.

By 1752 Newton had made the identification which is now so little questioned. 'We see that...[Milton] looked upon the book of Job, as a brief model of an epic poem: and the subject' of *PR* 'is much the same as that of the book of Job, a good man triumphing over temptation: and the greatest part of it is in dialogue as well as the book of Job, and abounds with moral arguments and reflections, which were more natural to that season of life, and better suited Milton's age and infirmities than gay florid descriptions' (ed. *PR*, 187–8). Newton supposes that Milton had collected materials for *PL* over a very long period of time; the scarcity in *PR* of 'allusions to poets either ancient or modern' (189) is to him consonant with what he takes (from Ellwood's story) to be the fact, that Milton 'was not long in conceiving, or long in writing' *PR* (188). He appears to intend by this no disparagement of the poem; indeed, many of his remarks upon it may have been intended as explanation, as an oblique defense against adverse criticism. Unfavorable comparison of *PR* with *PL*, leading to a neglect of *PR*, seems to have been a part of the history of the poems from the beginning. Thus in 1734 the Rev. John Jortin says that *PR* 'has not met with the approbation that it deserves. It has not the harmony of numbers, the sublimity of thought, and the beauties of diction, which are in' *PL*. 'It is composed in a lower and less striking style, a style suited to the subject.'[57]

Late 18th-century editors and critics attempted to remove the shorter poem from the shadow of the longer one. 'Uncommon energy of thought and felicity of composition,' says William Hayley, in his *Life of Milton*, 'are apparent in both performances, however different in design, dimension, and effect. To censure' *PR* 'because it does not more

---

[56] Francis Peck, *New Memoirs of the Life and Poetical Works of Mr. John Milton* (London, 1740), 6.

[57] The Rev. John Jortin, *Remarks on Spenser's Poems* (London, 1734), 171–2. Both Peck (84) and Newton (3) quote the somewhat longer passage in Jortin from which these observations are excerpted. Jortin's commentary on *PR* occupies altogether pp. 171–85 of the *Remarks*.

resemble the preceding poem, is hardly less absurd than it would be to condemn the moon for not being a sun, instead of admiring the two different luminaries, and feeling that both the greater and the less are visibly the work of the same divine and inimitable power.'[58] The comparison has its disadvantages. Dunster's attack on the problem, in his 1795 edition of *PR*, is more direct. He summarizes earlier remarks on the poem made by Johnson, Bentley, Newton, Thyer, and Warburton, then says, 'None of these learned critics seem to have considered what we may collect from our author himself, that he designed this poem for, what he terms, *the brief epic*, which he particularly distinguishes from the *great and diffuse epic*, of which kind are the great poems of Homer and Virgil, and his own' *PL* (1–2). Had Dunster not noticed that Newton had delivered himself of the same judgment? Dunster proceeds, at all events, to quote the relevant passage from *RCG*, and continues, 'His model then we may suppose to have been in a great measure the book of Job; and however the subject which he selected may have been considered as narrow ground, and one that cramped his genius,[59] there is no reason to imagine that it was chosen hastily or inconsiderately. It was particularly adapted to the species of poem he meant to produce, namely, the *brief*, or *didactic*, epic' (2).

That the brief epic is of its nature didactic is perhaps no more self-evident than that Hesiod's *Works and Days* (for example) is in a true sense epic. And what led a particular critic, no longer living, to the intertwining of definitions ordinarily kept separate may not be discoverable. Dunster's assignment of *PR* to the 'species' he denominates so crisply may on the other hand be in part explained by a comment in his concluding note to the poem: 'Though it may be said' of *PR*, 'as Longinus has said of the ODYSSEY, that it is the *epilogue* of the preceding poem, still the design and conduct of it is as different, as that of the GEORGICS from the ÆNEID' (267).

But difference did not, it must be emphasized, suggest to Dunster

[58] William Hayley, *The Life of Milton*, 2nd ed. (London, 1796), 188.
[59] See Richard Bentley's note to *PL* 10. 182 in his ed. of *Milton's Paradise Lost* (London, 1732), 314.

inferiority. Earlier in the same note he says, 'They who talk of our Author's genius being in the decline when he wrote his second poem, and who therefore turn from it, as from a dry prosaic composition, are, I will venture to say, no judges of poetry. With a fancy, such as Milton's, it must have been more difficult to forbear poetic decorations, than to furnish them; and a glaring profusion of ornament would, I conceive, have more decidedly betrayed the *poeta senescens*, than a want of it' (266–7).

Hayley had quoted from *RCG* Milton's remarks on the 'diffuse' and 'brief' models of the epic (69–70). In the margins of his copy of the 1796 edition of Hayley's *Life*, Coleridge wrote, commenting on the quotation,

These words deserve particular notice. I do not doubt, that Milton intended his Paradise Lost, as an Epic of the first class, and that the poetic Dialogue of Job was his model for the general scheme of his Paradise Regained. Readers would not have been disappointed in this latter poem, if they had proceeded to it with a proper preconception of *the kind* of interest intended to be excited in that admirable work. In it's kind, it is the most *perfect* poem extant; tho' it's *kind* may be [of] inferior Interest, being in it's essence didactic, to that other sort, in which Instruction is conveyed more effectively, because more indirectly, in connection with stronger & more pleasurable Emotions, & thereby in a closer affinity with action (Brinkley, 582–3).

Coleridge was not to be seduced into sun–moon comparisons, however: if we object to the style of *PR* as not being the style of *PL*, 'might we not as rationally object to an accomplished Woman's conversing, however agreeably, because it has happened that we have received a keener pleasure from her singing to the Harp?' (583).

But the battle was to have to be fought again and again. If Landor knew what Dunster and Coleridge thought of *PR*, the knowledge did not improve his own opinion of the poem. 'Invention, energy, and grandeur of design, the three great requisites to constitute a great poet, and which no poet since Milton hath united,' he says, in imaginary converse with Southey, 'are wanting here' (*Works and Life*, 4, 481). A part of the explanation is perhaps that 'Milton...took but little time in forming the plan' of *PR* (4, 489). Masson's judgment of the poem seems an unexplained mixture of Coleridge's and Landor's: *PR* 'is a different poem' from *PL*—'not so great, because not admitting of being so great; but it is as good in its different kind. The difference of kinds between the two poems is even signalized in certain differences in the language and versification.' *PR* 'seems written more hurriedly' than *PL*, 'and, though with passages of great beauty, with less avoidance of plain historical phrases, and less care to give to all the effect of continued song' (2, 14). And Mark Pattison too reviews 'the usual explanation[s] of the frigidity' of *PR*, that the poem 'betrays the feebleness of senility ...Or it is an "oeuvre de lassitude"...'[60] with such sympathy that his alternative explanation of the poem's effect as intended, as resulting from Milton's determination not to supplement the gospel narrative (193), seems to carry conviction not even for him. For 'it will still be capable of being alleged that the story told does not interest; that the composition is dry, hard, barren; the style as of set purpose divested of the attributes of poetry' (192). And this judgment in turn sorts oddly with the other 'possible view of the matter' Pattison proposes. 'Poetry ...[Milton] had said long before should be "simple, sensuous, impassioned" [*sic*] (Tractate of Education). Nothing enhances passion like simplicity.' In *PR*, therefore, 'Milton has carried simplicity of dress to the verge of nakedness. It is probably the most unadorned poem extant in any language. He has pushed severe abstinence to the extreme point, possibly beyond the point, where a reader's power is stimulated by the poet's parsimony' (193).

One of the most eloquent late 19th-century comparisons of *PL* and *PR* is Symonds' in *Blank Verse*. Not only was Symonds an admirer of Milton's, he was aesthetically extraordinarily responsive. This may have been one of his limitations as a critic, as well as one of his strengths:

In the 'Paradise Lost' we reach the manhood of the art of Milton. His elaborate metrical structure, supported by rich alliteration and assonance, here attains its full development. Already too there is more of rugged and abrupt sublimity in the blank verse of the 'Paradise Lost' than can be found in that of 'Comus.' The metre, learned in the school of the Elizabethan drama, is being used in

[60] Mark Pattison, *Milton*, English Men of Letters Series (London, 1879), 192.

accordance with the models of the Roman Epic. Yet the fancy of the poet has not yet grown chill or lost luxuriance, nor has his ear become less sensitive to every musical modulation of which our language is capable. 'Paradise Regained' presents a marked change. Except in descriptive passages, there is but little alliterative melody; while all the harsh inversions and rugged eccentricities of abnormally constructed verses are retained...No doubt there are admirers of Milton who would not allow that the metrical changes in 'Paradise Regained' are for the worse. Yet it is hardly to be denied that, in comparison with the 'Paradise Lost,' much of richness, variety, sonorousness, and liquid melody has been sacrificed (109–11).

The continuation of the passage, which characterizes the style of *SA* and reviews, briefly, all the comparisons made earlier, drawing on analogues from the world of painting, is not less interesting.

In *PR*, says Symonds, 'the master has grown older, and *his taste is more severe*' (112; my italics); yes, but in *PL* 'the fancy of the poet has *not yet* grown chill or lost luxuriance...' (110; my italics). It is, then, a matter of loss after all. 'Fortunately we know the dates of Milton's masterpieces,' Symonds remarks with a final calm of mind which the beleaguered 20th-century reader can only envy. 'There is therefore no uncertainty or subjectivity of criticism in the analysis of these changes in his manner; at the same time they are precisely what we might have expected *a priori*—the intellectual gaining on the sensual qualities of art as the poet advanced in age' (113).

Walter Raleigh changes the inflection of the often-repeated criticisms once again. He attributes 'the enhanced severity of a style which rejects almost all ornament...in part...to a gradual change in Milton's temper and attitude. It is not so much that his power of imagination waned, as that his interest veered, turning more to thought and reflection, less to action and picture.'[61] Compare Newton—and Hanford. Milton was right, Raleigh believes, not to think *PR* inferior to *PL*; 'Its merits and beauties are of a different and more sombre kind, yet of a kind perhaps further out of the reach of any other poet than even the constellated glories of *Paradise Lost* itself' (*loc. cit.*).

[61] Sir Walter A. Raleigh, *Milton* (London: E. Arnold, 1900), **159**.

So for two centuries the general criticism of *PR* depended on what must have seemed inevitable comparison with *PL*. The shorter poem was an inferior sequel to the longer one; or it was a drying up (perhaps natural enough) of the same flow. If *PR* was granted independence this was usually accorded it in terms of Milton's early reveries in *RCG*, with the added observation that the short epic is didactic in nature, and not capable of the greatness possible to the longer epic. In other words, the *kinds* were compared instead of the individual poems—but with similar effect. Even the most genuine admirers of *PR* have seemed to blur their own understanding of the poem, and ours, by overgeneralization. That general criticism should *be* general is of course not surprising; and it is as easy to misrepresent 'the' style of *PL* by overgeneralization as it is to misrepresent *PR*. But *PR* has suffered more from its misrepresentations, from oversimplified analysis, than has *PL*. *PR* is itself a long and complex poem, and it is an unusual poem. Perhaps it is unique. It requires, at all events, very careful, and very detailed, examination.

In his 1930 consideration of Milton's poetry, E. M. W. Tillyard speaks out firmly for judging *PR* on its own merits. It is not, he says, surprising that if the poem 'is not allowed a separate existence of its own, it should be frequently judged by wrong standards; that is, not by internal, but by the external standards' of *PL* or of *SA*.[62] For Tillyard, ultimately, *PR* 'is not an epic, it does not try to be an epic, and it must not be judged by any kind of epic standard' (316). Tillyard quotes Pattison on *PR* as an *oeuvre de lassitude*, and notes that

others, Landor and Saurat[63] for instance, allow many 'beauties' in the poem but consider it to lack vitality in general. Their assumption would be that, if he had been able, Milton would have written the whole poem as grandly as he wrote these excepted passages. In other words, the normal style of the poem is other than he wished it, and he had not the power to summon his sublimity at will. I can only deny this completely and say that the normal style of the poem is deliberately chastened or dimmed, and that Milton has complete command over his sublimity: he is not always sublime, simply because he does not wish to be (313–14).

[62] E. M. W. Tillyard, *Milton* (London: Chatto & Windus, 1949), 313. First published, 1930.
[63] See Denis Saurat, *Milton, Man and Thinker* (London: Dent, 1944), 195–7.

But if Milton is to be credited with having written *PR* as he wished to write it, the critic has only two alternatives. He may object to what Milton wished; or he may accept, may attempt both to understand the style (or styles) of *PR* and to determine their appropriateness to the poem. Tillyard himself chooses the latter course, and to his criticisms we shall return. W. W. Robson chooses the first alternative. Speaking for an anonymous confraternity, he says that *PR* 'has not usually been judged to be a failure...If critics are unenthusiastic, it is not as a rule because they find in the poem a discrepancy between intention and performance. It is rather that there is felt to be something unsympathetic, something even repellent, about the intention itself.'[64]

Robson makes his principal argument out of the contrast between two passages (presumably representative) from *PR* 2: lines 182–95, spoken by Satan, and 473–86, spoken by Jesus. The latter passage he finds 'strangely colourless and toneless. We have a sense of a mind behind it, but we have little or no sense of a voice expressing the mind. What made it poetry for the poet? Clearly the metre—the even beat of the remarkably regular verse, with that typical monosyllabic thud[65] at the end of so many of the lines, which, without interrupting the consecutive flow of the argument, reinforces the general effect of flat unincantatory assertion—the effect that makes it impossible to mistake the passage for even one of the more didactic parts' of *PL* (125–6). Robson finds the other passage 'tonally much more adequate,' and wonders why it is 'accepted as matter-of-course that Milton writes better poetry for "bad" characters than for "good"...Here we have a great poet writing on a theme with which he is beyond question seriously engaged, but producing work which considered by the standards of his own best writing is inert, jejune, and dull' (126).

Can this, we must ask, be what Milton intended?—to displease M1

---

[64] W. W. Robson, 'The Better Fortitude,' *The Living Milton*, ed. Frank Kermode (London: Routledge & Kegan Paul, 1960), 124–37, 124.

[65] The thud comes to us, I believe, as to Robson, courtesy of F. R. Leavis (*Revaluation*, 43). The reader is not asked here to try to imagine a non-monosyllabic thud—nor an atypical monosyllabic thud.

Robson so? There is, it turns out, a failure after all: a 'failure of incarnation' (134).

Milton's portrayal of Christ does not succeed in uniting the sacred figure with the epic hero...The peculiarity of *Paradise Regained* among Milton's poems is that the division of the poetic personality which prompts these strictures seems to be perfectly conscious. Milton gives all the imaginative and emotional appeal—the characteristic appeal of poetry—to the temptations: Christ rejects them as the spokesman of pure reason. But this involves Milton in an artistic contradiction. In allowing Christ to speak poetry at all, he is obliged to supply *some* tone, *some* presence, to the voice of pure reason. The result is the acerbity in Christ's speeches which strikes the ear so disagreeably (134–5).

'The Hero at the worst moments of the poem is made to sound like an irritable snob[66]...It was a tactical mistake to confine courtesy to the Devil' (136).

It is how we feel on days when cold / Climat, or Years damp our intended wing / Deprest, perhaps; but it is a bit too highly colored for perspicuity. And Robson does not say what he means: he does think *PR* a failure, and it is perverse and ultimately confusing of him to argue that the poem fails because Milton succeeds in doing what he should never have intended doing, rather than because an intention consonant with what we see in the poem, but more humane and more winning, is realized insufficiently well. Other critics, one hastens to say, find the poem *truly* successful, see in it the larger intention Robson pretends not to see, and are won—perhaps in part because they have no difficulty in imagining themselves 'in sympathy with certain religious and ethical doctrines' (134), but rather more because they find Jesus, though not indeed courteous to the Devil, more modest and gentle otherwise, more successfully realized, than Robson would allow. But 'The Better Fortitude' is very much worth reading. Robson does not think *PR* an

[66] This language in its original home, Northrop Frye's 'The Typology of *Paradise Regained*,' *MP* 53 (1956), 227–38, 234, is much more complex in bearing than it is as Robson uses it. Robson may be, as I am, one of those readers who at times assimilate unconsciously phrases of others which have a special resonance for them. Here it is none the less unfortunate that Frye's meaning and purpose, which do not carry with them a simple or obvious adverse judgment, are not acknowledged and differentiated from Robson's.

oeuvre de lassitude. He is centrally concerned with the 'plain style'; and while something—something in large part outside the poem, I think—prevents him from taking much pleasure in Milton's use of it, his remarks are continuously interesting, and provide a detailed and useful contrast with more sympathetic analyses given us by other 20th-century critics.

It will be recalled that Jortin spoke of *PR* as having been written in 'a lower and less striking style' than that of *PL*, 'a style suited to the subject.' W. Menzies is only one of many 20th-century commentators to suggest that behind the 'extreme simplicity and plainness' of the style of the poem is 'the style of the gospel story itself.'[67] This 'is a very simple, distinctive style, which never varies and is so closely associated with the person of Christ that the two are virtually inseparable' (105). For Jacques Blondel, also, 'L'attention doit être sans cesse ramenée au récit évangélique dont la brièveté interdit au poète de somptueuses évocations.'[68] Blondel's following argument seems a subtle and accomplished elaboration of points made less well by Pattison. 'Milton a renoncé à se placer devant la Bible en artiste, pour en magnifier la splendeur,' he says (110). Marjorie Nicolson as well finds the poem's New Testament materials basically determinative. 'The style of Jesus Christ, as it has come down to us, at least in the Synoptic Gospels, was simple, direct, clear, forceful, designed for simple men...As Jesus, Christ must and does speak in his own person and in his own style.'[69] Robson agrees that the style of *PR* 'takes its colour from the character of the Hero,' but finds him 'laconic and terse' with a 'Senecan terseness' (128).

The plainness of 'the plain style,' then, itself requires definition—or invites interpretation. For Beum, *PR* is 'a homelier kind of epic' than *PL*; understandably, if not altogether fortunately, its verse 'is looser

[67] W. Menzies, 'Milton: the Last Poems,' *Essays and Studies*, 24 (Oxford: Clarendon Press, 1939), 104.

[68] John Milton, *Le Paradis Reconquis*, étude critique, traduction et notes par Jacques Blondel (Paris: Aubier, [1955]), 109.

[69] Marjorie Hope Nicolson, *John Milton: A Reader's Guide to His Poetry* (New York: Noonday Press, 1963), 326.

and the verbal features are generally less intricate and exotic' (363). J. B. Broadbent finds a kind of 'efficiency' in the writing of the last books of *PL* and of much of *PR*, 'combining vividness with cool objective reflection...It could have become, but didn't, a model of how in a scientific world to respond realistically to the actual without losing the apperceptive control of poetic wit.'[70] Neither homeliness nor efficiency sounds much like what Edmund Blunden, and with him Tillyard, finds in *PR*, 'the perfection of that "Doric delicacy" that Wooton attributed to Milton's minor poems.'[71] And the coincidence between this opinion and Blakeney's, in turn, must be thought nominal: 'Apart from occasional glories of the lines, their superb and subtle embroideries...' there is throughout *PR* 'an astringency that is tonic in its effect...[Milton's] verse here reminds us, from another point of view, of the finest Greek statuary, which, for all its calculated severity, thrills with a spiritual emotion' (9). More than the stone of its medium separates that 'calculated severity,' finally, from the 'musicalité en mineur' that characterizes *PR* for Blondel, 'cette musicalité...aux tons assourdis, apaisés et limpides qui ne chantent que pour l'âme' (116).

Blondel, like many other critics, sees the range of verse effect in *PR* as deliberately reduced; Milton 'joue sur un nombre restreint de registres' (96), and this because 'il veut subordonner son art à des fins éthiques' (94). Broadbent thinks 'that as a poet...[Milton] came to trust less and less in art, and even that he always had a sense that the poetry does not matter.'[72] In art as decoration, perhaps, Milton came

---

[70] J. B. Broadbent, *Some Graver Subject* (London: Chatto & Windus, 1960), 272. Arnold Stein's characterization of the style of God's speech in *PL* 3 seems not dissimilar: 'Language and cadence are as unsensuous as if Milton were writing a model for the Royal Society and attempting to speak purely to the understanding' (*Answerable Style*, Minneapolis: University of Minnesota Press, 1953, 128). Stein continues, 'What Milton aims at is a particular kind of bare language that will rise above the familiar associations of such bareness with austerity and harshness. Much, not all, of God's speech is delivered in rhythms that are markedly shorter than usual with Milton, and yet successfully avoid the effects of brokenness or crabbedness.' Not a few critics associate the style of parts of *PL* 3, as well as that of *PL* 11 and 12, with the style of *PR*.

[71] E. M. W. Tillyard, *The Miltonic Setting* (London: Chatto & Windus, 1947), 116. First published, 1938.

[72] J. B. Broadbent, 'Milton's Rhetoric,' *MP* 56 (1959), 224–42, 234.

to trust less and less; but few critics would suggest that Milton's belief in art as control ever diminished. Says Menzies,

Two great features...largely account for...[*PR*'s] distinctive character. One is the almost ruthless self-restraint under which the poet's imagination works throughout, the other is the unsleeping alertness of his sense of style. This is why nothing in the poem for all its plainness is prose, and nothing, on the other hand, however elevated, is ever in the air or off the solid earth. The style of the *loftiest* passages is not the *least* severely controlled, and the very plainest are still poetry. Nor do the extremes of lowest and highest ever fall far apart in feeling; for they are kept firmly in touch by a common element present in both —the general style. The language of the poem, whether it rises or sinks, remains true to the subdued minor key in which it starts. The quiet spirit of the Visionary Wilderness would seem to have entered into it and rule in it throughout (109–10).

To the Visionary Wilderness we shall later return. Here we must proceed with the notion of 'the general style' of *PR*, a style which unites 'the extremes of lowest and highest.' In an article which has not, perhaps, the last word to say on its subject, but which makes nonetheless some essential preliminary observations, Donald L. Clark reminds us not merely that in *Ref* (*Works*, 3, 34) Milton praises 'the sober, plain, and unaffected stile' of the Scriptures, but that he was well acquainted with the classical tradition which distinguished three levels of style, the 'lofty, mean, or lowly' (*Educ*; *Works*, 4, 286), and assigned them appropriate uses. 'The lowly style,' Clark says, 'was called by Cicero *subtilis, tenuis*...Cicero says that this subtile or plain style is appropriate to the statement of facts and the presentation of logical arguments. Cicero also calls this style *humilis*...In Farnaby's summary statement of ancient doctrine: "The lowly (*humilis*) style is elegant, concise, modest, flowing gently, simple in neatness, but not uncultivated nor nerveless, nor arid."'[73] The style is appropriate, says Clark, to the discussion of 'the theological implications of free will, predestination, divine justice, and the vicarious atonement' in *PL* 3, and to 'the theo-

[73] Donald Lemen Clark, 'John Milton and "the Fitted Style of Lofty, Mean, and Lowly,"' *SCN* 11 (1953), Supp. 5–9, 8.

logical and moral argument and rebuttal between Satan and the Son of God' in *PR*. Clark reminds us too that Milton has Jesus, in *PR* 4. 357–60, commend the 'majestic unaffected stile' of the Hebrew Prophets (note the echo of Milton's own phrase in *Ref*) as a more appropriate teaching instrument 'Then all the Oratory of *Greece* and *Rome*' (*loc. cit.*). But, Clark says in conclusion, 'Milton's style was one of infinite variety. He practiced the lowly, the mean, and the lofty styles with such gradations and interminglings as seemed to him artistically appropriate to the subject, circumstances, audience, and literary form' (Supp. 9). A proper inference would seem to be that all three styles might be found in *PR* as in *PL*—though we might suppose the lowly and the mean styles to predominate in *PR*, the lofty in *PL*.

Expanding on a suggestion made by Tillyard (in *Milton*, 322), and on others, it may be, gathered from Dunster (see above, p. 298), Louis L. Martz finds special point in comparing the form and style of *PR* with the form and style of Virgil's *Georgics*. He reminds us that Virgil's *Aeneid* was for late Roman critics 'the model of the grand style, his *Georgics*, the model of the middle style, and his *Eclogues*, the model of the low style.'[74] Martz feels that 'the ground-style' of *PR* is the mean or middle style, as announced in *PR* 1. 1–7, and that here as elsewhere in the late poems Milton proposes 'to convert the modes of classic poetry into the service and celebration of Christianity.' In *PR* 'he has done this...by converting Vergil's georgic mode into a channel for religious meditation, with the result that the poem belongs, simultaneously, to the classical mode of didactic, instructive poetry, and to the Christian genre of formal meditations on the Gospel' (226). For Martz as for Tillyard, then, *PR* 'is not an epic...' (227).

'Cette préséance de l'élément méditatif et de l'argument n'est-elle pas le fait de la prose d'un controversiste plus que d'un poète qui cède librement aux images, aux sonorités qui s'imposent spontanément à lui?' asks Blondel (94). Whether the question is, to him, real or rhetor-

---

[74] Louis L. Martz, '*Paradise Regained*: the Meditative Combat,' *ELH* 27 (1960), 223–47, 224. The essay is reprinted in substantially the same form as Part 4 of Martz's *The Paradise Within* (New Haven: Yale University Press, 1964), 169–201.

ical, it would obviously be real to Robson, who finds some of the phrasing in the interchanges between Satan and Christ 'an overflow from the manner of Milton's controversial prose' (129). Robson admits that 'the plain style, with all its laconism...can have a certain ideal dignity of its own'; he cites the much—and very properly—admired ending of *PR* 1 as an example. But he finds few 'expansions' in the manner of *PL* and, when they occur, 'they stand out sharply in contrast with the surrounding verse' (*loc. cit.*). Yet 'the prevailing gravity and formality of the poem's characteristic manner forbid us any sense of having passed to a "lower" style or a less impressive subject-matter. On the contrary, Milton's way of contrasting the new poem with the old (*ille ego qui quondam*), in the first line' of *PR*, 'offers the promise of a *greater* sublimity': *PL* 'becomes in retrospect a song about a "happy Garden"; the poet is now to sing of deeds "above Heroic"' (130).[75]

It will already have been seen that the plain or lowly style of which Clark speaks and the middle style which Martz finds in *PR* have overlapping, if not identical, functions; and the confusion is not lessened by the fact that *PR* 2. 182–95, accorded grudging admiration by Robson (see above, p. 303), seems to F. W. Bateson "a triumph of the middle *or pastoral* style"[76] (my italics). Now, to climax our difficulties, we have in Robson the suggestion that *PR* 1. 1–7 (specifically identified by Martz, it will be recalled, as characteristic of the middle style) aspires in all its plainness to the sublime—unsuccessfully, to be sure, as we might expect considering that the poet is about to turn into a *controversiste*, and yet we must begin to wonder, at the very least, what 'the fitted style of lofty, mean or lowly' is 'fitted' to, and whether a single seven-line passage of verse may be written in all three styles at once—as well as, perhaps, secretly, in prose.

Stewart A. Baker might be responding directly to Robson, Bateson and Martz when he speaks of the *De partu virginis* of Jacopo Sannazaro (1458–1530) as creating a model of the short biblical epic in which the

---

[75] Cf. Arnold Stein, *Heroic Knowledge* (Minneapolis: University of Minnesota Press, 1957), 6–7.

[76] F. W. Bateson, '*Paradise Regained*: a Dissentient Appendix,' *The Living Milton*, 138–40, 140.

motifs of classical epic 'provide an indispensable cosmological and historical framework for meditation.'[77] Baker associates meditation explicitly and convincingly with the Virgilian pastoral. Both Sannazaro and Milton in *PR* employ 'the reductive idiom of pastoral,' Baker says, 'to test the values of classical epic' (121). In this 'interplay of genres' (131) the military motif of epic becomes 'a metaphor for defining a moral or theological idea' (123). Baker points out how in *PR* i. 8–11 Milton declares 'his stylistic and structural intentions by describing the pastoral setting through the military metaphor' (*loc. cit.*). In the event, 'It is through meditation, prophecy, debate, and the pastoral landscape that the values associated with...[the motifs of classical epic] are re-defined' (131). The role played in *PR* by the landscape, 'the inverted pastoral of "the waste Wilderness," the emblem of man's fallen state, which Jesus will transform spiritually into the ideal pastoral, "Recover'd Paradise"' (123), Baker illuminates, it seems to me, particularly excitingly.[78]

The idea that *PR* derives its unusual character from a studied 'interplay of genres' is an attractive one. Such an interplay, further, would seem likely to carry with it a necessary interplay of styles, not perhaps unlike those 'gradations and interminglings' of the lowly, the mean and the lofty which Clark finds in Milton. But must not such 'interplay,' such 'interminglings,' be licenced by a tradition, do they not require more countenance than the mere ingenuity of poets—or of critics recording what they perceive in poets—could afford them? '*Sermo Humilis*,' Chapter I of Erich Auerbach's *Literary Language and its Public*,[79] goes far, it seems to me, toward providing an answer to this question. A brief quotation will indicate here something of what, according to Auerbach, Christian writers made of the classical doctrine of the three levels of style:

In Augustine...the principle of the three levels hinged exclusively on the author's specific purpose, accordingly as he wished to teach (*docere*), to con-

[77] Stewart A. Baker, 'Sannazaro and Milton's Brief Epic,' *CL* 20 (1968), 116–32, 131.
[78] On the setting of *PR* see also below, p. 340.
[79] Erich Auerbach, *Literary Language and its Public in Late Latin Antiquity and in the Middle Ages*, tr. Ralph Manheim, Bollingen Series 74 (New York: Pantheon, 1965).

demn or to praise (*vituperare sive laudare*), or to persuade (*flectere*; *De doctr. chr.* 19). He found a similar view in Cicero; but he rejected Cicero's assumption that each level of style corresponded to a class of subject matter. The themes of Christian literature, he held, are all sublime; whatever lowly thing it may touch upon is elevated by its contact with Christianity. Nevertheless, the theory of the three levels of expression is useful to Christian teachers and orators; for Christian doctrine is not only sublime, but also obscure and difficult; yet since it is intended for all, since it is desirable that all should understand it and live in accordance with it, it should be set forth in the lowly, intermediate, or sublime style as the situation requires (38–9).

It must seem of fundamental importance also that to Christian writers *humilis* had almost of necessity to mean something far more than a quality of style: it 'became the most important adjective characterizing the Incarnation; in all Christian literature written in Latin it came to express the atmosphere and level of Christ's life and suffering' (40). And again, 'The humility of the Incarnation derives its full force from the contrast with Christ's divine nature: man and God, lowly and sublime, *humilis et sublimis...*' (41).

Whether *PR* has in these terms a 'general style,' a 'ground-style,' and if it has, whether that style is the plain or lowly style or the intermediate style, are not of course matters for offhand judgment. What Auerbach would seem to confirm is the appropriateness of the *sermo humilis* for simple narrative directly concerned with Jesus, and for those speeches of Jesus in which he must clarify truths obscured by Satan. But Jesus must also at times condemn Satan; and Satan must of course try, in various ways, and on various levels, the arts of persuasion. A testing of the materials and motifs of one genre by those of another would require further movements and contrasts between levels of style. There would seem to be more than sufficient occasion for the use of the higher as of the lower styles—and reason for seeking variety. Naturally a skilled writer would modulate with great care from one style into another, so that the language and manner in use at any given moment should always seem appropriate; thus the control, the coherence of style Menzies finds so striking. Nonetheless it makes more sense to look on the poem as displaying a complex intermingling of styles than as having been written largely in a single style, variously plain, showing here and there 'expansions,' 'purple patches,'[80] 'beauties' reminiscent of the grand style, that serve only to remind us how flat, or how relentlessly controlled, the 'general style' is.

One of Martz's most fruitful ideas is that 'the process of temptation' in *PR* is conveyed by the creation of 'what might best be called a contest of styles' (233). Thus after the 'humble, inward scenes' that begin *PR* 2, 'the process of temptation...bursts upon us in the high oratorical style' of *PL* (234). In general, 'The central contest, the full excitement, of the poem lies in...a meditative combat in which the flights of poetic splendor are consistently drawn back by the prevailing net of a frugal, georgic style to the ground of renunciation and temperance' (236).[81]

Martz is only one of a number of critics to have noted that 'the flights of poetic splendor' in *PR* seem in general to be associated with Satan, as plainness of style is associated with Jesus. Ants Oras says, 'One of the leading themes of *PR* is the systematic contrasting of temperance and self-control with the temptations of self-indulgent luxury and worldly glory. Into his descriptions of mundane magnificence Milton has concentrated much of his earlier brilliant coloring, reverting to many of his old stylistic and rhythmical methods...While the poet's philosophy condemns the things he depicts, he nevertheless depicts them in much

---

[80] See H. J. C. Grierson and J. C. Smith, *A Critical History of English Poetry*, 2nd revised ed. (London: Chatto & Windus, 1950), 169.

[81] Christopher Ricks replies to Martz in 'Over-Emphasis in *Paradise Regained*,' *MLN* 76 (1961), 701–4. Ricks gives a number of examples of what may seem a rather empty 'pointedness' or repetitiousness in *PR*, as in 1. 148, 149, 320, 411, 417, 429 and 435; 2. 403; 3. 2–3, 4, 13–14, 49–50 and 264; etc. If the 'contest of styles' is between 'the middle, georgic style which represents the way of temperance' and the 'self-indulgence of an elaborate style,' then Ricks feels the need of protesting (702) that 'there is certainly more than one way of being self-indulgent, and of being elaborate; Christ eschews some of the forms of self-indulgent elaboration, but not all.' Cf. what Baker says of the pastoral style, below.

Ricks discusses what he calls 'over-emphasis' in *PL* in *Milton's Grand Style* (Oxford: Clarendon Press, 1963), 17–20. *Milton's Grand Style* is a more than usually detailed, sensitive and valuable discussion of the diction and syntax of *PL*. It concerns itself, however, with qualities of style which as Ricks analyzes them have little or nothing specifically to do with versification, and accordingly I have not reviewed the book's argument in these pages.

the old manner' ('Milton's Blank Verse,' 188). In Blondel (to whom Martz makes acknowledgment) the same idea is at least nascent in such an observation as this: 'Le lyrisme intellectuel...trouve son unité dans l'opposition constante qu'il entretient entre deux éléments qui sans cesse s'appellent et se repoussent, la vérité morale et la beauté illusoire' (110). Fascinatingly, Blondel suggests that the originality of *PR* 'consiste non seulement à avoir donné aux tentations tout leur éclat à travers le miroir habile de Satan, mais aussi à laisser cette éphémère splendeur, jugée factice et fallacieuse par le Christ, exercer sur le lecteur toute la fascination d'un enchantement. Ainsi le charme subsiste parce que le poète sait qu'il n'est qu'enchantement passager devant la vérité austère et les valeurs jugées authentiques' (116). Compare Robson.

But Satan himself uses 'the plain style' at times, even though he represents generally, in contrast to Jesus, 'the polished orator' (Robson, 129). Baker speaks of the 'repetitive, pleonastic, parenthesis-filled style of the pastoral' (so described, it scarcely sounds 'plain') as being parodied by Satan in *PR* 1. 326–34;[82] the style of Jesus' reply, he says, is 'the simple and abrupt language of the "true" unaffected pastoral speaker' (125). Even the simpler style is one Satan may use, apparently. Says Clark: 'Satan knew he was addressing a superior intellectual and moral being. Hence his style is often plain and well adapted to the subtility of his arguments "addressed to a single judge, with whom there is very little room for rhetorical artifices," as Aristotle advised (*Rhet.* III, 12)' (Supp. 8). Barbara Lewalski makes a different suggestion still. Noting that Christ 'uses comparatively terse, pointed sentences to image the precision and rigor of his mind,' she suggests that often enough Satan is, precisely, 'endeavoring to imitate Christ's mode of

---

[82] It is perhaps an ironic affirmation of the complex and contradictory nature of the materials we are considering that a 'parenthesis-filled style' must be one in which 'the sense of the statement is suspended or interrupted' (*Italian Element*, 121); Prince is, of course, speaking of the 'magnificent' style as developed in Italian blank verse epic, not of the pastoral style. He also points out that 'the elaboration of language, the complexity of surface' of the epic style thus conceived 'are only justified if the poem requires a fullness of statement which often amounts to pleonasm. The element of pleonasm is one of the foundations' of *PL* (122–3).

speech.'[83] In commenting on the (relatively scant) use of rhetorical tropes in *PR*, she finds reason to emphasize the point: 'Analysis reveals a very close similarity in Satan's and Christ's use of the schemes, although Christ's speeches have some edge in regard to tightness of organization; the similarity lends further support to the observation that Satan in this poem is endeavoring to sound like Christ's alter ego, to imitate the voice of reason itself' (350). Discussing the use of tropes in *PR* also, John Carey makes a statement which may seem comparable to Baker's analysis (above) of *PR* 1. 326–36: 'More usually the distinction between Christ's rhetoric and Satan's, where any distinction can be made, is that Christ turns to rigorously intellectual and argumentative ends figures which Satan introduces to incite or to move.'[84]

However similar or different the rhetoric of the principals, then, the 'meditative combat' remains a combat. Perhaps no critic has more minutely analyzed the course of the struggle and its effect upon the styles of the combatants than Henry J. Laskowsky in his study of *PR* 3.[85] Laskowsky quotes (25–6) a long passage from John Dennis' 'The Impartial Critick' on 'the Didactick Stile' which is, Laskowsky says, Christ's: it is a style 'fit for instruction,' and must be 'pure, perspicuous, succinct, unaffected, and grave.'[86] Satan's style, on the other hand, is 'a sham style'; 'Satan assumes a variety of voices, all of which reflect a basic instability and lack of integrity.' But 'the authentic gravity of Christ ... constantly puts to rout the "false Gravity" of Satan, whose style is marked by "barbarity, obscurity and affectation"' (26; Spingarn, 3, 158).

As Laskowsky analyzes it, *PR* 3 begins with a series of antitheses in which Christ counters every argument Satan advances (27–8).[87] Christ breaks off the 'artificial debate' by saying:

[83] Barbara Lewalski, *Milton's Brief Epic* (Providence, Rhode Island: Brown University Press, 1966), 345.

[84] John Carey and Alistair Fowler, eds., *The Poems of John Milton* (London: Longmans, Green, 1968), 1073.

[85] Henry J. Laskowsky, 'Miltonic Dialogue and the Principle of Antithesis in Book Three of *Paradise Regained*,' *Thoth* 4 (1963), 24–9.

[86] Dennis' essay may be found in *Critical Essays of the Seventeenth Century*, ed. J. E. Spingarn, 3 vols. (Oxford: Clarendon Press, 1908–9), 3, 148–97. The quoted phrase is on 3, 157.

[87] The debate over glory becomes for Evans (43–4) an actual *metrical* duel, each speaker

> ...what moves thy inquisition?
> Know'st thou not that my rising is thy fall,
> And my promotion will be thy destruction?
> *(PR* 3. 200–2)

This, says Laskowsky, 'is an epigrammatic statement of the essential dramatic and dialectical movement' of *PR.* 'Therefore it is no wonder that Satan cannot endure this exposure of his Socratic pose and immediately launches into a more characteristically histrionic appeal to Christ' (28), the extraordinary lines 204–26. But Satan has lost; he has been 'forced...into the vulgarity of sheer display' (27). He does not, for a long time, give Jesus the opportunity to reply; when at length his display, and his argument, subside, Christ's necessary counterthrust begins —see 3. 387–93—'with that particular kind of epigrammatic terseness which is not simply a repudiation of Satan but also a rejection of his style' (29).

It is clear that Jesus himself would have no wish to use the style of *PR* 3. 204 ff. Presumably what he is rejecting in Satan, on the other hand, is the use of a 'sham style.' In what certain ways do 'barbarity, obscurity and affectation' betray themselves—how are *we* to recognize the false use of a style? By certain excesses (see below, pp. 343, 345) or unwitting lapses, inconsistencies, perhaps; but principally, I should think, the falsity must lie in the inappropriate use of the style—its use by the wrong person, in the wrong circumstances. 'None / But such as are good men can give good things,' says the Lady in *Comus* (701–2); and cf. *PR* 2. 319–22. The gift, the style, is (ordinarily) what it is; in the giver, the speaker, the circumstances, lies the falsehood. This is why, I think, so many readers have found Satan, in *PL* and *PR* alike, genuinely moving at times, Dalila genuinely persuasive in *SA.* Numbers of critics are on record as finding in *PR* 3. 204–26 far more than 'the vulgarity of sheer display.' And they are right. But so is Laskowsky. When Satan achieves a high style in *PR* it is likely to be, or to be imperfectly distinguishable from, an authentic high style. But Satan is Satan.

involving the word 'glory' in increasingly complex metrical compressions which climax in Christ's victorious display of virtuosity in *PR* 3. 134.

As with the high style, so with the lowly, the plain, the humble. Broadbent speaks of the 'flattened' diction he finds in *PL* after the fall (*Graver Subject*, 261); it has been on the whole a critical commonplace that the bareness of style of *PL* 11 and 12 is related to the bareness of style of *PR*. Listen to Oras' eloquent summation:[88]

After largely Elizabethan beginnings Milton created his own idiosyncratic, highly individual epic style, heroic and soaring, rather consistently sustained throughout somewhat more than the first half of *PL*. Then a change set in, gradually developing and persisting, with modifications, through all the rest of Milton's poetic career. A more austere style, less orotund, less reverberant and ornamental, briefer in its rhythms, shorter in the words it used, took Milton's poetry farther and farther away from the Elizabethan, and, more specifically, the Spenserian manner which had strongly influenced his early work. The style of deliberate magnificence was now used only intermittently, when the occasion seemed to demand it, as in Satan's attempts to convert Christ to worldliness in *PR*.

Granted that Oras is speaking here in the tradition which looks upon the development of Milton's style as a continuum, not differentiating the three levels of style and their uses. One might recall Hanford and his discrimination of two styles, the 'barer' style being that of Milton's 'ethical and intellectual intensity'; one might recall Clark and his discovery of the 'lowly' style in appropriate areas of *PL* as of *PR*. And still 'It would be a mistake,' Menzies assures us, speaking of *PR* (with admiration), '...to suppose that the style of the poem is just merely the style' of *PL* 'subdued and toned down to the proper pitch.' The style of *PR* 'is indeed more subdued, but that is not the chief difference. The style itself is a new one' (110). The reader will recall as well Robson's less admiring comment on 'the general effect' in *PR* 2. 473–86 'of flat unincantatory assertion—the effect that makes it impossible to mistake the passage for even one of the more didactic parts' of *PL* (126).

[88] Ants Oras, *Blank Verse and Chronology in Milton*, University of Florida Monographs, Humanities—No. 20 (Gainesville: University of Florida Press, 1966), 38. For further comment on some of the phrasing in this passage, see below, n. 89. Hereafter, *Blank Verse and Chronology* will be referred to in the text as *BV&C*; 'Milton's Blank Verse and the Chronology of his Major Poems' (see above, n. 21) will be referred to as 'MBV.'

I myself should doubt that the voice of Christ in *PR* could by any test of 'metrical movement' (Robson, *loc. cit.*) or style be differentiated always and without error from (say) the voice of Michael in *PL* 11 and 12. But this is not surprising, and it is not meant as approval nor as disapproval of style in either poem. There are not as many levels of style as there are speakers, situations and occasions. We may note in *PR* 1. 326–34 a curious mixture of balance and apparently aimless verbosity, of polish and simplicity; but I should doubt that we would recognize in the passage 'the superficial quality of Satan's pastoral style' (Baker, 125) if we did not know that the speaker was Satan. Again this is not surprising; and again neither we nor Milton are at fault. It is undoubtedly misleading to look on either *PL* or *PR* as a poem in (practically speaking) a single style from which nonetheless extended passages are somehow aberrant. We need not, on the other hand, try to identify a sublime style in *PL*, a separate sublime style in *PR* (in, e.g., 2. 337 ff.), and a false sublime into the bargain. We need not fracture the mean, nor endlessly subdivide the lowly. Style is only style. It is true that overgeneralization obscures distinctions we require for understanding. But there are limits also to the usefulness—not to say the feasibility—of differentiation.

III

Critics of the future will no doubt continue to differ about *PR* and its effectiveness as a poem. But disagreement over the value of a piece of writing is of most interest and of most use where those disagreeing have, and take account of, all real information that is available or that can be developed. The reader may recall Masson's scarcely elaborated observation that 'the difference of kinds' between *PL* and *PR* 'is even signalized in certain differences in the language and versification' (2, 14). To the degree that these differences are real, in what do they consist? How accurately, and in how much detail, have they been described?

Among the most important of the characteristic qualities of Milton's epic verse defined by Havens, and accepted by Hanford as fundamental to both the 'abundant' and the 'relatively plain' styles he distinguishes in the epics, are 'an unusual vocabulary,' the effect of which is 'to give splendor, as well as a certain strangeness or aloofness, to the poem,' 'parenthesis and apposition,' and 'inversion of the natural order of words and phrases' (Havens, 83, 81, 80). Prince too discusses 'the systematic deformation of "logical" word-order' in Italianate blank verse epic, and says that in Milton, this 'is made to serve the poetic effect both in a narrowly technical and in a more general aesthetic manner. By means of the phrasing the sense is suspended and diffused throughout a larger block of words than could otherwise be built into a unity; verses and sentences are thus bound together and brought into animated movement' (*Italian Element*, 122). In fact, then, 'What might appear superficially a mere complexity of ornament...contributes essentially to the structure of the verse...' (*loc. cit.*).

With this statement, intended principally as analysis of *PL*, we may compare John Carey's description of the style of *PR* as 'terser and tenser' than that of *PL*, and 'less involved.' 'The sentence length is abbreviated; the average in *PR* i, for example, is 7 lines...Brevity of sense-unit is a frequent mark of Christ's retorts (e.g. i *421–41* has 8 sentences: the most fragmented set of 21 lines in *PR*). Laconism features prominently in his speeches (e.g. i *335–6*;...i *354*;...i *496*; ii *317–18*, *321–2*;...iv *485–6*)' (1070).

'Undoubtedly Milton has simplified his language and cut down his unit of rhythm' in *PR*, Tillyard says (*Milton*, 315), and Martz compares 'the latinate suspension and compression' of the opening of *PL* with 'the normal movement and scope of educated English speech' in *PR* (226–7). Mrs Lewalski agrees, though with reservations which would seem finally to justify Hanford. 'A single sentence in the brief epic often extends over fifteen lines of verse, but seldom over twenty-five or thirty lines, as is very common' in *PL*, she says (344). While 'the Latinate inversions' in *PR* 'are neither so numerous nor so striking' as those in *PL*, however, 'yet they are used with some frequency...' (346–7). In short, *PR* 'will be found to use the same devices' as *PL*, 'albeit with restraint and with close attention to the decorum dictated by the subject' (344).

What are the implications for verse structure of the use of 'an unusual vocabulary' as against a simplification of language, or 'systematic deformation of "logical" word-order' as against the attempt to reproduce in poetry, more or less, 'the normal movement...of educated English speech'? To the extent that 'an unusual vocabulary' might contain a relatively high proportion of plurisyllables—one thinks of abstract terms derived from Latin or Greek, and the exotic proper names for which *PL*, especially, is famous—whereas a more characteristically English vocabulary might contain a higher proportion of monosyllables, some contrast in the movement of individual lines might be involved. There is a tendency for English monosyllables to be highly consonantal, and in lines composed entirely or principally of monosyllables there may be great variety, subtlety and sometimes difficulty of movement (cf. Prince, *Italian Element*, 143; above, p. 269). This effect is compounded by the fact that in a line composed of monosyllables, all or nearly all may be above the accentual threshold. One may not greatly approve Sidney's

> Rockes, woods, hilles, caves, dales, meads, brookes, answere me
> (*Certain Sonnets* 18. 13; Ringler, 147)

or Fairfax's

> Soft words, low speech, deep sobs, sweet sighs, salt tears
> (*Jerusalem Delivered* 3. 6. 1)
> Fire, aire, sea, earth, man, beast, sprite, place, and time (*ibid.* 14. 45. 4)

but their nature is clear, and what Milton might have learned from them is clear also. A greater number of comparable lines is to be found in *PL* than in *PR*; the most obvious of course is *PL* 2. 621,

> Rocks, Caves, Lakes, Fens, Bogs, Dens, and shades of death.

But *PR* contains remarkable monosyllabic lines:

> And now wild Beasts came forth the woods to roam (1. 502)
> Said'st thou not that to all things I had right? (2. 379)
> Let that come when it comes; all hope is lost (3. 204)
> Hail Son of the most High, heir of both worlds (4. 633)

Indeed, *asprezza* in English, as a quality of the sound of verse, must be achieved largely through the use of collocations of monosyllables to achieve a kind of sophisticated roughness, and monosyllables and polysyllables thus contribute to 'magnificence' in differing ways. In general, a highly polysyllabic verse moves smoothly and relatively swiftly. In it also there is likely to be a lightening and a spacing out of accent:

> *Daphne*, or *Semele, Antiopa* (*PR* 2. 187)
> *Artaxata, Teredon, Tesiphon* (*PR* 3. 292)

The tendencies here illustrated are, however, tendencies only; one must remind oneself that monosyllabic lines may move smoothly, and need not show increase of accent:

> I see thou know'st what is of use to know (*PR* 3. 7)

And lines largely made up of plurisyllables, while they are indeed likely to show a lightening of accent, need not be 'magnificent':

> Thy temperance invincible besides (*PR* 2. 408)

The felt character of individual lines containing (say) one polysyllable may depend somewhat on where the polysyllable falls in the line. Oras does associate the use of polysyllables with 'ornamentation,' with 'epic magnificence' (*BV&C*, 34); he graphs the occurrence of polysyllables, and their position in the line, in *Comus, PL, PR* and *SA* ('MBV,' 152–60). His figures show that a fairly constant percentage of the syllabic space in the poems is occupied by non-monosyllables (42·2% for *Comus*, 43·4% for *PL*, 43·3% for *PR*, 44·5% for *SA*; *BV&C*, 33).[89] Of the fifty-three words of four or more metrical syllables in *Comus*, thirty-eight, or 71·7%, occur in the last half of the line ('MBV,'

---

[89] Oras' remark, quoted above, p. 316, that Milton's later style is 'less orotund' than his earlier epic style, 'shorter in the words it used,' corresponds apparently to his figures for the use of words of four or more metrical syllables. The overall figures for *PL* and *PR*, in terms of the number of polysyllables per thousand lines, would not make the point—80·9 for *PL* 1–6, 83·3 for *PL* 7–12, 82·6 for *PR*. But the figure for *PR* 3—142·2—is markedly the highest in the two poems (see also text following), and very much raises the otherwise relatively low figures for *PR* (*PR* 1: 57·8; *PR* 2: 65·8; *PR* 4: 73·6). The figure for *SA*, however, is again high—101·6—leaving us to conclude that Oras' generalizations correspond less than perfectly with his statistics.

154); Oras finds roughly the same percentage in Marlowe and in such plays of Shakespeare as *Merchant*, *Caesar*, and *Much Ado* ('MBV,' 159). In Milton's later verse Oras notes a strong tendency rather for poly-syllables to occur predominantly in the first half of the line or medially ('MBV,' 156).

Of *PR* specifically he says, 'The number of longer words, not great in the earlier books, increases along with the splendor of the temptations with which Satan is trying to corrupt Christ. It reaches its culmination in Book III, in the vision of the kingdoms of the world and their military glory. In *PR* III. 267–347 [= 346], the passage presenting the central panorama of earthly might, the figures for non-monosyllables are excep-tionally high: for all words longer than one syllable, 478 syllables per hundred lines...' (*BV&C*, 34). The passage is one of the relatively few in *PR* rich in exotic place names, in the use of which, says Saints-bury, Milton 'has no rival in English'; in the specific passage in *PR* of which Oras is speaking, and in a few others, Saintsbury finds 'master-pieces of the kind' (2, 271). In general we are left to conclude, however, that *PR* shows the 'magnificent' use of plurisyllables less than does *PL*.

As for monosyllabic lines, 'rare in *PL*,' according to Carey, these 'are relatively plentiful in *PR*: *PR* i has 28 (an average of 1 in 18 lines), ii has 15, iii, 14 and iv, 34. Satan as the simple rustic has 4 in 23 lines (i *321–45*), the disciples ("Plain fishermen") 2 in 28 (ii *30–57*). Satan also uses them for the sake of insistence (ii *368*, *377*; iv *517*, *518*, *520*), and Christ for his steely parries (iii *396*, *398*, *407*; iv *152*, *153* and, the culmination of the action, iv *561*). When Satan makes his appeal to Christ's compassion, the monosyllabic lines cluster more thickly than anywhere else in the poem (iii *204*, *206*, *209*, *220*, *223*, *224*)' (1070). Carey's observations make it clear that monosyllabic lines have a wide range of tones and uses in *PR*; the reader must decide for himself whether the movement of the lines cited, and of others he may find for himself, conduces to simplicity of style or to difficulty, *asprezza*, and thus to a kind of magnificence.

Meaningful generalization about the effect on verse form of the use of 'an unusual vocabulary' is complicated further by the fact that words of any length may be unusual, and that ordinary words may be used in unusual ways. Thus in *PR* 2. 348–9,

> Alas how simple, to these Cates compar'd,
> Was that crude Apple that diverted *Eve*!

'diverted' is rich and surprising not in itself, but in its evocation of its literal, etymological meaning ('turned aside'), and in its suggestion of a kind of levity in Eve; 'crude,' which in one sense repeats 'simple,' in another makes us think of the undigested and the indigestible—and leads us to the wry reflection that neither Eve nor her descendants have found the Apple assimilable. The monosyllable 'Cates,' on the other hand, though used simply, is and was in less common use than any of the longer words in the passage. The effect of the lines is amazingly complex; but if the verse (with the minor inversion, the assonance between 'Alas' and 'Apple,' the triple alliteration on [k], the more elaborate '*compar'd*'–'*crude*' figuration, and the odd echo resulting from the occurrence of -*ple* as the fifth syllable of both lines) is also complex, its complexity is not a product of the 'unusual' qualities of the diction, though the two complexities support one another to make superb verse. Only the most limited and provisory generalizations about the effect on versification of the use of 'an unusual vocabulary' are, then, possible.

Of the practical effect on verse of 'systematic deformation of "logical" word-order,' 'latinate suspension and compression,' as against the attempt to achieve in verse 'the normal movement...of educated English speech,' it would seem that more could be said. Here too, however, we shall find that opposing principles may at times work locally in somewhat the same way, and that a single principle, consistently applied, may have effects surprisingly various. We shall find also that existing criticism, developed information we should have thought relevant to our study, is of less help than we might have supposed it would be.

It is best to begin by reminding ourselves that the *line* is metrically basic to verse. We have seen that there is reason to believe the English accentual-syllabic line to be made up of duple measures, two-syllable 'feet'; we have seen that to Prince the *effect* of the line is best accounted for by thinking of it as divided into two hemistichs (above, p. 372). Still we are speaking of the make-up of the *line*, of what gives the *line* its structural character. Critics like Havens, who feels that Milton maintained, as 'the fundamental feature of his prosody, the substitution of the free musical paragraph for the line as the unit of verse' (55), are simply phrasing inappropriately an entirely proper perception of those characteristics of Milton's epic verse—especially the verse of *PL*—of which Prince is speaking when he discusses the suspension and diffusion of sense in that verse 'throughout a larger block of words than could otherwise be built into a unity' (above, p. 318).

A verse paragraph could be said to serve as a *prosodic* unit, however, only if it were repeated, over and over, at precisely the same length—and probably then only if the lines that composed it did not themselves show a constantly repeated prosodic pattern: it would be metrically unitary only, in short, if it were a kind of unrhymed stanza. But a sentence shorter than a line does not become a prosodic unit; neither, then, does a sentence longer than a line. A syntactical unit is not a prosodic unit—though the two may be made to coincide. Havens intends to speak, in all probability, only of versification (general verse effect), not of prosody (the operation in verse of strict laws of meter). But we must have language to differentiate the two meanings.

The conception of the line as the prosodic unit of blank verse does not require the isolation of every line by grammatical pause; equally, it does not require the isolation and identification of the line by 'metrical' pause, theoretical or actually imposed. Arguing against T. H. Banks' belief 'that Milton thought in terms of verse paragraphs rather than single lines,'[90] John S. Diekhoff concludes 'that Milton considered the line as a more or less isolated unit of verse to be indicated as such by some sort of breath pause or lingering at the end.'[91] Sprott disagrees.

[90] Theodore H. Banks, Jr., 'Miltonic Rhythm: a Study of the Relation of the Full Stops to the Rhythm of *Paradise Lost*,' *PMLA* 42 (1927), 140–5, **144**.
[91] John S. Diekhoff, 'Terminal Pause in Milton's Verse,' *SP* 32 (1935), 235–9, **235**.

He thinks, however, that Milton

almost certainly indicated the ends of the lines by an inflexion of voice which would preserve their cadences...Probably too he indicated by vocal cadences the position of the breaks or *caesurae* within the lines. The cadences are determined partly by logical or rhetorical and partly by musical or metrical considerations; and ideally these factors co-operate. In practice, the rhetorical cadence or its break is much easier to recognize than the metrical. I think that when reading seventeenth-century verse we should endeavour to balance the half-lines against one another in rhythmical proportion, indicating the break by cadence (122–3).

This view of the 'balancing of half-lines against one another' is independent of Prince's view. Sprott implies that in lines showing more than a single break, one may be stronger than the other(s), and this may be the 'metrical' break, dividing the line into two parts; equally, however, metrical breaks may exist independent of sense pause. Recognizing 'the difficulty of preserving uniformity of interpretation,' however, Sprott, when he proceeds to statistical analysis, tabulates only rhetorical or grammatical pause.

The relationship between grammar and the prosodic unit, the line, central (one would suppose) to the effect of virtually all verse, is more important than any other single consideration to our sense of the character of blank verse. At one extreme of style, a poet will work with syntactical units, major and minor, long and short, singly and in combination, in such a way as to produce a flow of verse in which line ends and sense boundaries of varying degrees of strength coincide; at the other extreme he will enjamb, or break across the ends of lines, phrases too brief, their elements too strongly dependent on one another, to be divided comfortably. The effect of one kind of management is to produce lines of verse that have, in varying degrees, syntactical as well as metrical identity; the effect of the other is to put strain on meter and syntax by setting them at odds, to blur the syntactical identity of the line, and to postpone that moment when syntax and form will resolve together.

Note, however, that a very difficult enjambment may be followed by almost immediate resolution, while an easy coordination of symmetrically designed phrases may postpone the completion of a fairly naturally ordered sentence for many lines. 'The normal movement...of educated English speech'—or, alternatively, 'the repetitive, pleonastic, parenthesis-filled style of the pastoral' (Baker, 125)—may produce sense units, sense periods, brief or comparatively long. Inversions and suspensions may but need not lengthen the period of utterance, may but need not make strange the style; interruptions and inversions of certain kinds are familiar to us at all levels of speech. It is easy enough in reading to differentiate between, e.g., *PR* 2. 1–12, in which 'the new-baptiz'd,' line 1, is the subject of a verb which does not appear until line 11, and *PR* 2. 42–3,

God of *Israel*,
Send thy Messiah forth, the time is come;

but the difference *is* specifically syntactical. It is reflected in versification only imperfectly, and in ambiguous ways.

Five lines of the twelve of which the long passage is made up are, to be sure, enjambed:

> Mean while the new-baptiz'd, who yet remain'd
> At *Jordan* with the Baptist, and had seen
> Him whom they heard so late expresly call'd
> Jesus Messiah Son of God declar'd,
> And on that high Authority had believ'd,
> And with him talkt, and with him lodg'd, I mean
> *Andrew* and *Simon*, famous after known
> With others though in Holy Writ not nam'd,
> Now missing him thir joy so lately found,
> So lately found, and so abruptly gone,
> Began to doubt, and doubted many days,
> And as the days increas'd, increas'd thir doubt...

Enjambment permits a run of twenty-three syllables without pause in lines 2–4, a run of fifteen in lines 7–8. But parenthesis and qualification are used in familiar ways to draw out the total utterance, and parenthesis —interruption—involves pause: see, e.g., lines 6–7 and 10 above. In theory, enjambment and pause are opposite in effect; in practice we find both necessarily involved in the production of the verse paragraph, as both may be involved in the writing of suites of lines that do not give and are not intended to give the effect of the verse paragraph:

> But where delays he now? some great intent
> Conceals him: when twelve years he scarce had seen,
> I lost him, but so found, as well I saw
> He could not lose himself; but went about
> His Father's business; what he meant I mus'd,
> Since understand; much more his absence now
> Thus long to some great purpose he obscures.
>
> (*PR* 2. 95–101)

This is reverie, only slightly elevated in tone, and the sense units of which it is composed (all but the last) are brief, at times fragmentary. None the less four of the seven lines—a higher proportion than in *PR* 2. 1–12—are enjambed. Those that are not, let us note finally, do not impress us as whole single lines, since they must devote themselves in part at least to the completion of sense structures begun in earlier enjambed lines. Clearly pause and enjambment are of great importance to the movement and the structure of the heroic line; clearly they are evidences as well, the best signs we have of the relationship between syntax and meter. But as signs they are not easily read, and simple tabulations, mere records of occurrence, are not likely to tell us much.

Or perhaps it would be more accurate to say that they are not likely to tell us everything we should like to know, and we must learn not to expect from them what they cannot supply. Statistics on pause and enjambment in *PL* and *PR* exist; they give us an average sense, an overall sense, of one important element in the versification of the metrical unit, the line. But in verse like that of Milton's epics, in which the line is not ordinarily the *rhythmic* unit, we have an additional interest in the versification of structures larger than the line, up to and including the verse paragraph: this is, in effect, all that Havens and Banks are saying. And simple statistics—especially statistics for whole poems, or long subdivisions of poems—cannot tell us how pause and enjambment work in the verse paragraph, nor in adjacent lines nor groups of lines.

In verse in which the line is not the rhythmic unit, what is? a phrase or clause unbroken by punctuation? or a syntactical progression unbroken by *major* punctuation (semi-colon, or colon, or period)? or a full sentence only? If it is the first, certainly no figures at present available will tell us how frequently, in *PL* and *PR*, we may encounter runs unbroken by pause of (say) eleven to fifteen syllables, or sixteen to twenty syllables, or more. If it is the second, a simple count of strong pauses in *PL* and *PR*, book by book, will no doubt tell us something; but in long books especially, the averaging effect of statistics will tend to conceal even radical shifts, and to obliterate local distinctions we should think, in close analysis, characteristic and important. Oras tells us that in every hundred lines of *PL* there are 123·4 pauses marked by punctuation of all sorts; in every hundred lines of *PR* there are 126 pauses (*BV&C*, 59). The difference does not seem remarkable. The figure for strong pauses, marked by 'heavy punctuation marks,' is even less revealing: it is 34·5 per hundred lines for both poems (*BV&C*, 61. Carried to another place, the figures differentiate slightly—34·46/100 for *PL*, 34·54/100 for *PR*). If we break the figures for *PL* down, as Oras often does, to figures for the first six books and for the last six, we get 117·7:129 to *PR*'s 126 for all pauses, 33·89:35·06 to *PR*'s 34·54 for strong pauses. In both sets of figures *PL* 7-12 shows a higher incidence of pause than does *PR*. There are no figures for full stops only. Whatever it is—principally, no doubt, the management of syntax—that makes Oras (and others) feel that *PR* is 'briefer in its rhythms' than *PL* as a whole or even than *PL* 1-6 (*BV&C*, 38), obviously Oras' figures do not reveal it very clearly. It is time to turn from this inquiry and ask what the available statistics on pause and enjambment in *PL* and (particularly) *PR* can tell us—however much we may regret what they cannot.

Sprott's Chapter IX (112–28), entitled '"Paragraph Fingering" and the Break,' begins with a historical study of the caesura in English verse, gives examples (all from *PL*) of the use of pause in Milton's blank verse line, and concludes with tables for (1) the positions of breaks, and (2) the frequency of breaks, in the lines of *Comus*, *PL*, *PR* and *SA*. Exasperatingly, Sprott studies *PL* in the ten-book arrangement of the first edition. His figures are 'expressed as percentages of the total numbers of lines in the books or works' (126). Overall figures for positions of breaks in *PL* and *PR* thus expressed (*loc. cit.*) are as follows:

After syllable	1	2	3	4	5	6	7	8	9	10
PL	0·9	7·5	8·3	[1]8·8	8·3	20·6	9·2	7·6	0·8	41·9
PR	0·5	4·3	7·7	14·1	9·6	19·4	7·8	5·8	0·5	54·3

What is interesting here is (*a*) the high percentage of pauses, in both poems, after the 6th and, to a slightly lesser degree, the 4th syllable; Milton's use of pause is not in general, then, so unusual as some instances of it may have led us to suppose. I find interesting also (*b*) the fact that the figures for 'extreme pauses' (pauses after the first, 2nd, 3rd, 7th, 8th and 9th syllables) are invariably higher in *PL* than in *PR*; and (*c*) the considerably higher proportion of end-stopped lines in *PR* than in *PL*. Enid Hamer takes 'the enormous increase of endstopping' as one of the 'technical symptoms' of the decline 'in the power of sustained articulation' that *PR* shows from the 'mastery' of *PL*.[92] The 'increase' for *SA* is higher still; the figure Sprott gives for that poem is 57·3%. Not unexpectedly, the figure for *Comus* is highest of all—60·9% (126).

Sprott's figures for overall frequency of breaks in the four poems are as follows (127):

Number of breaks per line...	0	1	2	3	4	5	6	7
Comus	18·1	58·1	20·6	2·9	0·3	—	—	—
PL	13·5	57·2	25·0	3·4	0·7	0·1	0·02	0·03
PR	13·3	54·1	26·9	4·2	1·1	—	—	—
SA	15·3	52·4	26·0	5·0	0·9	0·2	—	—

Here what is most worth remarking, perhaps, is that both *Comus* and *SA* contain a distinctly higher proportion of lines without pause than do *PL* and *PR* (though punctuation in *Comus* is not fully comparable to

---

[92] Enid Hamer, *The Metres of English Poetry*, 4th ed. (London: Methuen, 1951), 102. First published, 1930.

punctuation in the later poems), and that while *PL* has lines that contain six and seven pauses, as the other poems do not, there is a higher percentage of lines containing two or more pauses in *PR* (32·2)—as in *SA*—than in *PL* (29·25). This may have a little to do with the impression of the critics that the 'unit of rhythm' in *PR* is briefer than that in *PL*. Commenting on the use of pause in *PR*, Blondel points out that multiple pauses slow the movement of the verse in, e.g., 1. 304 and 3. 115, lend it an air of nonchalance elsewhere, and so on. 'Au total, la fréquence des pauses ne traduit pas l'indifférence audacieuse du poète à l'égard d'une mesure trop régulière, mais elle rend perceptibles les mouvements de la pensée et les gestes' (114). Earlier (101–2) Blondel has remarked that inversions and disruptions of syntax enter the poem effectively with the commencement of the 'débat' between Christ and Satan; rather than showing a foreign use of English, however, the disruptions are, he says, close to those of the spoken language.

I have quoted from Oras several times without indicating the dimensions or the purposes of his studies; further information ought now to be supplied. 'Milton's Blank Verse and the Chronology of the Major Poems' (1953) is an elaborate statistical study of 'certain basic features of rhythm' in Milton's blank verse which, in Oras' opinion, 'would appear to be too deep-seated to have been radically affected' by the poet's 'feeling for "decorum"' ('MBV,' 129). In addition to the use and placement in the line of polysyllables, already discussed, the use of pauses, medial and terminal, marked by punctuation stronger than a comma, and the placement of pauses within the line, Oras considers (1) feminine endings, (2) recession of accent, (3) the use of the *-ed* suffix as a syllable in words (such as 'abhorrèd') in which it would normally be asyllabic, and (4) pyrrhic verse endings, as in (*a*) *Comus* 221 ('By a strong siding champion Con|sci-ence') and (*b*) *PR* 1. 7 ('And *Eden* rais'd in the wast Wil|derness'). The statistics Oras has gathered seem to him to fall into patterns which confirm the accepted chronology of *PL*, *PR* and *SA*. In brief, 'There is as a rule in the first half of *PL* a contrast with *Comus*—often very sharp...Most of the...tendencies contrasting with *Comus*...subside then in the second half of the epic and, usually even more distinctly, in *PR* and *SA*' ('MBV,' 149–50). There is, thus, in general, a movement from *PL* 7 or 8 on, through *PR* and *SA*, back toward *Comus*.

In a reply to Oras published in 1961, John Shawcross observes that Oras first arranged his statistics in the order dictated by the traditionally accepted chronology, then interpreted what he found as falling into a meaningful pattern. Using Oras' categories, the actual statistics somewhat revised by his own calculations, and at times re-combined or re-evaluated, Shawcross plots the figures for the last three poems as they rise or fall from the figures for *Comus*—and achieves a new chronology, *Comus*: *SA*: *PR*: *PL*. 'Rather we discover for the final form of these works a statistical ordering corroborating the investigations of Parker and Gilbert: *SA*; *PR* II, IV, III; *PL* VIII, IX, X; I, III, XII, XI; *PR* I; *PL* V, VII; IV, II, VI. The position of *PR* I does not probably represent an absolute place in the order of composition; it is more likely a relative order of the final completed text.'[93] Shawcross goes on to argue that most of *PR* was written early, as a drama, but that the poem was revised late, and appropriate additions made, to put it into epic form.

The controversy was closed (not decided) with the publication by Oras in 1966 of a monograph revising and supplementing his earlier study and reiterating its claims. That certain elements in Milton's versification—in general, (2), (3) and (4a) above—were Elizabethan in origin, and appear early in Milton, less and less frequently in his verse thereafter, Oras demonstrates, it seems to me, convincingly. But a great part of his argument lies elsewhere, and I find it very much less convincing. (This is not, of course, to say that I find Shawcross' argument more convincing.) For one thing, that Milton's use of pause was not 'radically affected' by his 'feeling for "decorum"' seems to me altogether unlikely; the frequency, the strength and the placing of pause have crucially important roles to play in the development of a style appropriate to the treatment of a given subject matter in a given form. The

[93] John T. Shawcross, 'The Chronology of Milton's Major Poems,' *PMLA* 76 (1961), 345–58, 352.

use of the feminine ending, as Oras in part admits, is comparable. For another thing, I cannot help feeling that both Oras and Shawcross have neglected the study of certain 'basic features of rhythm' that might also have repaid investigation. Milton's use of the accentual trochee initially, after a medial pause, and without preceding pause in the combinations x′′x, xx′x, ′x′x and ′′′x might be studied; the *kinds* of contraction and metrical compression Milton uses, as they increase or decrease, and as they relate to or differ from the kinds in use by his predecessors and contemporaries, might tell us something very interesting. But these are studies far larger than anyone has so far undertaken; and it could not be predicted that they would tell us anything certain about chronology. Statistics relating to verse practice are very difficult to interpret wisely. The careful accumulation and weighing of *instances*, on the other hand, must always be of value.

Whatever the validity of their claims for the meaning of their figures, Oras and Shawcross have analyzed the occurrence of pause in *Comus*, *PL*, *PR* and *SA* in overwhelming detail. There is not space here even for the briefest characterization of the charts, tables and lists to be found in the three studies; the interested reader will in any event wish to examine the figures tabulated, and decide for himself on their usefulness and bearing. Unfortunately, Sprott on the one hand and Oras and Shawcross on the other follow different principles in reducing their figures to ratios and percentages, so that their findings can seldom be compared. Oras (*BV&C*, 59) gives absolute figures for the incidence of pause after the various syllables of the line, for example, but when he converts these figures into percentages he gives us, not the percentage of lines in the total work which show pause after a given syllable, but the percentage of all the (internal) pauses in the poem which fall after each syllable, from 1 to 9:

After syllable		1	2	3	4	5	6	7	8	9
PL	abs.	88	796	869	1987	900	2178	942	802	78
	%	1·0	9·2	10·1	23·0	10·4	25·2	10·9	9·3	0·9
PR	abs.	10	99	153	297	205	398	165	126	12
	%	0·7	6·8	10·4	20·2	14·0	27·2	11·3	8·6	0·8

To divide Oras' absolute figures by the number of lines in the appropriate poem would convert those figures into percentages reckoned as Sprott reckons them; and one could then check the two sets of figures for agreement. If they did not agree, of course there would be no way of knowing which figures were the more nearly correct.

According to Oras' tabulations, *PR* 3 has altogether more strong pauses per thousand lines—379·2—than any other book in either *PL* or *PR* ('MBV,' 134); it also has the highest proportion of strong feminine pauses (that is, pauses following odd-numbered syllables) in the two poems ('MBV,' 148). Finally, *PR* 3 has a markedly higher proportion of extreme internal pauses than any other book of *PR*, and any book of *PL* but 7, with the figure for *PL* 8 just under that for *PR* 3. The ratio Oras gives for *PR* 3 is 38·6e:61·4m. In *PR* 4, however, the ratio decreases to 25·3e:74·7m. Oras says, 'This exceptional drop seems to be connected with the unusually calm, controlled tone of most of *PR* IV' ('MBV,' 141).[94] He adds in a footnote, 'The speeches in Book IV have only about half as many extreme pauses per 100 lines as those of Book III, where the debate between Christ and the Tempter is at its most animated, and considerably fewer than those of Books I and II. Except in the speeches few extreme pauses are used in any part of *PR*' ('MBV,' 141–2 n.). Seventy-five per cent of all extreme strong pauses in *PR*, says Oras, are used in run-on contexts; the figure for *PL* 1–6 is 79·4%, for *PL* 7–12, 78·2%, for *SA*, 62%, for *Comus*, 52·9% ('MBV,' 143 n.).

Of the 725 strong pauses Oras finds in *PR* ('MBV,' 134), 248, or 34·7%, are internal (one-third feminine, two-thirds masculine; 'MBV,' 148), while 467, or 65·3%, are terminal ('MBV,' 134). These compare with identical ratios of 30·5%:69·5% in *Comus* and *SA*; the corresponding ratios in *PL* 1–6 are 52·4%:47·6%, in *PL* 7–12, 48·1%:51·9%, in *PL* overall, 50·3%:49·7% (*loc. cit.*). The difference between the figures for *PL* and those for the other poems would seem significant. The

---

[94] *PR* 4 is also the only book of the poem in which strong pauses after the 4th syllable outnumber those after the 6th; the number (and percentage) of strong pauses after the 5th syllable in *PR* 4 are the highest in the poem as well (*loc. cit.*). And of *PL*, *PR* and *SA*, only in *PR* 4 is the figure for the occurrence of polysyllables in the last half of the line as high even as 40·4%; the next highest figure is the 30·8% of *PL* 10. See above, pp. 320-1.

relatively low use of strong internal pause in *PR* suggests to Oras 'an easing of that complex tension between syntax and meter characteristic of so much of *PL*: the strong syntactical pauses coincide more and more frequently with the expected rest at the end of the line. Milton's verse grows quieter, its flow becomes more even, more "classical"' ('MBV,' 137).

In Oras' 1966 monograph the figure given (*BV&C*, 61) for strong terminal pauses in *PR* remains 467 (Shawcross, 357, lists 475); the figure for all lines showing end-of-line punctuation Oras gives (*BV&C*, 59) as 1144. A comparison of these figures with the 1966 figures for *PL* shows 58·5% of the lines of the long epic as enjambed, only 44·7% of the lines of *PR* (*loc. cit.*). Shawcross' lists of run-on lines in *PR* (357–8) yield a figure of 44·6%. Sprott's statistics (126) would be 58·1% for *PL*, 45·7% for *PR*. One could not hope for much closer agreement.

Simple enjambment, 'the sense...drawn out from one Verse into another' merely, would not, presumably, play a sufficient part in bringing 'true musical delight'; a carefully ordered *variety* in the disposition of internal pause must and does, in *PR* as in *PL*, combine with the 'sense drawn out' to produce a kind of running counterpoint between the constant length of the metrical unit and the changing length of the phrase, the clause, the sentence. But we must not suppose that Milton's purposes in using enjambment—at an unusually high rate, even in *PR*—are fully accounted for in the wording of the brief note prefixed to *PL*. For one thing, enjambment may be looked on as alternative to rhyme in other ways than as it contributes to 'musical delight.' Rhyme in extended verse narrative, according to Trissino, 'would tend to check the flow of the verse by breaking it up into minor fragments (couplets, tercets, quatrains, or octaves) and would disrupt the continuity of matter, sense, and construction.'[95] That enjambment may be used as a major instrument of 'the continuity of matter' is obvious. At the same time, and to some degree paradoxically, Prince notes that 'the sense variously drawn out' serves verse that has abandoned rhyme as a

[95] John M. Steadman, 'Verse Without Rime: Sixteenth-Century Italian Defences of *Versi Sciolti*,' *Italica* 41 (1964), 384–402, 387.

substitute 'means of enforcing a continuity of pattern, inducing a continuity of expectation in the reader' (*Italian Element*, 112).

Broadbent takes 'the sense variously drawn out' to refer 'not to enjambement only but also to the iterative schemes of rhetoric' ('Milton's Rhetoric,' 242). He discusses, and illustrates in detail, Milton's use of the schemes to help give form to his unrhymed verse. It is *PL*, he says, 'that provides the most and clearest examples of the chief rhetorical devices—not only line-for-line but qualitatively: schemes, and tropes other than those we normally acknowledge to be "images," show up all the more when rhyme is absent, when images are few, and when the diction tends to be abstract. We should therefore expect a great deal of rhetoric' in *PR*, 'but...it is proportionately less' than in *PL*; 'if there were more, it would be obtrusive. It stands out most clearly in the third and fourth books...' (228). Broadbent quotes, and analyzes in terms of the relation between rhetoric and verse, *PR* 3. 44–53, 171–2, 175–6, and 4. 560–81 (228–9), and 1. 377–405 (235). He finds *PR* 'most like' *PL* 'in its rhetoric when Satan is tempting' (229).

'Though Broadbent's observation that the iterative schemes are less numerous' in *PR* than in *PL* 'is no doubt quantitatively true,' Barbara Lewalski says,

yet especially in the dialogue portions of the brief epic they occur very frequently and seem to serve an even more significant function than in the long epic. Through structural balance and sound repetitions they elevate and stiffen the language, providing the impression of a patterned verbal duel analogous to a single combat. Yet at the same time, paradoxically, they contribute to the impression of spontaneous speech, of a progressive and dramatic working out of meanings and understandings as Christ and Satan talk. More paradoxical still, those speeches which most critics designate as containing the greatest emotional realism and sincerity are among those contrived with the greatest rhetorical art (348).

In the following pages (349–55) Mrs Lewalski identifies and describes the principal rhetorical schemes of which Milton makes use in *PR*; she also quotes, and calls attention to the principal iterative patterns in, *PR* 1. 377–401, 1. 407–33, 3. 203–24, 4. 286–92, and 4. 516–81.

In his pp. 1073–4 Carey identifies and at times briefly discusses the rhetorical structuring of a great many passages in *PR*, among them 1. 1–7, 2. 9–12, 3. 44–107, 3. 109–20, 4. 163–9, 4. 182–7, 4. 286–92 and 4. 565–71.

The iterative schemes of rhetoric may, of course, be used to set off and unify individual lines:

> For where no hope is left, is left no fear (*PR* 3. 206)
>
> Light from above, from the fountain of light (*PR* 4. 289)

The customary use of the schemes, however, is to provide multilinear orders, emergent patterns—often overlapping patterns—which span varying numbers of lines within a larger syntactical structure, and thus serve as intermediate forms between the line and the verse paragraph. Critics have found other such intermediate forms. Thomas Wheeler notes that in both *PL* and *PR* numbers of 'blank verse couplets' are to be found, 'two-line units, grammatically independent and strongly linked by their sense and their construction.'[96] He instances (365–6) *PR* 1. 355–6, 2. 381–2, 3. 47–8 and 52–3, and 4. 291–2 and 309–12. But 'Milton's disdain for rhyme carries over to the couplets in his epics. They are usually put in the mouth of a character that Milton is officially "against." Temptation and false logic are likely to be voiced in couplets ...Belial's advice' in *PR* 2. 153–4 '... combines both temptation and fallacy' (367). Still, 'There is no rule here, merely a tendency. But we know so little about Milton's verse and so much about his intellectual development...that we need to spend some time listening to his voice' (*loc. cit.*).

When James Whaler is listening to Milton's voice he makes discoveries about the structure of the verse that are genuinely illuminating. Like many another critic, Whaler begins with the perception that while the five-beat line is the metrical unit, or base, or 'norm' in blank verse, a high rate of enjambment such as that in *PL* and *PR* 'is liable to obscure in the listener's mind—even obliterate—that norm' (15). And yet it

[96] Thomas Wheeler, 'Milton's Blank Verse Couplets,' *JEGP* 66 (1967), 359–68, 361.

must be preserved; to lose one's sense of the meter, in metrical verse, is to forfeit the ability to read the verse in any way other than as prose. How, in his construction of verse paragraphs long or short, does Milton keep us from losing our basic relationship to the meter?

In the first place, says Whaler, he does so by checking the flow of his verse, ceasing to enjamb, and writing 'integral lines' as often as we require them to preserve our orientation. Still, 'Less than a third of the lines of *PL* and less than half the lines of *PR* are integral' (16). An end-stopped line composed of a fragment which completes the syntax of the previous enjambed line, plus a short, complete phrase or clause, is presumably not an integral line; thus the discrepancy between Whaler's figures and those for enjambment versus end-stopping generally in Sprott, Oras, etc. Whaler distinguishes between slow-paced and quick-paced integral lines; both are direct safeguards of the metrical norm, and the quick-paced lines 'furnish an indispensable lyric touch' (17). Whaler is particularly interested in quick-paced lines; in his Appendix I (169–80) he analyzes the rhythmic patterns they may display (taking account of failure of stress, pause, inversion, etc.) and proceeds to list all the quick-paced integral lines in *PL* and *PR*, tabulated according to pattern. 'Compared with all other important writers of blank verse, Milton is frugal in his indulgence in quick-paced lines. Naturally: his paramount concern is with paragraph-structure' (180). Over 25% of Marlowe's and Shakespeare's blank verse lines, Whaler thinks, would be quick-paced integral lines. 'But in *PL* only 8 per cent, and in *PR* 12 per cent, of the lines are quick-paced' (*loc. cit.*).

Whaler turns back, then, to enjambment, and to the sense overlaps which contrast with the structure of the line. 'For anyone in the least acquainted with polyphonic music,' Whaler says, 'Milton's method of free overlapping compels comparison with the rhythmic management of voices in madrigal, motet, and anthem' (25).[97] The analogy ultimately carries Whaler farther than I for one find myself able to follow, but taken simply it seems apt and interesting enough. Verse is not, of course,

[97] Cf. Donald Ramsay Roberts, 'The Music of Milton,' *PQ* 26 (1947), 328–44, 338: 'The madrigal and kindred contrapuntal musical forms offer the closest analogue, and probably the prototype, of the Miltonic principle of continuous rhythmic movement.'

literally capable of carrying more than one voice at a time; but the notion that the same words may simultaneously form part of more than one recognizable structure seems undeniable. The multilinear structures Whaler goes on first to identify he finds in 'paragraphs...where enjambement is very active, involving at least half the lines'; in such paragraphs, we are told, Milton often keeps 'the 5-beat norm alive in the listener's consciousness' (27) by 'cross-rhythmic construction'— that is, by the construction of syntactical sequences of simple multiples of five beats which begin and end within lines, at once disguising the line unit and producing an arithmetic reminder of it. Whaler distinguishes two types of cross-rhythmic construction. In the first, T-construction, an integral line is led up to and followed by parts of lines totalling ten (or nine, or eleven) syllables, and containing five beats:

> Soon had his crew
> Op'nd into the Hill a spacious wound
> And dig'd out ribs of Gold.
> (*PL* 1. 688–90; Whaler, 29)

> ...for now the *Parthian* King
> In *Ctesiphon* hath gathered all his Host
> Against the *Scythian*...
> (*PR* 3. 299–301; cited, Whaler, 209)

In the slightly more complicated E-construction the central line is not integral, but contains a marked pause which falls in such a way as to divide unequally the twenty syllables of which the sequence is constructed; the result is that the syntax at first departs from, and then returns to, a pattern which underscores the line pattern:

> Who seekes
> To lessen thee, against his purpose serves
> To manifest the more thy might...
> (*PL* 7. 613–15; Whaler, 31)

> ...themselves were they
> Who wrought their own captivity, fell off
> From God to worship Calves...
> (*PR* 3. 414–16; cited, Whaler, 209)

Either kind of cross-rhythmic construction may be augmented, expanded, in various ways; Whaler gives examples of 'E expanded with intercalated T' (33), the 'E-chain' (34–7), etc. The more complex structures serve rather to compose the verse-paragraph 'as a finished contrapuntal piece' than to 'recall the metric norm' (37). Says Whaler, '*A paragraph textured with cross-rhythmic construction has, and is felt to have, a far different weave and movement from one in which such construction is scant or absent*' (160–1). A principal way in which 'we can distinguish the rhythmic style of PR from that of PL' is thus that 'cross-rhythmic construction is far less active in PR' (161); 42% of *PL* is involved in T- or E-construction, as against only 17% of *PR* (50). We may note as sample evidence of these proportions that in his Appendix II (181–210) Whaler lists the cross-rhythmic constructions he finds in *PL* 6, *PL* 10, and *PR* 3; even without explanatory notes the listing requires over eight pages for *PL* 6, twelve to thirteen for *PL* 10, only one (209) for *PR* 3.

PL 7. 613–15, quoted above, is composed of an ascending series of 2 / 4, 6 / 8 syllables; Whaler, counting 'beats,' represents such a series as $<^{1-2}_{3-4}>$, and says that whenever it occurs in Milton, 'whether in simple, expanded, or chain form, the context is one that stresses or implies an affirmative idea of perfection, absolute completeness, order, truth, harmony, power, or some virtue' (53). Whenever the alternative descending series $<^{4-3}_{2-1}>$ occurs, 'whether in simple, expanded, or chain form, the context is one that stresses or implies an idea of negation, imperfection, disorder, ruin, impotence, ignorance, hate, malice, abasement, or deadly sin' (56). He gives many illustrations for both series. Among those for the descending series he quotes *PR* 4. 622–4,

> ...yet not thy last and deadliest wound
> By this repulse receiv'd, and hold'st in Hell
> No triumph...;

it expresses, he says, 'Satan's ultimate destruction' (*loc. cit.*).

The chapter in which these observations occur is entitled 'Intimations of Numerical Symbol.' The intimations rapidly become declarations, grand affirmations, the symbolic structures 'discovered' and analyzed become more and more complex, at last bewilderingly complex, and 'Milton's Muse,' as Gunnar Qvarnström says, 'is metamorphosed into a higher mathematician.'[98] Again it seems, however, that *PR* does not lend itself to mathematical analysis as *PL* does; Whaler brings only *PR* 4. 551–9 (85–8) and *PR* 4. 486–98 (127–8) to the blackboard for complex symbolic demonstration. The phrase 'apt Numbers,' meanwhile, applies at least to the lesser mathematics of the verse proportions Whaler discusses in his first two chapters. And whatever scholars may ultimately decide about the relationship between Pythagorean number symbolism and the paragraphing of Milton's epic verse, Whaler will have contributed not insignificantly to our understanding of 'the sense variously drawn out' as a simple formal principle.

'What readers commonly fail to grasp,' says Beum, 'is that Milton's high incidence of enjambment is a tremendous paradox.' Though 'it is an inevitable concomitant of the long, complex periods Milton builds to achieve a texture of formality and elevation,' yet 'it does tend to create a feeling of what is lifelike, natural, and spontaneous' (356). The observation is particularly interesting as we contemplate the often reiterated fact that *PR* shows markedly less enjambment than *PL*. It is correspondingly interesting how often sympathetic critics of the shorter poem insist, without pejorative intent, that it is *not* lifelike. Tillyard, for example, comparing *PR* in some respects to the second book of the *Faerie Queene* and even to the earlier moralities, speaks of the 'allegorical twilight' of *PR*, and says eloquently,

---

[98] Gunnar Qvarnström, *The Enchanted Palace* (Stockholm: Almqvist & Wiksell, 1967), 143. It should be noted that Qvarnström is a firm believer in number symbolism; *The Enchanted Palace* is an analysis of *PL* in those terms. Qvarnström feels only that Whaler takes his analysis too far. Qvarnström himself points out (114) that there is just one 33-line speech in *PL* (9. 343–75) and one in *PR* (4. 451–83). 'It has been argued that 33 is the number of sorrow since it is the sum of the numbers constituted by the letters in the name of Abel (the Hebrew letters are numbers as well), and Abel means sorrow. It is...generally accepted...' also 'that Jesus was crucified when he was 33 years old, which reinforces the connection...The two 33-line speeches have a similar message. The Fall, against the hazards of which Adam warns Eve, will necessitate the crucifixion, against the pains of which Satan warns Jesus.'

The unearthly dialogue between Reason on the one hand and Passion in very subtle and sophisticated form on the other in the enchanted wilderness may indeed suggest some dramatised contest of virtues and vices for the possession of the human soul. But such dialogues are only part of *Paradise Regained*, for into the dimness are projected, like a sudden vision in a dream, the dazzling pageants of fair women, gorgeous banquet, and earthly pomp. And it is this contrast between brown shades and brilliant light that gives the poem its strong fascination. Nor is the contrast distracting, for its two parts are united by the common element of unnaturalness (*Milton*, 318–19).

Menzies too, we may recall, speaks of 'the quiet spirit of the Visionary Wilderness' (109–10) as ruling in the poem. 'About the visions, which are among its best-known scenes, there is something specially quiet and remote. The Banquet in the Wilderness, for example, distinct as it is, suggests an object viewed through the smaller end of a telescope. So, too, with the great nocturnal storm towards the close...it is a storm, indeed, but a storm in a dream' (110). To Blondel the physical background of the poem is

un décor dont Milton fait dès le début sentir la présence froide, abstraite. La nature n'éveille aucune sensation... '*the waste wilderness*' reste une notion morale sobrement définie, et les rares détails concrets (*wither'd sticks* (I, 316); *tough roots and stubs*: I, 339) rappellent qu'ils n'ont d'autre valeur que d'illustrer l'inimitié de la nature à l'égard du Christ, laissé seul, exposé à Satan. La nuit est *foul*: la conscience y participe, non la sensibilité; et les rocs, les arbres arrachés pendant la nuit de tempête sont dépouillés de toute suggestion autre que morale. L'art de Milton incline ici plutôt vers le style baroque où l'abstraction attire à elle l'image, sans la vider tout à fait de son contenu (106–7).

The desert in *PR*, says B. Rajan, 'is a place of destitution and clarity'.[99]

And in this emptiness there is human (Blondel, 101–2)—if 'unearthly' (Tillyard, 318)—speech. 'In this inward action of the meditative mind,' says Martz, 'all "characters," all speeches, are enveloped within, and suffused with, the controlling voice of the meditator himself. The meditative mind is exploring its own problems, as well as those of mankind, through the speeches of the "characters," who have indeed

[99] Balachandra Rajan, *The Lofty Rhyme* (London: Routledge & Kegan Paul, 1970), 7.

no separate existence, whose very function is to take upon themselves the meditative voice of the narrator' (239; and cf. Menzies, 111). The 'contest of styles' Martz finds in *PR* is itself, then, an internal contest. 'Satan and the Son of God in this poem speak within the mind of one who hopes himself to be a Son of God; both these actors use the human voice that this particular possible Son of God, John Milton, possesses...' (239–40).

The point for our purposes is not, I think, whether Martz is or is not 'right.' The point is that we must, when we read *PR*, adjust our expectations concerning the nature of dialogue to more complex imaginative conditions than we may have been prepared to recognize as being involved in the conception of the poem. Even if, as Shawcross theorizes, *PR* had been planned at first, and largely written, as an actual drama, the dialogue need not have been naturalistic. As we all know, the naturalness of even the most naturalistic dialogue is to an important degree an artifice; see, e.g., Mrs Lewalski (348; quoted above, p. 334). In *PR* Christ is man—but he is to begin with 'perfect man,' and by the end of the poem he is more. There is less inversion and latinate suspension in the dialogue of *PR* than in that of *PL*, especially *PL* before the fall—but the principal elements of the style of the longer poem survive in the shorter poem, not everywhere, perhaps, but appropriately, unobtrusively and (so to speak) proportionately disposed. The style of *PR* is bare—yet 'it is very easy to exaggerate this alleged bareness' (Tillyard, *Milton*, 315). What is, perhaps, as important as anything in the writing of *PR* is the scale to which it was constructed: a long poem, it is yet only a fifth as long as is *PL*. The rhythms of the one poem would for that reason have to be briefer than those of the other. And if the verse paragraph is in *PR* seldom sustained as it is in *PL*, the explanation may be in part, as Mrs Lewalski says, that 'the shorter poem might well seem unbalanced if constructed of such long units' (345). Even here we must be careful, for Blondel points out (115) that the movement of the verse paragraph, not merely in *PL*, but in *SA*, is more ample than that in *PR*. We come back in the end to a sense that, here as in every other poem Milton wrote, decorum governs—the decorum not simply of a 'kind,' but of the immensely subtle particular poem that took shape within Milton's imagination.

Other features of the versification of *PR* the critics have treated relatively more briefly. John Steadman reminds us that 'in justifying his own "*English* Heroic Verse without Rime," Milton appealed...to the precedent of poets rather than theorists' (385); Steadman none the less gives us an excellent brief account of the arguments of those 16th-century Italian theorists who felt the suitability of unrhymed verse for certain major narrative forms, and the relevance of the arguments to Milton's briefly stated theory, and to his general practice in *PL* and *PR*, would seem clear. At the same time, Milton's epics of course contain rhyme, so patterned that its presence could not everywhere be (and probably in few places is) accidental; for centuries this presence of rhyme was disregarded, or regarded as a blemish, or as having occurred by simple accident. Thus Blakeney (7–8) lists a few rhymed lines in *PR*, and quotes Cowper: 'Rime is apt to come uncalled, and to writers of blank verse is often extremely troublesome.'

Diekhoff's brief study of rhyme in *PL*,[100] as cursorily amended by J. M. Purcell,[101] should have called into existence more careful, extended and purposeful studies, but somehow did not. Pondering Diekhoff's evidence, and his conclusion that rhyme in *PL* is 'not mere accident' (543), nearly twenty years after the breakthrough article was published, Sprott for example found Milton's own rejection of rhyme in 'The Verse' an insuperable obstacle to serious entertainment of Diekhoff's view: 'Either...Milton spoke with his tongue in his cheek, or else the rhymes, if not accidental and unknown to their author, were at the least so definitely incidental to the general prosodic scheme that they were to be neglected (the term is Milton's own). The latter interpretation seems to me to be necessary...' (36–7). Beum, reporting Diekhoff's figures as emended by Purcell, accepts the 'rhymelessness' of *PL* as 'a relative matter' (349) but cannot himself take the matter as having more than passing importance. Milton's phrase 'the jingling sound of like

[100] John S. Diekhoff, 'Rhyme in *Paradise Lost*,' *PMLA* 49 (1934), 539–43.
[101] J. M. Purcell, 'Rime in *Paradise Lost*,' *MLN* 59 (1945), 171–2.

endings' suggests to Wheeler that what Milton was really attacking was 'that verse form which by 1667 dominated English poetry: the end-stopped decasyllabic couplet...' (359). This view would of course permit the acceptance of larger emergent structures of rhyme here and there in the epics, but Wheeler's purposes, as has been mentioned, lead him rather to insist on Milton's 'disdain for rhyme' (367); and in discussing Milton's 'blank verse couplets,' he does not find it convenient to speak of such complex structures of rhyme as that which occurs in *PL* 1. 183–91—nor of the seventeen actual rhymed couplets Diekhoff found in *PL*.

The 'considerable amount' of rhyme in *PL* 'has often been noted,' says Broadbent ('Milton's Rhetoric,' 230); 'what nobody has pointed out is that in blank verse rhyme is simply an iterative scheme like *epanalepsis* and *anadiplosis*. Identical rhyme was called, as a figure, *antistrophe*; near-rhyme is *prosonomasia* combined with *antistrophe*...' Rhyme is, then, one of the 'figures of sound' Milton uses, in combination with many other devices, to give the reader a sense of the sure and complex (though not mechanical nor obvious) construction of his blank verse. An unusual elaboration of rhetorical effect, in *PR* as in *PL*, may call attention to itself; what we then make of what we have discovered will depend on many things. Broadbent quotes *PR* 1. 377–405 and says, 'The extraordinary abundance of rhyme, *antistrophe*, *ploce* and *traductio*, and the final *anadiplosis*, are marks of Satan's factitious pathos' (235). Full terminal rhyme appears in the passage in 380–383 ('admire'–'desire') and in 384–387–398 ('know'–'foe'–'wo'). Mrs Lewalski (352–3) analyzes to somewhat different effect *PR* 3. 203–24, which contains terminal rhyme and half-rhyme, internal rhyme, and much supportive sound patterning, in addition, of course, to other iterative figures.

Lest it be thought that rhyme occurs in *PR* only as a kind of bauble, betraying in Satan a taste for the ornate bordering on vulgarity (cf. Laskowsky, 27–8; above, p. 315), one might call attention to 'aright' (*PR* 2. 475)–'delight' (480) and 'thought' (481)–'sought' (485) in lines spoken by Jesus—the lines, indeed, which Robson finds so 'colourless and toneless' (125). (I do not propose the rhyme as a 'saving grace,' but

343

then, I do not think that the passage needs saving.) Much more important, I should like to point out the unification of, e.g., *PR* 4. 394–450 by means of rhyme and related devices. The long passage begins, indeed, with Satan, and Satan's presence-in-absence is what unifies it conceptually:

> So saying he took (for still he knew his *power*
> Not yet ex*pir*'d) and to the Wilderness
> Brought back the Son of God, and left him there,
> Feigning to disap*pear*.

The 'there' ending line 396 introduces a long series 'sore'–'fire'–'there' –'fair'–'roar'–'dire' ending lines 402–412–421–426–428–431; this is supported by terminal 'day'–'gray'–'spray' in 400–427–437, 'dreams'–'beams' in 408–432, 'round'–'found' in 422–447, 'now'–'thou' in 409–424, *antistrophe* in 406–407 on 'head' (and see 'said' in 450), *antistrophe* in 438–439, and interweaving structures of alliteration, assonance and half-rhyme almost beyond count. The distance between words that exhibit full rhyme is often great, and it is no part of my purpose to suggest that we are intended to be specifically aware of all the sound patterns as we read—particularly when we first read. If, on the other hand, we have a sense of the unity of long sweeps of verse in Milton, as I think we do, we need not refuse evidences that help (only help) to explain that sense. And there is no point in arguing that the patterning to which attention has just been called is not what we are accustomed to thinking of as 'rhyming.' *PL* and *PR* are indeed unique. Milton could and did do things no other poet in English has done. And we as readers can and do respond, more and more fully as the poems come to be more and more deeply a part of us.

Milton's use of sound patterning to 'in-form' verse paragraphs is confirmed in part by Symonds. Milton 'confines his alliterative systems to periods of sense and metrical construction,' he says. 'When the period is closed, and the thought which it conveys has been expressed, the predominant letter is dropped. Thus there subsists an intimate connection between the metrical melody and the alliterative harmony, both aiding the rhetorical development of the sense' (103). Blondel finds more alliteration specifically in *PR* than does Symonds (110; above, p. 301), and he discusses at some length the importance of its use. 'Ce que la période poétique perd en ampleur,' he says, 'elle le retrouve ici dans l'harmonie plus subtile entretenue par la fréquence de l'allitération. Celle-ci donne au contenu de la pensée à la fois une plus grande élégance et une plus grande densité' (115). He points out a number of differing effects achieved by use of the device, including complex effects of dramatic irony.

The sense that an illusory yet haunting worldly beauty in *PR* is associated with Satan Blondel expresses again and again; that its effect on us may be at times intended to be undercut by an excessively rich local patterning of sound may be gathered also from his pages. He says, for example, 'A de rares moments, Milton évoque le souvenir de la légende arthurienne comme un motif d'ornement; il se mêle un sentiment lyrique à la réprobation que porte l'auteur aux mets trompeurs du Démon (II, 358–359). Ainsi le double effet de l'allitération donne toute son originalité à ce qui eût risqué de trop ressembler à un vers de Spenser' (116).

Beum writes briefly and generally on alliteration and assonance in Milton, finding most important 'their role in helping Milton achieve that *sine qua non* of all poetry—verbal conspicuousness' (354). He suggests that 'a thorough new study' of Milton's practice 'would do no harm.' I agree. In my essay on 'Blank Verse' in the *Milton Encyclopedia* I have myself written at somewhat greater length on musical patterning in *PL* and *PR*, including rhyme, than has been possible here; I shall write more fully still in the final volume of the *Variorum Commentary*.

Of the handling of accent in Milton's blank verse line, in *PR* especially, there is, again, little critical discussion. Where comment is to be found, one must be quite certain he understands the theoretical position taken by the critic offering evidence or interpretation before he accepts, or concludes that he knows how to interpret, statements made or statistics given. Enid Hamer, for example, finds the prosody of *PR* 'similar to that' of *PL*, 'except in one or two details. We notice an extension in the use of the more unusual and disturbing modulations, against which it is very difficult to keep the base in mind. The pyrrhic-trochee combination is the most important of these...' (101). She instances *PR* 1. 361, 2. 171, and 2. 180, but gives no statistics.[102] It happens that Mrs Hamer does not think much of double trochees; it happens also that she accepts not only the trisyllabic foot, but the monosyllabic foot. Thus she scans *PL* 6. 906

$$\text{Ăs ă | despíte | dŏn | ăgáinst | thĕ mŏst Hígh.}$$

She has her reasons: 'Emphasis and isolation combine with alliteration to enable the rather colourless word "done" to express the enormity of Lucifer's offence...and the extremely heavy final foot emphasizes the augustness of the "most High"' (94). Reluctantly she accepts the double trochee at the beginning of *PR* 1. 234, however. 'The alternative,

$$\text{Ăf|tĕr fórt| y̆ dáys fást|ing had remain'd}$$

is not here more attractive, as there is no particular reason for strong emphasis on the first syllable of "after"' (101). But now what of the 'extension' in *PR* 'in the use of the more unusual and disturbing modulations'? Mrs Hamer may—*may*—read ××′× much as I should; but how she 'keeps the base in mind' scanning *PL* 6. 906 as she does is not clear to me, so that the force her generalization might have—might even deserve to have—is dissipated.

Sprott's Chapter VII discusses inversion of feet in Milton. 'The rule, generally,' he says, 'is that in order that inversion may take place there must be a diaeresis between the inverting and the preceding foot'—that is, word division and foot division must coincide—'and the stress syllable of the preceding foot must be strongly accented or followed by a definite compensatory break...' (100). Sprott notes only one exception to these rules in Milton's verse, *PL* 3. 589, 'Astronomer in the Sun's lucent Orbe,' a line which does not seem to me to contain an inverted foot. What then of the 'disturbing modulation' ××′×, instanced so often in these pages? We begin to understand when we find Sprott listing

[102] *PR* shows, roughly, half as many instances of ××′× without saving pause as *PL* shows—something like fifteen or sixteen to thirty. Since *PR* is only a fifth as long as *PL*, this is perhaps an 'extension'; but more than simple statement is needed here.

PL 2. 880, 'With impétuŏus recoile and jarring sound,' and 11. 79, 'By the waters of Life, where ere they sate,' as showing inversion in the *first and* second feet (104), *PL* 5. 750, 'In thir triple Degrees, Regions to which,' in the first, second and fourth, *PL* 6. 906 (see Mrs Hamer) in the first, third and fourth (105), etc.

But if *PL* 2. 880 shows inversion of the first two feet, why, in Sprott's Chapter VIII, 'Loss of Speech Accent,' does *PL* 1. 511, 'With his enormous brood, and birthright seis'd,' show 'loss of accent' in the first foot (107)? 'The syllabic pentameter,' says Sprott (106), 'may lose one or two of its five speech accents without losing any of its stresses.' So he distinguishes between stress, as a *metrical* phenomenon, and speech accent. 'It is fundamental to understand that in syllabic verse[103] the lines are to be scanned according to theory irrespective of their audible rhythms. In this theory of verse there are no such feet as prosodical "pyrrhics" or "spondees". They may be heard in pronunciation, but they are not to be thought of as such in strict prosody...' (*loc. cit.*). So there is no inconsistency; the first foot in *PL* 1. 511 has lost *speech* accent, but presumably remains metrically—a trochee, like the first foot of *PL* 2. 880? Why is it not metrically an iamb? Perhaps it is. Is there no way of *knowing*? None of which I am aware. Still we must scan 'according to theory.'

My intention is not to belittle Sprott, whose work is in many ways valuable. I do, however, find his theory, his distinction between stress and accent (and the consequences thereof), incomprehensible. The matter comes up here because on his p. 101 Sprott offers us a table which should be extraordinarily useful, a table of inversions in the first, second, third, and fourth feet in the line in *Comus*, *PL*, *PR*, and *SA*. I shall

---

[103] Sprott follows Bridges in referring to Milton's verse as 'syllabic,' not as 'accentual-syllabic'; but since Bridges' use of the term 'syllabic' seems to be based on very questionable hypothetical distinctions (see below, p. 349); since there are, as has been shown, limits on the accentual variety metrically acceptable in the English line of counted syllables in rising rhythm; and since a syllabic verse in English in which there is *no* metrical requirement upon accent has come into existence, the term 'accentual-syllabic' for Milton's verse, and for all other verse in the same meter, must be preferred. See also Beum, 339.

reduce the figures (as always in Sprott, they are given as percentages of the total numbers of lines) to those that concern us most:

Inversion in foot	1	2	3	4
Comus	19·1	—	2·6	2·1
PL	18·2	0·5	2·6	2·4
PR 1	15·7	0·6	1·8	2·0
2	24·3	1·0	3·1	2·6
3	16·0	0·4	2·9	2·5
4	13·6	0·6	2·3	2·0
PR total	17·6	0·7	2·5	2·3
SA (blanks)	17·5	0·7	2·2	1·2

The figures are fascinating. Note, for example, that the percentages for *PR* 2 are in every position the highest for the poem; in the first two positions, as the complete table makes clear, they are the highest in all of Milton's blank verse. Why? we must wonder. And what effect does this have on us as we read? The percentages for *SA* for inversion in positions 2, 3 and 4 combined—that is, for inversion within the line—are on the other hand the lowest overall. What does *this* mean?

What, indeed, *does* it mean? Most of the trochees Sprott is tabulating would doubtless be trochees to anyone's ear. But Sprott is reducing what many others would call pyrrhics and spondees either to trochees or to iambs, judging each individual instance as he feels it. Doubtless he is as consistent as it is given to human beings to be. Still his results are not what (say) mine would be if I were to produce a comparable table; and of the difference I can tell only that my figures would in general be lower. It does *not* follow that my figures would be evenly and proportionately lower throughout. Bridges too tells us that in Milton's blank verse 'inversion...is most common in the first foot, next in the third and fourth, very rare in second, and most rare in fifth' (40); in the end I can get little more out of Sprott's table. There are no lines in *PR* which critics customarily cite as showing possible inversion in the fifth foot. 'Of course, if one is looking for inversion and determined to find it,' Sprott says (103), 'there are lines which might be quoted as possibilities.' Among other verses in Milton he instances *PR* 1. 2, 75, 356 (see below,

p. 353) and 368, and *PR* 3. 98 and 271. But 'None of these examples is certain; and they are all explainable without the supposition that they are to be inverted.'

Bridges does not believe in the existence of the accentual spondee; but 'unaccented or weak "feet"' (38) may in his view occur in any position in the line. He points out that 'the conjunction *and* occurs in stress-places in Milton's verse, where stressing it would make the verse ridiculous' (39); in illustration he cites *PR* 1. 99–109. 'There is no one place in the verse,' he concludes, 'where an accent is indispensable' (*loc. cit.*). The theory behind his various pronouncements on accent is obscure; even if one may work out a plausible guess as to what he means, for example, when he distinguishes 'accentual blank verse' from 'syllabic blank verse' (38), the distinction is idiosyncratic, and carries with it unrecognized difficulties of a formidable nature. But one does not go to Bridges, any more than to Sprott, for accentual theory.

Of most interest to us here is Bridges' study of recession of accent in Shakespeare and Milton. It is Bridges' opinion that while Milton's early verse shows a number of genuine examples of recession of accent in dissyllabic adjectives and participles used adjectivally—he gives eight examples (70), seven of them from *Comus*—Milton intended to exclude this 'obsolete mannerism' from his later verse, probably 'because the uncertainty which it introduces as to whether a syllable should be stressed or not, and the tendency which it has to make the verse smooth at all cost, would infect his inversions with uncertainty, and on these the character of his rhythm in a great measure depended' (71). He lists six 'doubtful' examples in *PL* (72), excluding from the reckoning altogether words like 'adverse' and 'unknown' which are, he says, 'in a double condition' (that is, capable of being accented on either syllable); he gives no instances from *PR*.

But words in a 'double' or 'uncertain' condition include dissyllabic prepositions and adverbs as well as adjectives and adjectival participles; Bridges notes as examples 'without,' 'beyond,' 'among,' 'before,' 'unless,' 'whereon' and 'whereby,' the first of which he thinks it justifiable to regard 'frankly as a word of indeterminate accent' (73).

He lists twenty lines in Milton in which the enforcement of regular alternating accent would produce the accentuation 'wíthout' (74–5); his examples include *PR* 1. 353,

And forty days *Eliah* without food,

but not *PR* 2. 442, 3. 197, 4. 391, 4. 541 and 4. 617, which show the word in the same situation. In most such instances he finds it preferable that 'neither syllable...be enforced' (74). Other prepositions and adverbs Bridges notes as being in 'uncertain' condition in the poem are 'wherein' in 1. 58, 'unless' in 3. 352 (a definite example of recession of accent, we are to understand finally) and 'among' in 4. 73. Bridges does not list 'henceforth' in *PR* 1. 142 and 1. 456, 'among' in 2. 68, 'forthwith' in 2. 236, 'therein' in 2. 463 and 3. 109, 'because' in 4. 156, or 'herein' in 4. 356. Of the examples he gives, he says, 'If these words are accented at all they must be a cause of uncertainty in the rhythm. The solution seems to be that they can be pronounced without any speech accent...' (75). It is a 'solution' which says more about Bridges, perhaps, than about Milton; but what Bridges discovers in Milton is surely of the greatest interest, and deserves further study. The fact is that use in 'a double condition' of the dissyllabic prepositions and adverbs listed, and more besides, was common in the verse of Milton's predecessors; what is the significance of Milton's continuation of it when he does in fact seem to have excluded recession of accent in dissyllabic adjectives and adjectival participles from *PR* and *SA*, and sharply reduced its incidence in *PL*?

Oras, including in his list 'unknown,' 'adverse' etc., still finds in *PL* only thirteen examples of such adjective-noun formulations as 'únblest féet,' 'óbscene dréad,' ten of them in the first four books (*BV&C*, 20). He finds none in *PR* or *SA*. It is his contention that Milton, 'moving away from Elizabethan and early Jacobean poetic conventions' (*BV&C*, 23), came increasingly to invert the position of adjective and noun where by doing so he might avoid the situation in which recession of accent might seem to be asked for. He lists (*BV&C*, 22) nineteen such inversions in *PR*; the first, *PR* 1. 35,

> Would not be last, and with the voice divine,

may for purposes of illustration be compared with *Comus* 468,

> The divine property of her first being.

Oras is silent on Milton's continuing to follow that 'Elizabethan and early Jacobean poetic convention' so closely related to recession of accent in adjectives and adjectival participles, the accentuation on either syllable of certain dissyllabic prepositions and adverbs.

The use of a proparoxytone trisyllable or polysyllable at the end of a line will result in a pyrrhic verse ending; see, e.g., *PR* 2. 187 and 3. 292, quoted above, p. 320, and see also p. 329 above. Oras believes that Milton uses pyrrhic endings for positive aesthetic reasons, though the reasons may have changed over the years. He calls attention to 'romantic and exotic effects' of the use of terminal pyrrhics in *PR* 2. 186–7, 2. 355–61, 3. 341–4 and 4. 34–75 ('MBV,' 188); he finds fewer effects of 'religious and ethical lyricism' in *PR* than in *Comus* or *PL*, but notes *PR* 1. 154–60, 2. 78–81, 2. 407–23, 3. 82–99, 3. 410–20, and 4. 607–9 ('MBV,' 188–9). These views would appear to conflict with Prince's view (already mentioned) 'that Tasso's practice' may have 'made Milton feel that the tenth syllable of his line must be its pivot, and must therefore be capable at least of receiving a strong stress when it did not demand one' (*Italian Element*, 135). Thomas Tyrwhitt, also invoking comparison between the English line and the Italian line, had said much the same thing as early as 1775;[104] Bridges, responding to Tyrwhitt, says, 'The truth seems to be that...[the] metrical position' of the tenth syllable 'in a manner exonerates it from requiring any accent' (39).

Blondel discusses all together, as 'weak endings,' pyrrhic endings (as in *PR* 1. 460), lightly accented terminal iambs (as in 1. 73 and 4. 419) and light feminine endings (as in 1. 425 and 3. 96); he says that such endings 'communiquent au mouvement de la pensée une grâce d'abandon ...' (112). This suggestion he expands into a subtle examination of the use of accent in *PR* generally, but especially in some of the speeches of Satan:

---

[104] Thomas Tyrwhitt, ed., *The Canterbury Tales of Chaucer*, 5 vols. (London, 1775–8), 4, 105 n.; the passage in question is quoted by Bridges, 84.

Ainsi l'adoucissement de la forme sonore corrige plusieurs fois la sévérité du fond. Mais d'autre part, lorsque cette même aisance dans le rythme aux contrastes plus atténués, se trouvera exprimer la pensée de l'Adversaire, elle fera mieux ressortir sa perfidie:

> '*Get Riches first, get wealth, and Treasure Heap*' (II, 427)
> ou   '*If Kingdom move thee not, let move thee Zeal*' (III, 171)

comportent dans la régularité monotone, très proche de la prose, une valeur de suggestion plus grande qu'il n'en eût été communiquée par un rythme plus heurté. Le rythme iambique traditionnel se met ici au service de l'artifice du démon et prend ainsi une valeur dramatique plus grande, lorsque pour montrer l'aisance de la tâche qu'il propose au Messie, il développe ensuite sa pensée en un vers où la familiarité a brisé la cadence '*Not difficult/if thou hearken to me*' (II, 428). A l'intérieur du vers, accents forts et accents faibles se répartissent avec une souplesse que les prosodistes ont reconnu plus grande que dans *Paradise Lost*...(112–13).

To the best of my knowledge, no verse critic who would find spondees in (say) the following lines,

> Will waft me; and the way found prosperous once (*PR* 1. 104)
>
> At these sad tidings; but no time was then (1. 109)
>
> Say and unsay, feign, flatter, or abjure? (1. 474)

has made a study of doubly-accented feet in *PR*, either alone or in relation to other feet—in *PR* only, or in comparison with the incidence of such feet in *PL*. Studies of the management of accent in *PR* must be accounted, then, not merely subjective, but few and fragmentary. To suggest that further concerted work, based on consistent, articulated assumptions, might profitably be done, is not necessarily, I think, to encourage that 'Higher Gradgrindism of charts and tables' which Beum finds so chilling (344).

One study of accent in Milton's verse, Albert Cook's 'Milton's Abstract Music,' is very different from anything else discussed thus far.[105] It is subjective, indeed, but very broad in its scope, and it defines and

[105] Albert Cook, 'Milton's Abstract Music,' *UTQ* 29 (1959–60), 370–85.

differentiates among the styles of Milton's poems, early and late, in ways the reader will wish to investigate and weigh for himself. Fortunately for us here, in discussing the 'poetic and rhythmic excellence' of *PR*, Cook makes a relatively brief, connected statement which sums up much of his argument:

One cannot say of the rhythm [of *PR*] that there are special major accents in the line (as in Shakespeare and most poetry), or that the major accents are levelled off in a syllabic pattern (as in Spenser, and in French poetry, for example), or that each accent becomes successively major as pronounced (as in *Paradise Lost*). The directness, or near prosiness, of the style, which acts as a severe limit on paragraph-long flights...is brought to bear on the rhythm in such a way that the syllabic pattern keeps the accents from being pronounced, and the accents keep the syllabic pattern from being incantatory...Just as Christ withstands temptation, the accents of the poetry that assert his steadfastness have a stark strength in their rugged, prosy resistance to absorption into the uniform syllabic norm of the poem. One could call it Biblical rather than classical...(381).

I have never, in the years since I first read these words, felt confident that my ear was capable of making the subtle discriminations Cook demands of it; I have never, indeed, felt confident that what Cook says with such authority and polish is consistent, or is or could be true. But the essay is an attempt to translate into words impressions which may not be translatable, and it is at the least genuinely stimulating.

Editors and critics of *PR* agree, as they must, that there is a higher incidence of final extrametrical syllables, or feminine endings, in *PR* than in *PL*; as would be expected, they do not agree on the reasons for the difference. Nor do they agree on the exact numbers involved, and that is understandable; if a word sometimes, or always, or often subject to contraction within the line occurs at the end of a line, is it contracted there or not? Compare, e.g., 'Heaven,' 'Heav'n' in *PR* 1. 30, 32, 55, 78 and 168, 'being' in *PR* 1. 62 and 2. 114. And what of those few lines which may or may not have feminine endings because they are genuinely ambiguous in structure? See, for example, *PR* 1. 356:

Knowing who | Í ám, | as Í | knów whó | thóu árt?

353

Knówing | who Í | am, as | Í knów | who thóu (árt?

Monosyllabic 'knowing' occurs in Shakespeare (see *2 H. VI* 1. 2. 97 and *Cor.* 2. 3. 155), in Chapman, Jonson, Sylvester, etc.; 'doing' is contracted to a monosyllable in *PL* 2. 162, 'flying' in *PR* 3. 323, 'saying' in *PR* 4. 394 and 541, etc. It is not possible to say how Milton intended *PR* 1. 356 to be read, though obviously each of us must make a choice *when* he reads.

J. C. Smith, at all events, finds seventy feminine endings in *PR*, 'or about 3 1–3 per cent,' only 'some ninety-three feminine endings, or less than 1 per cent' in *PL*.[106] Oras finds ninety-one feminine endings in *PR*, or 43·7 per thousand lines; eighty-six of the ninety-one are in speeches. In *PL* Oras finds 147 feminine endings altogether, or 13 per thousand lines ('MBV,' 161). Shawcross lists the lines in *PR* he reckons as having feminine endings; they total ninety. Sprott gives two sets of figures (57), the larger embracing 'all possible' feminine endings, the smaller, only those which are certain; the range for *PR* would yield sixty-two to ninety-seven such endings. My own figures for *PR* are ninety to ninety-three, counting 1. 356 (above), 3. 238 and 4. 73 as possible but deeply uncertain;[107] I find 142 in *PL*, 52 in Book 10.

Of the feminine endings in *PR*, eleven (1. 425, 1. 483, 2. 50, 2. 249, 2. 256, 3. 372, 3. 440, 4. 323, 4. 390, 4. 454 and 4. 532) are separate words or monosyllabic particles, three (3. 82, 3. 243 and 4. 324) are contractions, and one (1. 302, which parallels *PL* 9. 249; and see also *PL* 8. 216) is a kind of double feminine ending which gives something of the *sdrucciolo* effect even though the line remains hendecasyllabic by virtue of the compression of 'Socíe(ty' into a trisyllable (cf. dissyllabic 'día(monds' terminally in *Comus* 731, dissyllabic 'víolent' in *PR* 3. 87 and 'víolence' in *PR* 4. 388, etc.).[108] Only four feminine endings in *PL* are separate

---

[106] J. C. Smith, 'Feminine Endings in Milton's Blank Verse,' *TLS* No. 1818, Dec. 5, 1936, 1016.

[107] Of these, Shawcross accepts only 4. 73; he does not record 4. 390. Our findings are otherwise the same.

[108] Discussing *PL* 8. 216 and 9. 249 and *PR* 1. 302, Bridges says (5–6), 'It is possible that

monosyllables (10. 781, 871, 926 and 927), and apart from *PL* 8. 216 and 9. 249 and their *sdrucciolo* endings, mentioned above, only one line in *PL*, 12. 408, has a final extrametrical syllable which is itself a contraction.

More than half of the feminine endings in *PL* occur in Books 9 and 10, and various roughly interchangeable suggestions in explanation of this fact have been offered: the feminine ending is especially suited to the drama, and the materials of *PL* 9 and 10 are highly dramatic; 'Milton uses this type of verse deliberately to express agitation' (Smith); there is a 'deterioration in dignity' in this part of the poem (Sprott, 58); with the fall Adam and Eve become human in a sense in which they were not human before, and the relaxation in the strict form of the verse serves as a formal sign of this. That Jesus is human in *PR*; that the encounter between Satan and Jesus is highly dramatic also, and parallels the encounter between Satan and Eve in *PL*; that *PR* is 'a homelier kind of epic' than *PL*, and is 'located in a world familiar to us' (Beum, 363) might seem in some degree at least to explain the high proportion of feminine endings in *PR*. Saintsbury, however, has a simpler explanation: 'It may be noted that Milton accumulates redundant endings here, as he hardly does earlier; it is curious how this licence seems to be a Eurynome, or "wide-encroaching" temptation. . . ' (2, 252). To Symonds (110) the relatively high incidence of feminine endings in *PR* seems to 'add considerably to the heaviness' of the poem's movement; to Mrs Hamer (102) 'the repeated use of double endings gives a looser character to the versification' of *PR*.

Oras' view is as it were a positive version of Saintsbury's. Oras notes that the increase in the use of feminine endings *in the narrative* in *PL* 7–12 is almost as high as that in the speeches, and says, 'The evidence . . . suggests that. . . the growing predilection for double endings can have little if anything to do with dramatic decorum. . . The speeches in

these words *satiety* and *society* are allowed in this place because they admit of "elision". . . and can be therefore considered as single "hangers": but the elision being optional. . . all such endings, having two syllables extrametrical at the end, whether theoretically elidable or not, will still have a hexametric effect, and they do not differ from verses intended to have six feet.' For a discussion of 'optional' elision, see above, n. 26.

PR, with their greatly increased number of double endings, confirm the impression of a growing, probably spontaneous, change in rhythmical taste' ('MBV,' 162). 'Had Milton's experimentation with double endings in *PL* VII–XII satisfied him that his original stylistic restrictions were excessive and that such endings were fully capable of expressing dignity while adding variety to the style?' ('MBV,' 163). Oras recognizes, of course, that there is some connection between use of the feminine ending and the principles of decorum; observing that '*SA* outdistances the maximum figure in *PR* to an extent not encountered before'—he finds in *SA* 242 feminine endings, or 180·8 per thousand lines—he suggests in explanation of the sharp rise that 'most probably...a tendency progressively noticeable in Milton's nondramatic poems is here reinforced by a convention peculiar to the dramatic genre' ('MBV,' 162).

Whaler's discussion of the use of the feminine ending in Milton's blank verse is related to his discussion of enjambment, of 'free overlapping.' His principal concern is with *PL*, and he must ask, then, not why there are so many feminine endings in *PR*, but why there are so few in the longer poem. 'Wouldn't feminine endings serve well to demarcate and safeguard the metric line in the midst of steady enjambement?' (16). All too well, is his answer: 'A feminine ending creates a syllabic hedge against fluent overlapping. It is a streaming banneret that would demarcate the norm when Milton has other and less obtrusive means of demarcation, less perceptible because not extrametric.' And because Milton wishes, in *PL*, 'to move irregular rhythms above and below the ideal metric base, even as choir-voices slide freely above and below a cantus firmus' (*loc. cit.*), feminine endings would get in the way.

Prince, in a tart review of *Counterpoint*, takes this argument as illustrating Whaler's 'capacity for making bare-faced assumptions useful to himself.'[109] The scarcity of feminine endings in *PL*, he says,

has been generally taken to indicate that Milton wished to strengthen his line endings, and thus establish the line as a distinguishable unit amid the flow of his sentences. But this would not, of course, suit Mr. Whaler, who therefore asserts, as a truth too obvious to be challenged, that feminine endings have the

[109] *RES*, n.s. 9 (1958), 320–2, 321.

effect of *emphasizing* the line endings, and that they are rare in *Paradise Lost* precisely because Milton did *not* wish to establish the line as a unit. Yet most critics and metrists have accepted as obvious the fact that frequent feminine endings, at least in blank verse, tend to weaken and swamp the metric pattern... (*loc. cit.*).

And Prince's mentor, B. A. Wright, in a review even more contemptuous, says only of Whaler's reasoning on this point, 'There is no arguing with such views and such an ear.'[110]

Is Whaler quite wrong? Curiously enough, Beum—whether he is echoing Whaler, or has arrived independently at the same conclusion—says almost precisely what Whaler says: 'Short of a heavy stop, the feminine ending is probably the clearest way a poet has of demarcating the decasyllabic line. An abundance of such endings would have robbed Milton of the fluent run-on he was after. And they would have made less subtle the tension or effect of counterpoint Milton gains by enjambing, while at the same time ending his line on a strong (i.e., firmly stressed and usually long) syllable' (358–9). Beum seems to me, though not infallible, a sensitive reader. I do not think it likely that either side in this argument is in gross error; probably here, as so often, a single element of verse form will have differing effects in differing circumstances. My conjecture would be that in a passage showing heavy, frequent and varied internal pause combined with frequent enjambment and complex patterning of accent, the effect of an irregular but insistent use of feminine endings would be to blur the definition of the meter; in fairly regular verse, with few and light internal pauses, feminine endings would indeed help to demarcate lines. Neither effect would depend wholly on the use of the feminine endings. The matter is worth bringing to the reader's attention here because we have now, in fact, sufficient information from Oras, Shawcross, Whaler and others (though perhaps we have always had it from Milton himself!) to enable us to study the *real* effect of the high incidence of feminine endings in *PR*.

A final note on extrametrical syllables. As most Miltonists well know, *Comus* contains a number of lines which show what is called variously

[110] *MLR* 53 (1958), 244–5, 244.

'the extrametrical syllable at the caesura' and 'the midverse extra-metrical syllable'; for identification and discussion of these lines see my essay 'Studies of Verse Form in the Minor English Poems,' *Variorum Commentary*, 2, 1041–4. Bridges, discussing *SA* 748,

> Out, out *Hyaena*; these are thy wonted arts,

suggests that in that exceptional line 'we have apparently an extra-metrical syllable,' the *-na* of '*Hyaena*'; but he then proposes other solutions to the metrical problem the line poses, any of which he finds preferable 'as there is no other example of an extrametrical syllable within the line in all *P.L.*, *R.*, and *Samson*...' (50). On this most prosodists seem to agree. Sprott, however, says, 'The midverse extrametrical syllable...was wholly excluded from the prosody' of *PL* 'and admitted to' *PR* and *SA* 'only under very special conditions' (63). He neither explains nor illustrates.

Bridges devotes Part II of *Milton's Prosody* to a study of the verse of *PR* and *SA*; he gives almost all his space to the latter. It is his general conclusion that in the later poems (it did not occur to him to doubt that they were the later poems) 'Milton did not keep quite strictly to his laws of "elision", but...he approved of the great rhythmical experiments which he had made, and extended these' (46). Bridges then lists sixteen lines which would not 'have been admitted into *P.L.*' (47); three of these are from *PR*:

> And all the flour*ish*ing works of peace destroy (3. 80)
> Whose off-spring in his Territor*y y*et serve (3. 375)
> Thy pol*i*tic maxims, or that cumbersome (3. 400)

The italics are Bridges', and indicate the place of the metrical difficulty. In its remaining 2,067 lines, presumably, *PR* follows the rules for 'elision' laid down, in practice, in *PL*.

PR 3. 375, which has a parallel in *SA* 1171 (also listed), Bridges accounts for as an 'easy enough' synaloepha (blending) 'of a final vocalic *y* with initial consonantal *y*' (47). As for 'politic,' it is in principle not unlike dissyllabic 'capital' in *PL* 2. 924, 11. 343 and 12. 383, as Bridges notes (*loc. cit.*). The suggestion that 'politic' is to be contracted 'may seem to some,' Saintsbury says (2, 251), 'to justify Count Smorl-tork.' Naturally Saintsbury finds that the first two lines quoted above 'are clearly not reconcilable with the limitations sometimes tabulated' (2, 254); he misquotes *PR* 3. 375 in such a way as to make it, I should think, irreconcilable with *anyone's* limitations, including his own. But dissyllabic 'poĺitic' ('poĺitique') is to be found in, e.g., *Othello*, 3. 3. 13, Chapman's *Iliad*, 1. 313, Donne's 'Satire I,' 80, Jonson's *Volpone*, 4. 1. 144, etc. The *OED* records the spelling 'pol'tick.' I find dissyllabic 'flourishing' twice in Shakespeare, as in *R. II*, 1. 12. 18; I find it five times in Chapman, as in the *Iliad*, 2. 400; I find it in Jonson, in Sandys, in Heywood, and seven times in Cowley. Hunter (139) finds it in the metrical psalters—specifically, in the Scottish version of Sternhold and Hopkins. Far from agreeing with Saintsbury, one can only wonder— *what* great rhythmic experiments has Milton extended in *PR*? Nothing like *PR* 3. 375 and *SA* 1171 occurs in *PL*, true; but in Jonson's *Catiline* we find

> Yes, and they stud*y y*our kitchin, more then you (2. 191),

and that Milton 'would not' have used some appropriate version of the compression in (say) *PL* 9 or 10 seems too much to say. The contractions in *PR* 3. 80 and 400 are strange to us, but they were perfectly familiar to the 17th century, and the fact that they do not occur in *PL* hardly justifies us in supposing that Milton *excluded* them from that poem— or that their admission to *PR* constitutes either a 'relaxation' of the prosodic laws of *PL* or an 'extension' of 'great rhythmical experiments' *of Milton's*. It is time we assembled the information necessary to enable us to distinguish between what is original in Milton's versification and what is simply the verse practice of the times. Prince's remarks on the kinds of 'so-called elision' Milton tried to 'introduce...into English,' his examples of 'various elisions' which Milton 'devises' (133), are misleading and disconcerting in their oversimplification of the relation-ship, at this particular point, of Italian and English verse practice.

Sprott's general discussion of contraction, elision and synaloepha in Milton (63–74) is good; Sprott adduces historical evidence, and writes with thoroughness and care. He follows Bridges so closely, in so much, that his refusal to accept 'elision' as a mere theoretical device seems to me particularly admirable:

The probable conclusion to be drawn from phonetic spellings and the ideals of theorists is that in the seventeenth century vowel sounds actually were suppressed in the pronunciation of elision. The probability of the historical fact gives the probable lie to the modern, subjective criticism of Saintsbury and Masson. Since the status of glides is uncertain, however, the exact extent of the loss in each case cannot be determined...unless we find impeccable evidence for the absence of glides in average seventeenth-century speech (73).

Sprott's exemplification of the various kinds of metrical compression (74–98) is full, and his illustrations, some of them from *PR*, are carefully categorized. To our understanding of the verse of *PR* as an individual poem he adds little.

R. O. Evans' monograph *Milton's Elisions* is not without value, but it seems to me sadly—and, for the potential user, dangerously—uneven. In the first place, it seems hastily written; this is of importance when Evans reviews, slightingly, the work of such scholars as Prince and Helen Darbishire,[111] and represents them so nearly incomprehensibly as to make it impossible to tell whether he simply misunderstands them (as, indeed, I think he does), or whether he has a legitimate criticism which he has not found a sufficiently clear way of expressing. He reviews Bridges and Sprott—he is fairer to Bridges, though he condescends to both—revises the categories under which he will examine 'elision,' points out, justly, that earlier prosodists did not tell us 'how much elision of one variety or another occurred in any particular selection' (17), and proceeds to his study, which is in the main a study of *PL*. His Chapter 5, 'Milton's Qualitative Use of Elision,' is for the most part

[111] Evans discusses (19–23) the Introduction to Miss Darbishire's edition of *The Poetical Works of John Milton*, Vol. 1, *Paradise Lost* (Oxford: Clarendon Press, 1952), ix–xxxv. He makes a number of unsupported (and I think unfounded) charges against Miss Darbishire, and his 'examination' of her position discredits what it has in the first place misrepresented. Many Miltonists have wished that Miss Darbishire had not in fact gone to the length of producing a 'reformed text' of *PL*. But the evidence on which she bases her 'case' for such a text is of real interest and importance, and the understanding, and the scholarship, that would challenge hers must be impressive indeed.

acceptable, and students may wish to examine it as they examine the work of Bridges and Sprott, which it complements but does not supersede. The student must be warned, however, that Evans is capable of making mistakes. Having pointed out again and again, perfectly correctly, that 'Milton was operating in a well-known tradition' (14), he fails utterly (it would seem) to recognize monosyllabic 'i'th'' as familiar in that tradition (37–8); he appears to think that 'unshak'n' is dissyllabic in *PL* 4. 64 (35, 56). There are other errors. They make me somewhat distrustful of Evans' quantitative findings. Those findings for *PL* can be examined, if with difficulty, since Evans provides lists of all words and word groups involved in 'elision' in *PL*, category by category, book by book—but without line references—in an Appendix (51–64); his findings for *PR*, *Comus* and *SA*, however, are given only as totals, tabulated on p. 66. Where I am able to check his figures against my own they seldom agree. Evans finds 147 'elisions' in *PR* 1, 121 in *PR* 2, 155 in *PR* 3, and 174 in *PR* 4; I find 133 or 134 in *PR* 1, 106 in *PR* 2, 133 or 134 in *PR* 3, 177 or 178 in *PR* 4. What the causes of the discrepancy are there is no way of telling. It is particularly puzzling in that Evans says, 'There are a great many proper names in the poem ending in *-ia*, *-ian*, and very often Milton affords them their full complement of syllables' (45). I find *not one* certain example of this. My figures for 'elision' should thus be, or might well be, higher than Evans'; but they are in general much lower. Evans' figures would yield one 'elision' in every 3·16 lines of *PL*, one in every 3·46 lines of *PR*; mine would yield one in every 3·33 lines of *PL*, one in every 3·75 lines of *PR*.

Of the relatively low figures for 'elision' in *PR* 2, Evans at first remarks that they are close to the figures for *SA*; this gives him 'some reason...to suspect that Book II may have been the latest of the four books' of *PR* 'to be written' (42–3). A statement so mild, so qualified, it seems ungracious to dismiss; I can say only that if my figures for *PR* and *SA* were identical with Evans', they would not lead me to suspect what they lead him to suspect. In fact, however, my figures for *SA*, both for the blank verse lines and for all lines together, are very much higher than Evans'. But alternatively it may be, says Evans, that in *PR* 2

'Milton was beginning to experiment with elision not only as a metrical device, calculated primarily for euphonic variation, but was beginning to consider the possibilities of defining character in these terms. For example, simple characters, as the Virgin Mary, speak with very little elision. Satan and Christ are the great exponents of the device. In fact at places in Book II Satan and Christ seem to be engaged in a metrical duel...' (43; see also above, n. 83)—and so a suggestion which begins interestingly is confused or compromised, since unless (for once) Satan and Christ were trying to see who could use the *fewer* 'elisions,' their duel could scarcely result in the *low* figures Evans set out to explain. Still, the idea of 'elision' as a characterizing device—cf. Blondel on regularity of accent in some of Satan's lines—would seem to be worth further study.

Evans ends well:

Elision was primarily a device whereby a poet could secure variation in his lines and thus prevent euphonic monotony. It was also, especially in Milton, a device for securing economy; that is, by clever manipulation of elision a poet could pack his lines with much more meaning than would otherwise be possible. Very generally, then, the extensive system of metrical elision on which the English poets might draw helped them to secure something of the same effect that the inflectional system of Latin provided for the Roman poet. Finally, elision might be used functionally, almost symbolically, to help the poet indicate certain things about particular speakers, or certain passages, in his poem (50).

These are interesting, and thought-provoking, observations.

Most of the uses of 'elision' of which Evans speaks would it seems to me come under the heading of 'apt Numbers.' How this phrase, and the one immediately following in the note on 'The Verse' prefixed to *PL*, 'fit quantity of Syllables,' might relate specifically to *PR* has been little studied. Of course both phrases are often misunderstood, and misunderstood in precisely the same way; all too many critics have taken one formulation or the other as an expression of Milton's intention to write a line of ten syllables. But 'apt Numbers' means (briefly) 'suitable rhythms,' and 'fit quantity' means 'appropriate length or brevity' of syllables. The suggestion is not, of course, that Milton's blank verse is written in a quantitative meter, but that Milton was careful to use sounds of an appropriate length at particular places in particular lines. Helen Darbishire's studies suggest that some of Milton's preferred spellings, or alternative spelling forms, in *PL* have implications for quantity;[112] but the 1671 text of *PR* shows only a scattering of characteristic Miltonic spellings. A study of 'fit quantity' in *PR* remains to be made. Much of the sympathetic criticism of the poem, on the other hand, gives us insight into the 'aptness' of its 'Numbers,' and more than a few analyses of excellence of this kind have been recorded above. Still it will be evident that in this respect also there is more to do.

In his 1966 monograph Oras remarks that Shawcross' rejoinder to his own earlier study

would have been even more interesting if Shawcross had noticed what Louis L. Martz describes as the 'contest of styles' in the epic: the use of the 'middle style' in the earlier parts, the oratorical 'high style' of Satan, the simpler language of Christ. The way in which these contrasts, which doubtless were used deliberately, may be reflected in the prosody would be a fascinating subject to explore...Surprisingly, they do not affect the statistical averages for the work as a whole in a way that would make it seem out of place in the position it occupies close before the end of our graphs (*BV&C*, 40–1).

If the contrasts 'do not affect the statistical averages' the fact might suggest that the averages are averages for verse areas too large, and must of necessity obliterate such distinctions. Or it might be that the particular 'basic features of rhythm' studied have little to do with the differentiation of one style from another. Considering the crucial nature of pause, this would seem unlikely. The difficulty of interpreting the evidence is granted; but difficulty is not impossibility. At all events, 'the way in which these contrasts...may be reflected in the prosody [read 'versification'] would be a fascinating subject to explore,' indeed. Perhaps one day someone will explore it. Our knowledge of the verse of *PR*, and our understanding of how further that verse might profitably be examined, can surely be made to count for more than, at present, they do.

[112] See, e.g., Helen Darbishire, ed., *The Manuscript of Milton's Paradise Lost Book I* (Oxford: Clarendon Press, 1931), Introduction, xxx–xxxi; and see also the Introduction to Miss Darbishire's 1952 edition of *PL*, ix, xi, etc.

Index of Names and Titles

Index

Index

Index

Hagar, 126

Hakewill, George, *An Apologie for the Power and Providence of God*, 182, 191

Hall, Joseph
Contemplations, 23n., 51
Meditations, 146, 147

Hamer, Enid, *The Metres of English Poetry*, 328, 345–6, 347, 355

Hanford, James H.
John Milton, Englishman, 4, 5, 7
John Milton, Poet and Humanist, 166
A Milton Handbook, 295–6, 301, 316, 317, 318
The Poems of John Milton, 9, 47, 233

Harrington, James, *Oceana*, 65

Hastings, James
A Dictionary of the Bible, 143, 162
Encyclopedia of Religion and Ethics, 81, 148, 153, 196

Havens, R. D., *The Influence of Milton on English Poetry*, 294–5, 317–18, 323, 326

Hawkins, Edward, *Poetical Works of John Milton*, 9, 47, 81, 130

Hayley, William, *The Life of Milton*, 297, 299

Henry, N. H., 'The Mystery of Milton's Muse', 51

Herbert, George, *Outlandish Proverbs*, 59

Hercules, 241, 242, 243

Herodian, 148

Herodotus, *History*, 80, 96, 166

Herod the Great, 136, 154

Herrick, Robert, *A Country Life*, 158

Hershon, P. I., *The Pentateuch According to the Talmud*, 114

Hesiod
Theogony, 60, 63, 132
Works and Days, 85, 100, 298

Hesperides, 131

Heylyn, Peter, *Cosmographie*, 164

Heywood, Thomas, *The Hierarchie of the Blessed Angells*, 67, 69, 98, 112, 114, 359

Historia Augusta, 80, 184

Hobbes, Thomas, *Leviathan*, 97

Homer, 259, 285, 290, 298
Iliad, 63, 64, 68, 179
Odyssey, 60, 103, 216, 229

Homeric Hymns, 60, 119, 131

Hooker, E. N., 'The Purpose of Dryden's *Annus Mirabilis*', 54

Hooker, Richard, *The Laws of Ecclesiastical Polity*, 41, 57, 67, 97, 112, 218, 223

Hoopes, Robert, *Right Reason in the English Renaissance*, 41n.

Hopkins, Gerard Manley, *Correspondence*, 275n.

Horace
Ars Poetica, 202, 204, 221, 291
Carmen Saeculare, 181, 188
Carmina, 107, 116, 119, 123, 140, 192
Epistulae, 108, 119, 132, 135, 208
Epodes, 131
Odes, 284
Satirae, 135, 140

Howell, W. S., *Logic and Rhetoric in England, 1500–1700*, 179

Huet, Daniel, *Demonstratio Evangelica*, 219

Hughes, Merritt Y.
'The Christ of *Paradise Regained*', 14, 40n., 44, 137, 138, 146, 242
hn Milton: Complete Poems, 47, 57, 67–8, 76, 84, 92, 98, 120, 123, 138, 145, 185, 221, 228, 246
'Satan and the "Myth" of the Tyrant', 58

H[ume], P., 287

Hunter, William B.
'Eve's Demonic Dream', 228
'Milton's Arianism Reconsidered', 35n.
'The Sources of Milton's Prosody', 282, 292, 359

Huon of Bordeaux, 236

Hutton, James
The Greek Anthology in Italy, 155, 203
'Some English Poems in Praise of Music', 34n., 124

Hyginus, *Fabulae*, 118, 131

Hylas, 131

Hyrcanus II, 172

Innocent III, *De Contemptu Mundi*, 145

Irenaeus, St, *Contra Haereses*, 72

Index

Index

Index

Rajan, B.
'Jerusalem and Athens: the Temptation of Learning in *Paradise Regained*', 189, 198
'The Lofty Rhyme', 340
Rajna, Pio, *Le fonti dell'Orlando Furioso*, 238
Ralegh, Sir Walter, *Historie of the World*, 162, 163, 164, 233
Raleigh, Sir Walter A., *Milton*, 301
Rawlinson, G.
The History of Herodotus, 161
The Sixth Great Oriental Monarchy, 165
Regulus, 139
Rice, Warner, 'Paradise Regained', 50, 88, 101, 133
Richards, I. A., 93
Ricks, Christopher
'Over-Emphasis in *Paradise Regained*', 312n.
Milton's Grand Style, 312n.
Ritter, Constantin, *Platon*, 151
Roberts, Donald R., 'The Music of Milton', 336n.
Robson, W. W., 'The Better Fortitude', 37n., 303–5, 309, 313, 316, 317, 343
Rogers, R. S., *Studies in the Reign of Tiberius*, 190
Rohde, E., *Psyche*, 215
Ross, W. D., *Aristotle*, 41, 216
Rutilius Claudius Namatianus, *De Reditu Suo*, 185

Sackton, A. H., 'Architectonic Structure in *Paradise Regained*', 53, 69, 177, 241
Sacrobosco, Joannes de, *De Sphaera*, 187
Saintsbury, George, *History of English Prosody*, 265–6n., 280, 283, 291, 321, 355, 358–9
Sallust
Bellum Catilinae, 138
Bellum Iugurthinum, 187
Salmanassar, 162, 173
Samuel, Irene
'Milton on Learning and Wisdom', 209
Plato and Milton, 11n., 199–200, 210, 211, 217
'Semiramis in the Middle Ages', 162

Sandys, George
Metamorphoses (translation of Ovid), 242, 359
Relation of a Journey Begun An. Dom. 1610, 84, 87, 238
Sannazaro, Jacopo, *De Partu Virginis*, 16, 309–10
Saurat, Denis, *Milton, Man and Thinker*, 37n., 302
Sayce, Richard, *The French Biblical Epic in the Seventeenth Century*, 21n.
Schaff–Herzog *Encyclopedia of Religious Knowledge*, 36n.
Schultz, Howard
'Christ and Antichrist in *Paradise Regained*', 53
'A Fairer Paradise? Some Recent Studies of *Paradise Regained*', 125
Milton and Forbidden Knowledge, 53, 199, 209
Scipio Africanus, 26, 119, 144
Scot, Reginald, *Discoverie of Witchcraft*, 228
Scriptores *Historiae Augustae*, 80, 184
Selden, John
De Diis Syris, 175
Table Talk, 97
Semele, 118
Semiramis, 162
Senault, Jean François, *De l'Usage des passions*, 213
Seneca, 286, 305
Ad Helviam de Consolatione, 139
Ad Marciam de Consolatione, 156
Ad Polybium de Consolatione, 94
De Beneficiis, 183, 213
De Brevitate Vitae, 193
De Ira, 157
De Providentia, 156, 213
De Remediis Fortuitorum, 146
De Tranquillitate Animi, 190
De Vita Beata, 132, 213
Epistulae Morales, 139, 144, 145, 146–7, 193, 213, 214
Quaestiones Naturales, 233
Thyestes, 141
Severus, Alexander, 80

376

Index

Index

Index